Teaching the Middle Ages through Modern Games

Video Games
and the Humanities

Edited by
Nathalie Aghoro, Iro Filippaki, Chris Kempshall,
Esther MacCallum-Stewart, Jeremiah McCall
and Sascha Pöhlmann

Advisory Board
Alenda Y. Chang, UC Santa Barbara
Katherine J Lewis, University of Huddersfield
Dietmar Meinel, University of Duisburg-Essen
Ana Milošević, KU Leuven
Soraya Murray, UC Santa Cruz
Holly Nielsen, University of London
Michael Nitsche, Georgia Tech
Martin Picard, Leipzig University
Melanie Swalwell, Swinburne University
Emma Vossen, University of Waterloo
Mark J.P. Wolf, Concordia University
Esther Wright, Cardiff University

Volume 11

Teaching the Middle Ages through Modern Games

Using, Modding and Creating Games for Education and Impact

Edited by
Robert Houghton

ISBN 978-3-11-152137-4
e-ISBN (PDF) 978-3-11-071203-2
e-ISBN (EPUB) 978-3-11-071211-7
ISSN 2700-0400

Library of Congress Control Number: 2022939910

Bibliographic information published by the Deutsche Nationalbibliothek
The Deutsche Nationalbibliothek lists this publication in the Deutsche Nationalbibliografie; detailed bibliographic data are available on the internet at http://dnb.dnb.de.

© 2024 Walter de Gruyter GmbH, Berlin/Boston
This volume is text- and page-identical with the hardback published in 2022.
Cover image: Foundation (Polymorph Games, 2019)
Typesetting: Integra Software Services Pvt.

www.degruyter.com

Acknowledgements

This volume emerged from a conference strand at the International Medieval Congress at the University of Leeds in 2019. In the intervening years it has expanded and evolved substantially with the support of all the contributors, reviewers, and numerous friends and colleagues. It's been a long haul and I need to thank a number of people in particular:

Rabea, Ulla, Jana at DeGruyter for their organisational and editorial work and patience.

Phillipe and Michaël at Polymorph Games for creating and authorising our bespoke cover image.

Karen Cook for their swift and thorough compilation of the index.

And most of all, my wife Varan for her endless cheer and championing.

Contents

Acknowledgements —— V

Robert Houghton
1   Introduction: Teaching the Middle Ages through Modern Games —— 1

Part I: The Educational Impact of Games

Eve Stirling and Jamie Wood
2   Learning About the Past Through Digital Play: History Students and Video Games —— 29

Part II: Teaching through Commercial Games

Mike Horswell
3   Historicising *Assassin's Creed* (2007): Crusader Medievalism, Historiography, and Digital Games for the Classroom —— 47

David DeVine
4   Declaiming Dragons: Empathy Learning and *The Elder Scrolls* in Teaching Medieval Rhetorical Schemes —— 69

Ahmet Erdem Tozoğlu and Mehmet Şükrü Kuran
5   "What if you are a Medieval Monarch?": A *Crusader Kings III* Experience to Learn Medieval History —— 87

Part III: Creating Educational Games

Klio Stamou, Anna Sotiropoulou, Phivos Mylonas and Yorghos Voutos
6   A Video Game for Byzantine History – *Akritas*: Playing at the Byzantine Borders —— 113

Owen Gottlieb and Shawn Clybor
7   Collaborative Constructions: Designing High School History Curriculum with the *Lost & Found* Game Series —— 131

Courtnay Konshuh and Frank Klaassen
8 The Renaissance Marriage Game: A Simulation Game for Large Classes —— 155

Part IV: User Modification as Learning Practice

Erik Champion, Terhi Nurmikko-Fuller and Katrina Grant
9 Alchemy and Archives, Swords, Spells, and Castles: Medieval-modding *Skyrim* —— 175

Robert Houghton
10 Playing the Investiture Contest: Modding as Historical Debate in the Undergraduate and Postgraduate Classroom —— 201

Frank Klaassen
11 Game Development in a Senior Seminar —— 229

Part V: Games beyond the Classroom

Mariana López, Marques Hardin and Wenqi Wan
12 *The Soundscapes of the York Mystery Plays*: Playing with Medieval Sonic Histories —— 249

Robert Houghton
13 Beyond Education and Impact: Games as Research Tools and Outputs —— 279

List of Contributors —— 299

Index —— 303

Robert Houghton

1 Introduction: Teaching the Middle Ages through Modern Games

The scholarship which addresses the interaction between history and modern games is growing rapidly both in terms of volume and of approach. While academic critiques of games on the basis of historical inaccuracies represent a shrinking minority of this scholarship, lively debate continues around what exactly historical accuracy and authenticity mean in popular media in general,[1] and what they mean within games.[2] The role of historians and historical research in the production of games is increasingly well documented[3] and corresponds with a

---

[1] Christoph Classen and Wulf Kansteiner, "Truth and Authenticity in Contemporary Historical Culture: An Introduction to *Historical Representation and Historical Truth*," *History and Theory* 48, no. 2 (May 2009): 1–4, https://doi.org/10.1111/j.1468-2303.2009.00495.x; Konstantinos Andriotis, "Genres of Heritage Authenticity: Denotations from a Pilgrimage Landscape," *Annals of Tourism Research* 38, no. 4 (October 2011): 1613–33, https://doi.org/10.1016/j.annals.2011.03.001; Karl Alvestad and Robert Houghton, eds., *The Middle Ages in Modern Culture: History and Authenticity in Contemporary Medievalism* (2021), https://doi.org/10.5040/9781350167452?locatt=label:secondary_bloomsburyCollections.

[2] Andrew J. Salvati and Jonathan M. Bullinger, "Selective Authenticity and the Playable Past," in *Playing with the Past: Digital Games and the Simulation of History*, ed. Matthew Kapell and Andrew B. R. Elliott (New York: Bloomsbury Academic, 2013), 153–67; Tim Raupach, "Towards an Analysis of Strategies of Authenticity Production in World War II First-Person Shooter Games," in *Early Modernity and Video Games*, ed. Tobias Winnerling and Florian Kerschbaumer (Newcastle upon Tyne: Cambridge Scholars, 2014), 123–38; Robert Houghton, "It's What You Do With It That Counts: Factual Accuracy and Mechanical Accuracy in Crusader Kings II," *The Public Medievalist* (blog), September 30, 2014, https://www.publicmedievalist.com/ckii-houghton/; Tara Jane Copplestone, "But That's Not Accurate: The Differing Perceptions of Accuracy in Cultural-Heritage Videogames between Creators, Consumers and Critics," *Rethinking History* 21, no. 3 (2017): 415–38, https://doi.org/10.1080/13642529.2017.1256615; Martin Lorber and Felix Zimmermann, eds., *History in Games: Contingencies of an Authentic Past*, Studies of Digital Media Culture 12 (Bielefeld: Transcript-Verl, 2020); Robert Houghton, "If You're Going to Be the King, You'd Better Damn Well Act like the King: Setting Objectives to Encourage Realistic Play in Grand Strategy Computer Games," in *The Middle Ages in Modern Culture: History and Authenticity in Contemporary Medievalism*, ed. Karl Alvestad and Robert Houghton (IBTauris, 2021), 186–210.

[3] Stephen Totilo, "One Man's Year Making Assassin's Creed II," *Kotaku* (blog), December 21, 2009, https://kotaku.com/5431098/one-mans-year-making-assassins-creed-ii; Matthew Nicholls, "Digital Visualisation in Classics Teaching and Beyond," *Journal of Classics Teaching* 17, no. 33 (2016): 27–30, https://doi.org/10.1017/S2058631016000076; Lori Folder, "Thrones of Britannia – Campaign Map Reveal," *Total War Blog* (blog), November 12, 2017, https://www.total

growing demand for historical vigour amongst the playerbase.[4] The manner in which these games represent history and the past has been interrogated within various frameworks from diverse fields including Literary Studies,[5] Archaeology,[6] and Game Design,[7] and indeed has formed the basis for the construction of several new methodological approaches.[8] The potential of historical and pseudo-historical games to address serious and contemporary issues has been highlighted,[9] as

---

war.com/blog/thrones-campaign-map-reveal; Dominic Tarason, "Assassin's Creed Origins Becomes Edutainment Feb 20th," *Rock, Paper, Shotgun* (blog), February 13, 2018, https://www.rockpapershotgun.com/2018/02/13/assassins-creed-origins-becomes-edutainment-feb-20th/; Andrew Reinhard and Stéphanie-Anne Ruatta, "Consulting for Ubisoft on Assassin's Creed: Odyssey," *Archaeogaming* (blog), April 19, 2019, https://archaeogaming.com/2019/04/19/consulting-for-ubisoft-on-assassins-creed-odyssey/.

4 Erik Champion, *Critical Gaming: Interactive History and Virtual Heritage*, Digital Research in the Arts and Humanities (Farnham, Surrey: Ashgate, 2015); Copplestone, "But That's Not Accurate."

5 Janet Horowitz Murray, *Hamlet on the Holodeck: The Future of Narrative in Cyberspace* (Cambridge, Mass: MIT Press, 1998); Astrid Ensslin, *Literary Gaming* (Cambridge, Massachusetts; London, England: The MIT Press, 2014).

6 Shawn Graham, "Agent Based Models, Archaeogaming, and the Useful Deaths of Digital Romans," in *The Interactive Past: Archaeology, Heritage & Video Games*, ed. Angenitus Arie Andries Mol et al. (Leiden: Sidestone Press, 2017), 123–31; Andrew Reinhard, *Archaeogaming: An Introduction to Archaeology in and of Video Games* (New York: Berghahn Books, 2018).

7 Espen J. Aarseth, *Cybertext: Perspectives on Ergodic Literature* (Baltimore, Md: Johns Hopkins University Press, 1997); Robin Hunicke, Marc LeBlanc, and Robert Zubeck, "MDA: A Formal Approach to Game Design and Game Research," *Proceedings of the Challenges in Games AI Workshop, Nineteenth National Conference of Artificial Intelligence*, 2004, 1–5.

8 Jerremie Clyde, Howard Hopkins, and Glenn Wilkinson, "Beyond the 'Historical' Simulation: Using Theories of History to Inform Scholarly Game Design," *Loading . . . The Journal of the Canadian Game Studies Association* 6, no. 9 (2012), http://journals.sfu.ca/loading/index.php/loading/article/viewArticle/105; Adam Chapman, *Digital Games as History: How Videogames Represent the Past and Offer Access to Historical Practice*, Routledge Advances in Game Studies 7 (New York, NY: Routledge, Taylor & Francis Group, 2016); Vincenzo Idone Cassone and Mattia Thibault, "The HGR Framework: A Semiotic Approach to the Representation of History in Digital Games," *Gamevironments* 5 (2016): 156–204; Robert Houghton, "World, Structure and Play: A Framework for Games as Historical Research Outputs, Tools, and Processes," *Práticas Da História* 7 (2018): 11–43.

9 Josef Köstlbauer, "Do Computers Play History?," in *Early Modernity and Video Games*, ed. Tobias Winnerling and Florian Kerschbaumer (Newcastle upon Tyne: Cambridge Scholars, 2014), 24–37; Claire Taylor, "Serious Gaming: Critiques of Neoliberalism in the Works of Ricardo Miranda Zúñiga," in *Video Games and the Global South*, ed. Phillip Penix-Tadsen (Pittsburgh: Carnegie Mellon University, 2019), 47–58; Jörg Friedrich, "You Do Have Responsibility! How Games Trivialize Fascism, Why This Should Concern Us and How We Could Change It," in *History in Games: Contingencies of an Authentic Past*, ed. Martin Lorber and Felix Zimmermann, Studies of Digital Media Culture 12 (Bielefeld: Transcript-Verl, 2020), 259–75.

indeed has their potency as tools for right wing extremists.[10] The emergence of a new range of tropes and tendencies within historical games has been catalogued and is the subject of ongoing academic scrutiny from multiple disciplines.[11] Innumerable monographs, edited volumes, and journal articles have been published considering a vast and expanding range of periods,[12] regions,[13] and themes[14] which have contributed to a vibrant and diverse historiographical tradition. Be-

---

10 Jessie Daniels and Nick Lalone, "Racism in Video Gaming: Connecting Extremist and Mainstream Expressions of White Supremacy," in *Social Exclusion, Power, and Video Game Play: New Research in Digital Media and Technology*, ed. David G. Embrick, J. Talmadge Wright, and András Lukács (Lanham: Lexington Books, 2012), 85–100; Jules Skotnes-Brown, "Colonized Play: Racism, Sexism and Colonial Legacies in the DOTA 2 South Africa Gaming Community," in *Video Games and the Global South*, ed. Phillip Penix-Tadsen (Pittsburgh: Carnegie Mellon University, 2019), 143–53; Sam Srauy, "Professional Norms and Race in the North American Video Game Industry," *Games and Culture* 14, no. 5 (July 2019): 478–97, https://doi.org/10.1177/1555412017708936.

11 Matthew Kapell and Andrew B. R. Elliott, eds., *Playing with the Past: Digital Games and the Simulation of History* (New York: Bloomsbury Academic, 2013); Angenitus Arie Andries Mol et al., eds., *The Interactive Past: Archaeology, Heritage & Video Games* (Leiden: Sidestone Press, 2017); A. Martin Wainwright, *Virtual History: How Videogames Portray the Past* (Abingdon, Oxon; New York, NY: Routledge, 2019); Alexander von Lünen et al., eds., *Historia Ludens: The Playing Historian*, Routledge Approaches to History, vol. 30 (New York, NY: Routledge, 2020).

12 Carl Heinze, *Mittelalter Computer Spiele: Zur Darstellung und Modellierung von Geschichte im populären Computerspiel*, Historische Lebenswelten in populären Wissenskulturen 8 (Bielefeld: Transcript-Verl, 2012); Tobias Winnerling and Florian Kerschbaumer, eds., *Early Modernity and Video Games* (Newcastle upon Tyne: Cambridge Scholars, 2014); Daniel T. Kline, ed., *Digital Gaming Re-Imagines the Middle Ages*, Routledge Studies in New Media and Cyberculture 15 (New York: Routledge, 2014); Christian Rollinger, ed., *Classical Antiquity in Video Games: Playing with the Ancient World*, Imagines – Classical Receptions in the Visual and Performing Arts (London; New York: Bloomsbury Academic, 2020).

13 Vít Šisler, "Digital Arabs: Representation in Video Games," *European Journal of Cultural Studies* 11, no. 2 (2008): 203–20, https://doi.org/10.1177/1367549407088333; Fede Peñate Domínguez, "Steel-Clad Conquistadores on Horseback. A Case Study of Selective Authenticity and the Spanish Empire in Computer Games," *Presura* 23 (February 2017): 22–41; Phillip Penix-Tadsen, ed., *Video Games and the Global South* (Pittsburgh: Carnegie Mellon University, 2019).

14 Chris Kempshall, *The First World War in Computer Games* (Basingstoke, Hampshire; New York, NY: Palgrave Macmillan, 2015); Robert Houghton, ed., *Playing the Crusades*, Engaging the Crusades: The Memory and Legacy of the Crusades, Volume Five (Abingdon, Oxon; New York, NY: Routledge, 2021); Alyssa Goldstein Sepinwall, *Slave Revolt on Screen: The Haitian Revolution in Film and Video Games*, Caribbean Studies Series (Jackson: University Press of Mississippi, 2021).

yond this, games have been considered as scholarly historical research outputs, methods, and forums.[15]

A significant portion of this literature has focused on the use of games as learning tools. Historical games can have a phenomenal impact on their players' perceptions of the past – potentially to an even greater extent than any other form of popular media.[16] Anecdotal evidence and a growing number of quantitative and qualitative studies have demonstrated that impact extends into the classroom: for a sizeable minority of students, games play a pivotal role in the emergence of an interest in history as a subject, but also in their formative understanding of the discipline and the past.[17] The potency of games in this regard has contributed to their employment as elements of a growing range of educational programmes at almost every level of study, a development which has been accompanied by a corresponding emergence of a vibrant field of pedagogical research. There are of course limits to the capacities of games as educational tools and a number of authors have rightly highlighted potential pitfalls of using this medium in this manner ranging from the imperialist and colonialist tendencies of commercial games[18] to the difficulties inherent in securing

---

[15] Clyde, Hopkins, and Wilkinson, "Beyond the 'Historical' Simulation"; Jeremy Antley, "Going Beyond the Textual in History," *Journal of Digital Humanities* 1, no. 2 (2012), http://journalofdigitalhumanities.org/1-2/going-beyond-the-textual-in-history-by-jeremy-antley/; Dawn Spring, "Gaming History: Computer and Video Games as Historical Scholarship," *Rethinking History* 19, no. 2 (2015): 207–21, https://doi.org/10.1080/13642529.2014.973714; Vinicius Marino Carvalho, "Videogames as Tools for Social Science History," *Historian* 79, no. 4 (2017): 794–819, https://doi.org/10.1111/hisn.12674; Robert Houghton, "Scholarly History through Digital Games: Pedagogical Practice as Research Method," in *Return to the Interactive Past: The Interplay of Video Games and Histories*, ed. Csilla E. Ariese-Vandemeulebroucke et al. (Sidestone Press, 2021), 137–55.

[16] Robert Houghton, "Where Did You Learn That? The Self-Perceived Educational Impact of Historical Computer Games on Undergraduates," *Gamevironments* 5 (2016): 8–45; Sian Beavers, "The Informal Learning of History with Digital Games" (Open University, 2019).

[17] Andrew B. R. Elliott and Matthew Kapell, "Introduction: To Build a Past That Will 'Stand the Test of Time'- Discovering Historical Facts, Assembling Historical Narratives," in *Playing with the Past: Digital Games and the Simulation of History*, ed. Matthew Kapell and Andrew B. R. Elliott (New York: Bloomsbury Academic, 2013); Houghton, "Where Did You Learn That?".

[18] Stefan Donecker, "Pharaoh Mao Zedong and the Musketeers of Babylon: The Civilization Series between Primordialist Nationalism and Subversive Parody," in *Early Modernity and Video Games*, ed. Tobias Winnerling and Florian Kerschbaumer (Newcastle upon Tyne: Cambridge Scholars, 2014), 105–22; Sabine Harrer, "Casual Empire: Video Games as Neocolonial Praxis," *Open Library of Humanities* 4, no. 1 (2018): 5, https://doi.org/10.16995/olh.210.

student engagement across an entire cohort.[19] Much of the skepticism around the use of games as learning tools emerges from the poor reputation of "edutainment" games, which are frequently seen as failures both in educational and entertainment terms.[20] Perhaps most notably in recent years, the edutainment game *Playing History 2: Slave Trade*[21] has been widely criticized for a combination of simplistic mechanics drawn from franchises as diverse as *Tetris*[22] and *Crazy Taxi*[23] with a naïve and often trivial discussion of a serious issue with heavy contemporary resonance.[24] Nevertheless, ludic approaches are demonstrably effective teaching tools when delivered using suitable games, in an appropriate context, and through a critical approach.[25] The development of more complex and interesting games which permit education through play rather than gamifying classroom activities or rote learning can provide a pedagogically valid interactive technique and support student engagement.[26] Even the most serious historical issues may potentially be approached through appropriately designed and deployed games.

---

19 James Paul Gee, "What Video Games Have to Teach Us about Learning and Literacy," *Computers in Entertainment* 1, no. 1 (October 1, 2003): 1–20, https://doi.org/10.1145/950566.950595; David Leonard, "'Live in Your World, Play in Ours': Race, Video Games, and Consuming the Other," *SIMILE: Studies In Media & Information Literacy Education* 3, no. 4 (November 2003): 1–9, http://dx.doi.org/10.3138/sim.3.4.002; Jeremiah McCall, "Teaching History With Digital Historical Games: An Introduction to the Field and Best Practices," *Simulation & Gaming* 47, no. 4 (2016): 517–42, https://doi.org/10.1177/1046878116646693; Robert Houghton, "History Games for Boys? Gender, Genre and the Self-Perceived Impact of Historical Games on Undergraduate Historians," *Gamevironments* 14 (2021): 1–49, https://doi.org/10.26092/ELIB/918.
20 Richard Van Eck, "Digital Game Based Learning: It's Not Just the Digital Native Who Are Rest-Less," *Educause Review* 41 (2006): 16–30.
21 *Playing History 2: Slave Trade* (Serious Games Interactive, 2013).
22 *Tetris* (Alexey Pajitnov, 1984).
23 *Crazy Taxi* (Sega, 1999).
24 Wainwright, *Virtual History*, 196–99; Armond R. Towns, "Gamifying Blackness: From Slave Records to *Playing History: Slave Trade*," *Information, Communication & Society* 24, no. 12 (2021): 1–15, https://doi.org/10.1080/1369118X.2020.1739730.
25 Kevin Schut, "Strategic Simulations and Our Past: The Bias of Computer Games in the Presentation of History," *Games and Culture* 2, no. 3 (2007): 213–35, https://doi.org/10.1177/1555412007306202; Jeremiah McCall, "Navigating the Problem Space: The Medium of Simulation Games in the Teaching of History," *History Teacher* 1 (2012): 9–28; Jeremiah McCall, "Playing with the Past: History and Video Games (and Why It Might Matter)," *Journal of Geek Studies* 6, no. 1 (2019): 29–48.
26 Dennis Charsky, "From Edutainment to Serious Games: A Change in the Use of Game Characteristics," *Games and Culture* 5, no. 2 (2010): 177–98, https://doi.org/10.1177/1555412009354727; Simon Egenfeldt-Nielsen, *Beyond Edutainment: Exploring the Educational Potential of Computer Games* (S.l.: Selbstverlag bei www.lulu.com, 2010), Introduction.

Games may play a particularly important role in teaching which engages with the Middle Ages or medievalism. There is a growing body of evidence which suggests that historical games have a notably greater impact on their audience's perceptions of the pre-modern period than modern or contemporary history.[27] This trend is particularly noteworthy given that games which address the ancient world or, especially, the medieval world represent a significantly smaller proportion of published commercial games than those with a more modern setting.[28] There are numerous possible explanations for this anomaly, but ultimately these findings underline the potential utility of these games in teaching earlier periods of history. In combination with the unique and often unexpected tropes which emerge within games which employ medieval elements, games represent an important tool for the classroom in several fields, but one which must be deployed with particular care.

It is therefore vital that the use of games in the medieval history or medieval studies classroom is supported appropriately in order to ensure the effectiveness of the method and, moreover, to ensure that the exercise does not have a negative outcome for any students. This necessitates an understanding of emergent pedagogic approaches: of what games can teach and how. It also requires an engagement with the content of the games which will be used and, more generally, of the broader tendencies of historical representation within games.

Games for Teaching History

There is a well-established pedagogy of learning through play developed initially with regards to teaching through card, board, and tabletop games,[29] and teaching with videogames rests in large part on these traditions. Most games are inherently learning experiences: the player must learn to manipulate the

---

[27] Houghton, "Where Did You Learn That?"; Beavers, "The Informal Learning of History with Digital Games."
[28] Yannick Rochat, "A Quantitative Study of Historical Video Games (1981–2015)," in *Historia Ludens: The Playing Historian*, ed. Alexander von Lünen et al., Routledge Approaches to History, vol. 30 (New York, NY: Routledge, 2020), 3–19.
[29] Matthew Kirschenbaum, "Contests for Meaning: Playing King Philip's War in the Twenty-First Century," in *Pastplay: Teaching and Learning History with Technology*, ed. Kevin Kee (University of Michigan Press, 2014), 202, https://doi.org/10.2307/j.ctv65swr0.13; Philip Sabin, "Wargames as an Academic Instrument," in *Zones of Control: Perspectives on Wargaming*, ed. Pat Harrigan and Matthew G. Kirschenbaum, Game Histories (Cambridge, Massachusetts: The MIT Press, 2016), 424.

game's systems in order to progress and ultimately complete the game.[30] In the case of historical games, the player must learn how best to interact with the pseudo-historical environment presented by the game. Digital games are, in some ways, more potent educational tools than their traditional counterparts, although they also carry additional limitations and challenges in their use. These games have been used at almost every level of study of history from pre-school to postgraduate taught courses and deployed in various ways and to teach about a plethora of periods and themes.

At their most fundamental, historical digital games can introduce students to new periods, regions, and themes, and help to develop their basic understanding of elements of the past.[31] The audio-visual representations of environments and material culture within games such as *Assassin's Creed*,[32] *Call of Duty*,[33] *Age of Empires*,[34] or *Total War*[35] can allow student players to experience a simplified and stylised version of a historical world which can nevertheless form a strong introduction to the period and a valuable foundation for future study.[36] A particular example of this approach is found in Nicholls' extensive and painstakingly detailed digital reconstruction of fourth century Rome and the use of this evolving model within the classroom.[37] Through his teaching, Nicholls has demonstrated that the physical environments created within digital games can be more accessible to students than traditional maps and plans.[38]

Games can move beyond these simple introductions to present historical theories and models through their mechanics and rules. A game's mechanics represent an abstract and truncated model of reality, which is nevertheless functional, internally consistent, and extensively explorable. This model is in essence an argument about the events and systems it represents.[39] In the case of historical

---

30 Jesper Juul, *Half-Real: Video Games between Real Rules and Fictional Worlds* (Cambridge, Mass: MIT Press, 2005), 95–97.
31 Juan Francisco Jiménez Alcázar, "The Other Possible Past: Simulation of the Middle Ages in Video Games," *Imago Temporis* 5 (2011): 311; Houghton, "Where Did You Learn That?," 32.
32 *Assassin's Creed* (Ubisoft, 2007).
33 *Call of Duty* (Activision, 2003).
34 *Age of Empires* (Ensemble Studios, 1997).
35 For example: *Shogun: Total War* (Creative Assembly, 2000).
36 Spring, "Gaming History," 211–12; Chapman, *Digital Games as History*, 66; János Vas, "Four Categories Of Video Games in the Practice of History Teaching," *Staféta* 2 (2017): 217–19.
37 Nicholls, "Digital Visualisation in Classics Teaching and Beyond."
38 Nicholls, 27.
39 Ian Bogost, "The Rhetoric of Video Games," in *The Ecology of Games: Connecting Youth, Games, and Learning*, ed. Katie Salen Tekinbaş, The John D. and Catherine T. Macarthur Foundation Series on Digital Media and Learning (Cambridge, Mass: MIT Press, 2008), 117–40; Ian

games, the game mechanics represent arguments about historical systems and societies: they do not show historical events as they happened, but rather describe historical frameworks.[40] Within a learning environment, these games can be used to support the formative development of students' knowledge of historical systems through the presentation of arguments of cause and effect and by allowing the exploration of counter-factual histories.[41] Games such as *Empire: Total War*[42] or *Patrician*[43] have been used to teach economic history from basic concepts of supply and demand to more complex considerations of Imperial economics and mercantilism.[44] More complex games such as those of the *Civilization*[45] and *Europa Universalis*[46] series allow students to explore nuanced geopolitical situations in their entirety, highlighting the interconnected nature of politics, society, technology, economics, warfare, and a range of other factors.[47]

Bogost, *Persuasive Games: The Expressive Power of Videogames* (Cambridge, Mass.: MIT Press, 2010).
40 Rolfe Daus Peterson, Andrew Justin Miller, and Sean Joseph Fedorko, "The Same River Twice: Exploring Historical Representation and the Value of Simulation in the Total War, Civilization and Patrician Franchises," in *Playing with the Past: Digital Games and the Simulation of History*, ed. Matthew Kapell and Andrew B. R. Elliott (New York: Bloomsbury Academic, 2013), esp. p. 38; Adam Chapman, "Affording History: Civilization and the Ecological Approach," in *Playing with the Past: Digital Games and the Simulation of History*, ed. Matthew Kapell and Andrew B. R. Elliott (New York: Bloomsbury Academic, 2013), 61–73; Spring, "Gaming History," 215; Carvalho, "Videogames as Tools," 812; Houghton, "World, Structure and Play," 25–27.
41 Gary King, Robert O Keohane, and Sidney Verba, *Designing Social Inquiry: Scientific Inference in Qualitative Research*, 1994, http://www.dawsonera.com/depp/reader/protected/external/AbstractView/S9781400821211; Harry J. Brown, *Videogames and Education* (Armonk, N.Y.: M.E. Sharpe, 2008), 118; Alcázar, "The Other Possible Past," 300–301; Peterson, Miller, and Fedorko, "The Same River Twice," esp. p. 38.
42 *Empire: Total War* (Activision, 2009).
43 *The Patrician* (Ascaron, 1993).
44 Peterson, Miller, and Fedorko, "The Same River Twice," 41–42.
45 *Sid Meier's Civilization* (MicroProse, 1991).
46 *Europa Universalis* (Paradox Interactive, 2000).
47 Alex Whelchel, "Using Civilization Simulation Video Games in the World History Classroom," *World History Connected* 4, no. 2 (2007), http://worldhistoryconnected.press.uillinois.edu/4.2/whelchel.html; John K. Lee and Jeffrey Probert, "Civilization III and Whole-Class Play," *The Journal of Social Studies Research* 34, no. 1 (2010): 1–28; John Pagnotti and William B. Russell, "Using Civilization IV to Engage Students in World History Content," *The Social Studies* 103, no. 1 (2012): 39–48, https://doi.org/10.1080/00377996.2011.558940; Tom Apperley, "Modding the Historians Code: Historical Versimilitude and the Counterfactual Imagination," in *Playing with the Past: Digital Games and the Simulation of History*, ed. Matthew Kapell and Andrew B. R. Elliott (New York: Bloomsbury Academic, 2013), 185–98; Peterson, Miller, and Fedorko, "The Same River Twice," 43; Stephen Ortega, "Representing the Past: Video Games

Even games with a less obvious connection to history have been employed to teach the subject, such as Vas' use of the post-apocalyptic roleplaying series *Fallout*[48] to consider societal collapse.[49] Similar ludic teaching approaches have been deployed or suggested in neighboring fields including archaeology, international relations, and politics.[50] Historical games can allow students to discuss complex theoretical frameworks at various levels, extending all the way to postgraduate study.[51]

Play can also enable the critique of the historical arguments represented by game mechanics. Although these arguments are often questionable or outdated, this can present opportunities to interrogate flimsy historical arguments. Highlighting and analyzing shortcomings in the mechanics of a historical game mirrors the methods used to analyze the veracity of historical arguments put forth in more traditional academic media,[52] and this activity holds substantial learning potential.[53] Ortega has successfully used class criticism of the mechanics of *Civilization V* to engage students with the critique of historical arguments more generally.[54] In a similar manner, and despite his concerns about acritical use of the game, Donnecker has suggested that *Civilization* may be used educationally as a parody of nationalist history and ideology through the critique of the game's representation of historical figures and processes.[55] As McMichael

---

Challenge to the Historical Narrative," *Syllabus* 4, no. 1 (2015): 1–13; Vas, "Four Categories Of Video Games in the Practice of History Teaching," 215–17; Krijn H. J. Boom et al., "Teaching through Play: Using Video Games as a Platform to Teach about the Past," in *Communicating the Past in the Digital Age: Proceedings of the International Conference on Digital Methods in Teaching and Learning in Archaeology (12th-13th October 2018)*, ed. Sebastian Hageneuer (Ubiquity Press, 2020), 36–37, https://doi.org/10.5334/bch.
48 *Fallout* (Interplay Productions, 1997).
49 Vas, "Four Categories Of Video Games in the Practice of History Teaching," 221–23; Boom et al., "Teaching through Play," 37–38.
50 Nicolas de Zamaróczy, "Are We What We Play? Global Politics in Historical Strategy Computer Games," *International Studies Perspectives* 18, no. 2 (2017): 155–58, https://doi.org/10.1093/isp/ekv010; Tara Jane Copplestone, "Designing and Developing a Playful Past in Video Games," in *The Interactive Past: Archaeology, Heritage & Video Games*, ed. Angenitus Arie Andries Mol et al. (Leiden: Sidestone Press, 2017), 96; Boom et al., "Teaching through Play," 36–37.
51 A. Martin Wainwright, "Teaching Historical Theory through Video Games," *The History Teacher* 47, no. 4 (2014): 579.
52 Houghton, "World, Structure and Play," 27–29.
53 Jeremiah McCall, "Historical Simulations as Problem Spaces: Criticism and Classroom Use," *Journal of Digital Humanities* 1, no. 2 (2012): 21, http://journalofdigitalhumanities.org/1-2/historical-simulations-as-problem-spaces-by-jeremiah-mccall/.
54 Ortega, "Representing the Past," 1–4.
55 Donecker, "Pharaoh Mao Zedong and the Musketeers of Babylon," 120–21.

notes, the use of games in this manner can develop students' understanding of the presentation of history in society,[56] and Vas has argued that this critical approach may be used outside the strategy genre to consider the representation of history within the mechanics and world of games such as *Assassin's Creed*.[57] The limitations of the history presented in games can serve as a valuable means to explore and criticize historical arguments and viewpoints within a critical educational context.

Digital games can also be used to teach about the nature of history as a discipline. Custom built games have been created to teach historiographical approaches and to promote deconstructionist approaches to history. Clyde and Wilkinson developed *The History Game* to demonstrate their views on the construction of history as an abstract concept, formed by the selection of facts, evidence, interpretations, and conclusions made by their player historians.[58] More recently, Martínez has developed *Time Historians* where students collect data and interpretations relating to ancient Egypt in order to collaboratively create a historical account. He takes a loosely similar approach to Clyde and Wilkinson and utilizes a deconstructionist approach to demonstrate historiography and historical discourse while underlining the limits of empiricism.[59] Games have also been created to directly and explicitly support the development of other historical skills – a key example of this is Compeau and MacDougal's *Tecumesh Lies Here* which deploys augmented reality to direct students to learn about historical events and arguments through traditional methods including the use of libraries, archives, and the internet.[60]

A less abstract method to engage students with historical debate makes use of user modifications and game creation and has been deployed by several historians and teachers. As the mechanics of historical games represent arguments about given periods and themes, the alteration of these mechanics on the basis of historical research corresponds to the development of counterarguments and

---

[56] Andrew McMichael, "PC Games and the Teaching of History," *The History Teacher* 40, no. 2 (February 2007): 203–4.
[57] Vas, "Four Categories Of Video Games in the Practice of History Teaching," 219–21.
[58] Jerremie Clyde and Glenn R. Wilkinson, "More Than a Game . . . Teaching in the Gamic Mode: Disciplinary Knowledge, Digital Literacy, and Collaboration," *The History Teacher* 46, no. 1 (2012): 49–56.
[59] Manuel Alejandro Cruz Martínez, "The Potential of Video Games for Exploring Deconstructionist History" (PhD, University of Sussex, 2019).
[60] Timothy Compeau and Robert MacDougall, "Tecumseh Lies Here: Goals and Challenges for a Pervasive History Game in Progress," in *Pastplay: Teaching and Learning History with Technology*, ed. Kevin Kee (University of Michigan Press, 2014), 94–97, https://doi.org/10.2307/j.ctv65swr0.8.

debate.[61] Kee and Graham have demonstrated this in practice through student modification of *Civilization IV* as a conscious development of historical theses.[62] They have extended this method by having students construct digital games through a historically critical and scholarly approach.[63] Boom et al. have highlighted the widespread applicability of a similar method through the use of the text based game creator *Twine*: students develop gameplay based on their historical knowledge and research and in doing so create arguments about the past.[64]

Beyond these uses of game rules, mechanics, and modification as historical teaching methods, the use of this media as a platform for roleplay has substantial pedagogical merit. Bowman has constructed an extensive historical survey addressing the use of roleplaying games across a substantial range of fields,[65] and there is some evidence that roleplaying elements of games can extend their impact on players' understanding of history.[66] Within the study of history, roleplay has long formed an educational tool across periods and themes as a means to engage students with new periods and approaches,[67] and while these methods do not necessarily rely on formal game environments and structures, they nevertheless can form important elements of learning strategies through games. McDaniel's basic methodology for the deployment of educational roleplay (through preparing students with some knowledge of the subject matter, placing students in conflicting positions, providing direction and objectives for students within roleplay, managing students' progress through the exercise

---

61 Shawn Graham, "Rolling Your Own: On Modding Commercial Games for Educational Goals," in *Pastplay: Teaching and Learning History with Technology*, ed. Kevin Kee (University of Michigan Press, 2014), 226–27, https://doi.org/10.2307/j.ctv65swr0; Kevin Kee and Shawn Graham, "Teaching History in an Age of Pervasive Computing: The Case for Games in the High School and Undergraduate Classroom," in *Pastplay: Teaching and Learning History with Technology*, ed. Kevin Kee (University of Michigan Press, 2014), 279, https://doi.org/10.2307/j.ctv65swr0.17; Greg Koebel, "Simulating the Ages of Man: Periodization in Civilization V and Europa Universalis IV," *Loading . . . The Journal of the Canadian Game Studies Association* 10, no. 17 (2017): 72; Houghton, "World, Structure and Play," 27–31.
62 Kee and Graham, "Teaching History in an Age of Pervasive Computing," 279–81.
63 Kee and Graham, 281–85.
64 Boom et al., "Teaching through Play," 34–36.
65 Sarah Lynne Bowman, "Educational Live Action Role-Playing Games: A Secondary Literature Review," *The Wyrd Con Companion Book* 3 (2014): 112–31.
66 Houghton, "Where Did You Learn That?," 27–28.
67 Sharon M. Fennessey, *History in the Spotlight: Creative Drama and Theatre Practices for the Social Studies Classroom / Sharon M. Fennessey* (Portsmouth, NH: Heinemann, 2000); Avril Maddrell, "Teaching a Contextual and Feminist History of Geography through Role Play: Women's Membership of the Royal Geographical Society (1892–1893)," *Journal of Geography in Higher Education* 31, no. 3 (2007): 393–412, https://doi.org/10.1080/03098260601082305.

and ultimately embedding the roleplay activity within the broader curriculum[68]) was not designed around the use of games, but coincidentally follows much the same structure as McCall's framework for ludic education.[69] There is substantial potential for the further development of this overlap between roleplay and games in an educational environment.

Despite the wide-ranging and diverse potential for games as learning tools, it is important to acknowledge the limitations and peculiarities of the medium. The portrayal of history within commercial games is subject to the same pressures and trends found in any other media and, just as is the case with any other media, they tend to favor commercial interests, artistic spectacle, and popular expectations over historical veracity or depth.[70] Players' behavior within a game and their interpretation of the history it represents are inevitably influenced to a substantial extent by their understanding of this history: to an extent, the experience of history through games mirrors the players' expectations regardless of the intention of the creators of the game.[71] The focus on interactivity, player agency, competition, and progression within games can exaggerate these tendencies or create new and unexpected tropes and while the creation of custom games for learning purposes can alleviate many of these issues; this requires an understanding of how the fundamental differences in how games construct and communicate history in comparison to more traditional media. The creation of such games – and computer games in particular – can also require substantial investment of time and resources and requires a skillset removed from that of the traditional historian. Students also have a propensity to accept the history produced within games used for teaching as fact without challenging the arguments.[72] Most significantly, it must be acknowledged that proficiency, enthusiasm, and engagement with games can vary substantially within a class and there is alarming potential to alienate individuals and groups.[73]

---

68 Kathryn N. McDaniel, "Four Elements of Successful Historical Role-Playing in the Classroom," *The History Teacher* 33, no. 3 (May 2000): 357, https://doi.org/10.2307/495033.
69 McCall, "Teaching History With Digital Historical Games."
70 Donecker, "Pharaoh Mao Zedong and the Musketeers of Babylon," 116; Alessandro Testa, "Religion(s) in Videogames – Historical and Anthropological Observations," *Online – Heidelberg Journal of Religions on the Internet* 5 (2014): 271, https://doi.org/10.11588/REL.2014.0.12170; Adam Scott Glancy, "The 'I' in Team: War and Combat in Tabletop Tole-Playing Games," in *Zones of Control: Perspectives on Wargaming*, ed. Pat Harrigan and Matthew G. Kirschenbaum, Game Histories (Cambridge, Massachusetts: The MIT Press, 2016), 71–80; Houghton, "World, Structure and Play," 35–36.
71 Chapman, *Digital Games as History*, 36.
72 Schut, "Strategic Simulations," 228–29; Boom et al., "Teaching through Play," 31.
73 McCall, "Teaching History With Digital Historical Games," 532–33.

Nevertheless, the potency of games in the history classroom is evident. Despite their shortcomings, historical games can act as valuable and innovative methods for students to explore the past, but for this approach to be effective, they must be deployed critically. They must be used alongside formal teaching and accompanied by reflection before, during, and after play.[74] Furthermore, the limitations of individual games and the attitudes students bring to the medium and themes within these games must be addressed within the classroom.[75] McCall has emphasized the important role teachers should play in guiding students through the critical play and exploration of games,[76] and has developed extensive guidelines for the use of games as classroom tools.[77] In a similar manner, Pagnotti and Russell have produced an outline for the critical use of *Civilization IV*.[78] There is substantial pedagogical merit to these approaches and there is no reason why games should not be considered as valuable teaching tools when employed through the appropriate critical methods.

Modern Games and the Middle Ages

The place of the Middle Ages within modern games is peculiar. Representations of the period are driven by the confluence of medievalist and gaming tropes which often produce exaggerated or unexpected accounts. Games as a media tend to emphasize a number of factors including violence,[79] progression,[80]

---

[74] Ronan Lynch, Bride Mallon, and Cornelia Connolly, "The Pedagogical Application of Alternate Reality Games: Using Game-Based Learning to Revisit History," *International Journal of Game-Based Learning* 5, no. 2 (2015): 35–37, https://doi.org/10.4018/ijgbl.2015040102; Boom et al., "Teaching through Play," 31.
[75] Scott Alan Metzger and Richard J. Paxton, "Gaming History: A Framework for What Video Games Teach About the Past," *Theory & Research in Social Education* 44, no. 4 (2016): 556–58, https://doi.org/10.1080/00933104.2016.1208596.
[76] McCall, "Navigating the Problem Space," 23–24.
[77] McCall, 24–25; McCall, "Teaching History With Digital Historical Games."
[78] Pagnotti and Russell, "Using Civilization IV to Engage Students."
[79] de Zamaróczy, "Are We What We Play?," 165; Boom et al., "Teaching through Play," 33–34; Emil Lundedal Hammar, "Producing & Playing Hegemonic Pasts: Historical Digital Games as Memory-Making Media" (PhD, Arctic University of Norway, 2020), 64, https://munin.uit.no/handle/10037/17717; Houghton, "If You're Going to Be the King."
[80] Kaspar Pobłocki, "Becoming-State: The Bio-Cultural Imperialism of Sid Meier's Civilization," *Focaal – European Journal of Anthropology* 39 (2002): 165; Claudio Fogu, "Digitizing Historical Consciousness," *History and Theory* 48, no. 2 (May 2009): 117, https://doi.org/10.1111/j.

and competition[81] while abstracting, marginalizing or ignoring social interaction,[82] religion,[83] and morality.[84] Popular perceptions of the Middle Ages also typically focus on violence[85] but promote a vision of technological and social backwardness,[86] the centrality of religion,[87] and moral absolutes. Both sets of tropes tend towards eurocentrism and a white, male, and heterosexual world.[88] The combination of these tropes within modern games which employ medieval elements often produce easily anticipated exaggerations – such as extreme and endemic violence, implicit structural racism and sexism, or near absolute homogeneity of characters – but can also create more unexpected aberrations – Whiggish mechanics of technological progress accompanied by a "Dark Age" narrative, colorblind colonial empires in the eleventh century, or the segregation of religious paraphernalia and ritual from faith and morality.

1468-2303.2009.00500.x; de Zamaróczy, "Are We What We Play?," 166–67; Metzger and Paxton, "Gaming History," 554.

81 Espen J. Aarseth, "Quest Games as Post-Narrative Discourse," in *Narrative across Media: The Languages of Storytelling*, ed. Marie-Laure Ryan, Frontiers of Narrative (Lincoln: University of Nebraska Press, 2004), 365–66; Adam Smith and Soren Johnson, "Soren Johnson on Challenging the Norms of 4X Games," *Rock, Paper, Shotgun* (blog), April 6, 2018, https://www.rockpapershotgun.com/2018/04/06/soren-johnson-4x-strategy-interview/.

82 de Zamaróczy, "Are We What We Play?," 164–67; Wainwright, *Virtual History*, 102–11.

83 Domínguez, "Steel-Clad Conquistadores," 37; Wainwright, *Virtual History*, 141–48; Vít Šisler, "From Kuma\War to Quraish: Representation of Islam in Arab and American Video Games," in *Playing with Religion in Digital Games*, ed. Heidi Campbell and Gregory P. Grieve, Digital Game Studies (Bloomington, IN: Indiana University Press, 2014), 124–25.

84 William J. White, "The Right to Dream of the Middle Ages Simulating the Medieval in Tabletop RPGs," in *Digital Gaming Re-Imagines the Middle Ages*, ed. Daniel T. Kline, Routledge Studies in New Media and Cyberculture 15 (New York: Routledge, 2014), 21–22; Kathrin Trattner, "Religion, Games, and Othering: An Intersectional Approach," *Gamevironments* 4 (2016): 43–44; Hammar, "Producing & Playing Hegemonic Pasts," 65; Tilo Hartmann and Peter Vorderer, "It's Okay to Shoot a Character: Moral Disengagement in Violent Video Games," *Journal of Communication* 60, no. 1 (March 2010): 98, https://doi.org/10.1111/j.1460-2466.2009.01459.x.

85 Debra Ferreday, "Game of Thrones, Rape Culture and Feminist Fandom," *Australian Feminist Studies* 30, no. 83 (2015): 21–36, https://doi.org/10.1080/08164649.2014.998453; James L. Smith, "Medievalisms of Moral Panic:," in *Studies in Medievalism XXV: Medievalism and Modernity*, ed. Karl Fugelso, Joshua Davies, and Sarah Salih (Boydell and Brewer, 2016), 163–70, www.jstor.org/stable/10.7722/j.ctt19x3hn8.16.

86 Andrew B. R. Elliott, *Medievalism, Politics and Mass Media: Appropriating the Middle Ages in the Twenty-First Century*, Medievalism 10 (Woodbridge, Suffolk: D. S. Brewer, 2017), 55–77 esp. 77.

87 Heinze, *Mittelalter Computer Spiele*, 242–43.

88 Lisa Nakamura, "Queer Female of Color: The Highest Difficulty Setting There Is? Gaming Rhetoric as Gender Capital," *ADA* 1 (2012), https://doi.org/10.7264/N37P8W9V; Hammar, "Producing & Playing Hegemonic Pasts," 70–71.

These representations can easily influence their players perceptions of the Middle Ages, perhaps more so than for later periods of history.[89] Educational curricula largely marginalise or omit the medieval period leaving game developers and players to rely primarily on popular history and historical fiction to inform their understanding and play.[90] Medievalism is deeply embedded within the western popular imagination and has been employed to a substantial extent within the construction of modern political, cultural, and national identities,[91] and the reproduction of this medievalism within games serves to encourage players to accept their portrayal of the period.[92] The popularity of the fantasy genre within games and other media and the close association of this format with the medieval further complicates the representations within these games, but also contributes to their impact on their players' understanding of the period.[93] In combination, these factors contribute strongly to the potential influence exerted by these games.

As such, it is particularly important to consider the limitations of historical games for the teaching of the Middle Ages. They can be hugely influential both inside and outside the classroom and the complexity of influences behind their representations can lead to a sizeable range of deep and often unexpected depictions and receptions. In concert these issues can lead players towards unusual understandings of the period which must be interrogated carefully through critical play and integration with broader learning activities and approaches. This by no means disqualifies games as educational tools for the Middle Ages, and

---

89 Houghton, "Where Did You Learn That?," 25–26.

90 Houghton, 13–14.

91 Elliott, *Medievalism, Politics and Mass Media*; Paul B. Sturtevant, *The Middle Ages in Popular Imagination: Memory, Film and Medievalism*, New Directions in Medieval Studies (London; New York: I.B. Tauris, 2018).

92 Julian Wolterink, "Authentic Historical Imagery: A Suggested Approach for Medieval Videogame," *Gamevironments* 6 (2017): 104–31; Andrew B. R. Elliott and Mike Horswell, "Crusading Icons: Medievalism and Authenticity in Historical Digital Games," in *History in Games: Contingencies of an Authentic Past*, ed. Lorber Martin and Felix Zimmermann, Studies of Digital Media Culture 12 (Bielefeld: Transcript-Verl, 2020), 142.

93 Leigh Schwartz, "Fantasy, Realism, and the Other in Recent Video Games," *Space and Culture* 9, no. 3 (2006): 313–25, https://doi.org/10.1177/1206331206289019; Adam Chapman, "Playing the Historical Fantastic: Zombies, Mecha-Nazis and Making Meaning about the Past through Metaphor," in *War Games: Memory, Militarism and the Subject of Play*, ed. Phil Hammond and Holger Pötzsch (New York, NY: Bloomsbury Academic, 2020), 91–97; Aurelia Brandenburg, "'If It's a Fantasy World, Why Bother Trying to Make It Realistic?' Constructing and Debating the Middle Ages of *The Witcher 3: Wild Hunt*," in *History in Games: Contingencies of an Authentic Past*, ed. Martin Lorber and Felix Zimmermann, Studies of Digital Media Culture 12 (Bielefeld: Transcript-Verl, 2020), 201–20.

indeed as the chapters in this volume demonstrate they can be incredibly effective in this role, but it demands particular care when using them.

It should also be noted that the complex and convergent gaming and medievalist tropes present within these games pose some important learning and teaching opportunities. The web of influences behind these representations of the Middle Ages can form the basis for discussion of the development and dissemination of public medievalism and popular history.[94] In fact, the exaggerated tropes within this media in conjunction with the very visible and vocal popular discussion around these games can make them particularly useful case studies for this purpose – indeed this was a principle motivation for Heinze in selecting games with medieval elements as the subject of his *Mittelalter Computer Spiele*.[95] Beyond this, these games may be readily employed as demonstrations of the construction and interrogation of history: the selection and privileging of sources; the arrangement of data to support arguments through the creation of mechanics; and ultimately the consideration and debate of these arguments through play, counterplay, and user-modification. There are in sum a plethora of viable educational uses for representations of the Middle Ages in modern games.

This Volume

This volume presents a series of approaches to the use of historical games as learning and teaching tools for Medieval Studies and Popular Medievalism. In doing so it considers the use of physical and digital games as teaching tools at pre-university, undergraduate, and postgraduate levels; addresses the creation or modification of games for teaching; highlights the possibilities posed through user-modification as a learning activity; and ultimately notes the potential of games outside the classroom within museums and historical research. The volume balances the development of pedagogical theory with a substantial range of practical examples and highlights the overlap of effective teaching methods at pre-university and university level. This is facilitated through a tight focus on games as a medium and medieval history as the taught subject.

---

94 Andreas Körber, Johannes Meyer-Hamme, and Robert Houghton, "Learning to Think Historically: Some Theoretical Challenges When Playing the Crusades," in *Playing the Crusades*, ed. Robert Houghton, Engaging the Crusades: The Memory and Legacy of the Crusades, Volume Five (Abingdon, Oxon; New York, NY: Routledge, 2021), 103.
95 Heinze, *Mittelalter Computer Spiele*, 13–17.

Part I provides a consideration of the learning impact of games on their players within and outside the classroom. In their chapter, Eve Stirling and Jamie Wood use the results of an extensive online survey to examine the formative learning acquired by history students' casual play of historical video games. They explore how and why the respondents thought that some games were historical, and how playing games encouraged them to go beyond the digital world to further their understanding of the past. They consider students' roles as active agents in learning about the past through virtual play rather than as passive consumers of digital products. They draw on this analysis to provide suggestions about how games might be used productively to support students' learning.

Part II concerns the use of commercial games in education. Within this section, Mike Horswell sketches out ways in which crusading was presented in *Assassin's Creed*, and demonstrates how we might unpack its vision of crusading and the histories of perceptions of the past embedded in, and transmitted by, the franchise-launching game. David Devine continues in this vein to consider gamifying the composition classroom at university level by using *Skyrim* to allow the player to take on the identity of "the student of medievalist rhetoric." Mehmet Şükrü Kuran and Ahmet Erdem Tozoğlu describe their experiences using *Crusader Kings II* as a supplementary tool to teach medieval macro-history following a "history-as-a-process" philosophy and to provide an immersive teaching experience through the combination of lectures and discussions with personal gaming experience.

Part III moves on to consider the possibilities presented by custom built games within the classroom. In their chapter Klio Stamou, Anna Sotiropoulou, and Phivos Milonas describe the creation of a video game designed to familiarize pre-university students with the Byzantine era and aspects of its everyday life – such as military organization and public administration – and hence to develop students' historical thinking and social awareness. Next, Owen Gottlieb and Shawn Clybor address their experience of iterative curriculum design around the *Lost & Found* series set in Fustat (Old Cairo) in the twelfth century at high school level. In the final chapter of this section Coutnay Konshuh and Frank Klaasen explore the creation and deployment of their game – *The Renaissance Marriage Game* – as a supplementary educational tool and reflect on its use within a large class.

Part IV considers the potential of student led game design and modification as a pedagogical tool. Erik Champion, Terhi Nurmikko-Fuller, and Katrina Grant explore the ways in which *Skyrim* can be used and modified by undergraduate and postgraduate students to explain, through play, three related aspects of medieval society: the distinctive, related, and unique characteristics of Romanesque and Gothic architecture; the art, craft, and preservation of calligraphy, literature, inscription, and lore; and the importance of the medieval landscape in art history. Robert Houghton's chapter presents a teaching case study around the creation and modification of a board game representation of the Investiture Contest, underlines the importance of historical and digital literacies in the use of such methods, and considers techniques to counter underlying assumptions about the period and medium. Finally, Klaasen considers how theoretical models or concepts (such as race, class gender, anxiety, inversion, or repression) may be used as the basis for students to develop historical games which reflect and investigate these concepts through their mechanics.

Part V addresses the potential of historical games outside the classroom. Mariana Lopez, Marques Hardin, and Wenqi Wan discuss how gamification strategies have been combined with specialist knowledge on acoustical heritage, computer modelling, soundscape recreation, and medieval drama to create the online interface *The Soundscapes of the York Mystery Plays*. The final chapter by Houghton considers the potential of games as research tools for professional academic study. It considers the theory and practice surrounding this emergent field to highlight the possibilities and pitfalls presented by this medium and highlights divergent Gamic, Simulacrum, and Roleplaying approaches.

These chapters address numerous aspects of games as educational tools within various aspects of the field of medieval history and aligned and adjacent disciplines. Their approaches are hugely varied and present a cross section of the incredibly diverse array of teaching and learning methods surrounding the use of this media. Taken as a whole, they provide a substantial range of methods and methodologies which may be profitably transferred to teach almost any element of the Middle Ages or medievalism and to consider issues from other periods and fields. The pedagogical utility of games is undoubtedly limited by designer and audience expectations of the medium alongside its practical limitations, but the case studies and theory related through this volume do much to alleviate these issues and demonstrate the potency of games as educational tools.

Bibliography

Aarseth, Espen J. *Cybertext: Perspectives on Ergodic Literature*. Baltimore, Md: Johns Hopkins University Press, 1997.
Aarseth, Espen J. "Quest Games as Post-Narrative Discourse." In *Narrative across Media: The Languages of Storytelling*, edited by Marie-Laure Ryan, 361–76. Frontiers of Narrative. Lincoln: University of Nebraska Press, 2004.
Alcázar, Juan Francisco Jiménez. "The Other Possible Past: Simulation of the Middle Ages in Video Games." *Imago Temporis* 5 (2011): 299–340.

Alvestad, Karl, and Robert Houghton, eds. *The Middle Ages in Modern Culture: History and Authenticity in Contemporary Medievalism*. 2021. https://doi.org/10.5040/9781350167452?locatt=label:secondary_bloomsburyCollections.

Andriotis, Konstantinos. "Genres of Heritage Authenticity: Denotations from a Pilgrimage Landscape." *Annals of Tourism Research* 38, no. 4 (October 2011): 1613–33. https://doi.org/10.1016/j.annals.2011.03.001.

Antley, Jeremy. "Going Beyond the Textual in History." *Journal of Digital Humanities* 1, no. 2 (2012). http://journalofdigitalhumanities.org/1-2/going-beyond-the-textual-in-history-by-jeremy-antley/.

Apperley, Tom. "Modding the Historians Code: Historical Versimilitude and the Counterfactual Imagination." In *Playing with the Past: Digital Games and the Simulation of History*, edited by Matthew Kapell and Andrew B. R. Elliott, 185–98. New York: Bloomsbury Academic, 2013.

Beavers, Sian. "The Informal Learning of History with Digital Games." Open University, 2019.

Bogost, Ian. *Persuasive Games: The Expressive Power of Videogames*. Cambridge, Mass.: MIT Press, 2010.

Bogost, Ian. "The Rhetoric of Video Games." In *The Ecology of Games: Connecting Youth, Games, and Learning*, edited by Katie Salen Tekinbaş, 117–40. The John D. and Catherine T. Macarthur Foundation Series on Digital Media and Learning. Cambridge, Mass: MIT Press, 2008.

Boom, Krijn H. J., Csilla E. Ariese, Bram van den Hout, Angenitus Arie Andries Mol, and Aris Politopoulos. "Teaching through Play: Using Video Games as a Platform to Teach about the Past." In *Communicating the Past in the Digital Age: Proceedings of the International Conference on Digital Methods in Teaching and Learning in Archaeology (12th-13th October 2018)*, edited by Sebastian Hageneuer, 27–44. Ubiquity Press, 2020. https://doi.org/10.5334/bch.

Bowman, Sarah Lynne. "Educational Live Action Role-Playing Games: A Secondary Literature Review." *The Wyrd Con Companion Book* 3 (2014): 112–31.

Brandenburg, Aurelia. "'If It's a Fantasy World, Why Bother Trying to Make It Realistic?' Constructing and Debating the Middle Ages of The Witcher 3: Wild Hunt." In *History in Games: Contingencies of an Authentic Past*, edited by Martin Lorber and Felix Zimmermann, 201–20. Studies of Digital Media Culture 12. Bielefeld: Transcript-Verl, 2020.

Brown, Harry J. *Videogames and Education*. Armonk, N.Y.: M.E. Sharpe, 2008.

Carvalho, Vinicius Marino. "Videogames as Tools for Social Science History." *Historian* 79, no. 4 (2017): 794–819. https://doi.org/10.1111/hisn.12674.

Cassone, Vincenzo Idone, and Mattia Thibault. "The HGR Framework: A Semiotic Approach to the Representation of History in Digital Games." *Gamevironments* 5 (2016): 156–204.

Champion, Erik. *Critical Gaming: Interactive History and Virtual Heritage*. Digital Research in the Arts and Humanities. Farnham, Surrey: Ashgate, 2015.

Chapman, Adam. "Affording History: Civilization and the Ecological Approach." In *Playing with the Past: Digital Games and the Simulation of History*, edited by Matthew Kapell and Andrew B. R. Elliott, 61–73. New York: Bloomsbury Academic, 2013.

Chapman, Adam. *Digital Games as History: How Videogames Represent the Past and Offer Access to Historical Practice*. Routledge Advances in Game Studies 7. New York, NY: Routledge, Taylor & Francis Group, 2016.

Chapman, Adam. "Playing the Historical Fantastic: Zombies, Mecha-Nazis and Making Meaning about the Past through Metaphor." In *War Games: Memory, Militarism and the Subject of Play*, edited by Phil Hammond and Holger Pötzsch, 91–110. New York, NY: Bloomsbury Academic, 2020.

Charsky, Dennis. "From Edutainment to Serious Games: A Change in the Use of Game Characteristics." *Games and Culture* 5, no. 2 (2010): 177–98. https://doi.org/10.1177/1555412009354727.

Classen, Christoph, and Wulf Kansteiner. "Truth and Authenticity in Contemporary Historical Culture: An Introduction to *Historical Representation and Historical Truth*." *History and Theory* 48, no. 2 (May 2009): 1–4. https://doi.org/10.1111/j.1468-2303.2009.00495.x.

Clyde, Jerremie, Howard Hopkins, and Glenn Wilkinson. "Beyond the 'Historical' Simulation: Using Theories of History to Inform Scholarly Game Design." *Loading . . . The Journal of the Canadian Game Studies Association* 6, no. 9 (2012). http://journals.sfu.ca/loading/index.php/loading/article/viewArticle/105.

Clyde, Jerremie, and Glenn R. Wilkinson. "More Than a Game . . . Teaching in the Gamic Mode: Disciplinary Knowledge, Digital Literacy, and Collaboration." *The History Teacher* 46, no. 1 (2012): 45–66.

Compeau, Timothy, and Robert MacDougall. "Tecumseh Lies Here: Goals and Challenges for a Pervasive History Game in Progress." In *Pastplay: Teaching and Learning History with Technology*, edited by Kevin Kee, 87–108. University of Michigan Press, 2014. https://doi.org/10.2307/j.ctv65swr0.8.

Copplestone, Tara Jane. "But That's Not Accurate: The Differing Perceptions of Accuracy in Cultural-Heritage Videogames between Creators, Consumers and Critics." *Rethinking History* 21, no. 3 (2017): 415–38. https://doi.org/10.1080/13642529.2017.1256615.

Copplestone, Tara Jane. "Designing and Developing a Playful Past in Video Games." In *The Interactive Past: Archaeology, Heritage & Video Games*, edited by Angenitus Arie Andries Mol, Csilla E. Ariese-Vandemeulebroucke, Krijn H. J. Boom, and Aris Politopoulos, 85–97. Leiden: Sidestone Press, 2017.

Daniels, Jessie, and Nick Lalone. "Racism in Video Gaming: Connecting Extremist and Mainstream Expressions of White Supremacy." In *Social Exclusion, Power, and Video Game Play: New Research in Digital Media and Technology*, edited by David G. Embrick, J. Talmadge Wright, and András Lukács, 85–100. Lanham: Lexington Books, 2012.

Domínguez, Fede Peñate. "Steel-Clad Conquistadores on Horseback. A Case Study of Selective Authenticity and the Spanish Empire in Computer Games." *Presura* 23 (February 2017): 22–41.

Donecker, Stefan. "Pharaoh Mao Zedong and the Musketeers of Babylon: The Civilization Series between Primordialist Nationalism and Subversive Parody." In *Early Modernity and Video Games*, edited by Tobias Winnerling and Florian Kerschbaumer, 105–22. Newcastle upon Tyne: Cambridge Scholars, 2014.

Egenfeldt-Nielsen, Simon. *Beyond Edutainment: Exploring the Educational Potential of Computer Games*. S.l.: Selbstverlag bei www.lulu.com, 2010. Introduction.

Elliott, Andrew B. R. *Medievalism, Politics and Mass Media: Appropriating the Middle Ages in the Twenty-First Century*. Medievalism 10. Woodbridge, Suffolk: D. S. Brewer, 2017.

Elliott, Andrew B. R., and Mike Horswell. "Crusading Icons: Medievalism and Authenticity in Historical Digital Games." In *History in Games: Contingencies of an Authentic Past*, edited by Lorber Martin and Felix Zimmermann, 137–55. Studies of Digital Media Culture 12. Bielefeld: Transcript-Verl, 2020.

Elliott, Andrew B. R., and Matthew Kapell. "Introduction: To Build a Past That Will 'Stand the Test of Time'- Discovering Historical Facts, Assembling Historical Narratives." In *Playing with the Past: Digital Games and the Simulation of History*, edited by Matthew Kapell and Andrew B. R. Elliott. New York: Bloomsbury Academic, 2013.

Ensslin, Astrid. *Literary Gaming*. Cambridge, Massachusetts; London, England: The MIT Press, 2014.

Fennessey, Sharon M. *History in the Spotlight: Creative Drama and Theatre Practices for the Social Studies Classroom / Sharon M. Fennessey*. Portsmouth, NH: Heinemann, 2000.

Ferreday, Debra. "Game of Thrones, Rape Culture and Feminist Fandom." *Australian Feminist Studies* 30, no. 83 (2015): 21–36. https://doi.org/10.1080/08164649.2014.998453.

Fogu, Claudio. "Digitizing Historical Consciousness." *History and Theory* 48, no. 2 (May 2009): 103–21. https://doi.org/10.1111/j.1468-2303.2009.00500.x.

Folder, Lori. "Thrones of Britannia – Campaign Map Reveal." *Total War Blog* (blog), November 12, 2017. https://www.totalwar.com/blog/thrones-campaign-map-reveal.

Friedrich, Jörg. "You Do Have Responsibility! How Games Trivialize Fascism, Why This Should Concern Us and How We Could Change It." In *History in Games: Contingencies of an Authentic Past*, edited by Martin Lorber and Felix Zimmermann, 259–75. Studies of Digital Media Culture 12. Bielefeld: Transcript-Verl, 2020.

Gee, James Paul. "What Video Games Have to Teach Us about Learning and Literacy." *Computers in Entertainment* 1, no. 1 (October 1, 2003): 1–20. https://doi.org/10.1145/950566.950595.

Graham, Shawn. "Agent Based Models, Archaeogaming, and the Useful Deaths of Digital Romans." In *The Interactive Past: Archaeology, Heritage & Video Games*, edited by Angenitus Arie Andries Mol, Csilla E. Ariese-Vandemeulebroucke, Krijn H. J. Boom, and Aris Politopoulos, 123–31. Leiden: Sidestone Press, 2017.

Graham, Shawn. "Rolling Your Own: On Modding Commercial Games for Educational Goals." In *Pastplay: Teaching and Learning History with Technology*, edited by Kevin Kee, 214–27. University of Michigan Press, 2014. https://doi.org/10.2307/j.ctv65swr0.

Hammar, Emil Lundedal. "Producing & Playing Hegemonic Pasts: Historical Digital Games as Memory-Making Media." PhD, Arctic University of Norway, 2020. https://munin.uit.no/handle/10037/17717.

Harrer, Sabine. "Casual Empire: Video Games as Neocolonial Praxis." *Open Library of Humanities* 4, no. 1 (2018): 5. https://doi.org/10.16995/olh.210.

Hartmann, Tilo, and Peter Vorderer. "It's Okay to Shoot a Character: Moral Disengagement in Violent Video Games." *Journal of Communication* 60, no. 1 (March 2010): 94–119. https://doi.org/10.1111/j.1460-2466.2009.01459.x.

Heinze, Carl. *Mittelalter Computer Spiele: Zur Darstellung und Modellierung von Geschichte im populären Computerspiel*. Historische Lebenswelten in populären Wissenskulturen 8. Bielefeld: Transcript-Verl, 2012.

Houghton, Robert. "History Games for Boys? Gender, Genre and the Self-Perceived Impact of Historical Games on Undergraduate Historians." *Gamevironments* 14 (2021): 1–49. https://doi.org/10.26092/ELIB/918.

Houghton, Robert. "If You're Going to Be the King, You'd Better Damn Well Act like the King: Setting Objectives to Encourage Realistic Play in Grand Strategy Computer Games." In *The Middle Ages in Modern Culture: History and Authenticity in Contemporary Medievalism*, edited by Karl Alvestad and Robert Houghton, 186–210. IBTauris, 2021.

Houghton, Robert. "It's What You Do With It That Counts: Factual Accuracy and Mechanical Accuracy in Crusader Kings II." *The Public Medievalist* (blog), September 30, 2014. https://www.publicmedievalist.com/ckii-houghton/.

Houghton, Robert, ed. *Playing the Crusades*. Engaging the Crusades: The Memory and Legacy of the Crusades, Volume Five. Abingdon, Oxon; New York, NY: Routledge, 2021.

Houghton, Robert. "Scholarly History through Digital Games: Pedagogical Practice as Research Method." In *Return to the Interactive Past: The Interplay of Video Games and Histories*, edited by Csilla E. Ariese-Vandemeulebroucke, Krijn H. J. Boom, Angenitus Arie Andries Mol, and Aris Politopoulos, 137–55. Leiden: Sidestone Press, 2021.

Houghton, Robert. "Where Did You Learn That? The Self-Perceived Educational Impact of Historical Computer Games on Undergraduates." *Gamevironments* 5 (2016): 8–45.

Houghton, Robert. "World, Structure and Play: A Framework for Games as Historical Research Outputs, Tools, and Processes." *Práticas Da História* 7 (2018): 11–43.

Hunicke, Robin, Marc LeBlanc, and Robert Zubeck. "MDA: A Formal Approach to Game Design and Game Research." *Proceedings of the Challenges in Games AI Workshop, Nineteenth National Conference of Artificial Intelligence*, 1–5. 2004.

Juul, Jesper. *Half-Real: Video Games between Real Rules and Fictional Worlds*. Cambridge, Mass: MIT Press, 2005.

Kapell, Matthew, and Andrew B. R. Elliott, eds. *Playing with the Past: Digital Games and the Simulation of History*. New York: Bloomsbury Academic, 2013.

Kee, Kevin, and Shawn Graham. "Teaching History in an Age of Pervasive Computing: The Case for Games in the High School and Undergraduate Classroom." In *Pastplay: Teaching and Learning History with Technology*, edited by Kevin Kee, 270–91. University of Michigan Press, 2014. https://doi.org/10.2307/j.ctv65swr0.17.

Kempshall, Chris. *The First World War in Computer Games*. Basingstoke, Hampshire; New York, NY: Palgrave Macmillan, 2015.

King, Gary, Robert O. Keohane, and Sidney Verba. *Designing Social Inquiry: Scientific Inference in Qualitative Research*, 1994. http://www.dawsonera.com/depp/reader/protected/external/AbstractView/S9781400821211.

Kirschenbaum, Matthew. "Contests for Meaning: Playing King Philip's War in the Twenty-First Century." In *Pastplay: Teaching and Learning History with Technology*, edited by Kevin Kee, 198–213. University of Michigan Press, 2014. https://doi.org/10.2307/j.ctv65swr0.13.

Kline, Daniel T., ed. *Digital Gaming Re-Imagines the Middle Ages*. Routledge Studies in New Media and Cyberculture 15. New York: Routledge, 2014.

Koebel, Greg. "Simulating the Ages of Man: Periodization in Civilization V and Europa Universalis IV." *Loading . . . The Journal of the Canadian Game Studies Association* 10, no. 17 (2017): 60–76.

Körber, Andreas, Johannes Meyer-Hamme, and Robert Houghton. "Learning to Think Historically: Some Theoretical Challenges When Playing the Crusades." In *Playing the Crusades*, edited by Robert Houghton, 93–110. Engaging the Crusades: The Memory and Legacy of the Crusades, Volume Five. Abingdon, Oxon; New York, NY: Routledge, 2021.

Köstlbauer, Josef. "Do Computers Play History?" In *Early Modernity and Video Games*, edited by Tobias Winnerling and Florian Kerschbaumer, 24–37. Newcastle upon Tyne: Cambridge Scholars, 2014.

Lee, John K., and Jeffrey Probert. "Civilization III and Whole-Class Play." *The Journal of Social Studies Research* 34, no. 1 (2010): 1–28.

Leonard, David. "'Live in Your World, Play in Ours': Race, Video Games, and Consuming the Other." *SIMILE: Studies In Media & Information Literacy Education* 3, no. 4 (November 2003): 1–9. http://dx.doi.org/10.3138/sim.3.4.002.

Lorber, Martin, and Felix Zimmermann, eds. *History in Games: Contingencies of an Authentic Past*. Studies of Digital Media Culture 12. Bielefeld: Transcript-Verl, 2020.

Lünen, Alexander von, Katherine J. Lewis, Benjamin Litherland, and P. H. Cullum, eds. *Historia Ludens: The Playing Historian*. Routledge Approaches to History, vol. 30. New York, NY: Routledge, 2020.

Lynch, Ronan, Bride Mallon, and Cornelia Connolly. "The Pedagogical Application of Alternate Reality Games: Using Game-Based Learning to Revisit History." *International Journal of Game-Based Learning* 5, no. 2 (2015): 18–38. https://doi.org/10.4018/ijgbl.2015040102.

Maddrell, Avril. "Teaching a Contextual and Feminist History of Geography through Role Play: Women's Membership of the Royal Geographical Society (1892–1893)." *Journal of Geography in Higher Education* 31, no. 3 (2007): 393–412. https://doi.org/10.1080/03098260601082305.

Martínez, Manuel Alejandro Cruz. "The Potential of Video Games for Exploring Deconstructionist History." PhD, University of Sussex, 2019.

McCall, Jeremiah. "Historical Simulations as Problem Spaces: Criticism and Classroom Use." *Journal of Digital Humanities* 1, no. 2 (2012). http://journalofdigitalhumanities.org/1-2/historical-simulations-as-problem-spaces-by-jeremiah-mccall/.

McCall, Jeremiah. "Navigating the Problem Space: The Medium of Simulation Games in the Teaching of History." *History Teacher* 1 (2012): 9–28.

McCall, Jeremiah. "Playing with the Past: History and Video Games (and Why It Might Matter)." *Journal of Geek Studies* 6, no. 1 (2019): 29–48.

McCall, Jeremiah. "Teaching History With Digital Historical Games: An Introduction to the Field and Best Practices." *Simulation & Gaming* 47, no. 4 (2016): 517–42. https://doi.org/10.1177/1046878116646693.

McDaniel, Kathryn N. "Four Elements of Successful Historical Role-Playing in the Classroom." *The History Teacher* 33, no. 3 (May 2000): 357. https://doi.org/10.2307/495033.

McMichael, Andrew. "PC Games and the Teaching of History." *The History Teacher* 40, no. 2 (February 2007): 203–18.

Metzger, Scott Alan, and Richard J. Paxton. "Gaming History: A Framework for What Video Games Teach About the Past." *Theory & Research in Social Education* 44, no. 4 (2016): 532–64. https://doi.org/10.1080/00933104.2016.1208596.

Mol, Angenitus Arie Andries, Csilla E. Ariese-Vandemeulebroucke, Krijn H. J. Boom, and Aris Politopoulos, eds. *The Interactive Past: Archaeology, Heritage & Video Games*. Leiden: Sidestone Press, 2017.

Murray, Janet Horowitz. *Hamlet on the Holodeck: The Future of Narrative in Cyberspace*. Cambridge, Mass: MIT Press, 1998.

Nakamura, Lisa. "Queer Female of Color: The Highest Difficulty Setting There Is? Gaming Rhetoric as Gender Capital." *ADA* 1 (2012). https://doi.org/10.7264/N37P8W9V.

Nicholls, Matthew. "Digital Visualisation in Classics Teaching and Beyond." *Journal of Classics Teaching* 17, no. 33 (2016): 27–30. https://doi.org/10.1017/S2058631016000076.

Ortega, Stephen. "Representing the Past: Video Games Challenge to the Historical Narrative." *Syllabus* 4, no. 1 (2015): 1–13.

Pagnotti, John, and William B. Russell. "Using Civilization IV to Engage Students in World History Content." *The Social Studies* 103, no. 1 (2012): 39–48. https://doi.org/10.1080/00377996.2011.558940.

Penix-Tadsen, Phillip, ed. *Video Games and the Global South*. Pittsburgh: Carnegie Mellon University, 2019.

Peterson, Rolfe Daus, Andrew Justin Miller, and Sean Joseph Fedorko. "The Same River Twice: Exploring Historical Representation and the Value of Simulation in the Total War, Civilization and Patrician Franchises." In *Playing with the Past: Digital Games and the Simulation of History*, edited by Matthew Kapell and Andrew B. R. Elliott, 33–48. New York: Bloomsbury Academic, 2013.

Pobłocki, Kaspar. "Becoming-State: The Bio-Cultural Imperialism of Sid Meier's Civilization." *Focaal – European Journal of Anthropology* 39 (2002): 163–77.

Raupach, Tim. "Towards an Analysis of Strategies of Authenticity Production in World War II First-Person Shooter Games." In *Early Modernity and Video Games*, edited by Tobias Winnerling and Florian Kerschbaumer, 123–38. Newcastle upon Tyne: Cambridge Scholars, 2014.

Reinhard, Andrew. *Archaeogaming: An Introduction to Archaeology in and of Video Games*. New York: Berghahn Books, 2018.

Reinhard, Andrew, and Stéphanie-Anne Ruatta. "Consulting for Ubisoft on Assassin's Creed: Odyssey." *Archaeogaming* (blog), April 19, 2019. https://archaeogaming.com/2019/04/19/consulting-for-ubisoft-on-assassins-creed-odyssey/.

Rochat, Yannick. "A Quantitative Study of Historical Video Games (1981–2015)." In *Historia Ludens: The Playing Historian*, edited by Alexander von Lünen, Katherine J. Lewis, Benjamin Litherland, and P. H. Cullum, 3–19. Routledge Approaches to History, vol. 30. New York, NY: Routledge, 2020.

Rollinger, Christian, ed. *Classical Antiquity in Video Games: Playing with the Ancient World*. Imagines – Classical Receptions in the Visual and Performing Arts. London; New York: Bloomsbury Academic, 2020.

Sabin, Philip. "Wargames as an Academic Instrument." In *Zones of Control: Perspectives on Wargaming*, edited by Pat Harrigan and Matthew G. Kirschenbaum, 421–37. Game Histories. Cambridge, Massachusetts: The MIT Press, 2016.

Salvati, Andrew J., and Jonathan M. Bullinger. "Selective Authenticity and the Playable Past." In *Playing with the Past: Digital Games and the Simulation of History*, edited by Matthew Kapell and Andrew B. R. Elliott, 153–67. New York: Bloomsbury Academic, 2013.

Schut, Kevin. "Strategic Simulations and Our Past: The Bias of Computer Games in the Presentation of History." *Games and Culture* 2, no. 3 (2007): 213–35. https://doi.org/10.1177/1555412007306202.

Schwartz, Leigh. "Fantasy, Realism, and the Other in Recent Video Games." *Space and Culture* 9, no. 3 (2006): 313–25. https://doi.org/10.1177/1206331206289019.

Scott Glancy, Adam. "The 'I' in Team: War and Combat in Tabletop Tole-Playing Games." In *Zones of Control: Perspectives on Wargaming*, edited by Pat Harrigan and Matthew G. Kirschenbaum, 71–80. Game Histories. Cambridge, Massachusetts: The MIT Press, 2016.

Sepinwall, Alyssa Goldstein. *Slave Revolt on Screen: The Haitian Revolution in Film and Video Games*. Caribbean Studies Series. Jackson: University Press of Mississippi, 2021.

Šisler, Vít. "Digital Arabs: Representation in Video Games." *European Journal of Cultural Studies* 11, no. 2 (2008): 203–20. https://doi.org/10.1177/1367549407088333.

Šisler, Vít. "From Kuma\War to Quraish: Representation of Islam in Arab and American Video Games." In *Playing with Religion in Digital Games*, edited by Heidi Campbell and Gregory P. Grieve, 109–33. Digital Game Studies. Bloomington: Indiana University Press, 2014.

Skotnes-Brown, Jules. "Colonized Play: Racism, Sexism and Colonial Legacies in the DOTA 2 South Africa Gaming Community." In *Video Games and the Global South*, edited by Phillip Penix-Tadsen, 143–53. Pittsburgh: Carnegie Mellon University, 2019.

Smith, Adam, and Soren Johnson. "Soren Johnson on Challenging the Norms of 4X Games." *Rock, Paper, Shotgun* (blog), April 6, 2018. https://www.rockpapershotgun.com/2018/04/06/soren-johnson-4x-strategy-interview/.

Smith, James L. "Medievalisms of Moral Panic." In *Studies in Medievalism XXV: Medievalism and Modernity*, edited by Karl Fugelso, Joshua Davies, and Sarah Salih, 157–72. Boydell and Brewer, 2016. www.jstor.org/stable/10.7722/j.ctt19x3hn8.16.

Spring, Dawn. "Gaming History: Computer and Video Games as Historical Scholarship." *Rethinking History* 19, no. 2 (2015): 207–21. https://doi.org/10.1080/13642529.2014.973714.

Srauy, Sam. "Professional Norms and Race in the North American Video Game Industry." *Games and Culture* 14, no. 5 (July 2019): 478–97. https://doi.org/10.1177/1555412017708936.

Sturtevant, Paul B. *The Middle Ages in Popular Imagination: Memory, Film and Medievalism*. New Directions in Medieval Studies. London; New York: I.B. Tauris, 2018.

Tarason, Dominic. "Assassin's Creed Origins Becomes Edutainment Feb 20th." *Rock, Paper, Shotgun* (blog), February 13, 2018. https://www.rockpapershotgun.com/2018/02/13/assassins-creed-origins-becomes-edutainment-feb-20th/.

Taylor, Claire. "Serious Gaming: Critiques of Neoliberalism in the Works of Ricardo Miranda Zúñiga." In *Video Games and the Global South*, edited by Phillip Penix-Tadsen, 47–58. Pittsburgh: Carnegie Mellon University, 2019.

Testa, Alessandro. "Religion(s) in Videogames – Historical and Anthropological Observations." *Online – Heidelberg Journal of Religions on the Internet* 5 (2014): 249–78. https://doi.org/10.11588/REL.2014.0.12170.

Totilo, Stephen. "One Man's Year Making Assassin's Creed II." *Kotaku* (blog), December 21, 2009. https://kotaku.com/5431098/one-mans-year-making-assassins-creed-ii.

Towns, Armond R. "Gamifying Blackness: From Slave Records to *Playing History: Slave Trade*." *Information, Communication & Society* 24, no. 12 (2021): 1–15. https://doi.org/10.1080/1369118X.2020.1739730.

Trattner, Kathrin. "Religion, Games, and Othering: An Intersectional Approach." *Gamevironments* 4 (2016): 24–60.

Van Eck, Richard. "Digital Game Based Learning: It's Not Just the Digital Native Who Are Restless." *Educause Review* 41 (2006): 16–30.

Vas, János. "Four Categories Of Video Games in the Practice of History Teaching." *Staféta* 2 (2017): 211–27.

Wainwright, A. Martin. "Teaching Historical Theory through Video Games." *The History Teacher* 47, no. 4 (2014): 579–612.

Wainwright, A. Martin. *Virtual History: How Videogames Portray the Past*. Abingdon, Oxon; New York, NY: Routledge, 2019.

Whelchel, Alex. "Using Civilization Simulation Video Games in the World History Classroom." *World History Connected* 4, no. 2 (2007). http://worldhistoryconnected.press.uillinois.edu/4.2/whelchel.html.

White, William J. "The Right to Dream of the Middle Ages Simulating the Medieval in Tabletop RPGs." In *Digital Gaming Re-Imagines the Middle Ages*, edited by Daniel T. Kline, 15–28. Routledge Studies in New Media and Cyberculture 15. New York: Routledge, 2014.

Winnerling, Tobias, and Florian Kerschbaumer, eds. *Early Modernity and Video Games*. Newcastle upon Tyne: Cambridge Scholars, 2014.

Wolterink, Julian. "Authentic Historical Imagery: A Suggested Approach for Medieval Videogame." *Gamevironments* 6 (2017): 104–31.

Zamaróczy, Nicolas de. "Are We What We Play? Global Politics in Historical Strategy Computer Games." *International Studies Perspectives* 18, no. 2 (2017): 155–74. https://doi.org/10.1093/isp/ekv010.

Ludography

Age of Empires. Ensemble Studios, 1997.
Assassin's Creed. Ubisoft, 2007.
Call of Duty. Activision, 2003.
Crazy Taxi. Sega, 1999.
Empire: Total War. Activision, 2009.
Europa Universalis. Paradox Interactive, 2000.
Fallout . Interplay Productions, 1997.
Playing History 2: Slave Trade. Serious Games Interactive, 2013.
Shogun: Total War. Creative Assembly, 2000.
Sid Meier's Civilization. MicroProse, 1991.
Tetris. Alexey Pajitnov, 1984.
The Patrician. Ascaron, 1993.

Part I: **The Educational Impact of Games**

Eve Stirling and Jamie Wood
2 Learning About the Past Through Digital Play: History Students and Video Games

Abstract: This chapter examines history students' perceptions of their learning about the past through playing video games. We present a speculative design fiction that draws on data from a survey of student gamers' perceptions of their learning about history through videogaming. We used responses to the survey to create a story that explores both what students thought that they had learnt about history through playing "historical" video games in their free time and how they thought that they had learnt it. In addition, we explore why our respondents engaged in historical gameplay and what playing such games encouraged them to do beyond the digital world. Our aim is to understand students' roles as active agents in learning about the past through virtual play rather than as passive consumers of digital products.

The storyworld of MD 348211 – Playing the Past: making history in digital spaces 01

Motivation
Gaming for me is about escapism and challenge. I love it when I can't get off a game. I love the realism, action, the potential for strategy, the interaction, the attention to detail in the gameplay and the graphics. And the freedom in the game to explore. It's a draw like no other media.
So, a module based on playing computer games? Of course, I would choose that. I love gaming. My favourite? *Assassins Creed* because it is thoroughly enjoyable, and is what sparked my interest in history as a child, and led to me pursuing it at uni. As well as this, the game is fun, entertaining, well designed, challenging and, at the same time, educational. It (the module) was an opportunity to do something different where I could try out role playing as historical characters, rather than writing about them. I was also interested to see what it would be like to design a historical game that my friends could play.

Experience
The module runs twice a semester for seven days in total each time. It's tricky to get a place on it because there is a cap of 40 students. And it's popular because students like the idea of getting credit for playing video games! But many of us are also interested in the variety of different ways you are able to get involved, from RPG (role play game) aspects to working together and even getting the chance to design a game for the next group of students. I really like the concept of alternative history and wanted to see what it was like to see historical events play out in different ways from different perspectives.

https://doi.org/10.1515/9783110712032-002

We were told at the start of the module that we'd have to adopt a variety of different roles over the week. Some of the others were a bit nervous about this because they prefer playing solo, but I love the teamwork aspect of gaming so I was looking forward to it.

We all started the module in the first-person role and, although it was fun, at first, I couldn't really see what we were learning by rampaging around the medieval countryside. But as it went on, the prompts during gameplay, interactions with other characters, and the beauty of the architecture really drew me in and I learnt a lot about everyday life in medieval Italy as well as developing my combat skills. Every hour or so, we had to take a break and record a quick voice memo about what we had learned. At the end of the day, we had read a blog post about late medieval Italy that our tutor sent to us and had to write a paragraph or two in our online learning diaries.

I felt like I had a better idea of what was going on the next day when I joined three other students to complete a quest from Florence to Rome. It was good to work together and fun to be travelling around Italy and learning about all the different cities, although some of the others weren't taking it that seriously all the time. Then I got really into it and we played through the night on a side quest (not a module requirement). The learning center has 24-hour access and so we can still use the VR rooms to continue our game.

Then I slept . . .

On the fourth day I had the choice of doing the strategy game either on my own or in a group. I decided to pair up with one of my friends and we were given the position of a general in charge of the army of Milan planning a campaign against Florence. We're used to gaming together, so I think that we made a good team and we didn't have too many disagreements! The fact that if we made a mistake, we could go back and try again meant that we could think about alternative histories.

On the fifth and sixth days, I was part of a team that designed elements of the game for the next time the module runs. Some of my teammates are really into modding games to make them more interesting or accurate, so they really got into this task. We were given a pre-formatted "world" so we only had to add the details that we had researched about medieval life.

I prefer gameplay and experiencing different historical worlds so this was a bit less interesting to me. But I did learn a lot about how to use digital mapping software so that the game could be played in historical spaces, and about how important stories and characters are to game design.

Learning

Once we completed the week-long gameplay (equivalent to 40 hours of study) we then had a week to document and reflect on our experiences before the assessment submission.

I loved the module. Some of my friends said that it wasn't "proper" History, and I sort of understand that, but it was great to be able to bring my passion for gaming together with my love of History.

But playing this way meant that we explored different elements of living in a quasi-medieval world. We could do things that would not have been feasible in real life, let alone in other modules. Working through key decisions to be made with other students offered me insights into the complex nature of history. We were able to shape our own history through making choices based on real-life past events – it was so difficult! And we got assessed on how we engaged and reflected on these experiences.

I love that the university has offered this immersive experience. The world that the "game developer students" have created is filled with a rich back story and impressive environment (luckily, we have an agreement/relationship with a local games developer who donated the game engine so we had a prototype into which we could insert specific elements of the game, including historical information that we had researched).

Even though I wasn't as into the game design aspect of the module as some of the others, I feel like I learned a lot by getting to play with the past, rather than just observing it from a distance. It's not for everyone, but I think it could help some students understand how history "works" (rather than just about what happened in the past) by doing modules like this. When I looked back at my learning journal, I noticed that I enjoyed – or at least learnt something from – working through the "grind" of gameplay with other students. It also made me much more interested in Renaissance Italy than I'd ever have thought possible!

This speculative fiction draws on responses to a survey of how students' experiences of video gaming affected their understanding of and engagement with history. Over 200 students responded to our survey, from which we identified key themes and emblematic quotations to inform the above fiction, a student's account of their experience on the module *MD 348211 – Playing the Past: making history in digital spaces 01*. Our intention was to use this fiction to kick-start a discussion about how experiences of historical gaming might inform teaching and learning practice. In the next section, we present the results of our analysis of the survey by relating them to the three elements which structured our fiction: motivation, experience, and learning. Each of these elements is connected to our larger survey and relevant literature on video games and history.

Motivation

Students choose modules for a variety of reasons, broadly divided between intrinsic motivations, extrinsic motivations, and module characteristics.[1] Respondents to our survey were self-selecting and, as such, were unsurprisingly positive about the experience of playing video games in general and historical video games in particular. One said "History is made interactive, never before would I have taken such an interest in the Third Crusade or Italian Renaissance." Positivity about gaming suggested that there would be an intrinsic openness to taking a module that involved playing and making historical video games. This was expressed by some respondents through reference to the interest of the subject matter: "The game further drove my interest in medieval

---

[1] M. R. Hedges, G. A. Pacheco, and D. J. Webber, "What determines students' choices of elective modules?," *International Review of Economics Education* 17 (2014): 39–54.

conflict and on a very simplified level the idea of medieval wartime politics, and the difficulties of maintaining the identity of a nation during times of conflict."

Video games are often marketed and experienced as opportunities for players to exercise agency through their ludic structures and processes. Although this view has been critiqued on the grounds that what is cultivated is actually an illusion of gamer agency and subjectivity,[2] the key point is that historical games create a sense of agency on the part of those that play them. Respondents to our survey certainly felt this way: "The plot arc gives a real sense of empowerment . . . The tactical edge format means that I feel like I'm being engaged mentally, too." This reflects a certain level of self-awareness about the constructed and subjective nature of the gaming experience.

Research has suggested that gamers' sense of agency depends on a broad range of ludic, social, and psychological factors. Player immersion in game worlds does not, as is often assumed by designers and players, necessarily depend on the fidelity of graphics and sound within the virtual environment (i.e. "accuracy").[3] Indeed, Copplestone has suggested that players who are familiar with the media find that it offers a platform to "challenge how concepts of accuracy were formed and applied."[4] Rather, across different game types, a major predictor of player engagement and immersion is "the degree to which games satisfy motivational needs. Video game play that satisfies the needs for competence, autonomy, and relatedness increases a player's sense of immersion" considerably.[5] There is also an association between the authenticity of the virtual environment and player motivation, including their relationship to real world cognition and behavior. Importantly, playing video games can lead to a sense of fulfilment on the part of the gamer – the very act of gaming is thus potentially a motivating factor in and of itself.[6]

Studies of historical games have also suggested that they enable gamers to exercise a certain kind of agency. Uricchio, for instance, argued that historical

---

[2] A. Charles, "Playing with one's self: notions of subjectivity and agency in digital games," *Eludamos. Journal for Computer Game Culture* 3, no. 2 (2009): 281–94.

[3] E. Stirling, and J. Wood, "'Actual history doesn't take place': Digital Gaming, Accuracy and Authenticity," *Games Studies* 21, no. 1 (2021), accessed February 2, 2022, http://gamestudies.org/2101/articles/stirling_wood.

[4] T. J. Copplestone, "But that's not accurate: the differing perceptions of accuracy in cultural-heritage videogames between creators, consumers and critics," *Rethinking History: The Journal of Theory and Practice* 21, no. 3 (2017): 435.

[5] A. K. Przybylski, C. S. Rigby and R. M. Ryan, "A motivational model of video game engagement," *Review of General Psychology* 14 (2010): 162.

[6] Przybylski, Rigby and Ryan, "A motivational model," 154–166.

games do not so much represent the past as they simulate it.[7] Chapman and McCall have both suggested that the structures of historical games provide players with considerable opportunities to exercise agency within simulated historical environments.[8] In an earlier paper, Chapman also noted that because historical video games are "actively configured by their audiences" they open up additional layers of meaning and provide opportunities for individuals to exercise agency.[9] By embedding narrative and ludic structures in the simulated past, gamers are encouraged not just to imagine themselves in history, but to act through history. Simulated game-pasts enable gamers to actively work through shifting historical scenarios rather than passively consuming them, as was noted explicitly by a number of our respondents, including the following: "your actions have an actual, clear impact on the world around you based on which decisions you make, making you feel as though you can play how you want and not how the game tells you to play." The establishment of a sense of authenticity, by situating gameplay within realistic historical contexts and/or placing gamers in accurate representations of past places, is a further means of cultivating a sense of player agency in historical games.[10]

Some respondents to our survey certainly described themselves as exercising a strong sense of agency when playing historical games. They expressed a deep engagement with and ownership of the character (or dynasty, kingdom, country, empire, or other kind of polity) with which they were playing, with one stating, "Set in medieval Europe and parts of Asia you take the role of a medieval noble, have to manage your dynasty and Kingdom." There was sometimes a sense that the player progresses through history with their chosen polity, augmented by the "reality" of some of the events that are encountered: "It's a game of advancing your country of choice into an empire." On some occasions this was articulated in quite personalized language; one said, "You go back in time and play as one of your ancestors and live life as they did," indicating quite a deep level of engagement. Engaging directly in authentic historical processes, such as "advancing your country" by engaging with "real events"; living life "as they did" by

---

[7] W. Uricchio, "Simulation, history, and computer games," in *Handbook of Computer Game Studies*, ed. J. Raessens and J. H. Goldstein (Cambridge, MA: MIT Press, 2005), 327–338.

[8] A. Chapman, *Digital Games as History: How Videogames Represent the Past and Offer Access to Historical Practice* (London: Routledge, 2016); J. McCall, "Teaching History With Digital Historical Games: An Introduction to the Field and Best Practices," *Simulation & Gaming* 47, no. 4 (2016): 517–542.

[9] A. Chapman, "Privileging form over content: Analysing historical videogames," *Journal of Digital Humanities* 1, no. 2 (2012), accessed February 2, 2022, http://journalofdigitalhumanities.org/1-2/privileging-form-over-content-by-adam-chapman/.

[10] Stirling and Wood, "Actual history doesn't take place."

playing as a historical character was thus viewed as enabling players to exercise agency in quite an individualized manner, positioning themselves as historical actors within the gameplay environment.

In our fiction, we also wanted to acknowledge the importance of "modding" for some gamers by incorporating the option for some students to design elements of the game for others. One participant suggested: "It's very moddable and I am developing a mod for it to make the game more accurate, which other people have downloaded and play with too."

It was clear to us from the survey results that there was no single reason why a student might choose to take a module on historical gaming. The personal experience of gameplay, whether carried out solo, in collaboration or in competition with others, was pivotal, as was the sense that such gameplay was potentially individualized (or even individualizable). This led us to consider what the actual module experience might be like and how that might relate to the experience of playing historical games.

Experience

We wanted to provide a sense of how respondents' reflections on the process of playing digital games might relate to the student experience of taking our fictional module. Vital factors in generating a positive gaming experience included aesthetics, opportunities for social interaction, the ability to exercise choice, and the challenge of gameplay. We explore each of these features in turn in the next section.

Many of our respondents mentioned the aesthetic quality of games as being particularly important to their experience of gameplay. One suggested, "visual effects are stunning, plus there is presence of medieval history and mythical content all in one game," and another that "all of this in glorious graphics! It's perfect for any military history buff." The high aesthetic quality of games is something many of the participants in our survey mentioned. It was one of the factors that reportedly encouraged repeat playing. High-end graphics that offered accurate reconstructions of historical sites were viewed as encouraging gamers to immerse themselves in gameplay, in some cases helping to cultivate a deeper sense of engagement and ownership.[11] Music and other elements that added to the atmosphere also potentially heightened player engagement. It has been argued that the

---

11 Stirling and Wood, "Actual history doesn't take place."

creation of such atmospheric gaming environments opens up new ways of crafting and participating in the past.[12]

Although we emphasized the individual motivations for playing historical games in the last section, our survey revealed that social factors were also important for some gamers, a fact that we were keen to acknowledge in our fiction. The collaborative potential was emphasized by one respondent in particular: "Gaming has a somewhat incorrect reputation as being somehow antisocial. It is a highly social activity in which one can make friends and bond over mutual interests and activities. The co-operation element generates many hours of gameplay for me." Our fictional student so enjoyed the ability to work with others that they carried on into – even through – the night.

McCall has emphasized the role of choice in differentiating historical video games from other media.[13] Gameplay can replicate (in an approximate sense) some of the decisions that historical actors made which affected their lives and those of others, and this can be a powerful learning tool.[14] Some respondents to our survey demonstrated a sophisticated awareness of the potential of historical videogames to enable them to engage in counterfactual play.[15] For example, one respondent to the question about why they liked their favourite historical game stated that it: "placed the player in multiple different societies and cultures, leading the story and characters to consider their impact on the people they met." The process of gameplay in "authentic" historical contexts potentially enabled some gamers to exercise agency in shaping the course of in-game history: "It is set in Ancient Rome and contains a lot of real historical characters and events from the past, even if your actions may cause events to play out differently to how they actually occurred." For another respondent it was the chance to affect the course of history that was particularly attractive: "Although not very accurate, it is based on the past. I like how it gives a great opportunity to re-shape actual history." We were therefore keen to include a significant element of choice in our fictional module and wanted the student to reflect on what they had learnt by engaging in such simulated processes of historical choice-making (and re-making).

Students who responded to our survey repeatedly stressed their passion for playing challenging games. Difficulty was viewed positively in general terms with one respondent describing their favorite game as "difficult but interesting,

---

12 Copplestone, "But that's not accurate."
13 McCall, "Teaching History With Digital Historical Games"; J. McCall, *Gaming History: Using Video Games to Teach Secondary History* (London: Routledge, 2011).
14 Chapman, *Digital Games as History*; Copplestone, "But that's not accurate."
15 Stirling and Wood, "Actual history doesn't take place."

uses real events and people in history, casual game play is very interesting and there are always side quests to do during the game." The challenging nature of some games means that gamers may have to work through scenarios repeatedly in order to figure out effective gameplay strategies. Relatedly, as noted above, the inbuilt re-playability of historical games enables players to make different decisions and thus to explore a range of potential outcomes of different historical scenarios. This provides them with an opportunity to explore and learn about the nature of historical contingency.[16]

Learning

It was clear that some student gamers learnt a lot about history by playing games set in the past. As we have seen, this extends beyond learning information about history to engaging in processes of historical – or quasi-historical – thinking. For example, the challenges that historical games present in terms of limitations on resources and actions and the presence of obstacles and antagonists means that they "can illustrate the systemic context of people in the past, the complicated physical and even ideological milieus in which agents in the past found themselves."[17]

An important factor in deepening engagement with historical games is the extent to which they confirm respondents' pre-existing historical knowledge, as has been acknowledged by Chapman, who notes how gamers' ability to exercise agency is related to their knowledge of the past and broader discourses about history. For him, historical video games evoke "a player's historical understanding, invoke the larger historical discourse and [provide] a challenging space for the players to exercise their (narrative) agency."[18]

One of the respondents to the question "Why do you consider this game historical?" made a direct connection between prior historical knowledge and the design of the game, suggesting that once gameplay had commenced within an historical environment, gamers were able to "use familiar frameworks of history and mechanics built into the game to understand how historical figures, institutions and kingdoms interacted." Presumably prior knowledge was judged to give

---

[16] McCall, "Teaching History With Digital Historical Games," 525.
[17] McCall, "Teaching History With Digital Historical Games," 524.
[18] Chapman, *Digital Games as History*, 101. On gameplay narratives and agency more generally, see S. Domsch, *Storyplaying: Agency and narrative in video games* (Berlin: de Gruyter, 2013).

an advantage during gameplay within an historical scenario, a finding that aligns very well with Chapman's theories about the interrelationship between pre-existing historical knowledge and deepened engagement with games about the past.[19]

In order to understand students' roles as active agents in learning about the past through virtual play, we asked respondents to tell us what they did as a result of playing games. The results are presented in the following table (Table 2.1).

Table 2.1: From your experience of playing that game, did you? (n = 213).

Action	Frequency
Learn something	154
Try to find out more	148
Play another game	124
Talk to someone	93
Change the way you play the game	85
Visit a forum	47
Visit a place	43
Other	10

The most popular responses (try to find out more; learn something) both suggest that gamers thought that gameplay was connected to learning. This may be linked to the fact that some historical games encourage players to find out more about the past for themselves. For example, respondents reference the incorporation of encyclopaedias within games that allow players to find out about historic figures and key events. Responses to other questions indicate that respondents felt that historical games had piqued their interest in particular periods and introduced them to key historical actors. There was explicit recognition that games have the potential to engage people with history, including teaching them about specific places, ideas, and perspectives. Interesting too were responses that demonstrated the interplay between gameplay and the "real world," including participants who reported doing additional research into topics as a result of the game and even visiting places. Attempts to learn something were not restricted to the gameworld either, as was indicated by some of the free-text responses from those who selected "other":

---

19 Chapman, *Digital Games as History*.

- Used it to simulate the past so I can visualize it more;
- Got into historical reenactment;
- Found contextual knowledge that when researched, actually applied to school work I was working on and was correct;
- Actually got inspired to used real Norman weaponry;
- Start to make my own games;
- Watched Band of Brothers DVDs;
- Check the real history of it.

One of our follow-up questions asked about how gamers tried to find out more information, with the following options scoring highest: "online research" (149 responses), books (87), and Wikipedia (86). Free text responses mentioned TV documentaries, YouTube, discussions with friends and/or lecturers, and encyclopaedias, suggesting that respondents made use of a wide range of information sources when trying to find out more about the historical elements of games.

Respondents who selected "finding out more" and changing gameplay – and, potentially, talking to someone and/or visiting a forum – point towards the adoption of a strategic approach to the game. That a significant proportion (40%) of our respondents said that they changed the way that they played the game may be particularly significant. Working through different historical scenarios enables gamers to learn about the past, as discussed above. This was mentioned by one of the responses to a question about why a certain game was their favourite: "1. It has taught me about many nations and entities throughout history; 2. Although being alternate, does reflect perspectives of certain nations; 3. Alternate history." Re-playability is a fundamental feature of video gaming and the strategic decision to change one's approach to playing a game is not unusual, indicating that a baseline level of learning through reflection often takes place. However, as we have already noted, certain kinds of historical video games are particularly well-suited to engaging players in strategic thinking. Historical strategy games provide players with opportunities to engage in counterfactual play and to learn about the variability of historical contingency. One respondent reflected in a broader sense on what repeated gameplay can teach gamers: "It teaches you all about the grind. If you want something, go earn it."

Methodology

Video games are digital places of cultural meaning making[20] and those that are set in the past combine past and present in their storyworlds.[21] Historical video games (and to a lesser extent other genres, such as fantasy) implicitly – and sometimes explicitly – position themselves within historical and historiographical debates. Claims about games' historical "accuracy" and "authenticity" often figure prominently in marketing materials for historical video games. Video game designers engage in processes of research and occasionally employ historical consultants when developing games and, in the process, make explicit – and implicit – decisions about how to present history.[22] As a result, games can direct gamers towards very specific interpretations and understandings of the past and, particularly in the case of strategy games, encourage the reproduction and/or disruption of colonialist and hegemonic ideologies.[23] However, such pathways are often restricted and can reinforce established interpretations, a tendency that is often obscured by the fact that scenarios in (historical) games necessarily incorporate a degree of choice into the player experience, potentially creating something of an illusion of agency.[24] Copplestone suggests that "the move towards a less stratified and authoritative history has opened up new ways to think about and engage with the past, whilst refocusing attention on the role of the historian, or indeed the game developer in creating these accounts."[25] Drawing on user-centered approaches to the study of video games, our study was explicitly designed to let gamers tell us about their perceptions of the impact of playing historical video games on their understanding of history. We were particularly interested in probing one of the central paradoxes of historical gaming: that gamers are tightly constrained in their ability to experience

---

[20] K. Schut, "Strategic simulations and our past: the bias of computer games in the presentation of history," *Games and Culture* 2, no. 3 (2007): 213–235.

[21] D. Kirby, "The future is now: Diegetic prototypes and the role of popular films in generating real-world technological development," *Social Studies of Science* 40, no. 1 (2009): 41–70.

[22] D. N. Dow, "Historical Veneers: Anachronism, Simulation, and Art History in *Assassin's Creed II*," in *Playing with the Past: Digital Games and the Simulation of History*, ed. A. B. R. Elliott and M. W. Kappell (London: Bloomsbury, 2013), 215–231.

[23] H. J. Brown, "The Consolation of Paranoia: Conspiracy, Epistemology, and the Templars in *Assassin's Creed, Deus Ex,* and *Dragon Age*," in *Digital Gaming Re-imagines the Middle Ages*, ed. D. T. Kline (London: Routledge, 2013), 217–240; A. Chapman, A. Foka and J. Westin, "Introduction: what is historical game studies?," *Rethinking History: The Journal of Theory and Practice* 21, no. 3 (2017): 358–371.

[24] McCall, "Teaching History With Digital Historical Games."

[25] Copplestone, "But that's not accurate," 419.

the past due to the games' ludic, narrative, and formal structures but at the same time the gameplay experience can provide them with opportunities for sophisticated ways of engaging with history.

Design Fiction and Speculative Design

In creating the speculative design fiction with which this chapter began, we used narrative approaches to data analysis underpinned by our wish to create a design fiction prototype to help us to imagine alternative futures for (history) education. A design fiction, as described by science fiction author Bruce Sterling,[26] allows us to suspend disbelief about change while at the same time opening up space for discussion[27] by using prototypes within a "storyworld."[28] We used the speculative nature of the future-focused design fiction method to enable us to review our data in a way that is generative and exploratory. We used the module as a kind of "prototype" that enabled us to play with possible futures and to discuss alternative ways by which we might construct learning and teaching experiences within history education that are immersive, engaging, and draw on students' own experiences and perspectives.

Atkinson and Delamont propose that we should treat narratives as performance acts because they are forms of social action.[29] We were keen to make sure that our fiction was "loyal" to the data: it was written using 80% participant voices and 20% our narrative voice to give an insight into the range of different points of view articulated by respondents to our survey.[30] We based the fiction on an analysis of the data that drew on themes which we identified and refined after reviewing the dataset on several occasions.[31] We then worked separately to code the overall dataset and then came together to review and cross

---

[26] T. Bosch, "Sci-Fi Writer Bruce Sterling Explains the Intriguing New Concept of Design Fiction," *Slate*, March 2, 2012, accessed February 2, 2022, https://slate.com/technology/2012/03/bruce-sterling-on-design-fictions.html.
[27] A. Dunne and F. Raby, *Speculative everything: design, fiction, and social dreaming* (Cambridge, MA: MIT Press, 2013).
[28] Kirby, "The future is now."
[29] P. Atkinson and S. Delamont, "Analytical Perspectives," in *Collecting and interpreting qualitative materials*, 3rd edition, ed. N. K. Denzin and Y. S. Lincoln (London: Sage, 2005), 821–840.
[30] C. Bold, *Using narrative in research* (London: Sage, 2011).
[31] D. J. Clandinin and F. M. Connelly, *Experience and Story in Qualitative Research* (San Francisco: Jossey-Bass, 2000).

check codes and emerging themes. We then extracted representative quotes from the participants' responses to the questionnaire to help us to exemplify the key themes and codes.

Conclusions

This chapter adds further "much-needed" data to facilitate our understanding of patterns of user experience and perception.[32] We analyzed students' roles as active agents in learning about history through virtual play rather than as passive consumers of digital products that are set in the past. It complements an increasing amount of recent work that has sought to move beyond approaches focusing on how games represent the past by presenting gamers with fixed historical frameworks and instead to consider the various means by which historical games also construct individual and collective knowledge about the past.[33] For instance, McCall suggested that video games can play an important role in teaching high school students not just about historical knowledge, but also about historical processes.[34] The fiction sought to articulate not just what students thought they had learnt about history through playing "historical" video games in their free time, but also how they thought that they had learnt in a description of a learning context. Respondents to our survey – an admittedly self-selecting group of video gaming enthusiasts – almost without exception expressed positive opinions about video gaming, as noted above. We focused on three areas that had emerged in our survey. First, we were interested in why students were motivated to engage with historical video gameplay and how that might relate to choices that they make about learning. Second, we wanted to address the issue of the experience of historical videogaming and focused on how immersion seems to have been a powerful driver for engagement. Finally, we explored what students learn through historical videogaming. Our module prototype was a way of imagining how gaming could help to inform immersive teaching and learning experiences in history.

---

32 Chapman, Foka, and Westin, "Introduction."
33 Chapman, Foka, and Westin, "Introduction"; Copplestone, "But that's not accurate."
34 McCall, *Gaming History*.

Bibliography

Atkinson, P., and S. Delamont. "Analytical perspectives." In *Collecting and interpreting qualitative materials*, 3rd edition, edited by N. K. Denzin and Y. S. Lincoln, 821–840. London: Sage, 2005.

Bold, Christine. *Using Narrative in Research*. London: Sage, 2011.

Bosch, Torie. "Sci-fi writer Bruce Sterling explains the intriguing new concept of design fiction." *Slate*, March 2, 2012. Accessed February 2, 2022. https://slate.com/technology/2012/03/bruce-sterling-on-design-fictions.html.

Brown, Harry J. "The consolation of paranoia: conspiracy, epistemology, and the Templars in *Assassin's Creed, Deus Ex*, and *Dragon Age*." In *Digital Gaming Re-imagines the Middle Ages*, edited by D. T. Kline, 217–240. London: Routledge, 2013.

Chapman, Adam. *Digital Games as History: How Videogames Represent the Past and Offer Access to Historical Practice*. London: Routledge, 2016.

Chapman, Adam. "Privileging form over content: analysing historical videogames." *Journal of Digital Humanities* 1, no. 2 (2012). Accessed February 2, 2022. http://journalofdigitalhumanities.org/1-2/privileging-form-over-content-by-adam-chapman/.

Chapman, Adam, Anna Foka, and Jonathan Westin. "Introduction: what is historical game studies?" *Rethinking History: The Journal of Theory and Practice* 21, no. 3 (2017): 358–371.

Charles, Alec. "Playing with one's self: notions of subjectivity and agency in digital games." *Eludamos. Journal for Computer Game Culture* 3, no. 2 (2009): 281–294.

Clandinin, D. Jean, and F. Michael Connelly. *Experience and Story in Qualitative Research*. San Francisco: Jossey-Bass, 2000.

Copplestone, Tara J. "But that's not accurate: the differing perceptions of accuracy in cultural-heritage videogames between creators, consumers and critics." *Rethinking History: The Journal of Theory and Practice* 21, no. 3 (2017): 451–438.

Domsch, Sebastian. *Storyplaying: Agency and Narrative in Video Games*. Berlin: de Gruyter, 2013.

Dow, Douglas N. "Historical veneers: anachronism, simulation, and art history in *Assassin's Creed II*." In *Playing with the Past: Digital Games and the Simulation of History*, edited by A. B. R. Elliott and M. W. Kappell, 215–231. London: Bloomsbury, 2013.

Dunne, Anthony, and Fiona Raby. *Speculative Everything: Design, Fiction, and Social Dreaming*. Cambridge, MA: MIT Press, 2013.

Hedges, M. R., G. A. Pacheco, and D. J. Webber. "What determines students' choices of elective modules?" *International Review of Economics Education* 17 (2014): 39–54.

Kirby, David. "The future is now: diegetic prototypes and the role of popular films in generating real-world technological development." *Social Studies of Science* 40, no. 1 (2009): 41–70.

McCall, Jeremiah. "Teaching history with digital historical games: an introduction to the field and best practices." *Simulation & Gaming* 47, no. 4 (2016): 517–542.

McCall, Jeremiah. *Gaming History: Using Video Games to Teach Secondary History*. London: Routledge, 2011.

Przybylski, Andrew K., C. Scott Rigby, and Richard M. Ryan. "A motivational model of video game engagement." *Review of General Psychology* 14 (2010): 154–166.

Schut, Kevin. "Strategic simulations and our past: the bias of computer games in the presentation of history." *Games and Culture* 2, no. 3 (2007): 213–235.

Stirling, Eve, and Jamie Wood. "'Actual history doesn't take place': digital gaming, accuracy and authenticity." *Games Studies* 21, no. 1 (2021). Accessed February 2, 2022. http://gamestudies.org/2101/articles/stirling_wood.

Uricchio, William. "Simulation, history, and computer games." In *Handbook of Computer Game Studies*, edited by J. Raessens and J. H. Goldstein, 327–338. Cambridge, MA: MIT Press, 2005.

Part II: **Teaching through Commercial Games**

Mike Horswell
3 Historicising *Assassin's Creed* (2007): Crusader Medievalism, Historiography, and Digital Games for the Classroom

Abstract: This chapter will sketch out ways in which crusading was presented in the immensely popular 2007 game *Assassin's Creed*,[1] and demonstrate how we might unpack its vision of crusading and the histories of perceptions of the past embedded in, and transmitted by, the franchise-launching game. In discussing perceptions of the crusades from academic histories to those of Al-Qaeda and ISIS, Kristin Skottki has called for a *"relentless* historicization and contextualisation" to go beyond mere considerations of accuracy.[2] This chapter will model "relentless historicization" in order to play as a historian and to illustrate ways of productively bringing historical games into the classroom. It will locate the game in its historical and cultural contexts, its genealogies, inheritances, and assumptions about crusading. This will help us see the entwined nature of "academic" history and "popular" history and will treat the game as a historical artefact in and of itself – possessing a past, needing contextualization, and influencing perceptions of the past in turn.

Introduction

For many playing digital games represents an introduction to the crusades, complementing the basic knowledge of crusading from films, dramas, documentaries, *Wikipedia*, online videos, and history books. This chapter will outline ways in which crusading is presented in Ubisoft's popular, franchise-launching, 2007 game *Assassin's Creed* in order to employ it as an example of how we might unpack its vision of crusading in the classroom beyond considerations of accuracy or facticity.

The nature of video games which make historical claims has already generated productive consideration not merely of how to teach with (or against) them

---

1 *Assassin's Creed* (Ubisoft, 2007).
2 Kristin Skottki, "The Dead, the Revived and the Recreated Pasts: 'Structural Amnesia' in Representations of Crusade History," in *Perceptions of the Crusades from the Nineteenth to the Twenty-First Century: Engaging the Crusades, Volume One*, ed. Mike Horswell and Jonathan Phillips (Abingdon: Routledge, 2018), 124.

https://doi.org/10.1515/9783110712032-003

in terms of their accuracy, but of the types of history being produced, the entanglements between academic and popular visions of the past, and the work these games can do in understanding the past.[3] *Assassin's Creed* itself has provoked reflection from educators, attracting analysis from those who recognize the influence it exerts on perceptions of the Middle East, the Assassins, and other aspects of the history surrounding the Third Crusade (1189–92).[4] While discussions of the "accuracy" of a game can represent a useful starting point for educators which potentially bridges the forms of expertise of the educator and student,[5] Andrew B. R. Elliott has highlighted that the disjuncture(s) between games and scholarship present an opportunity to go deeper: "counterfactual histories are actually useful ways of revealing the contingent nature of history."[6] Similarly, Robert Houghton has argued that games themselves operate not only as "historical arguments," but offer unique possibilities for thinking about and engaging with

---

3 See Matthew Wilhelm Kapell and Andrew B.R. Elliott, ed., *Playing with the Past: Digital Games and the Simulation of History* (London: Bloomsbury, 2013); Kevin Kee, ed., *Pastplay: Teaching and Learning History with Technology* (Michigan: The University of Michigan Press, 2014); A. Martin Wainwright, "Teaching Historical Theory through Video Games," *The History Teacher* 47 (2014): 579–612; Jeremiah McCall, "Teaching History With Digital Historical Games: An Introduction to the Field and Best Practices," *Simulation & Gaming* 47 (2016): 517–542; Alan Metzger and Richard J. Paxton, "Gaming History: A Framework for What Video Games Teach about the Past," *Theory & Research in Social Education* 44 (2016): 532–564; Alexander von Lünen et al., eds., *Historia Ludens: The Playing Historian* (Abingdon: Routledge, 2020).

4 Magy Seif El-Nasr et al., "*Assassin's Creed*: A Multi-Cultural Read," *Loading . . .* 2 (2008): 1–32; Vít Šisler, "Palestine in Pixels: The Holy Land, Arab-Israeli Conflict, and Reality Construction in Video Games," *Middle East Journal of Culture and Communication* 2 (2009): 275–292; Nicholas Trépanier, "The Assassin's Perspective: Teaching History with Video Games," *Perspectives on History* (blog), May 1, 2014, www.historians.org/publications-and-directories/perspectives-on-history/may-2014/the-assassins-perspective; Mirt Komel, "Orientalism in *Assassin's Creed*: Self-Orientalizing the Assassins from Forerunners of Modern Terrorism into Occidentalized Heroes," *Teorija in Praksa* 1 (2014): 72–90; Andrew B. R. Elliott, "The *Assassin's Creed* Curriculum: Video Games and the Middle Ages" (paper presented at the International Medieval Congress, Leeds, UK, 2016), 1–11, www.academia.edu/26869807/The_Assassins_Creed_Curriculum_Video_Games_and_the_Middle_Ages [accessed May 25, 2020]; Lisa Gilbert, "'The Past Is Your Playground': The Challenges and Possibilities of *Assassin's Creed*: *Syndicate* for Social Education," *Theory & Research in Social Education* 45 (2017): 145–155; Lisa Gilbert, "'*Assassin's Creed* Reminds Us That History Is Human Experience': Students' Senses of Empathy While Playing a Narrative Video Game," *Theory & Research in Social Education* 47 (2019): 108–137.

5 Trépanier, "Assassin's Perspective."

6 Elliott, "*Assassin's Creed* Curriculum," 6.

history itself.[7] Both Elliott and Houghton see games as sites of historical creation located between the various parties involved in developing the game and each player.[8] Seeing the versions of history presented in games as "arguments" and sites of history-making allows historiographical study of these perceptions of the past; by situating them in the contexts of their production, educators engage with this form of historical perception *as history*.

In discussing perceptions of the crusades from academic histories to those of Al-Qaeda and ISIS, Kristin Skottki has called for a *"relentless* historicization and contextualisation" to go beyond mere considerations of accuracy.[9] It is this call I will take up in this chapter, modelling something of "relentless historicization" in order to play as a historian and historicize the game in its historical and cultural contexts – its genealogies, inheritances, and assumptions about crusading. This will help us see the entwined nature of "academic" history and "popular" history and will treat the game as a historical artefact in and of itself, needing contextualization, possessing a past, and requiring work to unpack. I am not offering the fruits of a quantitative audience-reception survey of what has been learned or transmitted about the crusades from these games – work which is sorely needed. Rather, this is a qualitative reflection on the perceptions of the past, and the entangled circumstances of the production of history.

Cutting Across the Third Crusade: *Assassin's Creed* (2007)

Despite its age, *Assassin's Creed* is important due to its huge popularity and cult following.[10] The series has generated a plethora of surrounding material, from merchandise, novels, and art books to online strategy guides, wikis, and discussions. The image of crusading it presents, especially of the Third Crusade, the Templars, Assassins, and eleventh-century cities, can be inferred to have significant impact amongst those who play it and beyond. Now a behemoth franchise having sold over 100 million copies, the *Assassin's Creed* brand is partly famous for allowing the players to explore 3D representations of historical locations –

---

7 Robert Houghton, "World, Structure and Play: A Framework for Games as Historical Research Outputs, Tools, and Processes," *Práticas Da História* 7 (2017): 14–16.
8 Houghton, "World, Structure and Play," 14; Andrew B. R. Elliott, "Simulations and Simulacra: History in Video Games," *Práticas Da História* 5 (2017): 28.
9 Skottki, "Structural Amnesia," 124.
10 Komel, "Orientalism," 73.

from the Near East, Renaissance Italy, Revolutionary United States, Paris, ancient Egypt, and the Greek Republics to "Viking Age" north-western Europe. The first game in the series was released in November 2007 and has sold roughly 10 million copies.[11] Set in AD 1191 at the time of the Third Crusade, it allowed the player to roam the imagined cityscapes of Damascus, Masyaf, Acre, and Jerusalem. As an assassin, the player had to kill various figures – both Muslim and Christian – before meeting King Richard I of England, "the Lionheart," killing the Grand Master of the Templars and facing off against the leader of the Assassins, the "Old Man of the Mountain." These enemies were linked – they were all secretly "Templars" who were part of an epoch-spanning conspiracy to subvert free will, and which persisted into the twenty-first-century segments of the game which framed the historical forays.

The first *Assassin's Creed* game dropped the player for the majority of the action into the middle of a land being contested by the Third Crusade. The Kurdish ruler Salah al-Din Ayyub, known to the West as Saladin, had united the Muslim powerbases of the Near East sufficiently to destroy the crusader Kingdom of Jerusalem's army at the Battle of Hattin in AD 1187 and retake the city in the same year, ending its 88-year occupation by Latin Christians. In response, three of the strongest sovereigns of Western Europe had answered the call of Pope Gregory VIII to embark on a crusade to attempt to reclaim Jerusalem and bolster what was left of the crusader kingdoms of "Outremer" on the Eastern Mediterranean coast. Most of what remained was Tyre, and the forces besieging Acre. The latter was recaptured by the crusaders under King Richard and King Philip Augustus of France; the Holy Roman Emperor, Frederick Barbarossa, had died on route. The crusade's other major military engagement was the Battle of Arsuf, regarded as a victory for Richard against Saladin's troops after Philip had returned to France. Subsequent infighting and strategic calculations saw Richard and Saladin negotiate a truce and the end of the crusade without the recapture of Jerusalem by the crusaders, although pilgrims were granted access to the Holy City.[12]

Almost all of the events which conventionally constitute the Third Crusade were peripheral to the game. Philip and Frederick were unmentioned and Saladin unseen. Richard was encountered in the concluding section, not as an opponent or target for the player's assassination but as the authority who set up a

---

[11] Richard Moss, "*Assassin's Creed*: An Oral History," *Polygon*, October 3, 2018, www.polygon.com/features/2018/10/3/17924770/assassins-creed-an-oral-history-patrice-desilets [accessed June 26, 2019].

[12] For the Third Crusade, see Thomas Asbridge, *The Crusades: The War for the Holy Land* (London: Pocket Books, 2010), 428–516.

fight with the Templar Grand Master. The historic leaders of the Hospitallers, Templars and Teutonic Knights (Garnier de Nablus, Robert de Sablé IV, and Master Sibrand respectively) were encountered and killed by the player, but other figures were either fictional or fictionalized. Although the city of Acre had been besieged by both sides in turn, when encountered in the game it was under the rule of the crusaders, locating it after their capture in July 1191. Indeed, the only "crusading" fighting occurs obliquely as the player approaches the crusader army engaged in the Battle of Arsuf offstage. This tactic, Lars de Wildt has argued, persists through the series: "Assassins are positioned as outsiders to allow the player a spectatorial and uncritical role in the predetermined fate of history."[13]

The tradition of side-lining crusader-Muslim fighting in this manner is an old one and a key tactic of the phenomenally popular nineteenth-century author Sir Walter Scott in his novel *The Talisman* (1825). It allowed the reframing of the narrative away from a Christian-Muslim dichotomy and foregrounded other conflicts: those in the crusaders' camp for Scott, and that between the Assassins and the Templars for the game.[14] This has the effect of resisting narratives overdetermined by the "clash of civilizations," an explanation of world history which pitches monolithic and enduring religio-civilizational entities as tautologically locked in bloody and inevitable conflict. In this view the crusades become symbols of an endless cycle of violence.[15] The "clash" interpretation of crusading – popular with US-presidential advisors after 9/11 and influential in some academic histories of the crusades even today – can be found in the game. The sermons of street preachers in Damascus and Jerusalem say of Saladin, "He has found the strength to fight for our civilisation. Make no mistake, it is our existence we are fighting for. The infidel king would see us wiped from the world. We must resist, we must push back!" However, at the heart of the *Assassin's Creed* series, the grain of intractable enmity runs between secret

---

13 Lars de Wildt, "'Everything Is True; Nothing Is Permitted': Utopia, Religion and Conspiracy in *Assassin's Creed*," in *Playing Utopia: Futures in Digital Games*, ed. Benjamin Beil, Gundolf S. Freyermuth, and Hans Christian Schmidt (Bielefeld: transcript Verlag, 2019), 168.
14 Mike Horswell, *The Rise and Fall of British Crusader Medievalism, c. 1825–1945* (Abingdon: Routledge, 2018), 69–72; Elizabeth Siberry, *The New Crusaders: Images of the Crusades in the 19th and Early 20th Centuries* (Aldershot: Ashgate, 2000), 112–130.
15 Skottki, "Structural Amnesia"; Kurt Villads Jensen, "Cultural Encounters and Clash of Civilisations: Huntington and Modern Crusading Studies," in *Cultural Encounters During the Crusades*, ed. Kurt Villads Jensen, Kirsi Salonen, and Helle Vogt (Odense: University Press of Southern Denmark, 2013), 15–26; Geraldine Heng, "Holy War Redux: The Crusades, Futures of the Past, and Strategic Logic in the 'Clash' of Religions," *PMLA* 126 (2011): 422–431.

societies rather than "civilizations": the Templars seeking world domination and the resistance embodied by the Assassins.[16]

The game possesses some important congruencies with the 2005 film by Ridley Scott, *Kingdom of Heaven*. It certainly influenced the game as the whole development team watched it together. Nicholas Cantin, an art director, reflected that it was a "kind of validation from Hollywood [. . .] plus it gave us a lot of references from the customs for the backgrounds."[17] The film also positioned itself obliquely to crusading, as it was set in the years prior to the Third Crusade. Instead of a crusade campaign it depicted the Battle of Hattin and the Fall of Jerusalem to Saladin in 1187. Scott's movie painted the violence as the result of the blinkered fanaticism of extremists on both sides: in the Christian Kingdom this was represented by the Templars, while the pragmatists sought peace through accommodation. In the game, the player's character, Altaïr Ibn-La'Ahad, was supposedly motivated to bring peace through assassination; the incongruity was expressed in conversation with Richard I, who chided the player: "You fight for peace, do you not see the contradiction?" Similarly, the game's marketing declared, "The Third Crusade is tearing the Holy Land apart. You, Altair, intend to stop the hostilities by suppressing both sides of the conflict."[18] In both game and film peace, and how to achieve it, are violently contested, reflecting perhaps the post-9/11 context of production.[19]

Perhaps the most obvious disjuncture from contemporary historical accounts of crusading which emphasize the role of religious devotion in motivating crusading, following the work of Jonathan Riley-Smith, is its relegation in the game.[20] This was a deliberate choice, Jade Raymond, the game's producer, related:

> Knowing that our subject is controversial by nature we have dealt with religion as a purely historical background element. We can not completely avoid religion because it was the impetus for the war. We have, however, worked with cultural experts throughout production to make sure that we treat sensitive topics with respect. As the Saracens and Crusaders battle one another for control – the Assassins are working to find a way to end the hostilities. They see the war as pointless. There is no reason Crusaders and Saracens

---

16 There is notable blurring, however, in the distinctions between sides as the series proceeds; de Wildt, "Everything Is True."

17 Nicholas Cantin, Art Director, 2018, in Moss, "*Assassin's Creed*."

18 From the description of the game on Steam, "*Assassin's Creed*: Director's Cut," *Steam*, store.steampowered.com/app/15100/Assassins_Creed_Directors_Cut_Edition [accessed July 17, 2019].

19 Paul B. Sturtevant, "*Kingdom of Heaven*'s Road Map for Peace," *Bulletin of International Medieval Research* 12 (2006): 23–39.

20 Jonathan Riley-Smith, *The Crusades: A History*, 3rd edn. (London: Bloomsbury, 2014), 13–20.

should not co-exist in peace. The Assassins are not allied with either side of the conflict, nor are they driven by a desire for profit or power. In *Assassins' Creed*, Crusaders (and the Saracens) are not the Assassins' true enemy. War is – as are those who exploit it.[21]

This anti-war perspective chimes with the war fatigue expressed by sympathetic characters in *Kingdom of Heaven*, who are similarly those who "put no stock in religion," as the Hospitaller character played by David Thewlis tells Orlando Bloom's Balian.[22]

Locating the game in the context of its production – the post-9/11 world which produced *Kingdom of Heaven* and academic debates about the nature of religiously-motivated violence – is an act of historicization which enables students to see and make connections to broader cultural moments and scholarly debates.[23]

Templar "Silhouette"

The Templars, as found in this incarnation of *Assassin's Creed*, are evil in terms a modern player can understand: they are willing to enslave, torture, and kill for dominion and are fanatically committed to their cause even in their dying moments. In history-defying fashion the brotherhood of Christian soldier-monks, despised by Saladin for their warmongering, are gradually revealed to include prominent Muslims, not least of whom is Al-Mualim, the head of the Assassins. This trope of the "bad Templars" and a Templar conspiracy needs to be seen in its history; a history which begins as the Templars were denounced and dismantled at the start of the fourteenth century by the French king and French Pope.[24]

Templar "continuations" or revivals have continued to sprout over the last two and a half centuries. Unencumbered by the inconvenience of continued existence, the Templars provided origin myths for Freemasonry and for conspiracy theorists looking for meaning in the reordering of societies amidst the

---

21 Jade Raymond, Producer, 2008, quoted in El-Nasr et al., "*Assassin's Creed*," 13.
22 Sturtevant, "Road Map," 35.
23 See Brian Johnsrud, "Metaphorical Memories of the Medieval Crusades after 9/11," in *Memory Unbound: Tracing the Dynamics of Memory Studies*, ed. Lucy Bond, Stef Craps, and Pieter Vermeulen (Oxford: Berghahn Books, 2017), 195–220; John D. Cotts, "The Academic Historiography of the Crusades and the Twenty-First Century Debate on Religious Violence," *International Journal of Military History and Historiography* 41 (2020): 343–376.
24 Malcolm Barber, *The New Knighthood: A History of the Order of the Temple* (Cambridge: Cambridge University Press, 1995), 280–314.

aftershocks of the French Revolution.[25] One abortive attempt to revive the Templars in England in the first half of the nineteenth century was centered on Sir Sidney Smith, Charles Tennyson d'Eyncourt, and the Duke of Sussex.[26] In the twenty-first century, alongside Norwegian terrorist Anders Breivik's imagined Templar identity, online groups claiming to resurrect the Templers persist, and a Mexican drug cartel has drawn on the rule of the Templars as a way of demanding loyalty and presenting themselves as having ancient Christian heritage. Umberto Eco parodied the Templars' ubiquity to conspiracy theories in his *Foucault's Pendulum* (1988), suggesting that the final way of identifying a lunatic was "by the fact that sooner or later he brings up the Templars."[27]

Harry J. Brown has characterized the Templars in *Assassin's Creed* as "a silhouette of the historical Templars"; they "represent a composite of previous Templar conspiracy theories."[28] He has cited the eighteenth-century appropriation of the Templars by Freemasons, and the penchant for linking both to conspiracies responsible for later social turmoil, as significant factors in creating and popularizing the idea that the Templars were (and continued to be) guardians of secret, world-changing knowledge. This was expounded by Dan Brown's novel *The Da Vinci Code* (2003, turned into a blockbuster film in 2006) and other novels and films, but has a long heritage of "mythistory" to draw on.[29] "The refiguring of the

---

[25] Barber, *The New Knighthood*, 314–334.

[26] Elizabeth Siberry, "Victorian Perceptions of the Military Orders," in *The Military Orders: Fighting for the Faith and Caring for the Sick*, ed. Malcolm Barber (Aldershot: Variorum, 1994), 366–368.

[27] Daniel Wollenberg, "The New Knighthood: Terrorism and the Medieval," *Postmedieval* 5 (2014): 21–33; Phil James, "Los Caballeros Templarios de Michoacán: Knights Templar Identity as a Tool for Legitimisation and Internal Discipline," in *The Crusades in the Modern World: Engaging the Crusades, Volume Two*, ed. Mike Horswell and Akil N. Awan (Abingdon: Routledge, 2020), 25–40; Umberto Eco, *Foucault's Pendulum*, trans. William Weaver (London: Vintage Book, 2001), 67. On the Templar myth, see also John Walker, "'From the Holy Grail and the Ark of the Covenant to Freemasonry and the Priory of Sion': An Introduction to the 'After-History' of the Templars," in *The Military Orders, Volume 5: Politics and Power*, ed. Peter Edbury (Aldershot: Ashgate, 2012), 439–447; Juliette Wood, "The Myth of Secret History, or 'It's Not Just the Templars Involved in Absolutely Everything'", in *The Military Orders, Volume 5: Politics and Power*, ed. Peter Edbury (Aldershot: Ashgate, 2012), 448–461; John Walker, "Sources for the Templar Myth," in *The Templars and Their Sources*, ed. Karl Borchardt et al. (London: Routledge, 2017), 360–371.

[28] Harry J. Brown, "The Consolation of Paranoia: Conspiracy, Epistemology, and the Templars in *Assassin's Creed*, *Deus Ex*, and *Dragon Age*," in *Digital Gaming Re-Imagines the Middle Ages*, ed. Daniel T. Kline (Abingdon: Routledge, 2014), 231–232.

[29] Brown, 229–230. "Mythistory" is Gary Dickson's term for a mythical, supposedly historical account, with its own life – he deploys it in relation to the legendary Children's Crusade; see

Templars as an ultramodern, ultrapowerful corporation in the *Assassin's Creed* series, as agents of the Illuminati in the *Deus Ex* series, and as an oppressive police force in the *Dragon Age* series," Brown argued, "suggests that they continue to embody the popular suspicion of covert and unaccountable power."[30] Indeed, pseudo-Templar orders continue to appear to the present day, not least with the advent of the internet. Modern groups include those set up in recent years to send Westerners to fight ISIS or as expressions of chivalry.[31] The Templars, then, are more historiographically interesting than just providing an opportunity to discuss their medieval history. Their long mythistory raises questions relevant to *Assassin's Creed* and other incarnations: why do they reoccur so frequently? What utility is there in the Templars to creators and consumers of digital games? What associations do they bring or invoke? They too need to be contextualized in their contemporary usage, not least amidst their invocations by white supremacists.[32]

Assassinating ... History

When it comes to the game's depiction of the Assassins at the core of the game's mythology and ideology, the developers cited the 1938 novel *Alamut*, written by Slovenian novelist Vladimir Bartol, as inspiration and guide.[33] The novel, hailed by Mirt Komel as "the most decisive and influential work of fiction" on the Assassins in the modern era, was translated into French in 1988/89 and English in 2003/4.[34] In the absence of autobiographical histories of the group, it aggregated many medieval legends about the Assassins, written by

---

Gary Dickson, *The Children's Crusade: Medieval History, Modern Mythistory* (Basingstoke: Palgrave Macmillan, 2008).
30 Brown, "Consolation of Paranoia," 234.
31 Rory MacLellan, "Far-Right Appropriations of the Medieval Military Orders," *The Mediæval Journal* 9 (2019): 175–198; Rory MacLellan, "Ordo Militaris Inc.: A Modern 'Military Order', Medieval History, and Historical 'Authenticity'", in *The Crusades and the Far-Right: Engaging the Crusades, Volume Eight*, ed. Charlotte Gauthier and Jonathan Phillips (Abingdon: Routledge, forthcoming 2022).
32 Nicholas L. Paul, "Modern Intolerance and the Medieval Crusades," in *Whose Middle Ages?: Teachable Moments for an Ill-Used Past*, ed. Andrew Albin et al. (New York: Fordham University Press, 2019), 34–43; Adam Bishop, "#DeusVult," in *Whose Middle Ages?: Teachable Moments for an Ill-Used Past*, ed. Andrew Albin et al. (New York: Fordham University Press, 2019), 256–264.
33 Nicolas Cantin, an Art Director for the first *Assassin's Creed* game in 2018 Polygon interview; Jade Raymond, Producer of *Assassin's Creed* quoted in 2006 in Komel, "Orientalism," 83.
34 Komel, "Orientalism," 83.

their Christian and Muslim enemies, and perpetuated the orientalist stereotypes of nineteenth-century Europeans.³⁵ Not least of these was the labelling of the sect as "Assassins," rather than Nizari Ismailis.

Geraldine Heng has identified "Benjamin of Tudela, Arnold of Lübeck, William of Tyre, Jacques de Vitry, Marco Polo, Odoric of Pordenone, and the author of Mandeville's Travels, among others" as medieval contributors to a mythistory of the Assassins in the West, as well as thirteenth-century Persian historian Alauddin Ata-Malik Juvaini's account in which he accompanied the Mongols and read works from the Nizaris library before he ordered it burned down.³⁶ "Commonly known" elements of the "Assassins" myth derive from this corpus, including: the identity of the "Old Man of the Mountain" as the leader; the fanatically devout followers prepared to commit suicide at his command; and the artificial paradise garden with servile virgin women into which young would-be assassins were tricked into thinking was the paradise which awaited them upon their martyrdom. These elements appeared in *Assassin's Creed* in various forms: the aged Al-Mualim in the Masyaf fortress has a garden zone unlocked by the player behind his castle complete with young women, and the player performs a "leap of faith" in the game which appears to attackers to be a suicide jump.³⁷ Finally, Komel has suggested that the mantra of the assassins (the creed of the game's title) that "nothing is true, everything is permitted" was also a nineteenth-century invention which can be traced back to Silvestre de Sacy through Gustav Flügel, Fredrich Nietzsche, and Bartol's novel.³⁸ According to the game's creative director, Patrice Désilets, this creed expressed the foundational principle of the whole series: "the creed is what the franchise like stands upon – that you can do what you want in an *Assassin's Creed* game."³⁹ The phrase resonated more broadly. In 2018 Désilets asserted that "it's not only a way of playing; it's the way of living. [. . .] 'nothing is

---

35 Geraldine Heng, "Sex, Lies, and Paradise: The Assassins, Prester John, and the Fabulation of Civilizational Identities," *Differences* 23 (2012): 7–13; Komel, "Orientalism," 78.
36 Heng, "Fabulation," 4, 7.
37 Komel, "Orientalism," 84; Frank Bosman, "'Nothing Is True, Everything Is Permitted': The Portrayal of the Nizari Isma'ilis in the *Assassin's Creed* Game Series," *Online: Heidelberg Journal of Religions on the Internet* 10 (2016): 6–26; Oana-Alexandra Chirală, "'Show This Fool Knight What It Is to Have No Fear': Freedom and Oppression in Assassin's Creed (2007)," in *Playing the Crusades: Engaging the Crusades, Volume Five*, ed. Robert Houghton (Abingdon: Routledge, 2021), 56–57.
38 Komel, "Orientalism," 84–85.
39 Patrice Désilets, quoted in Moss, "*Assassin's Creed*"; see also Chirală, "Freedom and Oppression," 59–66.

true; everything is permitted' is real. And I receive messages almost every day about it – about that. I get people who got tattoos on their body."[40]

If the Templars possessed an ostensible contemporary relevance, so did the Assassins. Heng and Komel have shown how in popular and academic works the mythologized Assassins are corralled into presentist histories of 9/11 as the first terrorists, not least by historian Bernard Lewis.[41] However, in *Assassin's Creed* the Assassins are transmuted into freedom fighters. In deference to modern expectations the game takes pains to point out that the killings are surgical strikes and the assassins do not kill innocents. Again, interrogating the presentation of the Assassins in the game leads to the illumination of several levels of historical re-presentation. This enables investigators to evaluate the version of Assassins being depicted, and locate that image in its historical and contemporary contexts. At the least, it complicated the overlaying of the binaries employed by the "Clash" rhetoric of West-crusaders-good against East-assassins-evil.[42] Going further, considering the impact of role-playing a medieval assassin in a twenty-first-century context has led at least one commentator to ask whether players are being invited to "work through" modern anxieties of terrorist enemies hidden in plain sight by (in the logic of the game) "returning to the medieval source of Arab terrorism, assuming the role of a professional, well-nigh supernatural assassin."[43] Considering the perlocutionary effects of the game provokes us to think about how the act of playing, consuming and imaginatively engaging with these forms of historical media generates identities and practices as well as perceptions of the past.

A History for Today

Discussing where the game's designers developed their presentation of history from highlights the intersection of popular and academic perceptions of the past, and disjunctions between the nature of historical knowledge claimed by the "historical" game and scholars. The game credited two recognized crusade historians, David Nicolle and Paul M. Cobb (also a consultant on *Kingdom of Heaven*),

---

40 Désilets, quoted in Moss, "*Assassin's Creed*".
41 Heng, "Fabulation," 3–5; Komel, "Orientalism," 79.
42 Chirală, "Freedom and Oppression," 55.
43 Nickolas Haydock, "Introduction: "The Unseen Cross Upon the Breast": Medievalism, Orientalism and Discontent," in *Hollywood in the Holy Land: Essays on Film Depictions of the Crusades and Christian-Muslim Clashes*, ed. Nickolas Haydock and Edward L. Risden (London: McFarland & Company, 2009), 6.

who work on military history and the crusades from the Islamic perspective respectively.[44] Any discussion of the game's historicity needs to include these influences as well as those already described – clearly the designers felt the need to be "historical" and that translated to the inclusion of crusade specialists. The historians brought in a further stream of information. Raymond commented, "We have used the web, documentaries, old medieval encyclopaedias, paintings, and novels. The historian helped us with some harder to find information such as original city plans of Jerusalem, Damascus, and Acre that date back to the 3rd crusade."[45] The experts provided the game validation in terms of its historicity. Raymond again recalled, "we got comments back from both of them [the historians] saying, 'It's clear that you guys went to Jerusalem . . . it's exactly like being there!' And not one on the team actually went! We just got really good research material."[46]

The use of the terms "historical" and "accuracy" by the game's designers and marketers provides an excellent opportunity to discuss the nature of those terms and how they are understood by creator, player and critic. Gabrielle Spiegel has argued that historical knowledge can be understood as making specific "truth claims" about the past.[47] In this sense, *Assassin's Creed* appeared to be attempting to have its cake and eat it; it played on its historicity at times and disavowed it at others. Raymond exemplified this approach:

> *Assassin's Creed* is a speculative fiction and it's a fun genre to work in. By grounding a story in reality, you increase its credibility. Suspension of disbelief becomes easier because it's happening in our world. You're exploring cities that still exist today – encountering infamous individuals whose names everyone knows – witnessing battles that really occurred.[48]

The marketing asserts that the game "immerses you in the realistic and historical Holy Land of the 12th century, featuring life-like graphics, ambience and the subtle, yet detailed nuances of a living world"; the series' tagline is "the past is your playground."[49] Creative Director Désilets argued that "I strongly believe that video games are really our own time machine, it's a way to go back in time,

---

[44] David Nicolle, *The Third Crusade, 1191: Richard the Lionheart, Saladin and the Struggle for Jerusalem* (Oxford: Osprey, 2006); Paul M. Cobb, *The Race for Paradise: An Islamic History of the Crusades* (Oxford: Oxford University Press, 2014).
[45] Raymond quoted in El-Nasr et al., "Assassin's Creed," 14.
[46] David Knight, *Assassin's Creed: Limited Edition Art Book* (Prima Games, 2007), 122. Given to me by Ubisoft, with thanks to Ben Westerman.
[47] Gabrielle M. Spiegel, *The Past as Text: The Theory and Practice of Medieval Historiography* (London: Johns Hopkins University Press, 1997), xii–xiii.
[48] Raymond quoted in El-Nasr et al., "Assassin's Creed," 6–7.
[49] "*Assassin's Creed*," Steam.

basically."⁵⁰ Despite consultation of historians and historical sources, both Raymond and Cantin shrugged off the constraints of history when it suited them. "When you work with history, you need to take it a little bit more seriously, I think," Cantin reflected, "And without, you know, making sure that everything is like the history. We had to let ourselves open windows on that side, creatively. [. . .] We needed to be credible instead of being authentic on the visual aspect and the gameplay aspect."⁵¹ Claude Langlais, the Technical Director, wanted the behavior of the characters to be "believable" rather than accurate.⁵² Discussing the decision to replace Conrad of Montferrat with William as an assassination target, Raymond narrated this tension:

> We strove for accuracy, even for the guys that you assassinate. We had Conrad of Montferrat at first in our game. Then when we did research into the specific year 1191, we found out he was actually killed mysteriously, but it wasn't in 1191. So then we decided; "Oh, we can't put him in our game," because we didn't want to have a guy who didn't actually die in that year as one of the guys you kill, because we wanted it to be historically plausible. So, then we found out that William, who was related to Conrad, was actually in Acre in 1191. So then we thought, "Oh cool, we'll stick William there instead."⁵³

These comments push at a helpful tension for students to consider and open up conversations about what constitutes credibility, plausibility, believability, and authenticity – and to what uses they can be put. If, as Spiegel suggests, claims about the past have a particular cultural status, we can productively ask what work they are doing in the context of the game's narrative and marketing. "Texts," Spiegel wrote of cultural forms which I suggest includes games, "both mirror and generate social realities, which they may sustain, resist, contest, or seek to transform, depending on the case at hand."⁵⁴

The visual elements bear witness to the tension between the demands of "accuracy" and appeal, a theme often returned to by its creators. Medieval clothing, Raymond recalled, did not vary much and those without means "pretty much walked around wearing variations on a brown sack of potatoes with tights."⁵⁵ The art team therefore deliberately introduced more variety and color into the outfits of the population of the cities. For the Templars and other crusaders (see Figure 3.1) the team took historical designs but Art Director Raphael Lacoste commented:

---

50 Knight, *Art Book*, 118.
51 Cantin quoted in Moss, "*Assassin's Creed*."
52 Knight, *Art Book*, 65.
53 Knight, *Art Book*, 94.
54 Spiegel, *The Past as Text*, 24.
55 Knight, *Art Book*, 60.

> We based our population on information that was historically as accurate as possible, but, you know, we are still artists, so we are creating, we aren't trying to focus exactly on reality but we're trying to make something more stylized. It was based on historical designs, so we kept the cross, the Lionheart's lion, and for the tunics, we also kept the designs of the different factions but we tried also to make this more dramatic.[56]

Emphasized by the *Art Book* produced by the makers of the game, *Assassin's Creed* was designed to be visually sumptuous. Indeed, the cities exemplify the tensions between the constraints of the game's mechanics, historical facticity, and the need to present a spectacular experience. Creating a life-size replica of each location visited (Jerusalem, Damascus, Acre, and the fortress and village at Masyaf) would have impeded the gameplay experience, however each place had to "feel" authentic. To this end, cities were constructed out of base units laid out on historical maps with attention paid to iconic landmarks and cinematic vistas. Lacoste explained: "We didn't want to recreate the cities exactly as they were, but we still used the real landmarks [. . .] we exaggerated the proportions a bit and made some [. . .] things maybe more organic and interesting for our visual composition."[57] Each city had its own "filter" to convey a mood, distinct architectural styles, and iconic viewpoints (Figures 3.2–3.6).[58]

In these ways we can see the impact of other, non-historical media. As well as *Kingdom of Heaven*, artists working on the game cited *The Name of the Rose* and *Black Hawk Down* as influences, as well as *One Thousand and One Nights*, *Sands of Time*, and *Prince of Persia 3* for their rendering of Damascus.[59] The visual echoes of nineteenth-century orientalist painters, particularly David Roberts, are legion.[60] Cumulatively, what this complex visual melange of meticulously rendered landmarks, repeated "Lego blocks" of buildings, visually distinct themes, and a variety of populations aimed to achieve was "affective authenticity," a sufficiently "medieval" feel to convince the player to suspend disbelief. The techniques employed recognise the relative – and modern – nature of what is perceived to be medieval.[61]

---

56 Knight, *Art Book*, 77.
57 Knight, *Art Book*, 133.
58 Knight, *Art Book*, 121–150; Chirală, "Freedom and Oppression," 62–64.
59 Knight, *Art Book*, 140, 144, and 129.
60 See Annabel Jane Wharton, *Architectural Agents: The Delusional, Abusive, Addictive Lives of Buildings* (Minneapolis, MN: University of Minnesota Press, 2015), Plate 5.
61 For "affective authenticity" see Andrew B. R. Elliott and Mike Horswell, "Crusading Icons: Medievalism and Authenticity in Historical Digital Games," in *History in Games: Contingencies of an Authentic Past*, ed. Martin Lorber and Felix Zimmerman (Bielefeld: transcript Verlag, 2020), 137–156 and other chapters in this book. Also, chapters in Rob Houghton ed., *Playing the Crusades: Engaging the Crusades, Volume Five* (Abingdon: Routledge, 2021).

Figure 3.1: King Richard (second from left) and Templar knights confront the player (centre, hooded) amidst the Battle of Arsuf.

Figure 3.2: View of Jerusalem with the Dome of the Rock prominent (left).

Figure 3.3: View of Damascus.

Figure 3.4: View of the streets of Damascus with repeating elements visible.

3 Historicising *Assassin's Creed* — 63

Figure 3.5: View of Acre cathedral.

Figure 3.6: Detail of stained glass window of Acre cathedral.

Conclusion

I have shown how *Assassin's Creed* can be employed in the classroom in deeper ways than merely considering its accuracy, through appreciating the game as a historical artefact in its own right. Accuracy can be a useful starting point for classroom discussion, though I have tried to show how questions of authenticity and plausibility facilitate deeper study of the historiographic entanglements of the game's presentation of the past. These include novels, films, paintings, and contemporary political and scholarly debates. While a comprehensive evaluation of these influences and interrelationships – and the game's reception and influence – is beyond the scope of this chapter, it has pointed the way towards resources which would facilitate further study; the large and varied body of work referenced in the notes and bibliography is merely the tip of the iceberg of scholarly evaluation of *Assassin's Creed* and historical games.

This "relentless historicization" is eminently applicable to other historical or pseudo-historical games – indeed, it will help reframe them as themselves historical products and producers of perceptions of the past. Moreover, appreciating the ways in which games' technical features structure and limit images of the past helps us see how history is being reflected and made beyond the academy. And, as recent work has discussed, it has moved considerations of accuracy to the more productive conversations about constructions of authenticity.[62]

Assassin's Creed sits within, and contributes to, a history of perceptions of the crusades, crusader states, military orders, and assassins which is complex and yet has the power to influence contemporary employments of all these historical elements.[63] *Assassin's Creed*, and crusading computer games more broadly, are a rich resource from which to draw connections between historiography, medievalism, and contemporary culture in the classroom.

Bibliography

Asbridge, Thomas. *The Crusades: The War for the Holy Land*. London: Pocket Books, 2010.
Barber, Malcolm. *The New Knighthood: A History of the Order of the Temple*. Cambridge: Cambridge University Press, 1995.

---

[62] Especially Lorber and Zimmerman, eds., *History in Games*.
[63] E.g. Thomas Lecaque and Joshua Call, "Knives in the Dark and the Death of History: Validating Himmler's Middle Ages through *Assassin's Creed*," in *The Crusades and the Far-Right: Engaging the Crusades, Volume Eight*, ed. Charlotte Gauthier and Jonathan Phillips (Abingdon: Routledge, forthcoming 2022); see also Elliott and Horswell, "Crusading Icons."

Bishop, Adam. "#DeusVult." In *Whose Middle Ages?: Teachable Moments for an Ill-Used Past*, edited by Andrew Albin, Mary C. Erler, Thomas O'Donnell, Nicholas L. Paul, and Nina Rowe, 256–264. New York: Fordham University Press, 2019.

Bosman, Frank. "'Nothing Is True, Everything Is Permitted': The Portrayal of the Nizari Isma'ilis in the *Assassin's Creed* Game Series." *Online: Heidelberg Journal of Religions on the Internet* 10 (2016): 6–26.

Brown, Harry J. "The Consolation of Paranoia: Conspiracy, Epistemology, and the Templars in *Assassin's Creed, Deus Ex*, and *Dragon Age*." In *Digital Gaming Re-Imagines the Middle Ages*, edited by Daniel T. Kline, 227–239. Abingdon: Routledge, 2014.

Chirală, Oana-Alexandra. ""Show This Fool Knight What It Is to Have No Fear": Freedom and Oppression in Assassin's Creed (2007)." In *Playing the Crusades: Engaging the Crusades, Volume Five*, edited by Robert Houghton, 53–70. Abingdon: Routledge, 2021.

Cobb, Paul M. *The Race for Paradise: An Islamic History of the Crusades*. Oxford: Oxford University Press, 2014.

Cotts, John D. "The Academic Historiography of the Crusades and the Twenty-First Century Debate on Religious Violence." *International Journal of Military History and Historiography* 41 (2020): 343–376.

Dickson, Gary. *The Children's Crusade: Medieval History, Modern Mythistory*. Basingstoke: Palgrave Macmillan, 2008.

Eco, Umberto. *Foucault's Pendulum*. Translated by William Weaver. London: Vintage Book, 2001.

Elliott, Andrew B. R. "Simulations and Simulacra: History in Video Games." *Práticas Da História* 5 (2017): 11–41.

Elliott, Andrew B. R. "The *Assassin's Creed* Curriculum: Video Games and the Middle Ages," 1–11. Paper presented at the International Medieval Congress, Leeds, UK, 2016. www.academia.edu/26869807/The_Assassins_Creed_Curriculum_Video_Games_and_the_Middle_Ages.

Elliott, Andrew B. R., and Mike Horswell. "Crusading Icons: Medievalism and Authenticity in Historical Digital Games." In *History in Games: Contingencies of an Authentic Past*, edited by Martin Lorber and Felix Zimmerman, 137–156. Bielefeld: transcript Verlag, 2020.

El-Nasr, Magy Seif, Maha Al-Saati, Simon Niedenthal, and David Milam. "*Assassin's Creed*: A Multi-Cultural Read." *Loading . . .* 2 (2008): 1–32.

Gilbert, Lisa. "'*Assassin's Creed* Reminds Us That History Is Human Experience': Students' Senses of Empathy While Playing a Narrative Video Game." *Theory & Research in Social Education* 47 (2019): 108–137.

Gilbert, Lisa. "'The Past Is Your Playground': The Challenges and Possibilities of *Assassin's Creed: Syndicate* for Social Education." *Theory & Research in Social Education* 45 (2017): 145–155.

Haydock, Nickolas. "Introduction: "The Unseen Cross Upon the Breast"; Medievalism, Orientalism and Discontent." In *Hollywood in the Holy Land: Essays on Film Depictions of the Crusades and Christian-Muslim Clashes*, edited by Nickolas Haydock and Edward L. Risden, 1–30. London: McFarland & Company, 2009.

Heng, Geraldine. "Holy War Redux: The Crusades, Futures of the Past, and Strategic Logic in the 'Clash' of Religions." *PMLA* 126 (2011): 422–431.

Heng, Geraldine. "Sex, Lies, and Paradise: The Assassins, Prester John, and the Fabulation of Civilizational Identities." *Differences* 23 (2012): 1–31.

Horswell, Mike. *The Rise and Fall of British Crusader Medievalism, c. 1825-1945*. Abingdon: Routledge, 2018.

Houghton, Robert. "World, Structure and Play: A Framework for Games as Historical Research Outputs, Tools, and Processes." *Práticas Da História* 7 (2017): 11–43.

Houghton, Robert, ed. *Playing the Crusades: Engaging the Crusades, Volume Five*. Abingdon: Routledge, 2021.

James, Phil. "Los Caballeros Templarios de Michoacán: Knights Templar Identity as a Tool for Legitimisation and Internal Discipline." In *The Crusades in the Modern World: Engaging the Crusades, Volume Two*, edited by Mike Horswell and Akil N. Awan, 25–40. Abingdon: Routledge, 2020.

Jensen, Kurt Villads. "Cultural Encounters and Clash of Civilisations: Huntington and Modern Crusading Studies." In *Cultural Encounters During the Crusades*, edited by Kurt Villads Jensen, Kirsi Salonen, and Helle Vogt, 15–26. Odense: University Press of Southern Denmark, 2013.

Johnsrud, Brian. "Metaphorical Memories of the Medieval Crusades after 9/11." In *Memory Unbound: Tracing the Dynamics of Memory Studies*, edited by Lucy Bond, Stef Craps, and Pieter Vermeulen, 195–220. Oxford: Berghahn Books, 2017.

Kapell, Matthew Wilhelm, and Andrew B. R. Elliott, eds. *Playing with the Past: Digital Games and the Simulation of History*. London: Bloomsbury, 2013.

Kee, Kevin, ed. *Pastplay: Teaching and Learning History with Technology*. Michigan: The University of Michigan Press, 2014.

Knight, David. *Assassin's Creed: Limited Edition Art Book*. Prima Games, 2007.

Komel, Mirt. "Orientalism in *Assassin's Creed*: Self-Orientalizing the Assassins from Forerunners of Modern Terrorism into Occidentalized Heroes." *Teorija in Praksa* 1 (2014): 72–90.

Lecaque, Thomas, and Joshua Call. "Knives in the Dark and the Death of History: Validating Himmler's Middle Ages through *Assassin's Creed*." In *The Crusades and the Far-Right: Engaging the Crusades, Volume Eight*, edited by Charlotte Gauthier and Jonathan Phillips. Abingdon: Routledge, forthcoming 2022.

Lünen, Alexander von, Katherine J. Lewis, Benjamin Litherland, and Pat Cullum, eds. *Historia Ludens: The Playing Historian*. Abingdon: Routledge, 2020.

MacLellan, Rory. "Far-Right Appropriations of the Medieval Military Orders," *The Mediæval Journal* 9 (2019): 175–198.

MacLellan, Rory. "Ordo Militaris Inc.: A Modern 'Military Order', Medieval History, and Historical 'Authenticity'." In *The Crusades and the Far-Right: Engaging the Crusades, Volume Eight*, edited by Charlotte Gauthier and Jonathan Phillips. Abingdon: Routledge, forthcoming 2022.

McCall, Jeremiah. "Teaching History With Digital Historical Games: An Introduction to the Field and Best Practices." *Simulation & Gaming* 47 (2016): 517–542.

Metzger, Alan, and Richard J. Paxton. "Gaming History: A Framework for What Video Games Teach about the Past." *Theory & Research in Social Education* 44 (2016): 532–564.

Moss, Richard. "*Assassin's Creed*: An Oral History." *Polygon*, October 3, 2018. www.polygon.com/features/2018/10/3/17924770/assassins-creed-an-oral-history-patrice-desilets.

Nicolle, David. *The Third Crusade, 1191: Richard the Lionheart, Saladin and the Struggle for Jerusalem*. Oxford: Osprey, 2006.

Paul, Nicholas L. "Modern Intolerance and the Medieval Crusades." In *Whose Middle Ages?: Teachable Moments for an Ill-Used Past*, edited by Andrew Albin, Mary C. Erler, Thomas

O'Donnell, Nicholas L. Paul, and Nina Rowe, 34–43. New York: Fordham University Press, 2019.
Riley-Smith, Jonathan. *The Crusades: A History*. 3rd edn. London: Bloomsbury, 2014.
Siberry, Elizabeth. *The New Crusaders: Images of the Crusades in the 19th and Early 20th Centuries*. Aldershot: Ashgate, 2000.
Siberry, Elizabeth "Victorian Perceptions of the Military Orders." In *The Military Orders: Fighting for the Faith and Caring for the Sick*, edited by Malcolm Barber, 365–372. Aldershot: Variorum, 1994.
Šisler, Vít. "Palestine in Pixels: The Holy Land, Arab-Israeli Conflict, and Reality Construction in Video Games." *Middle East Journal of Culture and Communication* 2 (2009): 275–292.
Skottki, Kristin. "The Dead, the Revived and the Recreated Pasts: 'Structural Amnesia' in Representations of Crusade History." In *Perceptions of the Crusades from the Nineteenth to the Twenty-First Century: Engaging the Crusades, Volume One*, edited by Mike Horswell and Jonathan Phillips, 79–106. Abingdon: Routledge, 2018.
Spiegel, Gabrielle M. *The Past as Text: The Theory and Practice of Medieval Historiography*. London: Johns Hopkins University Press, 1997.
Sturtevant, Paul B. "*Kingdom of Heaven's* Road Map for Peace." *Bulletin of International Medieval Research* 12 (2006): 23–39.
Trépanier, Nicholas. "The Assassin's Perspective: Teaching History with Video Games." *Perspectives on History* (blog), May 1, 2014. www.historians.org/publications-and-directories/perspectives-on-history/may-2014/the-assassins-perspective.
Wainwright, A. Martin. "Teaching Historical Theory through Video Games." *The History Teacher* 47 (2014): 579–612.
Walker, John. "'From the Holy Grail and the Ark of the Covenant to Freemasonry and the Priory of Sion': An Introduction to the 'After-History' of the Templars." In *The Military Orders, Volume 5: Politics and Power*, edited by Peter Edbury, 439–47. Aldershot: Ashgate, 2012.
Walker, John. "Sources for the Templar Myth." In *The Templars and Their Sources*, edited by Karl Borchardt, Karoline Döring, Philippe Josserand, and Helen J. Nicholson, 360–371. London: Routledge, 2017.
Wharton, Annabel Jane. *Architectural Agents: The Delusional, Abusive, Addictive Lives of Buildings*. Minneapolis, MN: University of Minnesota Press, 2015.
Wildt, Lars de. "'Everything Is True; Nothing Is Permitted': Utopia, Religion and Conspiracy in *Assassin's Creed*." In *Playing Utopia: Futures in Digital Games*, edited by Benjamin Beil, Gundolf S. Freyermuth, and Hans Christian Schmidt, 149–186. Bielefeld: transcript Verlag, 2019.
Wollenberg, Daniel. "The New Knighthood: Terrorism and the Medieval." *Postmedieval* 5 (2014): 21–33.
Wood, Juliette. "The Myth of Secret History, or 'It's Not Just the Templars Involved in Absolutely Everything.'" In *The Military Orders, Volume 5: Politics and Power*, edited by Peter Edbury, 448–461. Aldershot: Ashgate, 2012.

Ludography

Assassin's Creed. Ubisoft, 2007.

David DeVine
4 Declaiming Dragons: Empathy Learning and *The Elder Scrolls* in Teaching Medieval Rhetorical Schemes

Abstract: James Murphy notes that so-called Classical "Sophistic rhetoric" made its way into the Medieval schoolroom through the form of *declamatio* and *progymnasmata* exercises.[1] *Declamatio* or "declamations" were faux speeches that students would put on to gain experience in various genres, such as legal or political speech. While on the other hand, Hermogenes' *progymnasmata*, or "preliminary exercises," had students compose short speeches on character, *topoi*, proverbs, and other elements that would become larger works, later. Murphy notes that these exercises were "transmitted directly into the Middle Ages by Priscian,"[2] where today, these same exercises make up the contemporary composition classroom bulletin.[3] Then, how can we teach these medieval schemas to contemporary students? One proposal is by gamifying the composition classroom.[4] By drawing on scholarship from composition and rhetoric and game studies this project proposes using a fantasy medieval video game, *The Elder Scrolls V: Skyrim*,[5] to help students take on the identity of "the student of medievalist rhetoric." By means of the game, students gain empathy through playing as their character, someone far different from themselves. As students play with and within the gamespace, they take on the projective identity of their characters in the medievalist-inspired Tolkienesque world of Skyrim and write, speak, and create as their characters. The *declamatio* and *progymnasmata* they produce "fits in" to the world of the gamespace as they declaim jarls and rebels, salute thanes and holds, and write encomiums or invectives of states and empires. Students, with

---

[1] James Jerome Murphy, "Introduction: The Medieval Background," in *Three Medieval Rhetorical Arts*, ed. James Jerome Murphy, Medieval and Renaissance Texts and Studies Studies, vol. 228 (Tempe, Ariz: Arizona Center for Medieval and Renaissance Studies, 2001), xii.
[2] Murphy, xii.
[3] George Alexander Kennedy, "Introduction," in *Progymnasmata: Greek Textbooks of Prose Composition and Rhetoric*, ed. George Alexander Kennedy, Writings from the Greco-Roman World, v. 10 (Atlanta: Society of Biblical Literature, 2003), ix–xvi.
[4] Justin Hodgson, "Developing and Extending Gaming Pedagogy: Designing a Course as Game," in *Rhetoric/Composition/Play through Video Games*, ed. Richard Colby, Matthew S. S. Johnson, and Rebekah Shultz Colby (New York: Palgrave Macmillan US, 2013), 45–60, https://doi.org/10.1057/9781137307675_5.
[5] *Skyrim* (Bethesda Game Studios, 2011).

their projective identities, then take those skills taught through Classical and medieval rhetoric and interest garnered through *Skyrim* and write for "real world" communities beyond the university. This project addresses both the theory and pedagogy of medieval rhetoric, and proposes one curriculum for such a class.

Introduction

Some of the most significant lessons I've learned about teaching – and consequently about learning – have been through engaging with fantasy games. Fantasy, as a reflection of reality, is a lens we can use to magnify or distance ourselves from the reality of a given situation. This amplification enables us to learn, understand, critique, and persuade others about the grounded realities we live in in a way that captures our imaginations. While fantasy stories and novels give us the ability to sit as a fly-on-the-wall and look into other worlds or alternative histories, fantasy video games offer a practical exercise – an engaging one – in acting out those other worlds and the problems that take place there.

Games are not only enriching and engaging, encouraging us to become heroes or villains, take on new identities, solve problems, or source entertainment for ourselves and our families, but they are also, in the words of James Paul Gee, exceptionally good at teaching us how to play them.[6] As we play through the level of a *Tomb Raider* adventure, Gee explains that the player, playing as Lara Croft, in ignoring Professor Von Croy in the tutorial to *Tomb Raider: The Last Revelation*,[7] is learning multiple things at once. They are learning how to be Lara, how to manoeuvre through the gamespace, how to manipulate objects in her world, and consequently how to play the game itself.[8] And if games have this potential to teach us multiple things at once, which Gee argues they do throughout his 2004 *What Video Games Have to Teach Us about Learning and Literacy*, I have sought to ask how we might translate gameplay, especially the captivating worlds of fantasy video games, into the classroom.

In this project, I propose one such curriculum for teaching a first-year composition (FYC) course with a Medieval fantasy video game, *The Elder Scrolls V: Skyrim*, in order to teach the critical thinking skills, writing and composition, and Classical and Medieval rhetorical schemes that the Writing Programs

---

6 James Paul Gee, *What Video Games Have to Teach Us about Learning and Literacy*, Education (New York, NY: Palgrave Macmillan, 2004), 2–4.
7 *Tomb Raider: The Last Revelation* (Core Design, 1999).
8 Gee, *What Video Games Have to Teach Us about Learning and Literacy*, 114–16.

Administrators' Outcomes statement and other scholars of rhetoric and composition have prioritized in their own classrooms. Additionally, *Skyrim*'s setting enables conversations about race, racism, and fantasy tropes, which make up the context of the writing course I propose.

The Content of Composition

Rhetoric, to quote the rhetorician Quintilian, is the "art of the good man speaking well"[9] and involves learning how to invent, arrange, style, memorize, and deliver arguments, according to the Roman orator and statesman Cicero.[10] Where the original art or "*techne*" of rhetoric was developed with public speaking in mind, much of what we know about rhetorical arts can be, and has been, translated into the composition process, to the end that teaching rhetoric, today, is about writing. Rhetoric, Classical, Medieval, and modern, is worked into many textbooks on teaching writing such as *Everything's an Argument*,[11] *They Say, I Say*,[12] *The Harbrace Guide to Writing*,[13] and many other contemporary textbooks at use in college composition classrooms, today. The guiding body for that curriculum is the Council of Writing Programs Administrators (WPA).

According to their 2014 update to the WPA Outcomes Statement for First-Year Composition, rhetorical knowledge is "the ability to analyze contexts and audiences" and "is the basis for composing" (wpacouncil.org).[14] As the guiding statement for FYC in U.S. postsecondary education, this "Outcomes Statement" sets the expectations for FYC across institutions, and prioritizes rhetorical knowledge, in addition to critical thinking, reading, composing, and writing and research processes. Students in the FYC classroom are expected to "Learn and use key rhetorical concepts through analyzing and composing a variety of texts," "Gain and experience reading and composing in several genres to understand how genre conventions shape and are shaped by readers' and writers

---

[9] Marcus Fabius Quintilianus, *The Institutio oratoria of Quintilian. 1: Books I–III*, Reprint, The Loeb classical library 124 (London: Heinemann, 1996), bk. 12.1.1.
[10] Marcus Tullius Cicero, *De Inventione*, trans. Charles Duke Yonge (United States: ReadHowYouWant.com, 2006).
[11] Andrea A. Lunsford and John J Ruszkiewicz, *Everything's an Argument* (Bedford: St Martin's, 2016).
[12] Gerald Graff and Cathy Birkenstein, *They Say / I Say: The Moves That Matter in Academic Writing* (New York: W. W. Norton & Co, 2010).
[13] Cheryl Glenn, *The Harbrace Guide to Writing* (Boston, MA: Cengage Learning, 2012).
[14] Council of Writing Program Administrators, n.d., www.wpacouncil.org.

practices and purposes," and "Develop facility in responding to a variety of situations and contexts calling for purposeful shifts in voice, tone, level of formality, design, medium, and/or structure," among others. So, with rhetoric at the forefront of the FYC classroom, we might ask how rhetorical knowledge and critical thinking can best be taught to college students.

While no two FYC classrooms are identical, college composition teachers, inhabiting English departments, or standalone departments of rhetoric, in some cases, as well as writing programs divorced from other academic units, are responsible for teaching this rhetorical knowledge to their students. In my classroom, as it was the way in which I learned as a student, I have decided to teach those rhetorical arts and knowledge in the way that they were taught to ancient and Medieval students: through the *progymnasmata* and *declamatio* exercises of Sophists. According to Sharon Crowley and Debra Hawhee, in their *Ancient Rhetorics for Contemporary Students*,[15] which pairs together the history of the discipline – that of rhetoric – with contemporary examples and exercises for the composition process, the *progymnasmata* or "preliminary exercises" were tasks that students took on such as memorizing fables, composing tales and proverbs, and writing commonplaces and descriptions.[16] These tasks, the authors of the exercises believed, would help their students become "competent rhetors if they combined study of rhetorical principles with lots of practice composing."[17] This is the philosophy that I take into my own classroom. But one question arises, which is "how do we teach Medieval and Classical schemes in a way that keeps students engaged with the content, rather than feeling as though the exercises are arcane or grounded in some long-lost practice?" In other words, "how do we keep the content relevant to students' lives, today?"

Gee said that "Real life works something like a massively multiplayer game."[18] Games, consequently, he argued, have a lot to teach us about how the world works, as they are coded and designed in ways that make us want to play them and engage with their content. Citing the fantasy, massively multiplayer online game *World of Warcraft*[19] as one of his examples, Gee explains that through playing a game, we experience and learn about the game's world as we take on different identities within the game's space.[20] By playing as a male

---

[15] Sharon Crowley and Debra Hawhee, *Ancient Rhetorics for Contemporary Students* (Boston: Pearson, 2012).
[16] Crowley and Hawhee, 28.
[17] Crowley and Hawhee, 24.
[18] Gee, *What Video Games Have to Teach Us about Learning and Literacy*, 7.
[19] *Word of Warcraft* (Blizzard Entertainment, 2004).
[20] Gee, *What Video Games Have to Teach Us about Learning and Literacy*, 47–51.

tauren (a type of minotaur) shaman, Gee experiences the world of *World of Warcraft* in a particular way. The same player (the human piloting the in-universe game character) may have an entirely different experience playing as a female elf warrior, and the player is capable of taking on different identities within the game's space. The point Gee is making by comparing our world to a game world such as *World of Warcraft* is that where the player navigates the world with the identity of the character they're playing as, we, as academics or teachers or citizens navigate our own world(s) by taking on identities like "student" or "researcher" and playing with them to figure out how they work and who we are.

As a teacher of writing and composition, as a student, and as an avid player of video-games, I similarly use different identities to navigate the world-space I share with my family, my co-workers, my students, and others, and taking to heart what Gee and others have said about the persuasive, learning potential of video games, I sought a way to marry together games with my curriculum of FYC. By doing so, I argue that such a curriculum – a composition and rhetoric course designed with a game or games as one of the course's required texts enables participation and engagement with the subject material – is an ideal way to introduce new or foreign concepts to students in a way that challenges them, much like a video game.

Then, how do we leverage the way that games work to teach and engage our students with the content of the *progymnasmata* and ancient and Medieval rhetoric? I argue: through playing *Skyrim*. But before diving into the world of Nords and epic battles with dragons, I first want to cover how Medieval rhetorics answer the WPA's call for rhetorical knowledge being taught in the college composition classroom.

Medieval Rhetoric in Teaching FYC

Medieval and Classical rhetoric, or, at least, the rhetoric that was taught in the Medieval and Classical schoolroom, answer the calls for making arguments in formal and informal settings, as well as demonstrate the rhetorical knowledge and sophisticated audience-awareness that the "Outcomes Statement" calls for.

According to James Murphy, Classical, Sophistic rhetoric was transmitted into the classroom through the *progymnasmata* and *declamatio* exercises. And of the *progymnasmata*, George Kennedy explains that "a Latin version of the Greek handbook attributed to Hermogenes was made by Priscian about A.D. 500" which "preserved [Hermogenes'] extensive works on grammar, and [was] given some use in medieval schools."[21] Kennedy continues "The handbooks of progymnasmata may also interest modern teachers of composition, for they present a sequence of assignments in reading, writing, and speaking which gradually increase in difficulty and in maturity of thought from simple story-telling to argumentation, combined with study of literary models."[22] These progymnasmata, or "preliminary exercises" were designed for young students and consisted of early education in the Classical and Medieval schoolrooms. Of the more advanced exercises, the *declamatio*, Crowley and Hawhee note of both *progymnasmata* and *declamatio* that "Students of ancient rhetoric did engage in a good deal of practice with artificial rhetorical situations taken from history or literature or law" where "this practice was aimed at teaching them something about the community they would later serve, as well as about rhetoric."[23] Of *declamatio* or "declamations" specifically, they explain that Romans who lived during the first centuries CE held rhetorical contests called declamations, the object of which was to compose a complicated and innovative discourse about some hackneyed situation involving pirates or angry fathers. The winner was the person who could compose the most unusual arguments or who could devise the most elaborate amplifications and ornamentations on an old theme,[24] or in other words, schoolchildren in the classroom would construct arguments that took situated knowledge and invented (composed) new arguments, through a form of argumentative game, about tried and tested topics. They were learning by playing with rhetoric. In this way, they were gaining rhetorical knowledge through play in a way that we can learn from as FYC teachers, now.

One question I found myself asking as an instructor of rhetoric is how do we capture the same magic of retelling old knowledge with new and innovative turns? I set my students on the task of creating similar, frivolous parables and tales within the composition classroom; students would compose stories not unlike the fables of Aesop that they would read and memorize for their first progymnasmata exercise: the fable. The knowledge that they were recording, through talking animals and old adages, was in some ways critical to the contemporary moment. As students would read through the fable exercises in the Crowley and Hawhee text and begin their work in rhetoric by memorizing one such light-hearted tale of ants and birds and fish and lions and such, they were

---

21 Kennedy, "Introduction," ix.
22 Kennedy, x.
23 Crowley and Hawhee, *Ancient Rhetorics for Contemporary Students*, 20.
24 Crowley and Hawhee, 23.

beginning to learn about rhetorical appeals and learn how to package cultural wisdom into writing.

By doing the work of the *progymnasmata*, and, later, declamations, my students began to engage with these cultural logics in a way that got them thinking about values and writing, paired together. But some of what they were learning may have come off as divorced from actual practice. At this point early in my teaching career, I knew I wanted to teach Classical and Medieval rhetorics to fulfil the WPA Outcomes Statement's call for rhetorical knowledge-centered classrooms. But I wanted to find a way to engage students with the content of ancient and Medieval rhetoric in a way that suited the modern moment and exigence. So, I began to ask myself, how can I teach these cultural logics and exercises in a grounded, thoughtful way, that also engages them to think critically about the content they are producing and the environment they are critiquing.

One way that scholars of composition and rhetoric have answered this call is through the play Gee and others discuss and propose is already at work within learning (and teaching). In their edited collection *Rhetoric/Composition/Play through Video Games*, Richard Colby, Matthew S. S. Johnson, and Rebekah Shultz Colby[25] collect a myriad of answers as to how we might marry play – through video games – with the content of the composition classroom.[26] One contributor, Justin Hodgson, explains that gamifying the classroom itself is one way we can incorporate games and play into the composition classroom.[27] Hodgson explains that not long ago "James Paul Gee challenged us to reconsider the relationships between video games and the learning principles structuring many classrooms" which encouraged him to develop a gaming pedagogy with the principle in mind that "if one wants to teach a course about games, one should do so *as a game*" (emphasis in original).[28] I took this to heart when given the reins of my own FYC classroom and decided to follow Hodgson and Gee's call to develop pedagogies involving play in – what I hope is – an innovative way that engages and answers the WPA Outcomes statement.

I set out, then, on the task of designing a course teaching Medieval rhetorical schemes with a gamified syllabus. Students, in this proposed curriculum, play

---

25 Many other resources for gamification exist, such as *The Multiplayer Classroom: Designing Coursework as a Game* (2012) that either engage with teaching with games or gamification of the classroom and the syllabus itself, like the aforementioned.
26 Richard Colby and John Alberti, eds., *Rhetoric/ Composition/Play through Video Games: Reshaping Theory and Practice of Writing*, Digital Education and Learning (New York: Palgrave Macmillan, 2013).
27 Hodgson, "Developing and Extending Gaming Pedagogy."
28 Hodgson, 45–46.

through a series of exercises over the course of the semester to learn rhetorical knowledge, critical reasoning skills, and writing processes. In this curriculum, students would not only play with writing and conventions, but also would play through one Medieval fantasy video game to get into the setting of Medieval rhetoric: that game is *Skyrim*. By teaching a course on Medieval rhetorical schemes alongside one Medieval fantasy video game, this curriculum enables a handful of advantages over the more traditionally "four-walled classroom" approach. Those follow, here:

> Students are able to learn the 36 principles that Gee espouses in his *What Video Games Have to Teach Us about Learning and Literacy*, which is also a text students in the course read over the semester.
>
> Students are able to immerse themselves in a Medieval world, gaining some context into (one interpretation of) the Medieval world of high-fantasy without, say, having to read all of Tolkien.
>
> Students are presented with a space to watch rhetoric play out – as it does in the game – and then speak to that rhetorical power in their writing assignments, composing setting-specific writings.

In the following pages, I introduce the setting of *Skyrim*, as I would to my students, and walk through the gamified syllabus, a sort of "game instruction manual" and the major and some of the minor assignments of a "gamified FYC" with *Skyrim*. I will comment on how to incorporate the game's setting of "Skyrim" into the gamified coursework of the FYC environment. I hope to lay out one road map for how such courses might be taught, but I can feasibly see the theoretical grounding, herein, being applied to composition classes teaching Classical, Renaissance, or modern[29] rhetorical schemes with various different games appropriate to the genre-settings that may apply to those eras.

The Context of Medieval Fantasy

Skyrim provides a unique setting for a composition course because it deftly touches on all the content I want to cover in a semester. The world is rich and complex, and is grounded in older fantasy tropes such as those found in Tolkien.

---

29 As a consideration, adventure and role-playing games such as the Assassin's Creed settings of *Assassin's Creed: Odyssey*, *Assassin's Creed 2*, or other games may map onto these settings nicely. Other game franchises, like Sid Meier's *Civilization*, which span multiple eras might work for a survey course in rhetorical practice, not focusing on one particular era.

Paul B. Sturtevant covers these quite nicely in his "Race: the Original Sin of the Fantasy Genre" where he examines how tabletop fantasy games and the fantasy video games stem from the problematic depictions of race found in earlier fantasy media.[30] And those tropes enable engagement with a landscape that may feel foreign, yet familiar, to students navigating a contemporary rhetoric course.

Race and racisms exist. The world is in conflict. There are protagonists. There are antagonists. And at the same time, while some of these, maybe universal tropes, exist, there is an element of fantasy that students can indulge in as a form of escapism. Yes, in its bones, the land of Skyrim is fraught with dangers, conflict, and paranoia, but also mystery, beauty, and importantly: dragons. To quote the back of the game's box, *Skyrim* is "Epic fantasy reborn" and that "Skyrim reimagines and revolutionizes the open-world fantasy epic, bringing to life a complete virtual world for you to explore any way you choose. The legendary freedom of choice, storytelling, and adventure of The Elder Scrolls is realized like never before." Of the world-space, Bethesda, *Skyrim*'s producing company, explains that "Dragons, long lost to the passages of The Elder Scrolls, have returned to Tamriel [the game's setting planet] and the future of the Empire hangs in the balance." Skyrim, then, not unlike the settings of *Dungeons & Dragons*, or *The Hobbit*, is a land brimming with conflict where you – the player – have the chance to tip the scales of fate.

Unlike Tolkien's epics, the *Dungeons & Dragons* source novels, and other written fantasy tales, *Skyrim*, as a game, puts the player in control of the destiny of the world. In a recent article on *The Atlantic*, Luke Winkie comments on how games, in this case tabletop board games like *Catan* or *Puerto Rico*, have made exploitation or plunder "part of their game mechanics" ("The Board Games that Ask You to Reenact Colonialism").[31] Of those games, Winkie says that the player or group of players "reenact human history's grimmest episodes." These games, as well as games like *Skyrim* or other fantasy video games such as *Dragon Age*,[32] *Assassin's Creed*,[33] and others, through the game's mechanics, put the player in the driver's seat. The world reacts to them, the player, and the player can shape the world.

---

[30] Paul B. Sturtevant, "Race: The Original Sin of the Fantasy Genre," The Public Medievalist, May 12, 2017, https://www.publicmedievalist.com/race-fantasy-genre/.
[31] Luke Winkie, "The Board Games That Ask You to Reenact Colonialism," The Atlantic, July 22, 2021, https://www.theatlantic.com/culture/archive/2021/07/board-games-have-colonialism-problem/619518/.
[32] *Dragon Age: Origins* (Bioware, 2009).
[33] *Assassin's Creed* (Ubisoft, 2007).

When discussing tabletop board games like *Puerto Rico*, the narrative booklets that come with the game may do a lot of the scene-setting, but in three-dimensional exploratory video games like *Tomb Raider*, *Skyrim*, and others, the game's antagonists or setting can be much more in-their-face. For example, guards in *Skyrim* comment on the race of the player. If the player is playing as a Nord, the resident race of Skyrim's province within the empire, guards will react positively, saying things such as "How can I help a brother Nord?," but when the player plays as an Imperial, seen by a large portion of Skyrim's population as an outside conqueror or oppressor, the player is met with suspicion. Guards will often comment "Staying out of trouble, Imperial?" and other such phrases.

There are also episodes where skin tone comes into play. Redguards, a race of Black humans with a heritage – or at least aesthetic – based loosely on real-world North African tribes, and Dark Elves, who are based loosely on *Dungeons & Dragons*' "Drow" race of dark-skinned fantasy elves, can come into conflict with the Nords of Skyrim. In one incident, a group of Redguards are kicked out of the settlement of Whiterun while looking for a mysterious woman. The Redguards are seen as foreign and state to the player that they are clearly "not welcome here," where they enlist the player's aid in finding their mark. In another instance in Windhelm, a Dark Elf minding her own business is accosted by a group of Stormcloak veterans (think toned-down Nord nationalists with strong senses of racial pride) for being an "imperial spy," after which the Nords threaten violence against the Dark Elves' borough in Windhelm – named in the source material as the "Grey Quarter" presumably for their skin tone.

The game is problematic, in that it presents race in a way that blindly follows a kind of reductive nativism. Within *Skyrim*, either you're a Redguard or you're not – you're an Argonian (a kind of lizardman) or not – and there are no sliders for how much of one race you want to be. You just are the race you play as. Some races are better at certain things, think magic or martial prowess, than others, and that nativism is hard baked into the game's mechanics. So in a game that promotes "the legendary freedom of choice" as the back of the box for *Skyrim* claims, there is actually very little you can do in the character customizer when it comes to the background of the player – a background that in some way or another the world of *Skyrim* responds to.

This is not the content of my course. It is ultimately not a course on race or racism, or a course on game design, or a course on tabletop or video game mechanics. There are a few things that my English courses are not, as it relates to games. What they are about is writing and rhetorical practice. While the game is problematic in places, and *Skyrim* is not the only offender, those problems come to the surface as students play through the game's space with a critical lens. As students experience the game world, the "setting" of the course, they come across these incidences of racial tension, or epic fantasy, or the sometimes-glorified violence, and other instances that give them grimaces or "a-ha" moments. They ask why the game is that way, or why the world is that way, and that is the context for my course. They are engaged with topics, all of which I cover or provide resources for students to learn more about when it comes to race and rhetoric, the environment and rhetoric, war and demagoguery and rhetoric, etc. And they are presented with opportunities and challenges for creating persuasive writing.

How to Argue with Dragons: Intersections of Writing and *Skyrim*

This is where the content of writing and rhetoric mix with the context of Medieval fantasy: students come into the class with a wealth of knowledge and a set of expectations about what they are going to learn, what they are going to get out of a college writing class, and what they want to do in the world. The context of Medieval fantasy provides a sort of setting for the content of writing. In short, *Skyrim* gives my students something to write about. It also provides a way to talk about race or racism, or gender identity, or digital representation in a lower-stakes environment. You might ask "is anyone going to get offended or put off by racist claims against Elves?" While some students in the class might play as an elf or like elves in fantasy, at the end of the day, there are no elves in my composition course. For that reason, we can talk about race, in the context of what it might be to be an elf, or to act like an elf, or to be excluded from elf life in ways that students understand but are not directly impacted by. While I have a zero-tolerance policy for hate in my classroom, talking *about* "elf-hate" enables difficult conversations and provides opportunities for students to learn about real-world issues in a less tense environment: as Poor outlines, fantasy racism provides a safer space to explore racial issues, although care must be taken to ensure that these fantasy elements do not end up providing a way to avoid facing these problems.[34] Likewise, as Leonard explains, while games can

---

34 Nathaniel Poor, "Digital Elves as a Racial Other in Video Games: Acknowledgment and Avoidance," *Games and Culture* 7, no. 5 (2012): 391–92, https://doi.org/10.1177/1555412012454224.

provide interpretations of racial dynamics,[35] they frequently act as "tourism" for white players to experience a vision of other, typically black, communities.[36] In a related vein, Higgin correctly notes that representation of race within fantasy games frequently relies on colonial perceptions.[37] Games like *Skyrim* must therefore be deployed with caution, but can nevertheless provide an important tool for exploring these issues.

Students in my class have plenty of opportunities to write about the game-world and issues they care about that occur in the real world. Some low-stakes assignments may ask students to become an observer of a racially tense moment within *Skyrim*; they are then asked how that makes them feel, a kind of reactive writing from their own perspective. Then, I may ask them how they would handle that situation as they are playing as their character. If the student is encountering the Dark Elf in Windhelm sequence I described above for the first time, I might ask them to reflect on how it made them feel through their different identities. What did it mean for my student – as a student – to witness that, what did it mean for them to witness that as a fellow Dark Elf or a Nord, or as a third race.

This is generally how I combine the content of writing with the context of Medieval fantasy: I take the fantasy setting of Skyrim, with all of its tensions and problems, and I ask the students how they would solve those disputes – with writing. The Civil War sequence between the Nords and Imperials provides a wealth of opportunity for *encomiums* or *invectives*, short speeches on the character or nature of a figure. Jarl Ulfric Stormcloak, the leader of the nationalistic Nord-supremacists I mentioned above, could become the subject for a justification speech or defence speech. A writing prompt may ask a student to consider "Is the violence of the Civil War [in Skyrim] justified?"

As students play through the game-world and solve these disputes, conversation, and really rhetoric, are out in full force. One of the most polarizing decisions, according to many sources and fan-sites online, within *Skyrim* is whether or not to ally with a sect of dragon-slaying warriors known as the Blades in slaying the dragon Paarthurnax, or to let the dragon, who is said by the blades to be

---

[35] David Leonard, ""Live in Your World, Play in Ours": Race, Video Games, and Consuming the Other," *SIMILE: Studies In Media & Information Literacy Education* 3, no. 4 (November 2003): 2–3, http://dx.doi.org/10.3138/sim.3.4.002.
[36] Leonard, 4–5.
[37] T. Higgin, "Blackless Fantasy: The Disappearance of Race in Massively Multiplayer Online Role-Playing Games," *Games and Culture* 4, no. 1 (2008): 21–22, https://doi.org/10.1177/1555412008325477.

inherently evil (a kind of black-and-white perspective), live in isolation at the top of the tallest mountain in the world. The drake asks the player – in my class my students – "What is better? to be born good or to overcome your evil nature through great effort?". There is a discourse within the game about good and evil, about race and racial heritage, about pastoral life, about all kinds of things that just, in my opinion, make for good writing assignments. And whether the student is arguing with a dragon about the nature of good and evil, declaiming a Jarl (a Nord "king") for starting a war that lost thousands of lives, or engaging in other rhetorical practices and activities, the setting of Skyrim, as well as the mechanics of *Skyrim*, set the stage for some truly fun interactions by presenting issues and characters in a setting that players and students can play with and learn from.

Taking *Skyrim* Into the Classroom on Monday

While I've already included some ideas on potential writing assignments such as the declamations or *encomiums* and *invectives* that were commonplace in the ancient and Medieval classroom, now with a *Skyrim* twist, you may be asking how to scaffold the content or bring an exercise into your own classroom for next week. For that, I have a few suggestions. Those follow:

Give Historical Examples

When having your students engage with Medieval and ancient rhetorical frames and schemas, one of the most helpful things I have found is to use examples. When talking about *encomium* for example, the type of "defence of character" speech, I have my students read Gorgias' *Encomium of Helen*.[38] In that text, Gorgias defends the mythical Helen of Troy from blame for causing the Trojan War by demonstrating the power of *logos*, which roughly means "speech." Gorgias in his *encomium* explains that Helen cannot be blamed for the War because she was persuaded or bound by fate, thus laying the blame elsewhere. In my classes, we also read some secondary material about Gorgias' *Encomium of Helen*, critiquing it and how it works. For this, I strongly recommend Sprague's *The Older Sophists*.[39]

---

[38] Gorgias, *Gorgias, Encomium of Helen*, ed. Douglas M. MacDowell, Repr. (Bristol: Bristol Classical Press, 1999).
[39] Hermann Diels and Rosamond Kent Sprague, eds., *The Older Sophists: A Complete Translation by Several Hands of the Fragments in Die Fragmente Der Vorsokratiker, Edited by Diels-*

Then, for students who side with the Stormcloaks in their playthrough of *Skyrim*, I ask students to defend the leader of the rebellion, Jarl Ulfric. By having an example of an *encomium* speech to look at and reference, they can mimic the style or arrangement of a piece and use the example to their advantage. I may expect to see students copying the same logical structure, or mimicking the tone of Gorgias' piece when trying to absolve Ulfric from blame for the war in Skyrim.

Explore the Game-world with Students

Secondly, don't leave students to explore the gamespace alone. In my class, I leave a boilerplate notice on my syllabus that explains, in the introduction to the course's material: "This class does not assume you have *any* previous video-game experience, and all concepts will be thoroughly explained as we continue in the virtual space." By exploring the game world with students, you can teach them the mechanics or give them an opportunity to see how I – the instructor – digest material and look for unique experiences within the gamespace. For using a game like *Skyrim*, I think this is especially important as the game is just big.

By highlighting certain experiences students can have within the game world, like the Dark Elf in Windhelm interaction, or other notable sequences where the themes of the course are on display, you can help students understand and navigate the world-space that the game takes place in. One thing I have done in the past is have the game on-screen in the class, either through a recording or by hooking up my laptop to a projector within the classroom, and showing a particular sequence that I think is in some way related to the thematic context of the course. Then, I have students reflect, through a short writing assignment, on what they saw or share their thoughts on the scene in small groups. Then, with the examples that they have already digested, they can begin the work of writing *progymnasmata* or *declamatio* exercises, or other rhetorical forms.

Kranz. With a New Edition of Antiphon and Euthydemus, 1st ed. (Columbia: University of South Carolina Press, 1972).

Issue Content Warnings and Contextualize What Students are Seeing In-Game

It should be said that the content of fantasy video games, especially ones like *Skyrim,* may not be for everyone. For that reason, either due to the graphical depictions of violence, the presence of racially motivated violence, or depictions of murder and other items, I issue a content warning at the beginning of my course. *Skyrim,* at times, can be a brutal game compared to what students are used to playing in their home environments. There are decapitations, blood, and pillaging. While I think all of these elements help us dig into the setting of Medieval and Classical rhetoric, that content may not be what everyone has signed up for, and for that reason I flag certain things in my syllabus and give disclaimers when exploring the game world with students in the classroom.

It's also critically important to contextualize what students are seeing within the game. If there's not a deliberate nod to what the educational value of what students are seeing, you may experience pushback from the more vocal students in your course. For all the games I've paired my courses with, teaching Medieval rhetorical frames with *Skyrim* has had a few instances of students asking things like "What's the point?" or "How does this relate to writing?" I answer those by talking about the rhetorical situation or audiences or some other lesson in rhetorical practice. Writing is always situated. There is writing within the game, through the script of the characters or the in-game books to analyse. Writing presupposes an ongoing conversation that the student is joining. These are some of the ways you can contextualize your gamespace to the classroom, to varying effect.

Have Students Take Sides

Especially when teaching rhetoric, it's important to foster a safe environment for learning, but that doesn't mean there can't be disagreement and conflict within the classroom. The declamation exercises and debates, or tetralogies (four-part legal speeches of defence and opposition) are all good places for students to take sides within the classroom. For more frivolous exercises I might have students divide themselves within the classroom on ideas such as whether or not hot dogs are sandwiches, or what the ideal first date location might be, or local issues that connect with the classroom like "should we expand the light-rail to campus?" Each of these give students the opportunity to use rhetoric. They can say, "Yes, a movie is a good ideal first date location because it gives you something to do" or "No, that's not an ideal location because you can't speak with your partner for a majority of the date."

By getting students to take sides on issues, especially ones that come up about games or about *Skyrim*'s setting specifically, students are presented with the opportunities to use the rhetoric their learning to debate with each other, persuade each other, and come to terms with the course's material. Issues may arise in your class about the nature of violent video games being educational resources. There might be concerns about other issues that come up. Embrace those disagreements within the classroom and have students write about them or see how writing can be used to resolve them; that's the nature of rhetoric.

Conclusions and Cautions

In this chapter, I've covered some recommendations for incorporating one Medieval fantasy video game into a curriculum for a FYC writing course at the university or college. What I would like to leave you with are some conclusions and cautions for doing this work.

To begin with cautions, firstly, consider where your students are at in terms of technology. If you plan to use games in your course as I have proposed, students will have some technical limitations and different technological access that you need to consider when designing a course with a game. If not everyone in the classroom has access to a laptop capable of running *Skyrim*, make accommodations for them to play on their desktop computer at home; if they do not have a desktop at home, make your own technology available to them in office hours, etc. Accessibility is one of my primary concerns when drafting syllabi for courses such as these because I want to make sure everyone has an equitable opportunity to succeed within my classes. And it may come down to that some students simply cannot access the game. In those instances, have them read from a game's source material or watch *YouTube* play-throughs of games where they can experience the setting, although not the participation in that setting, with ease.

One other caution I might advise is that by playing through a single-player experience like *Skyrim*, students are deprived the opportunity to interact – and compete – with each other within the gamespace. Other, more online enabled games, such as *The Elder Scrolls Online*, *World of Warcraft*, *Minecraft*, or *ECO*, might give students more opportunities to work together (or not) than a single-player experience like *Skyrim*, so depending on how much connectivity you want your students to have with each other, you may consider a multiplayer online game, or even a co-op game, depending on what your course's goals are.

To conclude, teaching rhetorical efficaciousness is increasingly important in our world, and learning how to learn is, I argue, universally relevant. By pairing a course, with its source materials and textbooks, with a video game, or even a board game or tabletop game, students have an opportunity to engage in a setting that gives them context for their writing. It gives them things to talk about, to critique. But if you have ever had a particular "a-ha" moment when playing a game yourself, or just want to consider using games as resources within your class, try thinking about the ways in which games can reinforce or provide context for the content that you want to teach. Is it for everyone? No, maybe not. But games have an expressive power, to quote Ian Bogost, that help us get into "someone else's shoes" and think from different angles and perspectives.[40] And that, I believe, is what rhetoric and writing are about.

Bibliography

Bogost, Ian. "Proteus: A Trio of Artisanal Game Reviews." *Gamasutra* (blog), February 15, 2013. http://bogost.com/writing/proteus/.

Cicero, Marcus Tullius. *De Inventione*. Translated by Charles Duke Yonge. United States: ReadHowYouWant.com, 2006.

Colby, Richard, and John Alberti, eds. *Rhetoric/ Composition/Play through Video Games: Reshaping Theory and Practice of Writing*. Digital Education and Learning. New York: Palgrave Macmillan, 2013.

Council of Writing Program Administrators. n.d. www.wpacouncil.org.

Crowley, Sharon, and Debra Hawhee. *Ancient Rhetorics for Contemporary Students*. Boston: Pearson, 2012.

Diels, Hermann, and Rosamond Kent Sprague, eds. *The Older Sophists: A Complete Translation by Several Hands of the Fragments in Die Fragmente Der Vorsokratiker, Edited by* Diels-Kranz. *With a New Edition of Antiphon and Euthydemus*. 1st ed. Columbia: University of South Carolina Press, 1972.

Gee, James Paul. *What Video Games Have to Teach Us about Learning and Literacy*. Education. New York, NY: Palgrave Macmillan, 2004.

Glenn, Cheryl. *The Harbrace Guide to Writing*. Boston, MA: Cengage Learning, 2012.

Gorgias. *Gorgias, Encomium of Helen*. Edited by Douglas M. MacDowell. Repr. Bristol: Bristol Classical Press, 1999.

Graff, Gerald, and Cathy Birkenstein. *They Say / I Say: The Moves That Matter in Academic Writing*. New York: W.W. Norton & Co, 2010.

---

40 Ian Bogost, "Proteus: A Trio of Artisanal Game Reviews," *Gamasutra* (blog), February 15, 2013, http://bogost.com/writing/proteus/.

Higgin, T. "Blackless Fantasy: The Disappearance of Race in Massively Multiplayer Online Role-Playing Games." *Games and Culture* 4, no. 1 (2008): 3–26. https://doi.org/10.1177/1555412008325477.

Hodgson, Justin. "Developing and Extending Gaming Pedagogy: Designing a Course as Game." In *Rhetoric/Composition/Play through Video Games*, edited by Richard Colby, Matthew S. S. Johnson, and Rebekah Shultz Colby, 45–60. New York: Palgrave Macmillan US, 2013. https://doi.org/10.1057/9781137307675_5.

Kennedy, George Alexander. "Introduction." In *Progymnasmata: Greek Textbooks of Prose Composition and Rhetoric*, edited by George Alexander Kennedy, ix–xvi. Writings from the Greco-Roman World, v. 10. Atlanta: Society of Biblical Literature, 2003.

Leonard, David. ""Live in Your World, Play in Ours": Race, Video Games, and Consuming the Other." *SIMILE: Studies In Media & Information Literacy Education* 3, no. 4 (November 2003): 1–9. http://dx.doi.org/10.3138/sim.3.4.002.

Lunsford, Andrea A., and John J Ruszkiewicz. *Everything's an Argument*. Bedford: St Martin's, 2016.

Murphy, James Jerome. "Introduction: The Medieval Background." In *Three Medieval Rhetorical Arts*, edited by James Jerome Murphy, vii–xxiii. Medieval and Renaissance Texts and Studies Studies, vol. 228. Tempe, Ariz: Arizona Center for Medieval and Renaissance Studies, 2001.

Poor, Nathaniel. "Digital Elves as a Racial Other in Video Games: Acknowledgment and Avoidance." *Games and Culture* 7, no. 5 (September 2012): 375–96. https://doi.org/10.1177/1555412012454224.

Quintilianus, Marcus Fabius. *The Institutio oratoria of Quintilian. 1: Books I–III*. Reprint. The Loeb classical library 124. London: Heinemann, 1996.

Sturtevant, Paul B. "Race: The Original Sin of the Fantasy Genre." The Public Medievalist, May 12, 2017. https://www.publicmedievalist.com/race-fantasy-genre/.

Winkie, Luke. "The Board Games That Ask You to Reenact Colonialism." The Atlantic, July 22, 2021. https://www.theatlantic.com/culture/archive/2021/07/board-games-have-colonialism-problem/619518/.

Ludography

Assassin's Creed. Ubisoft, 2007.
Dragon Age: Origins. Bioware, 2009.
Skyrim. Bethesda Game Studios, 2011.
Tomb Raider: The Last Revelation. Core Design, 1999.
Word of Warcraft. Blizzard Entertainment, 2004.

Ahmet Erdem Tozoğlu and Mehmet Şükrü Kuran
5 "What if you are a Medieval Monarch?": A *Crusader Kings III* Experience to Learn Medieval History

Abstract: This chapter is about the authors' experiences and observations on a blended world history course that combines classical lecture and discussion components of teaching with video game sessions. The students play strategy video games with a heavy historical focus. The course, named Playing with The Past, is designed to experiment on how to integrate video games on teaching history, especially in order to achieve a higher understanding of the contemporary social, political, economic, and technological context of a given era for different cultures and civilizations. This chapter presents the utilization of *Crusader Kings*, a renowned grand strategy game series, to teach medieval history, which constitutes an integral part of our course. It also examines how the game provides advantages for an immersive learning environment and how it fails to model medieval history at specific points. Our experiments and observations may be beneficial for designing a general world history course and any history course on specific periods, cultures, and nations that aims to utilize alternative tools to deliver a course.

Introduction

It can be argued that one of the most challenging aspects of a history course is letting the students understand certain events, decisions, and choices for a given historical period through their contemporary lenses instead of their personal, complete modern points of view. Although classical teaching methodologies allow some techniques for this purpose, tools that will enable experimenting with the social, political, economic, and technological norms could also be used for teaching these historical lenses. Following a "history as a process" philosophy, physical or virtual tools could be developed based on primary and secondary

---

Acknowledgments: This course is designed and implemented in Abdullah Gül University (AGU) by the instructors. In the 2021 spring semester, the course was remotely offered at both AGU and Bahcesehir University (BAU). We ran the course five times between 2015 and 2021 with different video game titles and their different historical models and observing students' experiences and learning based on the quality of their essays and blog posts. We would like to thank all students for their contributions to the class content from the beginning.

https://doi.org/10.1515/9783110712032-005

sources with which a student can (at least partially) "experience" a given historical era which will significantly improve their understanding of the era in question.

Many video games chose a particular historical setting (medieval Europe, crusades, warring states era Japan for example) as the game's setting since their advent in the early 1980s. Although most of these games only utilize some aspects of the historical context in their gameplay, some games build their gameplay on extensive models representing various elements of the chosen historical setting. Therefore, they create "as-if-worlds" which are flexible in their temporal and spatial setting, and allow players to experience a time travel in countless parallel histories.[1] Utilized mainly by strategy games, the focus of these models varies greatly from political, economic, technological to militaristic. A well-known example of such strategy games is the long-running *Sid Meier's Civilization* series.[2] In this series, the player takes control of a "nation" starting from 4000 BCE to 2020 CE and experiences various aspects of the nation such as technological and cultural development, expansion, military conflict, and city development.

It can be argued that these strategy games with detailed historical models could be utilized as supportive tools in history courses by considering the aforementioned "history as a process" philosophy.[3] By playing these games, students can freely experiment on these models to achieve a higher understanding, called an immersion process by Radetich et al., of the historical setting in question.[4] To quote Sid Meier: "When games are done right, players don't even realize they're learning."[5]

---

[1] Annette Vowinckel, "Past Futures: From Re-Enactment to the Simulation of History in Computer Games," *Historical Social Research / Historische Sozialforschung* 34 (2009): 330–331.

[2] *Sid Meier's Civilization* (MicroProse, 1991); *Sid Meier's Civilization II* (MicroProse, 1996); *Sid Meier's Civilization III* (Infogrames, 2001); *Sid Meier's Civilization IV* (Firaxis Games, 2005); *Sid Meier's Civilization V* (Firaxis Games, 2010); *Sid Meier's Civilization VI* (Firaxis Games, 2016).

[3] For recent examples of this approach, see John Pagnotti and William B. Russell III, "Using Civilization IV to Engage Students in World History Content," *The Social Studies* 103 (2011): 39–48; A. Martin Wainwright, "Teaching Historical Theory through Video Games," *The History Teacher* 47 (2014): 579–612; Jeremiah McCall, "Teaching History with Digital Historical Games: An Introduction to the Field and Best Practices," *Simulation and Gaming* 47 (2016): 517–542; Hao Wang, Wen-Wen Chen, and Chun-Tsai Sun, "Play Teaches Learning?: A Pilot Study on How Gaming Experience Influences New Game Learning," in *Interactivity and the Future of the Human-Computer Interface*, edited by Pedro Isaias and Katherine Blashki, 147–168 (Hershey, PA: IGI Global, 2020).

[4] Laura Radetich and Eduardo Jakubowicz, "Using Video Games for Teaching History. Experiences and Challenges," *Athens Journal of History* 1 (2015): 1–14.

[5] Sid Meier and Jennifer Nee Noonan, *Sid Meier's Memoir! A Life in Computer Games* (New York: W. W. Norton & Company, 2021), 234.

We have designed an undergraduate-level course named "Playing with The Past," which aims to introduce world history via a blended methodology, including a classical lecture and discussion (L & D) session and game experience session. The course covers the time span stretching from Middle Ages to the modern age in different modules. Each module starts with an L & D session and continues with a game experience session. The students are introduced to the mechanics of a strategy game, focusing on the historical context of the module. After each module, the students are asked to play the video game on their own with specific goals and write an essay explaining their experiences and compare and contrast the historical sources on the historical setting and their individual game experiences. In addition to these short essays, they are also asked to choose a nation or culture at a specific era, play a corresponding strategy game for an extended time (15 to 20 hours) with that nation or culture, and write down a comprehensive report focusing on their game experiences and historical sources on the same historical setting as an end-of-the-semester assignment.

Over the years, we have experimented on using different video games in our course, namely: *Sid Meier's Civilization* series by Firaxis games, *Total War* series by Creative Assembly,[6] and several Grand Strategy games by Paradox Interactive (*Crusader Kings II & III, Europa Universalis IV, Hearts of Iron IV*).[7] All three of these game series have a different modelling focus. In the first two years of the course, we used one game from each series (*Civilization IV, Crusader Kings II*, and *Empire: Total War*) and observed the students' experiences with the modelling concepts of each series. Based on our observations, the games from the Grand Strategy series provided the most comprehensive experience due to their level of detail, high historical accuracy, and versatility in modelling different cultures and nations based on their specific features. Consequently, we switched to using three games in the Grand Strategy series starting from *Crusader Kings II* (CK2) for medieval ages, *Europa Universalis IV* (EU4) for early modern to the industrial age, and *Hearts of Iron IV* (HoI4) for early to mid-twentieth century following a distinct periodization concept.[8] In the final version of the course (as of Spring 2021 semester), we utilized *Civilization VI, Crusader Kings III*, and *Europa Universalis IV* in order.

---

6 For example: *Medieval: Total War* (Creative Assembly, 2002); *Shogun 2: Total War* (Creative Assembly, 2011).
7 *Crusader Kings II* (Paradox Interactive, 2012); *Crusader Kings III* (Paradox Interactive, 2020); *Europa Universalis IV* (Paradox Interactive, 2013); *Hearts of Iron IV* (Paradox Interactive, 2016).
8 Greg Koebel, "Simulating the Ages of Man: Periodization in Civilization V and Europa Universalis IV," *The Journal of the Canadian Game Studies Association* 10 (2017): 60–76.

In the rest of this chapter, first we explain the course structure in detail, then briefly explain the main mechanics of each Grand Strategy game used in the course, and finally elaborate on our observations in combining the classical L & D based learning and video game experience-based learning in a world history course context in detail.

Course Structure

Our course is designed as a free elective course targeted to students whose major program is not history. Since its beginning, the course has evolved a lot in terms of the topics of discussion and the flow of the semester. In the latest version, the course content is divided into three main parts: thematic introduction to concepts and ideas, Middle Ages, and the early modern period (Table 5.1). Each part is covered by several two-week modules, which include a game playing and learning & discussion (L & D) session consecutively. Each module is composed of a one-week L & D session and a one-week game experience session.

Table 5.1: Structure of the course content in relation to games.

Introduction to the Historical Concepts	Middle Ages (867–1453)*		Early Modern Ages (1444–1812)**		
Fail or rise of civilizations? Periodization of history. History vs. historiography, games, and history since the 1980s.	Catholic Christian Feudal Dynasty	Muslim Clan Dynasty, Tribal Dynasty	Castille, Portuguese or Morocco: geographical explorations & colonization	Ottomans: the gunpowder empires and land and naval trade routes	The Holy Roman Empire: religious conflicts, capitalist economy, and the unique structure of the HRE.

*start and end dates of Crusader Kings III.
**start and end dates of Europe Universalis IV.

Introduction to Concepts, Ideas, and Cultures

The classes at the beginning of the semester are used to provide students with some critical thinking tools about several concepts they may encounter through history games or history courses at any level. These include but are not limited to history versus historiography, the periodization of history, and the progressive interpretation of history, civilizations, and cultures. Students are asked to consider what makes cultures flourish or fail? What does cultural or territorial expansion mean from a historical point of view? How did different games model these themes in their interface from the 1980s to 2020s? A game-playing session accompanies this discussion. Since it is easy to play and many students may be already familiar with it, *Civilization VI* was the chosen game among several alternatives. The students played from the beginning till the Early Modern ages to observe how a civilization emerges, grows, and expands in time from a "game" perspective. Finally, the students wrote their first blog posts to synthesize the gaming and L & D session outcomes.[9]

Medieval Section

This part of the course aimed to give a broader understanding of cultures through different geographical settings and provide students with critical evaluation skills through game playing and L & D sessions. In this part, we focus on the Christian and Islamic Cultures in the Middle Ages in two consecutive modules in a reciprocal manner. In the gaming session, the students played in Ireland first, as mostly suggested for the beginners, then another Christian character in the Iberian Peninsula. By playing a Catholic landlord in CK3, the students learned the basic game mechanics on the geopolitical components, religion, titles, regions, and, most importantly, the relationships between the characters, which are essential to understand the feudal system configuration of the game. Then, in the following week, an L & D session was used to evaluate how several themes of Catholic Christian Feudal Europe were modelled in the game and how "accurate" they are from the point of the written history. After taking the first module, the students wrote their second blog posts to reflect their opinions and blend game playing and L & D session experiences.[10]

The following module repeats the same approach for Islamic cultures in the Middle Ages. The students are asked to play as a Muslim ruler in the Iberian Peninsula first, then any "tribal" system in the rest of the world. In the game playing sessions, the students learned the fundamentals of how the game models the Islamic cultures through clan government system and various Islamic

---

[9] "Blogpost 1," Playing with the Past, accessed June 20, 2021, https://playingwithpast.wordpress.com/tag/blogpost1/.
[10] "Blogpost 2," Playing with the Past, accessed June 20, 2021, https://playingwithpast.wordpress.com/tag/blogpost2/.

faiths and in what ways is it similar or different from the Christian feudal counterparts. As usual, in the following week, the L & D session covered the Islamic culture during the Middle Ages concerning their neighboring cultures and provided some critical thinking tools to evaluate the accuracy of the CK3 model for non-Christian cultures from a historic point of view. The students wrote their third blog post to demonstrate their personal understanding.[11]

After the two modules on the Middle Ages, the students also wrote their mid-semester reviews to evaluate how *Crusader Kings III (CK III)* helps them learn about medieval history. In particular, the students described their previous knowledge about the medieval history of the Western and non-western civilizations before playing CK3. Then, they explained in what ways playing the game helped them conceive European and non-European medieval institutions (such as the feudal system, medieval titles, and the authority of religions) and finally to evaluate the role of the L & D sessions to cast a critical eye on the emulation of these themes in the game.[12]

Early Modern Section

The third part of the course examines the emergence of the pre-modern world by referring to cross-cultural and geographical diversity. During the game experience sessions of this second part, we switch to EU4 and explain the differences and similarities with CK3. Unlike CK3, EU4 focuses on nations instead of landlords, and each of these nations have mission trees which follow their historical progress. We elaborate on these missions by discussing the reasons for choosing these paths in terms of game mechanics for a more immersive learning experience.

Each module in this part is dedicated to different aspects of the pre-modern world. The first module is for understanding the global connections from a commercial point of view. The emphasis is on geographical exploration, beginning of colonization, and establishment of colonial empires in the sixteenth century. The students experience these themes through EU4 by playing as the Kingdom of Castille, Portugal, or Morocco starting in 1444 to establish the first colonies in Africa and the Americas. The following week, the L & D session is about the historical background of all events, institutions, and ideas they

---

[11] "Blogpost 3," Playing with the Past, accessed June 20, 2021, https://playingwithpast.word press.com/tag/blogpost3/.
[12] "Blogpost 4," Playing with the Past, accessed June 20, 2021, https://playingwithpast.word press.com/tag/blogpost4/.

experienced in the gaming session. Consecutively, the second module is on the Islamic world in the pre-modern period by focusing on the Gunpowder Empires of the sixteenth century; the Ottomans, Safavids, and Mughals. Students played as Ottomans in 1444 in the course session. They were asked to play alternative scenarios, such as Persia in 1504 or Aceh in 1579, to examine how Islamic cultures adapted themselves to the changing global context.

The second L & D session examines the game mechanics about chronologically increasing the East-West gap in EU4 and the overall discussion of why many non-western cultures lagged behind technologically and could not resist European colonization. The third module of this part is about a particular topic in the game, the Holy Roman Empire (HRE). The game session dwells on the unique mechanics of the HRE, and the students play as Austria and try to lead this loose confederation and try to control the spread of Protestant teachings in their territories. The following L & D session examines the unique game mechanics of HRE and verifies their historical accuracy. It also addresses the background of the emergence and spread of religious conflicts across Europe in the sixteenth and seventeenth centuries by revisiting several events and institutions of the game.

Learning Assessment

We used three different evaluation criteria for assessing the learning of the students: weekly blog posts, a term project, and a classical midterm exam.

After each module, the students are asked to write 500-to-600-word long reflection essays on the course's blog website. In these essays, students blend their gaming experiences with the theoretical discussions of the following weeks and critically reflect on their personal perspectives. Therefore, they are not summaries of the thematic modules but individual assessments of different learning paths.

The midterm exam is an interpretation-based essay-style exam that aims to assess to what extent the students internalize the topics discussed in different modules. There are three sets of exam questions, one regarding examination of history, one regarding game mechanics, and on counterfactual history or "what if scenarios." Here, they are expected to utilize their knowledge of historical sources, in-class discussions, and game experiences to develop their own hypothesis following the aforementioned "history as a process" philosophy.

The final project is an extended version of gaming sessions. Other than the games played during the semester, the students may choose from a wide range of games, including *Hearts of Iron IV*, *Imperator Rome*, *Total War* Games, *Victoria II*, or *Kingdom Come: Deliverance*. They initially submit a proposal of what

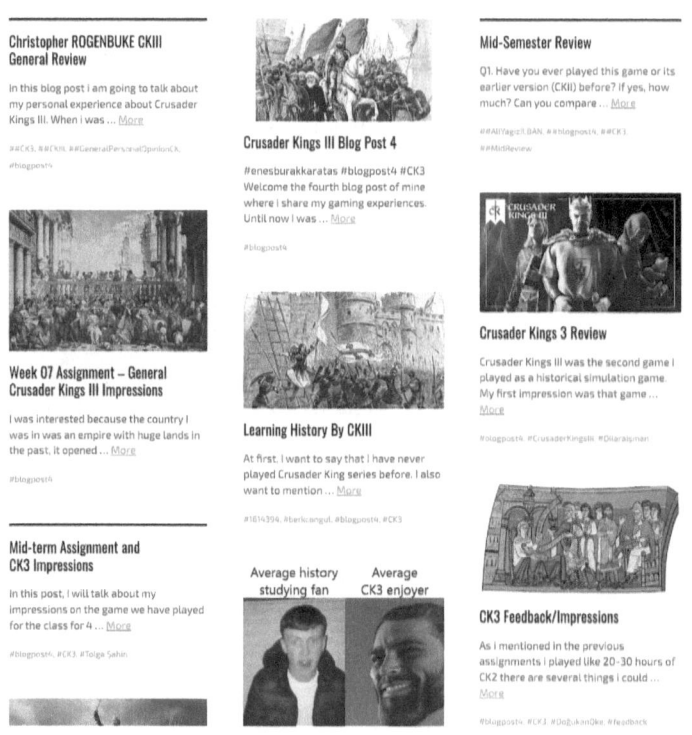

Figure 5.1: Example posts from the blog of our course at playingwithpast.wordpress.com (retrieved on June 22, 2021).

they would like to play, what period, what culture, and their primary objectives. After receiving feedback from the instructors, they play for about 16–20 hours and write a 2,000-word blog post whose objectives are similar to the bi-weekly posts.

History Game Mechanics

The Middle Ages has been one of the most popular themes and settings in video games starting from the emergence of the video game industry in the early 1980s. While occasionally such themes are used on their own, frequently they have been used in conjunction with fantasy elements such as magic, demons, mythical beasts, and Tolkienesque concepts (such as elves and dwarves). When we focus on medieval era-themed games having no such fantasy elements, regarding surface-level aspects, they generally provide a good level of representation of the era in question. This is especially prevalent in terms of audio-visuals, basic terminology, and the overall "feel" of the age. Though historical misconceptions (i.e., Vikings having horned helmets) and cliches had been quite dominant in the early historical video games, recent titles generally tend to pay more attention to historical accuracy and, at worst, try to avoid the most common mistakes.

On the other hand, when we look at the in-depth socio-political aspects of the medieval era, the representative quality of these games varies widely. Here, the representative quality mainly depends on the genre of the game since this determines its main focus areas. Based on well-established video game industry lexicon, Medieval-era themed video games are generally divided into four broad categories:[13]

a. Action, Adventure games
b. City builders
c. Simulation and Role-playing games
d. Grand strategy games

The action and adventure games (such as the *Assassin's Creed* series) generally let the player play as a certain character (usually a soldier, a knight, or a thief) and mainly focus on action elements (traversing the environment, combat) as well as some story elements. So, the experience is usually limited to honing physical reflexes and deduction skills, which do not offer in-depth knowledge. In the city builders (i.e., the *Anno* series), the player is usually tasked to build a medieval city, care for its inhabitants, and eventually form a stable working economy with the given limitations and resources. Here the focus is mainly on the economic aspects of the era. The game asks the player to find the "optimal" way of building the economy given particular constraints and values. Therefore, the challenge and in-depth experience in these games can be considered an optimization problem-solving exercise with a medieval flavour.

Simulation and role-playing games (i.e., *Kingdom Come: Deliverance, The Guild* series) again focus on a single individual but allow a more in-depth experience, including role-playing, details of craftsmanship, day-to-day life, and interaction between social classes. Gameplay in these games can offer a rich microhistory experience but will be limited to a particular geographical area and a particular time period. Finally, the grand strategy games (i.e., *Crusader*

---

13 Alternatively, Houghton introduces another classification based on the objectives of this genre of games. See Robert Houghton, "If you're going to be the king, you'd better damn well act like the king: Setting authentic objectives to support learning in Grand Strategy Computer Games," in *The Middle Ages in Modern Culture: History and Authenticity in Contemporary Medievalism*, ed. Karl C. Alvestad and R. Houghton (London: Bloomsbury Academic, 2021), 190.

Kings series, *Total War* series) allow the play to rule over a realm and have a much broader and deeper view of the era in question, including its sociopolitical, technological, militaristic, economic, and religious aspects. Since the goal of the game is to understand and "play" according to the historical versions of these institutions, it can be argued that grand strategy games can offer the best and most inclusive experience of the era in question.

Among the variety of grand strategy games available on the medieval era, we choose the *Crusader Kings* series in our course due to their vast number of mechanics emulating various aspects of the medieval era (i.e., social hierarchy, the relationship between secular and religious leaders, geography and its implications, army composition, taxation, and trade) and its inclusivity of different parts of the medieval Eurasia and Africa region. Although the name of the series, *Crusader Kings*, implies that the game is limited to Catholic Europe, over the years the game has expanded to include the Muslim world, the non-Catholic Christian world, the Nordic pre-Christian nations, the Indian subcontinent, nomadic tribes in central Asia as well as part of sub-Saharan Africa. Initially, we had used *Crusader Kings II*, but in our latest iteration of the course we utilized the recently launched *Crusader Kings III*, which is designed to be more accessible to non-gamer audiences without sacrificing in-depth mechanics.

In this section, we first explain the key mechanics of *Crusader Kings* games mainly over *Crusader Kings II* (CK2) and then talk about the critical changes in *Crusader Kings III* (CK3), then underlining some emergent gameplay as a result of these mechanics.

Core Features and Mechanics of *Crusader Kings* Series

Crusader Kings games have been designed to simulate the feudal system in Catholic Western Europe during the Middle Ages. Other geopolitical entities are added as playable realms with additional content, such as the Islamic world, the Nordic pre-Christian societies, and Indian nations. As of 2021, the game map of CK2 encompasses Europe, Middle East, North Africa, the Indian subcontinent, and Central Asia regions. In these games, the smallest geopolitical entity is a province that is ruled by a count or countess (or their equivalents in other cultures such as "Earl" in English culture and "Bey" in Turkic culture). Each province is further divided into several settlements as castles (governed by the nobility, a baron or baroness), cities (governed by a mayor), and bishoprics (managed by the clergy, a bishop). Several provinces nearby form a third-level entity called a duchy. In turn, several duchies form a fourth-level entity called a kingdom. Finally, several kingdoms form an empire that is the fifth and biggest geopolitical entity in the game. Each one of these entities has an associated "title" which is may be held by a dynasty and at a given time controlled by one character from that dynasty who is the designated "owner" of that title. The title owner is entitled to collect the tax and military levy income from the province, which constitute the primary sources of economic and militaristic power in the game, respectively. Lastly, each title has its own hereditary laws which dictate the rules of succession upon the death of the current owner.

Based on an idealized system of feudalism, these geopolitical entities have a rigorous hierarchical relation in the game. Since every province is part of a duchy, the owner of the duchy title is considered as the "de-jure" liege of all the owners of the provinces under that particular duchy. In reverse, the owners of the provinces under a particular duchy are called "de-jure" vassals of the owner of the duchy title. However, the CK games have a clear differentiation between "de-jure" liege and a "de-facto" liege who may or may not be the same character. A weak de-jure duke may risk its vassals rebelling against him and form independent county-level realms. On the other hand, a strong de-jure duke can press his de-jure claim over an independent count's belonging to his duchy and subjugate them after a victorious war. The same system and relationship are repeated between dukes and kings, and kings and emperors.

A single character can theoretically hold as many titles as they wish (either at the same level, or different levels). In practice though, there is a limit on this number called the "demesne size" which is mainly based on the administrative skill of the character. A character can exceed their demesne size, but this excess causes an increasingly heavy penalty on both tax and levy income which can swiftly turn the realm into a very ineffective political entity. To alleviate this issue, a ruler can give some of their titles to other characters who at that point become his vassals. These vassals are tasked to take care of the entity associated with that title in the name of their liege and in return earn money and levies from the land. Also, these vassals are required to send some of their tax income, and upon request, lend soldiers (levies) to their lieges.

In these games, the player controls the highest-ranking member of a particular dynasty. All other characters in the game are controlled by the computer (AI characters).[14] Based on many traits (including genetic, social, and cultural

---

14 As Johnson pointed out, rather than allocating "great men" model as the central pillar of the game, CK established less-known and ordinary individuals as the basis and the role of the player is not just to make decisions about the political and economic system but to rebuild these individuals as the outcomes of these events. See Mark R. Johnson, "The Place of Culture, Society, and Politics in Video Game World Building," in *World-builders on World-Building: An Exploration of Subcreation*, ed. Mark J. P. Wolf (New York: Routledge, 2020), 110–131.

traits) each character has an opinion on each other character in the game at a level between −100 (complete hatred and mistrust) and 100 (complete fidelity and admiration) that affects many aspects of the game. As a simple example, a vassal with a bad opinion of his liege will send less tax and fewer levies to his liege and will stop sending anything at all if his opinion is low enough. There is also collective AI behavior based on these opinion levels. If many of a lord's vassals have a very bad opinion of them, these vassals may start conspiring to revolt, found independence movements, or trigger events to overthrow their lord. A liege can revoke the title of their vassal if they feel threatened by that character, but such drastic action can have serious consequences:
a) All the other vassals' opinion of the liege will be lowered
b) The vassal whose title is about to be revoked can declare war on the liege

The *Crusader Kings* games aim to emulate the precarious balance in the feudal system by forcing the player to have vassals and to engage with them using these character relationship mechanics.

When we come to the religions aspects of the feudal system, the bishopric in each province has a different mechanic than the other types of settlements in the Catholic world. The owner of a bishopric, a bishop, has different liege, taxation, levy, and inheritance rules than the secular lords and ladies. In practice, a bishop has two lieges: his feudal lord and the Pope. By default, the bishop sends his tax and levy to the Pope regardless of the geographical location of the bishopric. However, if the bishop's opinion of his feudal lord is higher than his opinion of the Pope, he will send his tax and levy to his feudal lord. Moreover, the bishop's title is not hereditary. Upon the death of a bishop the Pope assigns a new bishop to the bishopric which happens outside the control of the feudal lord. The feudal lord can change this law (the investiture law) to reserve the right of appointing the bishops in their lands. Although this alternative investiture law (free investiture) has direct benefits to the lord, it, in turn, angers the Pope. If a lord angers the Pope too much, the Pope can excommunicate them from the Catholic faith, which allows neighboring Catholic lords to declare war, seize lands, and ultimately depose them. Considering this religious mechanic, a Catholic ruler has a second precarious relationship, this time with the bishops in their lands and the Pope.

In these grand strategy games, the players can conduct wars with other nations. Since wars are mainly the most "action-oriented" parts of grand strategy games, in earlier grand strategy games, it was straightforward to wage war with a country by simply declaring a war whenever the player wishes. Here, the *Crusader Kings* series again follow a more detailed and arguably more realistic path and have a "casus belli" system. In these games, in order to declare war, a character must have a valid "casus belli" against the target. The game offers numerous types of casus belli ranging from political-based de-jure claims to religious-based conquests, excommunication wars, or even full-scale crusades or jihads. The type of available casus belli is also affected by the type of government you have. For example, a nomadic tribe has many casus belli against its neighbors, while a feudal Catholic lord surrounded by other Catholic lords is greatly limited to only political-based de-jure claims.

The *Crusader Kings* series implement a partially different ruleset when moving east and southward to the Muslim world. In particular in CK2, the game tries to emulate the differences of the *iqta* system, which was the prevalent political system in the Muslim world in the medieval era. First of all, a Muslim lord can revoke a duchy level vassal title without angering his other vassals. Here the game tries to emulate a fundamental difference of the *iqta* system in which the land is not granted to a dynasty but instead granted to a single person, and the liege (the sultan or emir) reserves the right to revoke this choice of his whenever he wishes. Next, regarding the religious settlements, since there is no centralized religious hierarchy in Islam, the bishopric settlement in a Muslim province (interestingly called a Mosque in the game) can be governed by any character and only the sultan is the liege of the holder of the mosque title. Here, the game tries to emulate the lack of any bishopric concept in the Islamic world. However, it can be argued that it is a partially successful emulation at best.

A key difference when playing as a Muslim character is the decadence mechanic. Every Muslim dynasty has a decadence rating which ranges from 0 (no decadence, fully abiding with the Islamic laws) to 100 (complete decadence, clear well-known acts against the tenets of the Islamic faith). CK2 assumes 25 as the average decadence rating and gives bonuses to dynasties that have a lower decadence rating (higher taxes, higher morale of the army) while punishing dynasties with high decadence ratings (i.e., lower taxes, lower morale of the army). Moreover, a dynasty which has at least 75 decadence risks a massive decadency revolt in which a powerful rebellious army appears and tries to overthrow and eradicate the whole dynasty due to their extremely decadent activities. Decadence is mainly increased by male relatives of the dynasty without any titles to govern or by losing wars to non-Muslim countries. On the other hand, it is decreased by pious activities (such as going to Hajj) and successful wars against non-Muslim countries.

Similar to the systematic changes in the Muslim world, the *Crusader Kings* series offer unique mechanics in pre-feudal or pre-*iqta* governments. In CK2, Nordic, Germanic, and Slavic tribes follow a particular tribal government system that is much less organized but has its own advantages like recruiting levies based on the ruler's prestige instead of taxation. On the other hand, Central

Asian nomadic tribes such as the Turkic or the Mongolian tribes have the nomadic government system, reflecting that these societies are composed of different clans whose relationships must be managed by their rulers. As for the Indian subcontinent, which was a very late addition to CK2, the game uses the Western European feudal system with some minor tweaks and changes.

Crusader Kings III and Newer Mechanics in the Series

The newest iteration in the *Crusader Kings* series, *Crusader Kings III* (CK3), was released in late 2020. Retaining the core design principles and level of detail of the earlier entry in the series, CK3 aims to address several issues of its predecessor:
1. Having a much more accessible, readable, and clear visual interface
2. Increasing the character focus of the game to accommodate the personality traits affecting many mechanics directly
3. Having a more inclusive core game system by designing the main game architecture from scratch to accommodate Catholic Western Europe, Orthodox East Europe, the Muslim world, the Indian subcontinent, and the various tribal and nomadic people right from the get-go

Since CK3 retains the core design principles of CK2, here only the main differences and additions over the former game will be noted.

CK3 has much more appealing visuals regarding all aspects of the game, such as provinces, characters, and differences between different cultures. Moreover, the menu items, potential actions a player can take, and the numerous modifiers are much easier to understand and follow than in CK2 (Figure 5.2). Some of these changes also affect the gameplay of the game; for example, unlike in CK2, in CK3 the first level entities (castles, cities, and bishoprics) are clearly visible in the game map and are distinct geographical regions for army movement. Aside from such visual changes affecting gameplay directly, the pure visual changes make the game much more accessible to players and especially players new to the series and grand strategy games in general. This is a critical aspect, especially in our educational case study, and we have experienced much less frustration and difficulty from the students trying to understand and play the game.

A core design principle of the *Crusader Kings* games has always been the provision of a character-oriented experience. It can be argued that besides the socio-political aspects of society, the personality traits of rulers also played a significant role in the unravelling of events during the medieval era. Therefore, the player is no more an omnipotent figure who controls an entire civilization,

 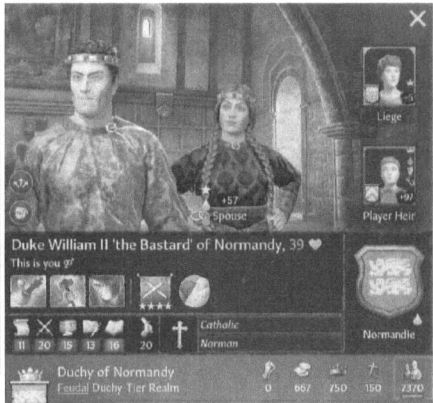

Figure 5.2: Character screens in Crusader Kings games. (Left) William the Conqueror from Crusader Kings II, (right) William the Conqueror from Crusader Kings III.

but controlling a lineage of individuals a medieval royal family.[15] CK2 already had a personality trait system that marks a certain character as humble, compassionate, wrathful, sadistic, or zealot amongst a substantial range of other possibilities. These personality traits develop mainly during the childhood of the character and affect many of their decisions. CK3 goes one more step regarding these traits and directly connects them with many actions using a "stress" system. In this system, a character behaving against their personality traits gains stress (i.e., a merciful ruler executing a criminal, a sadistic ruler letting go of a criminal, a shy ruler participating in feasts) (Figure 5.3). When the stress level of a character reaches certain thresholds, the character suffers a mental break, and the severity of the break increases with high levels of stress, which can cause the character to kill some random person in the court out of anger or even commit suicide. Therefore, the game directly incentivizes the player to play according to the personality traits of the ruler and find some ways of managing this stress.

Similar to CK2, there are several governmental systems in CK3 including feudal, clan, and tribal. The feudal system is very similar to the feudal system in CK2 with a notable difference. The amount of tax and levies a vassal gives to his/her liege is determined by individual feudal contracts between the liege and the vassal and is mainly independent of the relationship level between the two. This contract can be modified however, if the liege asks to increase the

---

[15] Kirk Lundblade, "Watch Me Make History: Reenacting and Remaking the Past in Historical Game Live Streams," *Popular Culture Studies Journal* 9 (2021): 73–74.

amount of tax or levy the vassal is expected to provide; this will be considered as a tyrannical action and will lower the opinion of all vassals of the same liege. However, with intrigue-based actions, this increase can be done without such negative connotations.

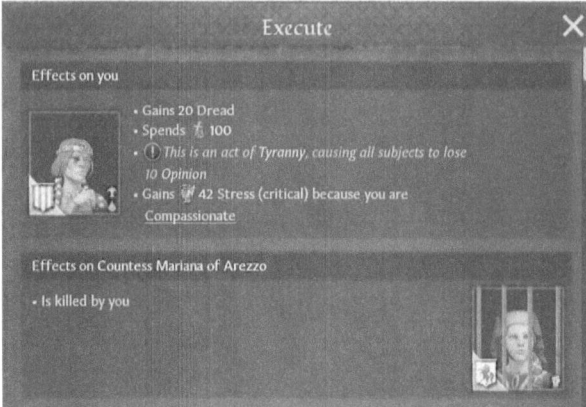

Figure 5.3: A compassionate character gains a considerable amount of stress if they execute a prisoner regardless of the legitimacy of the execution in terms of the laws of the country.

In the Muslim world, instead of the *iqta* system from CK2, the game uses the term "clan" governmental system. Again, this is similar to the feudal system; however there are no feudal contracts, and the amount of tax and levy given by the vassal to the liege is determined by the relationship between the current holders of the two titles. Also, powerful Muslim vassals expect to have family relations with their liege since they too want to become part of the ruling "clan." As a side note, CK3 completely removes the decadence system from the Muslim realms.

This difference between the feudal and the clan/*iqta* system has profound implications. The Catholic Western European world is basically modelled to follow a more static law-based system between the owners of titles, whereas the Muslim world is depicted as much more dynamic and purely based on current relationship levels between the title owners. So, one can criticize the governmental systems depicted in both games, where each has better representations on certain aspects and poor oversimplifications on others. An initial observation could highlight that the Catholic Western World seems to be following a more written rule-based system and mainly immutable. On the other hand, the Muslim world is a more oral relationship-based system and is very dynamic.

Arguably one of the biggest changes of CK3 is the faith and religion system. The game tries to systematically model every religion based on a core "Religion Family, Tenet, Virtue/Sin, Doctrine" system. In the game, each character and province have a "faith" such as Catholicism or Ash'arism, each of which represents a denomination of a religion such as Christianity for Catholicism and Islam for Ash'arism. Depending on its core religion, each faith belongs to a Religion Family, which determines its relationship with other faiths. Each faith has three tenets representing the three most important rites, rituals, and traditions. These tenets allow some special mechanics and capabilities such as "communion" in Catholicism, enabling the excommunication concept within the faith by the spiritual leader of the faith. Virtue/Sins represent what types of traits are considered virtuous and sinful by the adherents of that faith, such as the drunkard being considered sinful by all Muslim faiths.[16] A character who has these traits will have relationship bonuses or penalties against other characters based on the other character's faith. For example, a "temperate" character will be considered virtuous by both Christians and Muslims since temperate is a virtue in the faiths of both religions. Finally, doctrines determine the importance of gender, the tolerance of other faiths, the clergy, and what kind of behaviour is considered a crime in that faith. Adultery of a female character is considered as "criminal" behaviour for the Catholic faith. Therefore, the lord/lady of a realm has the religious right to imprison an adulterous woman if such actions of her are known to the public. The list of these tenets, virtue/sins, and doctrines of each faith is extensive,[17] but a short list of some major medieval era Abrahamic faiths is given as a reference in Table 5.2.

Having such a consistent religion system covering all religions and faiths of the medieval era offers ease in game development irrespective of different geographical regions and cultures. However, the representative accuracy of complex structures like faith and religion based on a strict mechanical system is obviously very debatable. A glaring example is the game's division of Islamic faiths along with theological schools similar to the division of Christian faiths, not based on the more well-known and established "mainly" political branching such as Sunni,

---

16 Despite its highly-detailed religion configuration, many mechanics and in-game concepts about non-Christian religions are still western-oriented. For a critical approach to its religious content, see Piotr Pawel Skora, "Deus Vult, the Representation of the Conflicts with the Religious Other in Grand Strategy Video Games: *Crusader Kings*," *Conflict, Justice, Decolonization: Critical Studies of Inter-Asian Societies* (2021), accessed March 23, 2022, https://cjdproject.web.nctu.edu.tw/wp-content/uploads/sites/105/2021/06/Skora_2021_Deus-Vult.pdf.
17 An exhaustive list can be found in "Faith," *Crusader Kings III Wiki*, accessed June 20, 2021, https://ck3.paradoxwikis.com/Faith.

Table 5.2: Tenets of some major Abrahamic faiths during the medieval era in CK3.

Religion	Faith	Tenets		
Islam	Ash'arism	Fatwa	Struggle & Submission	Jizya
	Maturidism	Fatwa	Struggle & Submission	Literalism
	Muwalladism	Adaptive	Struggle & Submission	Jizya
	Isma'ilism	Taqiya	Struggle & Submission	Jizya
	Zayidism	Taqiya	Struggle & Submission	Legalism
Christianity	Catholicism	Communion	Armed Pilgrimages	Monasticism
	Orthodoxy	Communion	Pentarchy	Monasticism
	Apostolic	Communion	Communal Identity	Aniconism
	Coptic	Alexandrian Catechism	Communal Identity	Monasticism
	Insular Christianity	Pastoral Isolation	Vows of Poverty	Monasticism
Judaism	Haymanot	Esotericism	Communal Identity	Halakha

Shia, Kharijite/Muhakkima. Such a division implies that different theological schools in Islam (such as Ash'arism and Maturidism in Sunni Islam) have a similar relationship with each other as the Catholic Church and the Orthodox Church did.

All things considered though, such a complex and consistent system allows the player to understand and experience the immense effect of religion not only on the social life but also the political sphere in an obvious fashion.

As for the non-Christian, non-Islamic world, the game offers the tribal system for the rest of the world except for the Indian Subcontinent, which is represented again by the feudal system. Although these realms can be played and playing as rulers of such realms offer some unique experiences and gameplay opportunities, since the game is a much more recent entry compared to CK2, currently, these lands lack considerable detail with the notable exception of the Nordic realms.

Student Reflections

This section explains our observations on the students' experiences in our blended world history course and underlines the key advantages of using such a methodology. Houghton has shown that computer games can influence university students' interest in history and their reflexive knowledge of history by means of a comprehensive student survey.[18] With a different approach, we base our observations on the in-class discussions and, more specifically, a special blog post assignment where students summarized their experiences on using *Crusader Kings III* as part of their learning on the Middle Ages. A great majority of the students who participated in this special blog post assignment (30 out of 32) mentioned that using gaming sessions considerably enhanced their learning process one way or another. This enhancement seems to be different in many students, however some common items underlined by the students are as below:

> *Crusader Kings III* taught the importance of several key medieval concepts such as inner workings of feudalism, the importance of religion not only at the societal level but also at the political level, and courtly intrigue to name a few. Unlike a classical learning, this is a very immersive learning experience since the students want to excel at the game instinctively and they can only achieve this goal by mastering the game mechanics hence understanding the actual historical institutions and concepts.

> Game sessions incentivize students to search more on the state/dynasty/kingdom they are playing with. They want to understand who the person they are playing as and what they actually did. So, the game becomes a positive motivator for further learning.

> After a gaming session, the L&D sessions start to become more interesting since the content of these L&D sessions become related to the game.

A potential criticism of such a blended learning methodology could be that students focus too much on the games and lose focus on the actual learning. However, many students observed that gaming sessions alone are not enough for learning history. Instead, in-depth L & D sessions are crucial. The gaming sessions and *Crusader Kings III* in particular offer a good complementary tool to the L & D sessions. It should also be noted that such comments are mainly given by students who are already good at playing such games. To quote a student's remark: "That is why having a [L & D] session that entirely focuses on these [history knowledge] matters are helpful. Also that is what makes this course a course, not a gamer community."

The character-focused aspect of *Crusader Kings III* also let the students understand that all historical key figures are human beings, not some mythical

---

18 Robert Houghton, "Where did you learn that? The self-perceived educational impact of historical computer games on undergraduates," *Gamevironments* 5 (2016): 8–45, accessed June 20, 2021, http://elib.suub.uni-bremen.de/edocs/00105656-1.pdf.

creatures or larger-than-life characters. To quote another student's remark: "History happened the way it did for a vast range of remarkable, exciting, and stupid reasons, and grasping that requires you to imagine yourself in the position of those making the decisions."

When we add our own observations on the students' reflections and observations, we can itemize the benefits of utilizing *Crusader Kings III* and the gaming sessions roughly as below:

In-depth geographical knowledge: first, utilizing an interactive world map, which directly or indirectly affects many game mechanics, dramatically increases the student's knowledge of world geography and its socio-political and economic implications in history. By allowing the students to interact with the map (army/navy movement, trade routes, regional development, terrain types, and so forth), they internalize concepts like strategic and economic importance, which in turn helps them understand various key decisions taken by countries, nations, or leaders in the past.

Increased awareness of the interaction between various societal issues: having an interactive tool (such as *Crusader Kings III*) that allows experimenting on various societal issues by making decisions greatly increases students' understanding of such topics. They become more aware of the complex set of interactions between economic, religious, technological, political, and cultural elements and realize that in most cases none of these elements stand on their own. Instead, they affected each other profoundly throughout history.

Experience-based, immersive learning: most students report that learning history through a video game has a critical immersive component. They can look at the game, experiment on a given strategy, and get immediate feedback from the game. Based on the feedback, they can alter their strategy and try it again to see the differences in the outcome. After a while, this trial-and-error methodology allows them to internalize the intricate interactions of the various systems in the game and lead to more immersive learning of the subject matter.

One important side note here is that most of the students who could not achieve the goals we put to them in the game-based assignments incentivized themselves to try again by different tactics and decisions. Even though we explicitly stated to the students that success or failure is not important in the game-based assignments, they prefer to try again and learn how to succeed in these goals. Since these additional trials become personal assignments they set up for themselves, they have a very high motivation which in turn further increases the immersiveness of their experience.

Moreover, since all the games we have used cover a long period of time in history, after a few game sessions, students surmise the fact that their previous decisions affect their current situation profoundly and understanding of the concept of contingency in the history-as-a-process philosophy.

Understanding the concept of different "readings" of history via modelling decisions of the games: on many occasions, either after we have explained a certain game mechanic or after a game-based assignment, students started criticizing the modelling choices of the game regarding these mechanics. We observe that discussing an interactive model is much easier to follow than discussing over a passive reading of history in a historical text. The key advantage of discussing an interactive model is checking how it works with the other game mechanics and the implications of such a model in the greater context of the whole game. Such discussions immediately connect with different possible readings of history, the fact that the same history can be read differently, why there is a need for different readings, and how to use multiple sources, tools, and so forth to better understand history as a whole.

An excellent example of such a modelling decision is the controversial "westernization" mechanic of EU3, which has been replaced by the more versatile "institutions" mechanic in EU4. Although the "institutions" mechanic can still be criticized as Eurocentric, the "westernization" mechanic was vastly more Eurocentric and led all non-western European nations to either become a backward country in the long run or change their culture and "westernize."

Contextualizing key events and major developments: finally, we observe that students' understanding of the societal systems of the past increases considerably after a couple of game sessions. Afterwards, they start to elaborate on events more from a historical perspective instead of a modern viewpoint. This change of perspective greatly increases their understanding of certain historical key events and developments being part of a greater process instead of thinking of them as strange occurrences that happened with little connection to their contemporary surroundings.

Conclusion

In this chapter, we introduced our experiences and observations on a blended world history course with a classical lecture and discussion sessions and game sessions in which students can play complex strategy games that model various institutions of certain historical eras. We organize the course in three major parts: an introduction and two main parts exploring the Middle Ages and Early Modern Age with *Crusader Kings III* and *Europe Universalis IV*, along with Lecture and Discussion sessions. This paper particularly focuses on the challenges of the teaching of the Middle Ages and our use of *Crusader Kings* series as an alternative strategy game as a supporting tool to learn and discuss history. As demonstrated above, the *Crusader Kings* series is a remarkable attempt at modelling the medieval societies and their economic, religious, and administrative features. By experimenting with the mechanics of the game, students internalize historical knowledge as active participants instead of passive readers. As pointed out, the game still requires extra mechanics and concepts to become more comprehensive in a global manner. In time, with the release of the new patches and Downloadable Content (DLCs), the gaming experience would be relatively equal for many non-European cultures as well. Although it requires some effort to set up such a blended history course, we observe that the gains of gaming experience outweigh the challenges and allow for a more profound and immersive learning experience. In a nutshell, the new immersive technologies would not be sole tools for the educative purpose, but along with lecture and discussion sessions, they would serve as complementary tools for immersive learning.

Bibliography

"Faith." Crusader Kings III Wiki. Accessed June 20, 2021. https://ck3.paradoxwikis.com/Faith.

Houghton, Robert. "If you're going to be the king, you'd better damn well act like the king: Setting authentic objectives to support learning in Grand Strategy Computer Games." In *The Middle Ages in Modern Culture: History and Authenticity in Contemporary Medievalism*, edited by Karl C. Alvestad and R. Houghton, 186–210. London: Bloomsbury Academic, 2021.

Houghton, Robert. "Where did you learn that? The self-perceived educational impact of historical computer games on undergraduates." *Gamevironments* 5 (2016): 8–45. Accessed June 20, 2021. http://elib.suub.uni-bremen.de/edocs/00105656-1.pdf.

Johnson, Mark R. "The Place of Culture, Society, and Politics in Video Game World Building." In *World-builders on World-Building: An Exploration of Subcreation*, edited by Mark J. P. Wolf, 110–131. New York: Routledge, 2020.

Lundblade, Kirk. "Watch Me Make History: Reenacting and Remaking the Past in Historical Game Live Streams." *Popular Culture Studies Journal* 9 (2021): 69–87.

Koebel, Greg. "Simulating the Ages of Man: Periodization in Civilization V and Europa Universalis IV." *The Journal of the Canadian Game Studies Association* 10 (2017): 60–76.

McCall, Jeremiah. "Teaching History with Digital Historical Games: An Introduction to the Field and Best Practices." *Simulation and Gaming* 47 (2016): 517–542.

Pagnotti, John, and William B. Russell III. "Using Civilization IV to Engage Students in World History Content." *The Social Studies* 103 (2011): 39–48.

Radetich, Laura, and Eduardo Jakubowicz. "Using Video Games for Teaching History. Experiences and Challenges." *Athens Journal of History* 1 (2015): 1–14.

Meier, Sid, and Jennifer Nee Noonan. *Sid Meier's Memoir! A Life in Computer Games*. New York: W. W. Norton & Company, 2021.

Skora, Piotr Pawel. "Deus Vult, the Representation of the Conflicts with the Religious Other in Grand Strategy Video Games: Crusader Kings." *Conflict, Justice, Decolonization: Critical Studies of Inter-Asian Societies* (2021). Accessed June 20, 2021. https://cjdproject.web.nctu.edu.tw/wp-content/uploads/sites/105/2021/06/Skora_2021_Deus-Vult.pdf.

Wainwright, A. Martin. "Teaching Historical Theory through Video Games." *The History Teacher* 47 (2014): 579–612.

Wang, Hao, Wen-Wen Chen, and Chun-Tsai Sun. "Play Teaches Learning?: A Pilot Study on How Gaming Experience Influences New Game Learning." In *Interactivity and the Future of the Human-Computer Interface*, edited by Pedro Isaias and Katherine Blashki, 147–168. Hershey, PA: IGI Global, 2020.

Vowinckel, Annette. "Past Futures: From Re-Enactment to the Simulation of History in Computer Games." *Historical Social Research / Historische Sozialforschung* 34 (2009): 322–332.

Ludography

Crusader Kings II. Paradox Interactive, 2012.
Crusader Kings III. Paradox Interactive, 2020.
Europa Universalis IV. Paradox Interactive, 2013.
Hearts of Iron IV. Paradox Interactive, 2016.
Medieval: Total War. Creative Assembly, 2002.
Shogun 2: Total War. Creative Assembly, 2011.
Sid Meier's Civilization. MicroProse, 1991.
Sid Meier's Civilization II. MicroProse, 1996.
Sid Meier's Civilization III. Infogrames, 2001.
Sid Meier's Civilization IV. Firaxis Games, 2005.
Sid Meier's Civilization V. Firaxis Games, 2010.
Sid Meier's Civilization VI. Firaxis Games, 2016.

Part III: **Creating Educational Games**

Klio Stamou, Anna Sotiropoulou, Phivos Mylonas and Yorghos Voutos

6 A Video Game for Byzantine History – *Akritas*: Playing at the Byzantine Borders

Abstract: Integration of new technologies into the learning process lies among the objectives of the contemporary educational approach related to historical periods. Thus, students familiar with the use of technology approach the traditional history lesson by participating in modern educational games of historical content. To intrigue them more into deepening their knowledge in history, we propose a history-based video game, so that they can familiarize themselves with Byzantine era and interact with aspects of its everyday life, such as military organization and actual public administration. The latter will be achieved through digitized copies of artifacts, so as to endorse and resemble a regular Byzantine life, e.g., as a commoner, a soldier, a high-level official, or even an emperor. By participating in these educational scenarios the students will have the opportunity to acquire direct knowledge about artifacts placed in Byzantine museums or the architecture of buildings, e.g., a Byzantine church, a palace or a house. The motivation behind this educational video game that is based on real cultural data/metadata is the development of students' historical thinking and social awareness, and the production of a valuable teaching tool to make the learning process as appealing as possible.

Introduction – Byzantine history in Greek Schools

Byzantine History has been a topic in Greek schools that usually has been treated with dismay by both students and teachers. The theocratic spirit of the Empire, the lack of qualification of teaching history by the teachers, and the normal dislike of students about the past have all created a vicious cycle making this part of history a difficult course to study and teach.

Byzantine history has been taught in Greek primary and secondary education as the connecting link between Ancient and Modern Greek history, in three different grades in primary and secondary education. That is students in the fifth grade of elementary School (ages 9–10), in the second grade of High School (ages 13–14), and in the second grade of Lyceum (ages 16–17) are being taught Byzantine History. Generally, the syllabus starts with a summary of

Roman history, while Constantine's decision to move the capital from Rome to Constantinople marks the beginning of the journey to what Greek students come to know as Byzantium.

The syllabus – which is designed by the Ministry of Education and the ministry-supervised Institute of Educational Policy[1] and must be followed by all educators, is directed mainly to facts, emperors, and battles. In fifth grade of primary school only two of 38 lessons about Byzantine history concern everyday life, while one is about women in the Byzantine society, and six more about art and letters. In High School, Byzantine history is presented in the context of an era starting in 330 and finishing in the eighteenth century. Four of the book's seven chapters are about Byzantine history. The first three present – in chronological order – events, information about the administration, economy, and society, while the fourth takes into account everyday life, literature, art, and science.

Finally, in Lyceum, Byzantine history is presented in the context of the era 565–1815, with four chapters concerning mainly Byzantine history (events, diplomacy, economy, and society), along with some mention of Arab expansion, and Western Medieval Europe. A fifth chapter presents the civilization in Byzantium, Western Mediaeval Europe, Balkans, and Russia and the caliphates.

In order to make Byzantine history more attractive to students – especially those at elementary and high school level – a number of digital approaches have been proposed through "Photodentro"[2] (Tree of light – a Ministry of Education supported repository for digital approaches to courses). Regarding Byzantine History most of the resources are PowerPoint presentations, which are supposed to be used by the teachers during their lectures as to make them more attractive or interesting to the students.

Our proposition gives more power to the student. Elementary and high school students being taught Byzantine history know their way around technology. Most of them own a smartphone or a tablet, or they are using one owned by another family member. They know how to use a PC – computer usage has been included in the curriculum of the first grade in Greek elementary schools – and some of them even have a video–game console like PlayStation[3] or Xbox.[4] Gaming is something normal for them, and they do play medieval oriented games like

---

[1] "Institute of Educational Policy," accessed May 20, 2021, http://www.iep.edu.gr/en/.
[2] "Photodentro – Greek National Aggregator of Educational Content," accessed May 20, 2021, http://photodentro.edu.gr/aggregator/?lang=en.
[3] "Playstation," accessed May 20, 2021, https://www.playstation.com/en-us/.
[4] "Xbox," accessed May 20, 2021, https://www.xbox.com/en-US.

Age of Empires: Castle Siege,[5] *Clash Royale*,[6] and so forth. The use of video games in teaching history – as we shall show in the following paragraphs – is an established educational method,[7] which promotes the collaboration in the classroom and provokes the interest of the students.

The rest of the chapter is organized as follows. First we give a short presentation of recent works (state of the art) regarding video games technology in educational practice. Next, we present how to integrate video games in the teaching of history, in general. Finally, we shall present the video game we propose and how we expect it will encourage students to study Byzantine History.

Integration of Video Games in the Teaching of History

Good Practices of Teaching Strategies

Over the past four decades, many researchers have discussed how and why to use digital video games effectively in the history classroom. Studies on historical games in history education have increased significantly since then. The 1990s, with the exception of Taylor's discussion of *Civilization*,[8] were largely silent on the use of simulation games in history lessons, although Corbeil[9] wrote an article in defence of learning through play and simulations. However, several new studies have emerged in the twenty-first century. One of the most important analyses comes from Squire's unpublished dissertation, "Replaying History."[10] Squire investigated the use of *Civilization III* with several groups of

---

5 *Age of Empires: Castle Siege* (Smoking Gun Interactive Inc., 2014).
6 *Clash Royale* (Supercell, 2016).
7 Marco Rüth and Kai Kaspar, "Commercial Video Games in School Teaching: Two Mixed Methods Case Studies on Students' Reflection Processes," *Frontiers in Psychology* 11, no. 11 (2021): 3802, https://doi.org/10.3389/fpsyg.2020.594013.
8 Tom Taylor, "Using the Simulation 'Civilization' in a World History Course," *History Microcomputer Review* 10, no. 1 (1994): 11–16, http://survey.hshsl.umaryland.edu/?url=http://search.ebscohost.com/login.aspx?direct=true&db=eric&AN=EJ493946&site=ehost-live.
9 Pierre Corbeil, "Learning from the Children: Practical and Theoretical Reflections on Playing and Learning," *Simulation and Gaming* 30, no. 2 (1999): 163–80, https://doi.org/10.1177/104687819903000206.
10 K. Squire, "Replaying History: Learning World History through Playing Civilization III," *Indiana University, Indianapolis* (Bloomington, IN: University of Indiana, 2004), http://website.education.wisc.edu/kdsquire/dissertation.html.

teens to examine how such a game could affect the learning of world history. What Squire found, among many pieces of information, is that the game itself was not the most important variable when evaluating the usefulness of the gaming experience for learning world history. Instead, what was most important were the types of learning communities and learning practices cultivated through play, discussion, critique, and expansion of play.

An important reference to how to use digital gaming with historical content comes from educator and researcher McCall and his book *Gaming the Past*.[11] The book focuses on the use of digital games to simulate historical content in classrooms. His research begins with the reasons why one can get students to play historical simulation games and how to engage them with digital games. The book is focused on the educational strategies for the utilization of digital games, in the historical education with specific types of learning exercises.

Utilization of a video game refers to the category of game-based learning, as explained above in the text. Below we present five cases in which, according to McCall,[12] the video game could be used in the teaching of history:

1. **Game Overview:** Introduces students to a critical analysis of games, helping them to think about the limits and possibilities of the video game, while encouraging them to think about how the story is created.
2. **Immersion in the game:** Students immerse themselves through the rules of the game emphasizing causes, consequences, and strategies without focusing on deeper historical analysis.
3. **Exploring a historical problem:** Students contrast primary and secondary sources with assumptions that emerge from the game.
4. **Reflection:** Students discuss the representation of the past unfolding in the game, which can be compared to other visual and non-visual sources. Students can evaluate the existing representations of some games and reflect on why they were created in this way.
5. **Game reliability:** Develops a critical attitude of students towards the game, avoiding comparisons with how the situation really was. A reflection is made on the significance of a historical event.

Recent works indicate that video games are potential motivators for extracurricular learning in history class, by enabling students to experience a given

---

[11] Jeremiah McCall, *Gaming the Past: Using Video Games to Teach Secondary History*, Gaming the Past: Using Video Games to Teach Secondary History (New York: Routledge, 2012), https://doi.org/10.4324/9780203831830.
[12] McCall, *Gaming the Past*.

narrative.[13] Furthermore, Metzger and Paxton[14] identified the dangers of subjectivity in the conception of a historical game and highlighted the dangers of a biased representation of the given historical context, an element that is also found in written texts. On the other hand, it is believed that games give enough orientation to empower students' critical engagement with the medium and its content.[15]

Bass[16] proposed a method for games as an interactive mean of teaching medieval history under the notion of enhancing the learning experience. He presented a collection of games that could be utilized in a classroom environment, which offer a narrative for better understanding the medieval era. Moreover, students are challenged to deepen enquiry into specific events and their effects through formal and secondary sources.

Boom et al.[17] argued the idea that historical video games support experiential learning, while students as actors relive the past from the "first person" perspective. Although aggressive behavior is prevalent in most commercial video games, they indicated that several applications offer educational capabilities through specific mediated approaches in a wide variety of contexts and for different audiences.

On the other hand, Fokides, Polydorou, and Mazarakis[18] dealt with the use of modern tools such as smartphones and Google Cardboard[19] compatible devices for history teaching within the high school environment. Essentially, they introduced enjoyable activities into classroom practice under the scope of creating an animating environment for teaching history.

---

13 Scott Alan Metzger and Richard J. Paxton, "Gaming History: A Framework for What Video Games Teach About the Past," *Theory and Research in Social Education* 44, no. 4 (2016): 532–64, https://doi.org/10.1080/00933104.2016.1208596.
14 Metzger and Paxton.
15 Richard Pfeilstetter, "Gamifying Anthropological Theory Teaching. Critique, Learning and the Video Game Civilization," *Disparidades-Revista De Antropologia* 75, no. 2 (2020).
16 Ian Bass, "The Potential of Video Games for Enhancing Teaching History," *International Journal of Management and Applied Research* 7, no. 3 (2020): 308–18, https://doi.org/10.18646/2056.73.20-022.
17 Krijn H. J. Boom et al., Teaching through Play: Using Video Games as a Platform to Teach about the Past. In: Hageneuer, S (ed.), *Communicating the Past in the Digital Age*. London: Ubiquity Press. DOI: https://doi.org/10.5334/bch.c.
18 Emmanuel Fokides, Eleni Polydorou, and Panos Mazarakis, "Using Google Cardboard Compatible HMDs and Spherical Videos for Teaching History to High School Students," *International Journal of Smart Education and Urban Society* 11, no. 4 (2020): 18–34, https://doi.org/10.4018/ijseus.2020100102.
19 "Google Cardboard," accessed May 20, 2021, https://vr.google.com/cardboard/.

Li[20] argued that game enthusiasts are taking part in a new form of storytelling – an emergent form of public consent – due to their interactions with historical context video games. These games are constructed into a historic field and consequently involve "people as well as nations and communities in the creation of their own histories." More specifically, the issue of historical narrative is to represent the past according to the developers' own means and concerns and allow the player to take part in a constructive dialogue about the past. His research indicated the relation between designer and gamer, in order to collectively shape the historical consciousness of players. The educational practice which can be gained from the pedagogical virtue of historical video games can potentially yield a new generation of public historians.

Hanes and Stoen[21] proposed a model that defines how historical context can be presented in a video game at a content level and demonstrate how it can be applied to the analysis of the content in a commercial historical game. They tried to examine games' mechanics and contents to calculate and explore the educational factors of each commercial computer game. Also, the authors tried to trace non pre-defined learning objectives, making them exploitable in history class by educators as an additional analysis tool to assist in the selection of an appropriate historical context. Furthermore, this method proposed the integration of games along with history classes to assist them in converting real and feasible serious game designs into heritage informational content and learning objectives and vice versa.

The aforementioned works indicate the special scientific interest in the search for the benefits in the pedagogical practice found in games. We gathered a small selection that underlines useful information related to the expert's[22] requirements. The following sections provide an overview of the proposed methodology to the reader that can be applied in different historic backgrounds.

---

20 Na Li, "Playing the Past: Historical Video Games as Participatory Public History in China," *Convergence*, 2020, https://doi.org/10.1177/1354856520967606.
21 Laurence Hanes and Robert Stone, "A Model of Heritage Content to Support the Design and Analysis of Video Games for History Education," *Journal of Computers in Education* 6, no. 4 (2019): 587–612, https://doi.org/10.1007/s40692-018-0120-2.
22 Teacher, game designer, scientist or enthusiast.

Creating a Video Game for the Teaching of History

Many video games deal with historical events, creating digital representations which communicate with the players. According to Chapman,[23] historical games have become one of the most widespread and successful forms of public history. Atkins[24] calls video games a "new form of historical text" that is very popular and also promises to change the way history is consumed by the general public. Furthermore, the immense virtual worlds are characteristic to modern computer games, which allow the player to be part of the narrative separately from the words and symbols which exist in written text.[25]

Šisler[26] records his research endeavor by creating a digital game (serious game). He defines a reference framework for creating the game, which aims to address the above issues by incorporating the following five design principles:

1. **Versatility:** Unlike storytelling, digital games are a form of representation that can offer many alternative perspectives.
2. **Authenticity of historical content:** The main challenge of a serious game with historical content is related to authenticity: how can a game whose main advantage is to run and execute procedures and systems deal with real historical memories?
3. **Constructivism:** Players must critically evaluate the gathered information, use social skills and empathy to critically approach the social aspect of history.
4. **Participation:** As Schut[27] argues, most historical digital games focus almost exclusively on politics, economics, and war. Köstlbauer[28] adds that

---

[23] Adam Chapman, "Is Sid Meier's Civilization History?," *Rethinking History* 17, no. 3 (2013): 312–32, https://doi.org/10.1080/13642529.2013.774719.

[24] Bary Atkins, "'History Is Bunk?: Historiographic Barbarism in Civilization' Published as 'La Storia è Un'assurdità: Civilization Come Esempio Di Barbarie Storiografica?,'" in *Civilization: Storie Virtuali, Fantasie Reali*, ed. Matteo Bitanti (Milan: Costa & Nolan, 2005).

[25] David Williamson Shaffer et al., "Video Games and the Future of Learning," *Phi Delta Kappan* 87, no. 2 (2005): 105–11, https://doi.org/10.1177/003172170508700205.

[26] Vít Šisler, "Procedural Religion: Methodological Reflections on Studying Religion in Video Games," *New Media and Society* 19, no. 1 (2017): 126–41, https://doi.org/10.1177/1461444816649923.

[27] Kevin Schut, "Strategic Simulations and Our Past: The Bias of Computer Games in the Presentation of History," *Games and Culture* 2, no. 3 (2007): 213–35, https://doi.org/10.1177/1555412007306202.

[28] J. Köstlbauer, "The Strange Attraction of Simulation: Realism, Authenticity, Virtuality," in *Playing with the Past: Digital Games and the Simulation of History*, ed. A. B. R. Elliot and M.W. Kappel (New York, NY: Bloomsbury, 2014), 169–83, https://doi.org/10.5040/9781628928259.ch-011.

many historically inspired digital warfare games exclude aspects such as political casualties or the unintended socio-political and economic long-term consequences of military action. However, in part as an attempt to correct the hegemonic bias of traditional historical research, the discipline of history has expanded its scope to include a wide variety of topics. Engaging players with content that was not edited due to dominant narratives is a challenge for serious games.

5. **Historical context:** Galloway[29] argued that a realistic game must maintain some kind of relevance, for example some kind of environmental fidelity, which translates from the player's social reality to the game environment. Galloway calls it a "necessary agreement" to achieve "realism" in gaming.

Teaching Practices

The didactic practices applied in the digital serious game are not limited to simple citation, decoding texts, and comprehension questions, but push to highlight the opposing views of the main characters (such as Akrites) at the negotiating table and in the field of diplomacy, organization, planning, and in the execution of warfare, with the aim of understanding and discussing their argumentation and logic. For teachers, the digital game is desirable to be an educational tool that motivates students to learn about the history of the Middle Ages, and specifically Byzantine history. The purpose of designing this educational digital game is to stimulate students' critical discussion and willingness to research, as well as to provide a multifaceted perspective on historical events.

The digital game must be useful, provide clear targeting, and necessary or even immediate feedback in order to facilitate the streaming experience. The feedback helps the student to look for better solutions to problems that arise, resulting in the extension of knowledge.[30]

Considering serious games as a type of intentional learning as they are designed with a specific educational goal in mind, Anderson[31] structures this type of learning around four organizational questions:

1. **The learning question:** What should the student learn?

---

29 Alexander R. Galloway, "Social Realism in Gaming," *Game Studies* 4, no. 1 (2004), http://www.gamestudies.org/0401/galloway.
30 Šisler, "Procedural Religion."
31 J. B. Anderson, K. J. Swick, and J. Yff, "Service-Learning in Teacher Education: Enhancing the Growth of New Teachers, Their Students, and Communities," in *AACTE* (Washington, DC, 2001), accessed May 21, 2021, http://files.eric.ed.gov/fulltext/ED451167.pdf.

2. **The teaching question:** How should instruction be provided in order to achieve high learning requirements?
3. **The evaluation question:** How should accurate evaluation instruments be designed or selected?
4. **The alignment question:** How should learning, teaching and assessment be balanced?

Game-based Learning is a way of teaching where students explore content learning through digital games, which have predetermined learning outcomes, according to Prensky.[32]

Scenarios and Digital Games

In recent years, the design of educational or teaching scenarios, which concern proposed ways of teaching sections of History, has gradually evolved and been integrated into the teaching practice. A scenario can last more than one teaching hour and is implemented through a series of educational activities, which are parts of the scenario, integrated in either simple or complex form. A typical structure of an educational scenario includes the scenario identity, the scenario implementation framework, the teaching process, and the implementation.

Collaborative scenarios can provide the supportive framework for the teacher to make use of digital games, guiding student interactions. Scenarios can provide the structure and guidance that students need, so that the game experience can help them reap significant cognitive and meta-cognitive benefits, even if the digital game does not actually support some form of collaboration. To this end, we suggest to the teacher the following basic stages of work for the utilization of learning games and the integration of cooperative scenarios in them:
1. **Preparation**
2. **Cooperation**
3. **Reflection**

The benefits of this effort are expected to come primarily from the motivation for increased engagement with the game, which is expected to be enjoyed by student-players. The student will want to play the game in order to experience

---

32 Mark Peterson, "Computer Games and Learning," in *Computer Games and Language Learning*, ed. J. Raessens and J. Goldstein (Cambridge, MA: The MIT Press, 2013), 33–50, https://doi.org/10.1057/9781137005175_3.

the interesting emotions that this experience creates. As a consequence, it must activate the cognitive processes required by the learning mechanism, the one integrated in the game. The result is expected to be increased engagement and interaction (students with each other, with the teacher, with the game and the educational material), which will gradually lead to the achievement of essential learning objectives such as:

- **Emergence of the cognitive object** (learning basic / advanced knowledge, familiarity with multiple perspectives / interpretations, connection of knowledge with everyday situations, analysis of strategies, etc.),
- **Development of skills** (self-action for problem solving, cooperation, social interaction (communication), project time planning, search and organization of information, etc.).

However, creating an educational and, at the same time, fun game is not a simple matter. It requires an understanding of human nature and what is really fun for the student group. An additional difficulty is related to the possible contradiction between educational goals and game features. Winning orientation in a game may lead student users not to try strategies they deem inappropriate. This may prevent them from fully investigating the consequences of specific strategies.

Also, the efficiency of learning using games should not be expected to be high if the only thing that will be counted as a learning outcome is the knowledge of the subject. The game is not expected to be as efficient as a traditional form of educational activity, because in the game the student spends time on secondary – but necessary – activities, such as learning instructions and getting acquainted with how to play.

Perhaps the most important design element of a learning or educational digital game is the relationship that the game develops between the scenario and the learning method. The learning method should be aptly integrated in the scenario and gameplay of the game, so that the student learns in their attempt to play the game, without feeling that the learning effort interferes with and interrupts the smooth development of the game. Depending on how successfully this relationship is formed, it can be characterized as Intrinsic, Relevant or Arbitrary.[33]

---

[33] Michela Bernarducci, *Multimedia for Learning: Methods and Development (3Th Edition) – Book Review*, European Journal of Education Studies, vol. 1 (Boston, MA: Pearson Education, 2016), accessed May 21, 2021, http://oapub.org/edu/index.php/ejes/article/view/5/53.

Intrinsic: The most efficient way to design a learning game is when the game script effortlessly activates the learning method, that is the learning elements jump straight out of the scenario, effectively promoting the game. It simply means that the student-player activates the necessary cognitive learning processes, because he feels that this way he will play the game successfully and not because he has to learn something foreign in relation to the game.

Relevant: In many games the learning elements logically influence the development of the game (for example the position of the player on the game board); it is therefore relevant to the scenario, but without being well integrated and springing from the scenario as in the previous case.

Arbitrary: Finally, the relationship is characterized as arbitrary when the learning method seems completely foreign (and therefore arbitrary) in relation to the game scenario.

In the context of creating a digital serious game, it is essential to present the teaching strategies, which are based on the digital game and will be followed in the design of the educational scenarios and consequently the serious game, as their use engages students in alternative forms of learning and satisfies modern learning needs. The utilization of digital games in the teaching of History provides students and teachers with many possibilities in relation to the management of the historical past. Also, in the educational digital game (serious game) the educational goal setting and the playful way of approaching the knowledge coexist with the didactic practices of the game per Mission. On the other hand the role of the teacher is strengthened in the modern educational environment and especially in the case of the digital serious game. It must be emphasized that the teacher assumes the role of the thoughtful-critical teacher, both during the implementation of the activities, which are closely intertwined with the plot, as it develops in the individual missions of the game, and during the reflection of the process.

A Game to Play

What we propose is a video game that will allow students to interact with life in the times of the Byzantine Empire. The students, playing individually or in a group, will start by choosing the era they are going to explore. The options will be the early Byzantine period (330–717), the middle Byzantine period (717–1025), and the later years (1025–1453), as these are defined in the school curriculum.

Subsequently, the students will have to decide the area in which their mission is going to take place: an agricultural area, the borders, Constantinople or another city like Salonica, or the palace. The student's final choice will be the character with whom they will identify. Available characters may be an everyday man, woman or child, as well as a priest, monk or a nun. Characters specific to missions or regions may include merchants, teachers, administrative personnel (tax collecting officers or cabinet members) and military personnel (soldiers or officers), as well as persons like the emperor or the empress (both as a consort and as the titular empress) and the regent.

Depending on the choices the student makes, a number of missions will be available for the student to follow. Depending on their choices the mission may be impossible – for example choosing a monk or a tax collecting officer to play a military mission would probably lead to the failure of the mission and the defeat of the army. This way the student will be able to learn the consequences of their choices, while the mission repetition will allow for the better understanding of the historical facts and issues behind the mission.

Use-case Scenarios

A Woman in the Byzantine Empire

A number of missions would take into account the everyday life of a woman, giving the player the opportunity to play as a woman or a young girl. The woman will have the goal to take care of the household chores and provide her family with their everyday needs, while the girl may be helping her mother. The student will be called to perform certain chores that were normal for an everyday woman: praying, helping around the house, taking care of her children, preparing meals for the family, looking after the elderly, but also getting dressed, using her jewellery and so on. Depending on the region in which the mission takes place the woman will have different chores, as a woman in an agricultural area would have to take part in the cultivation of the land, along with her household, while a woman in one of the Empire's cities will probably have to take care of a small garden.

Meanwhile, choosing a woman that is part of the palace, either as part of the court or even as the empress herself, will mean that a different mission will be at hand. Many things will be the same, as in the case of a commoner, but in this case palace intrigue will also be part of the mission. Diplomacy will thus be part of the mission, presenting yet another aspect of the Byzantine Empire.

During these missions the students will be called to use artifacts which will already be known to them through their lessons. Their teacher may use the web pages of the Museum of Byzantine Culture in Salonica, or the one of the Byzantine and Christian Museum of Athens, in order to introduce the students to the artifacts that will be used in their missions. When such an artifact is chosen, the student may remember the information about it and correctly use it in their mission. Thus, students are immersed into the historical setting by incorporating the authentic scenery of the heritage sites into the game environment.[34]

Ruling the Empire

For the more ambitious students, another scenario of the game will be to play as an emperor, an empress or a regent, the ruler or sovereign. In this case the student will be presented (depending on the time they have chosen) with choices such as going to war, raising taxes, and making diplomatic decisions. In this scenario, the user will have access to information about the person they are impersonating. Also, there will be available information about the allies and enemies of the Byzantine Empire, both to the east and to the west – information that will aid them to better understand the connections and interrelations among Byzantium and the rest of the world at this period of time, and make the appropriate choices in diplomatic dilemmas.

Of course, the choices the student might make in such a scenario won't be infinite. The choices the student will be presented with may change the course of history, providing for a different outcome in certain cases. A battle may not be won, making the student go back and take the mission again, so as to make those choices that will get him or her to the correct outcome.

Fighting for the Empire's Borders

The largest use case is that of the "Akritas," the soldiers whose duty was to defend the Empire's borders. The very word, *Akritas*, originates from the Greek word akri (*άκρη*) meaning edge, or border in a wider sense. Akritas is a collective name used to define the soldiers stationed at the borders of the Empire,

---

[34] Michał Mochocki, "Heritage Sites and Video Games: Questions of Authenticity and Immersion," *Games and Culture* (2021), accessed May 21, 2021, https://doi.org/10.1177/15554120211005369.

those who replaced the Roman Empire's *milites limitaneos*, as well as the inhabitants of the borderland in general. Akrites gained the peak of their importance during the ninth to eleventh centuries, when the expansion of the Caliphate was threatening the Empire. A mixture of military troops and militia (as part of the *Themata* system), they were both soldiers and farmers living in the borders. Soldiers were given land to cultivate and live in it, with their families, with the obligation of defending the borders. Land would be passed to their children, along with the military obligation.

The Akrites were part of folk culture, especially through songs, called the "Akritika" (of the Akrites or of the border), songs that would praise their valor. The epic poem of Digenes Akritas[35] written in the late eleventh to early twelfth century describes the life of the most prominent of the Akrites and is the basis of a number of later folk songs written about Digenes Akritas. The epic poem can be found in six different manuscripts with variations in each one.[36]

Who was Digenes? Vassilios "Digenes" Akritas was not a historical person, but rather one of legends. He was the son of an Arab – the Saracen Amir – who had converted to Christianity to marry Digenes' mother. So Digenes was of two origins, of two races – of two geni – and this gives him his nickname (duo geni – δύο γένη – Digenes). He is presented as the best of each race, creating a kind of superhero. His diversity is an advantage, even if he is still a man of his time with all the problems one can imagine, that will surface when creating a video game. For the folk tradition he is a kind of superhero and this provides us with the narrative needed to grab the attention of children who are hooked on Captain America or Spider-Man.

Digenes was sent to defend the borders and performed very well. He lived with his wife somewhere near the Euphrates river, on the "farm," while he completed a number of deeds he had to perform. He started with killing two bears and a lion at the age of 12 (long before meeting his wife). When his father-in-law (a general) didn't accept him, he abducted his favorite daughter and managed to defeat her father's army, and after their marriage he protected her from a number of dangers (animals and persons) and of course he protected the borders.

Local legend has it that he was in charge of protecting the islands of Cyprus and Crete, so he would leap from mainland (Asia) to Cyprus, and then Crete, to take care of Saracens who might be trying to invade. His handprint was said to be imprinted on the Cyprus' mountain, when he fell, granting its name Pentadaktylos (five fingers) and his footprint is said to be on the Psiloritis mountain of Crete.

---

35 John Mavrogordato, ed., *Digenes Akritas* (Oxford: Oxford University Press, 1970), https://archive.org/details/DigenesAkritesGreekEnglish.
36 Eliso Elizbarashvili, "The Formation of a Hero in *Digenes Akrites*," *Byzantine Studies* 50, no. Bristol (2010): 437–60.

The legend provides us with more than enough stories to add into our narrative, with the best of all being his fight with Death: the only fight that Digenes lost. The story cannot be found in the epic poem, but variations of it can be found in different folk songs both of Cyprus and mainland Greece. And this will be one fight that we expect to be thoroughly used and fought in our game. After all who wouldn't like to fight with Death and win?

Having all this information, this narrative, so many missions can be made available for the student to choose. The student will enter the game and they will have to choose from a number of Akrites to play as. There is always the question of how to deal with diversity, how a feminine Akrites would fit in this very much masculine role. There is the possibility to allow for a feminine hero, based on the modern Greek meaning of the word Akritas: both male and female inhabitants of borders. Having this in mind, a woman living in the borders may well be one of the options presented to the student. Another kind of mission that the student might also choose to play with may be the narrative of an "akritiko" song, that is try to recreate the story the song narrates.

As the Akrites were at the time both farmers and soldiers, another mission may be a fully peaceful one. The student may decide to have their hero cultivate the land and manage the farm. The hero's mission would not be to defend the borders, but to provide for their family, and take care of the farm and every day chores. A battle happens even in the fully peaceful mode, as invasions were something expected in the life in the borders of the Byzantine Empire. The student would be able to choose to decline a battle, if they did not want to participate. This mission would have the option to continue, even without the battle. Of course cultivation of land is a difficult mission by itself, allowing for play to continue without getting boring for the students.

On the other hand the soldier Akritas would have to deal with invasions and battles, and dealing with all sort of enemies (including Saracens and Apelatai). During these battles every win will provide more "points" to the hero to pass their mission. As the hero wins more battles the student will be presented with more options for their missions.

At some point the student will be able to choose a mission in which Digenes will be the hero. Most of the Digenes' missions would be about invasions that need to be defeated, giving more points to the player. When playing as Digenes, the battles will be fiercer and the enemies will be more difficult to deal with. Just like real Digenes had to pass "stages of self-establishment,"[37] as Elizbarashvili remarks, the student has to pass different stages in the game to get to the final stage.

---

37 Elizbarashvili, "The Formation of a Hero."

The final mission when playing as Digenes will be the final battle of Digenes himself: the battle with Death. The option of winning this battle is available, provided that the student makes the correct decisions in a number of cross-points, however it will be difficult. Digenes did lose that battle and the students know that, but they do have the opportunity – difficult as it may be – to get a different outcome.

Conclusions

The primary purpose of the implementation of an educational video game for the history of the Byzantine Empire will be the development of historical thinking and social awareness of the student. This will allow them to understand the historical facts, to link causes and results, to interpret human behavior through time with the aim of realizing that the modern world is a continuation of the past and that it is directly connected with their life.

By proposing an educational video game on the subject of the study of Byzantine History, we aid the fundamental goal of every teacher, to make their course more interesting and effective for their students; the approach will guide students towards self-driven learning and the discovery of knowledge through the investigation of the aforementioned historical period.

Finally, application of such methodology ensures the students' ability to identify factors, causes, and consequences of historical events, and in addition it allows them to correlate, compare, draw conclusions, and exercise their historical knowledge, thus nurturing their historical thinking.

We do keep in mind the fact that Byzantine history, at least as it is presented in the curriculum of the Greek Ministry of Education, covers a vast time period, increasing the potential educational scenarios in an almost exponential manner. We can therefore conclude that both the choice of appropriate educational scenarios and the choice of missions that will be implemented in the game is a huge undertaking.

Bibliography

Anderson, J. B., K. J. Swick, and J. Yff. "Service-Learning in Teacher Education: Enhancing the Growth of New Teachers, Their Students, and Communities." In *AACTE*. Washington, DC, 2001. Accessed May 20, 2021. http://files.eric.ed.gov/fulltext/ED451167.pdf.

Atkins, Bary. "'History Is Bunk?: Historiographic Barbarism in Civilization' Published as 'La Storia è Un'assurdità: Civilization Come Esempio Di Barbarie Storiografica?'" In

Civilization: Storie Virtuali, Fantasie Reali, edited by Matteo Bitanti, 65–81. Milan: Costa & Nolan, 2005.

Bass, Ian. "The Potential of Video Games for Enhancing Teaching History." *International Journal of Management and Applied Research* 7, no. 3 (2020): 308–18. https://doi.org/10.18646/2056.73.20-022.

Bernarducci, Michela. *Multimedia for Learning: Methods and Development (3Th Edition) – Book Review*. European Journal of Education Studies. Vol. 1. Boston, MA: Pearson Education, 2016. Accessed May 20, 2021. http://oapub.org/edu/index.php/ejes/article/view/5/53.

Boom, Krijn H. J., Csilla E. Ariese, Bram van den Hout, Angus A. A. Mol, and Aris Politopoulos. "Teaching through Play: Using Video Games as a Platform to Teach about the Past." In: Hageneuer, S (ed.), *Communicating the Past in the Digital Age*, London: Ubiquity Press. https://doi.org/10.5334/bch.c.

Chapman, Adam. "Is Sid Meier's Civilization History?" *Rethinking History* 17, no. 3 (2013): 312–32. https://doi.org/10.1080/13642529.2013.774719.

Corbeil, Pierre. "Learning from the Children: Practical and Theoretical Reflections on Playing and Learning." *Simulation and Gaming* 30, no. 2 (1999): 163–80. https://doi.org/10.1177/104687819903000206.

Dias, Diogo. "Teaching History and Geography with Video Games Auckland, New Zealand." Media Design School New Zealand, 2020. Accessed May 20, 2021. https://www.researchgate.net/publication/343166486_Teaching_History_and_Geography_with_Video_Games_20200611.

Elizbarashvili, Eliso. "The Formation of a Hero in *Digenes Akrites*." *Byzantine Studies* 50, no. Bristol 1990 (2010): 437–60.

Fanise, Yoan, and Paul Tumelaire. "Valiant Hearts: The Great War," 2014. Accessed May 20, 2021. https://www.ubisoft.com/en-us/game/valiant-hearts.

Fokides, Emmanuel, Eleni Polydorou, and Panos Mazarakis. "Using Google Cardboard Compatible HMDs and Spherical Videos for Teaching History to High School Students." *International Journal of Smart Education and Urban Society* 11, no. 4 (2020): 18–34. https://doi.org/10.4018/ijseus.2020100102.

Galloway, Alexander R. "Social Realism in Gaming." *Game Studies* 4, no. 1 (2004). http://www.gamestudies.org/0401/galloway.

"Google Cardboard." Accessed May 20, 2021. https://vr.google.com/cardboard/.

Hanes, Laurence, and Robert Stone. "A Model of Heritage Content to Support the Design and Analysis of Video Games for History Education." *Journal of Computers in Education* 6, no. 4 (2019): 587–612. https://doi.org/10.1007/s40692-018-0120-2.

"Institute of Educational Policy." Accessed May 20, 2021. http://www.iep.edu.gr/en/.

Köstlbauer, J. "The Strange Attraction of Simulation : Realism, Authenticity, Virtuality." In *Playing with the Past: Digital Games and the Simulation of History*, edited by A.B.R. Elliot and M.W. Kappel, 169–83. New York, NY: Bloomsbury, 2014. https://doi.org/10.5040/9781628928259.ch-011.

Li, Na. "Playing the Past: Historical Video Games as Participatory Public History in China." *Convergence*, 2020. Accessed May 20, 2021. https://doi.org/10.1177/1354856520967606.

Mavrogordato, John, ed. *Digenes Akritas*. Oxford: Oxford University Press, 1970. https://archive.org/details/DigenesAkritesGreekEnglish.

McCall, Jeremiah. *Gaming the Past: Using Video Games to Teach Secondary History. Gaming the Past: Using Video Games to Teach Secondary History.* New York: Routledge, 2012. https://doi.org/10.4324/9780203831830.

Metzger, Scott Alan, and Richard J. Paxton. "Gaming History: A Framework for What Video Games Teach About the Past." *Theory and Research in Social Education* 44, no. 4 (2016): 532–64. https://doi.org/10.1080/00933104.2016.1208596.

Mochocki, Michał. "Heritage Sites and Video Games: Questions of Authenticity and Immersion." *Games and Culture*, 2021. Accessed May 20, 2021. https://doi.org/10.1177/15554120211005369.

Peterson, Mark. "Computer Games and Learning." In *Computer Games and Language Learning*, edited by J. Raessens and J. Goldstein, 33–50. Cambridge, MA: The MIT Press, 2013. https://doi.org/10.1057/9781137005175_3.

Pfeilstetter, Richard. 2020. "Gamifying Anthropological Theory Teaching. Critique, Learning and the Video Game Civilization." *Disparidades. Revista de Antropologia* 75(2): e016. https://doi.org/10.3989/dra.2020.016.

"Photodentro – Greek National Aggregator of Educational Content." Accessed May 20, 2021. http://photodentro.edu.gr/aggregator/?lang=en.

"Playstation." Accessed May 20, 2021. https://www.playstation.com/en-us/.

Rüth, Marco, and Kai Kaspar. "Commercial Video Games in School Teaching: Two Mixed Methods Case Studies on Students' Reflection Processes." *Frontiers in Psychology* 11, no. 11 (2021): 3802. https://doi.org/10.3389/fpsyg.2020.594013.

Schut, Kevin. "Strategic Simulations and Our Past: The Bias of Computer Games in the Presentation of History." *Games and Culture* 2, no. 3 (2007): 213–35. https://doi.org/10.1177/1555412007306202.

Shaffer, David Williamson, Kurt R. Squire, Richard Halverson, and James P. Gee. "Video Games and the Future of Learning." *Phi Delta Kappan* 87, no. 2 (2005): 105–11. https://doi.org/10.1177/003172170508700205.

Šisler, Vít. "Procedural Religion: Methodological Reflections on Studying Religion in Video Games." *New Media and Society* 19, no. 1 (2017): 126–41. https://doi.org/10.1177/1461444816649923.

Squire, K. "Replaying History: Learning World History through Playing Civilization III." *Indiana University, Indianapolis*. Bloomington: University of Indiana, 2004. Accessed May 20, 2021. http://website.education.wisc.edu/kdsquire/dissertation.html.

Taylor, Tom. "Using the Simulation 'Civilization' in a World History Course." *History Microcomputer Review* 10, no. 1 (1994): 11–16. Accessed May 20, 2021. http://survey.hshsl.umaryland.edu/?url=http://search.ebscohost.com/login.aspx?direct=true&db=eric&AN=EJ493946&site=ehost-live.

Toh, Weimin, and Fei Victor Lim. "Using Video Games for Learning: Developing a Metalanguage for Digital Play." *Games and Culture*, 2020. Accessed May 20, 2021. https://doi.org/10.1177/1555412020921339.

"Xbox." Accessed May 20, 2021. https://www.xbox.com/en-US.

Ludography

Age of Empires: Castle Siege. Smoking Gun Interactive Inc., 2014.
Clash Royale. Supercell, 2016.

Owen Gottlieb and Shawn Clybor

7 Collaborative Constructions: Designing High School History Curriculum with the *Lost & Found* Game Series

Abstract: This chapter addresses design research and iterative curriculum design for the *Lost & Found* games series. The *Lost & Found* card-to-mobile series is set in Fustat (Old Cairo) in the twelfth century and focuses on religious laws of the period. The first two games focus on Moses Maimonides' Mishneh Torah, a key Jewish law code. A new expansion module which was in development at the time of the fieldwork described in this article that introduces Islamic laws of the period, and a mobile prototype of the initial strategy game has been developed with support National Endowment for the Humanities. The series pays close attention to period details and provides numerous entry points for curriculum. Featured at the 2019 Smithsonian American Museum of Art (SAAM) Arcade, winner of the best non-digital game at International Meaningful Play, and a Bronze medal winner at the International Serious Play competition, these games combine engaging table-top play across game genres with opportunities to learn about medieval religious history. The first game in the series is a strategy game which combines competitive and collaborative play as players make trade-off decisions to balance the needs of their family with needs of the wider community. The second game in the series is a party game which focuses on legal reasoning. This chapter addresses approaching learning environments, from design with experts and playtests with learners to participant observation and narrative reports at a high school where the game is being used to teach history. Crucial to learning games is the way in which they relate to, are interwoven with, and are ultimately embedded in curriculum, especially learning outcomes and objectives. This chapter will examine strategies and processes that explore that interweaving.

Introduction

The dynamics of classroom environments vary and range across diverse contexts. Game design for the classroom thus requires playtesting and integration for particular audiences, typically determined by age and grade. Focusing on the specific learner population is a critical component of design in order to ensure the game is developmentally appropriate, engaging, and can be integrated into the classroom. Ideally, the work of games-for-learning designers and classroom teachers intersects early in the learning game design process and continues at each successive iterative phase of game design. But what happens when the educator and/or designer's target population broadens, changes, and shifts? Once learning games are already developed, how might game designers and classroom educators work together to optimize the use of a game for different audiences and classrooms, honing the curriculum and the use of the game for those classrooms?

This design case examines how a game designer-researcher (Gottlieb) and a history scholar and classroom educator (Clybor) collaborated over the course of three years to explore opportunities to integrate *Lost & Found*, a series of three learning games (one of which was still in development), into a series of high school history classrooms. Over the course of their explorations, the designers developed three primary design approaches to take forward following their classroom observations and analyses:

- tailoring the emphasis of classroom reading and lecture preparation to focus on topics that would later be instrumentalized in gameplay.
- using more scaffolding of the particular history-relevant skill sets used for competition in gameplay.
- teaching game media literacy regarding how the game designers approached representing history in the game, which includes leveraging any available designer publications, discussions, and statements.

Through our shared experiences of exploration, observation, analysis, and design decision-making, we intend to provide this design case as precedent for other designer/educator teams seeking to adapt learning games to build curricula for new classroom environments.

Design Case

This chapter is presented as a design case. Design cases include thick descriptions of an intentionally designed artifact or experience.[1] While designers have long used design analysis to advance their professional practices, the use of design cases in learning designs is exemplified by scholarly works such as the *International Journal of Designs for Learning*. This tradition of the use of design cases draws from naturalistic research traditions originating in anthropology and sociology.

---

1 Elizabeth Boling, "The Need for Design Cases: Disseminating Design Knowledge," *International Journal of Designs for Learning* 1, no. 1 (2010), https://doi.org/10.14434/ijdl.v1i1.919.

Learning designers apply design iteration, observation, thick description, and checks on interpretations to provide record of and accounting of design decisions, failures, and practices. These cases are not oriented towards generating generalized knowledge, but rather seek to provide precedents for designers – cases which will assist in the practices of design. This is distinct from design-based research, which uses iteration of designed artifacts for the establishment of new social science knowledge.[2] Though design cases on games for learning involve iteration, the iteration is focused on the process of design as opposed to determining new learning theory.

This design learning case is related but different in intent and approach from action research practices in the classroom. In action research, teachers use systematic inquiry to gather data about teaching, school operation, and student learning in order to increase insight, develop teaching practices, and bring about positive change in the learning environment, student outcomes, and the experience of those involved.[3] In the case described in this chapter, because our goal was curriculum development (see Background below), we focus on the curriculum and its process of development as design artifacts to explore and iterate. We use ethnographic methods and formal IRB procedures to gather data, which would provide us with options beyond the initial design study in terms of methodological analysis approaches. While the data is gathered such that it could be used for social science research, we deploy the data in the service of a design project: seeking design questions and exploring design approaches. Such a design-case oriented process allowed us to respond with flexibility to student responses as well as shifting classroom environments over time, while also capturing and preserving data for more varied research use in the future.

Background: Designers in Collaboration

Co-authors Gottlieb and Clybor met in 2018 at the Game Developers Conference (GDC) in San Francisco when they were both presenting history learning games, and quickly found they had related design interests and complementary skills.

---

2 (DBRC) The Design-Based Research Collective, "Design-Based Research: An Emerging Paradigm for Educational Inquiry," *Educational Researcher* 32, no. 1 (January 1, 2003): 5–8, https://doi.org/10.3102/0013189X032001005.
3 Geoffrey Mills, *Action Research: A Guide for the Teacher Researcher*, 6th edition (NY, NY: Pearson, 2017).

Gottlieb, a professor, researcher, and designer in the fields of games and interactive media for learning, with a specialty in history and religion, was presenting on his team's 2017 tabletop learning game releases *Lost & Found*[4] and *Lost & Found: Order in the Court*.[5] These two games, one a strategy game and one a legal-reasoning party game, focus on Jewish religious laws of lost and found objects in twelfth century Fustat (Old Cairo), a crossroads of Islam, Judaism, and Christianity, as a means to teach about pro-social aspects of religion (collaboration, cooperation, and sustainable governance practices). The first two games in the series deal with Moses Maimonides' laws for the Jewish community found in the *Mishneh Torah* (1170–1180). In *Lost & Found*, players both collaborate and compete while navigating the laws of lost and found objects with the ability to choose how they respond in each situation such as when and whether to follow the law. They must balance the needs of their family and those of the community, making trade-off decisions. *Order in the Court* is a legal reasoning game in which players create stories to explain how a law might have arrived in a court in the first place. The latest release in the series, *Lost & Found: New Harvest*,[6] introduces Islamic law by Ibn Rusd and Al-Marghinani. When combined with the original *Lost & Found*, *New Harvest* allows players to play as Jews and Muslims living side by side, and to compare the contemporaneous legal systems of Muslim and Jewish neighbours.

Clybor, a published historian with a Ph.D. in history and independent school teacher with ten years of experience in the classroom, was attending the parallel Independent Games Festival (IGF) with the Czech Game development studio Charles Games, whose serious game *Attentat 1942* been nominated for the award "Excellence in Narrative."[7] Clybor played various roles for Charles Games, including translator, localizer, game designer, and curriculum writer on two different video game projects: *Attentat 1942* and its sequel *Svoboda 1945: Liberation*.[8] Set in Czechia, the games are historically-situated narrative adventures comprising multimedia elements (Full-Motion Video, documentary

---

[4] Owen Gottlieb, Ian Schreiber, and Kelly Murdoch-Kitt, "Lost & Found," *Initiative in Religion, Culture, and Policy, MAGIC Spell Studios*, January 1, 2017, https://scholarworks.rit.edu/other/904/.

[5] Owen Gottlieb and Ian Schreiber, "Lost & Found: Order in the Court – The Party Game," *Initiative in Religion, Culture, and Policy, MAGIC Spell Studios*, January 1, 2017, https://scholarworks.rit.edu/other/903/.

[6] Owen Gottlieb and Ian Schreiber, "Lost & Found: New Harvest," *Initiative in Religion, Culture, and Policy, MAGIC Spell Studios*, November 4, 2020, https://scholarworks.rit.edu/other/947/.

[7] *Attentat 1942* (Charles Games, 2017).

[8] *Svoboda 1945: Liberation* (Charles Games, 2021).

footage, and interactive comics). The goal of both games is for players to conduct interactive interviews of friends, family, and other "everyday people" in the near-present, and then relive with them their experiences of the Second World War and its aftermath. Through his work with Charles Games, Clybor had developed a keen interest in the possibilities of game-based learning and teaching history through commercial video games.

Clybor and Gottlieb discovered that they shared a passion for teaching history in the classroom through games. Having focused the design of the *Lost & Found* series for undergraduates, Gottlieb was looking to develop approaches and curricula to bring *Lost & Found* to high schools. Clybor had just completed a curriculum guide for *Attentat 1942*, and was looking for innovative ways to incorporate other games and game-based learning in his classroom. This synchronicity led us to collaborate on curriculum development for the *Lost & Found* games series.

Gottlieb and his team had primarily focused on undergraduates as their target audience with additional limited play observation of teens. Gottlieb's team, based at a university game design and development program, has access to many undergraduate players for playtesting and iteration. Gottlieb also reasoned that a tabletop game that would be initially compelling for undergraduates could also have the capability to interest high schoolers, as had been the case with classics such as *Dungeons & Dragons* and *Magic: The Gathering*. Gottlieb wanted to work on a high school curriculum with an expert high school history teacher who was literate in the medium of games. Meanwhile, Clybor recognized an opportunity to work with a game designer on building game-based curricula while enhancing his history classroom offerings, especially because the setting of the *Lost & Found* series coincided with subjects he was teaching. We would work together to design something new that we hoped would engage and excite students while deepening their history skills.

Goals and Approach

We decided that the eventual curriculum should be iterated in the classroom and stimulating for high school students, while also serving the teaching goals of educators. We sought to maximize a diversity of teaching opportunities and learning experiences given the variety and volume of material designed into the games: historical, legal, ethical, art history, and religious studies. To achieve these goals, we decided to explore the use of games in Clybor's classroom with a focus on deeper historical understanding and historical empathy (see section below on this topic).

In terms of collaboration, we worked to share expertise areas, design a playful approach to curriculum development, and respond to what arose in the shifting classroom contexts. In order to capture what occurred, Clybor would gather audio and video recordings on the ground, keep journals of preparation and classroom observations, and share his reflections with Gottlieb.

We conferred on Clybor's lesson plans prior to the in-class events, then, following the sessions, we discussed and analyzed the observations that Clybor had gathered. The initial iteration was initiated following Clybor's instincts for what might work best in his classroom. Gottlieb provided sources in advance to Clybor regarding the history of the period as it pertained to the game. This included secondary sources, original primary source texts of the legal material that was used to develop the game, and a design rationale for how the game incorporates this material. Clybor suggested ways to introduce the material, ways to frame the game or use the game to frame the lessons, and potential approaches to reflection that he felt would be effective. Gottlieb helped Clybor prepare an introductory lesson for the game by providing demo tutorial material and offering suggestions from what Gottlieb and his team had gathered from a variety of playtests and play sessions. After each set of classes, we debriefed, reviewed observations, discussed student responses, actions, and reflections, and considered different interpretations of what we observed. Each year, we drew on the previous years' experience to consider new approaches for iteration: how we might maximize the classroom experience for the learners with regards to exploration of the topic, with each step advancing the lesson plans and approaches.

Historical Thinking, Historical Empathy, and Games

Although it was important to Clybor that the historical content in *Lost & Found* aligned thematically and chronologically with content covered in his curriculum, his core objectives were skill-based: to develop students' historical thinking and historical empathy. In the case of the first two games, this meant historically situating Judaism in the specific context of old Fustat. The third game meant also historically situating Islam in old Fustat. Building upon Samuel Wineburg's work, Clybor's understanding of historical thinking entails remaining aware of our modes of thinking in the present while avoiding the projection of these modes of thinking onto the past. According to Wineburg, the reconciliation of this contradiction makes historical thinking a counterintuitive or "unnatural" act because it requires us to both embrace and escape our presentism – understanding the past with contemporary values that are based on modern concepts.[9] Peter Seixas similarly argues that historical thinking occurs when students negotiate solutions to six different "problems" that revolve around tensions between history and the historian, who "is a temporal being immersed in time, investigating and writing at a particular historical juncture, with particular lenses, questions and methods," necessarily, with interpretive lenses defined by experiences in the present.[10] One of these key problems, particularly challenging in our curriculum development, is historical perspective taking, the act of juggling historical continuity and change to develop an understanding of "the minds of peoples who lived in worlds so different from our own."[11] Jason Endacott and Sarah Brooks have also provided helpful retrospectives on different scholarly approaches to conceptualizing and building historical empathy. One approach cautions that emotional and affective empathy can lead to presentism, whereas a more cognitive and reason-based approach to empathy draws upon contextualization to reconcile the tensions between our understandings of the past with our inescapable present.[12] In other words, we can never truly know the emotional world of

---

9 Samuel S. Wineburg, *Historical Thinking and Other Unnatural Acts: Charting the Future of Teaching the Past* (Temple University Press, 2001), 84.
10 Peter Seixas, "A Model of Historical Thinking," Educational Philosophy and Theory 49, no. 6 (2015): 6, https://doi.org/DOI: 10.1080/00131857.2015.1101363; cf. Peter Seixas et al., *The Big Six: Historical Thinking Concepts* (Toronto: Nelson Education, 2013). The website of the Historical Thinking Project (https://historicalthinking.ca/historical-thinking-concepts) based on Seixas' work articulates the problems/concepts succinctly as:
1. Establish historical significance
2. Use primary source evidence
3. Identify continuity and change
4. Analyze cause and consequence
5. Take historical perspectives, and
6. Understand the ethical dimension of historical interpretations.

11 Seixas, "*A Model of Historical Thinking*, 9.
12 See: Wineburg 2001; cf., Stuart J. Foster and Elizabeth Anne Yeager, "The Role of Empathy in the Development of Historical Understanding," *International Journal of Social Education* 13, no. 1 (1998): 1–7; Stuart J. Foster, "Using Historical Empathy to Excite Students about the Study of History: Can You Empathize with Neville Chamberlain?," *The Social Studies* 90, no. 1 (January 1, 1999): 18–24, https://doi.org/10.1080/00377999909602386; Bruce VanSledright, "From Empathetic Regard to Self-Understanding: Im/Positionality, Empathy, and Historical Contextualizations," in *Historical Empathy and Perspective Taking in the Social Studies*, ed. O. L. Davis Jr., E. A. Yeager, and S. J. Foster (Lanham, MD: Rowman & Littlefield Publishers, 2001), 51–68; Stéphane Lévesque, *Thinking Historically: Educating Students for the Twenty-First Century, Thinking Historically: Educating Students for the Twenty-First Century* (University of Toronto Press, 2008); Jeffrey Nokes, *Building Students' Historical Literacies: Learning to Read and Reason with Historical Texts and Evidence* (Routledge, Taylor & Francis Group, 2012).

historical actors, but we can know the context that framed their potential emotional responses. Another approach to historical empathy drawing upon Keith Barton and Linda Levstik, among others, notes the dangers of erasing emotion and affect from the study of history.[13] Summarizing this approach, Lisa Gilbert argues:

> While they [Barton and Levstik] agreed that imagining the emotions of others as though they were one's own represents a problem for historical reasoning, they reminded readers that this action should rightly be categorized as sympathy rather than empathy. Further, Endacott and Brooks (2013) suggested that "students must be able to find an affective connection between the experiences faced by historical figures and similar experiences in their own lives" as one of the skills necessary for historical empathy (p. 46). They indicated that this approach to historical empathy "can help students develop a stronger awareness of needs around them and a sense of agency to respond to these needs. (p. 45)"[14]

Here Gilbert transitions from Barton and Levstik to settle on a definition of historical empathy oriented in the work of Endacott and Brooks; namely that historical empathy is a "dual dimensional" act of cognitive perspective recognition plus affective connection (what Barton and Levstik describe as "caring.")[15] By this approach, learners perform the cognitive work of empathy to avoid presentism, but they also need to care about whom they are learning about. They need to care in the sense that they are able to make moral judgements about the material, develop compassion for people's experiences in the past, and take civic action

---

[13] Keith C. Barton and Linda S. Levstik, *Teaching History for the Common Good* (New York: Routledge, 2004), https://doi.org/10.4324/9781410610508; Sarah Brooks, "Historical Empathy in the Social Studies Classroom: A Review of the Literature," *Journal of Social Studies Research* 33, no. 2 (Fall 2009): 213–34; Jason L. Endacott, "Reconsidering Affective Engagement in Historical Empathy," *Theory & Research in Social Education* 38, no. 1 (January 1, 2010): 6–47, https://doi.org/10.1080/00933104.2010.10473415; Jason L. Endacott and Sarah Brooks, "An Updated Theoretical and Practical Model for Promoting Historical Empathy," *Social Studies Research and Practice* 8, no. 1 (2013): 41–58; Elif M. Gokcigdem, *Fostering Empathy Through Museums* (Rowman & Littlefield Publishers, 2016); Jason L. Endacott and Sarah Brooks, "Historical Empathy: Perspectives and Responding to the Past," in *The Wiley International Handbook of History Teaching and Learning*, ed. Scott Alan Metzger and Lauren McArthur Harris (John Wiley & Sons, 2018): 203–25, https://doi.org/10.1002/9781119100812.ch8.

[14] Lisa Gilbert, "'Assassin's Creed Reminds Us That History Is Human Experience': Students' Senses of Empathy While Playing a Narrative Video Game," *Theory & Research in Social Education* 47, no. 1 (January 2, 2019): 6, https://doi.org/10.1080/00933104.2018.1560713.

[15] Endacott and Brooks, "An Updated Theoretical and Practical Model for Promoting Historical Empathy," 44; cf. Barton and Levstik, *Teaching History for the Common Good*, 228–243.

based upon what they learn.[16] Caring requires affect, and is key for empathetic engagement in history.

Attuned to the affective power of the medium of games, both Gottlieb and Clybor seek to leverage both the cognitive and affective opportunities for learners through historical empathy. James Gee has long noted the importance of role-taking in games in terms of its exploration of identity.[17] Game designers also understand the power of emotion in play. For example, Tracy Fullerton devotes an entire section of her text on game design to "Working with Dramatic Elements:" [T]hese elements are what engage players with the formal system – what gets them and keeps them emotionally involved in the game. Challenge, play, and story can all provide emotional hooks that captivate players and invest them in the outcome so that they will keep playing.[18]

The medium of games and the act of play is attuned to affective experience as well as cognitive experience. Therefore, approaching the teaching of history with games should attend to both cognitive and affective historical empathy. What might the students think while problem solving? And how might they engage, in terms of affect?

In the Classroom

In 2018, Clybor brought the strategy game *Lost & Found* to his ninth-grade honours ancient world history course as the culminating activity of a larger unit that focused on the Middle Ages in the Mediterranean World. The school is a private high school in the Northeastern United States. The population of the school includes both non-Jewish and Jewish students, some of whom may have had previous exposure to some of the Jewish texts. All student names have

---

[16] At the core of Barton and Levstik's approach is understanding the purpose of history education as preparing learners to be citizens in a pluralist democracy, and so students must learn history to develop a sense of caring about that role and responsibility. Gilbert, "Assassin's Creed Reminds Us That History Is Human Experience," 6–7; see for example, Barton and Levstik, *Teaching History for the Common Good*, Chapter 2, Chapter 12.
[17] James Paul Gee, "Stories, Probes, and Games," *Narrative Inquiry* 21, no. 2 (January 1, 2011): 353–57, https://doi.org/10.1075/ni.21.2.14gee; James Paul Gee, *What Video Games Have to Teach Us About Learning and Literacy. Second Edition: Revised and Updated Edition*, 2nd ed. (Palgrave Macmillan, 2007).
[18] Tracy Fullerton, *Game Design Workshop: A Playcentric Approach to Creating Innovative Games, Third Edition*, 3 edition (Boca Raton: A K Peters/CRC Press, 2014): 341.

been replaced with pseudonyms in this article.[19] The class included nine students in total (five girls and four boys), ranging in age from 14 to 15 years old. Clybor's initial lesson goals were for students to:

- Explore the possibilities and limitations of religious co-existence in the Fatimid Caliphate, and compare this milieu to other civilizations in the Mediterranean world.
- Explain how Jews, as a religious minority, used religious laws to define and manage their communities in the Middle Ages.

These goals connected to larger themes central to his course, such as cultural blending and religious co-existence, and melded nicely with the kinds of design intent that motivated the game's development.

Clybor's *Lost & Found* mini-unit took four days to complete. The first class began with a short lecture and finished with a guided group discussion on two assigned readings: a short secondary source article from the *Jerusalem Post* about the Fatimids,[20] and a primary source excerpt in Hebrew and with English translation from Maimonedes' *Mishneh Torah*.[21] Some of the game's core mechanics and many of the scenarios were based on and inspired by a particular chapter of *Mishneh Torah, Gezelah va'Avedah*, that deals with the return of lost belongings. The next two days were devoted to the play sessions. On the first day, Clybor organized the class into two groups of four to five students, provided a 10-minute tutorial, and then walked students through their first round of play. The rest of this class and the entire next class were devoted to independent game play. The last day was devoted to a class-wide reflection, during which the students proved so eager to discuss the game that Clybor rarely needed to pose the questions he had prepared in advance; instead he reacted to comments, asked follow-up questions, and offered observations to channel the conversation.

Clybor's initial expectation was that students would use their historical reasoning skills to connect content from the game to content from the assigned primary and secondary sources to develop an argument about how Jews used religious law to define their communities in the Middle Ages. This occurred primarily with the *Mishneh Torah* excerpts, which the students referenced throughout their play

---

[19] Students and parents all consented to participation in adherence to IRB procedures. Use of pseudonyms for students is specifically for publisher specifications.

[20] Seth J. Frantzman, "To Pray Where Maimonides Prayed," The Jerusalem Post | JPost.com, February 14, 2017, https://www.jpost.com/diaspora/to-pray-where-maimonides-prayed-481462.

[21] Rabbi Eliyahu Touger, *Rambam Mishneh Torah: Sefer Nezikin* (Moznaim Publishing, 1997).

sessions and group discussion. One of the groups even called Clybor over to read an excerpt with them to confirm that their understanding of the text was correct in terms of how they were applying it to make a decision regarding their gameplay. Another student, Marc,[22] reported to Clybor that on his way home after the first day of play that he saw another student unknowingly drop a quarter while exiting the school bus. That evening Marc called the student to announce that he had found a piece of his lost property. The student he called was dumbfounded as Marc explained to him that because they were both Jewish he had an obligation in "the spirit of the *Mishneh Torah*."

An unexpected theme that emerged almost immediately during the class-wide debrief was whether it was the additional historical context such as the lecture and readings or the game itself that provided the richest opportunities for learning. Initially, Marc, Larry, and Paul expressed the opinion that the game was not particularly useful for learning history beyond the supplemental context, such as the class readings and overview of the rules. Danica disagreed with this opinion, leading to the following exchange between her and Clybor:

> Danica: "Once you learn the rules, I agree that's where the historical context ends, but I think it really helps, as someone who isn't Jewish, and who doesn't have a lot of experience with Judaism, to learn what the essence of the Mishneh Torah really is, and what the overall themes of it are in relation to . . . to . . . "
>
> Clybor: "How the religion functions?"
>
> Danica: "Yes. Like how it functions in the historical context that we're learning about."
>
> Clybor: "As opposed to?"
>
> Danica: "As opposed to just learning the basic facts of the period."

Here Danica discussed her interpretation of play through its procedures and her role within them, which, she expressed, gave her a sense that she was learning through direct experience about the perspective of someone following their daily life in the context of *Mishneh Torah* laws. In other words, Danica was speaking to a different type of context, which she believed allowed her to understand an "essence" of a historically located cultural experience through the play process. We can see here both the risks of presentism, and essentialism, but also the potential for players, through following procedures and roles in a game, to develop a sense of first-hand connection to a historical experience. The game's mechanics,

---

[22] Pseudonym, as is the case with all student names in article.

the carefully researched illustrations on the cards, and the overall social milieu of gameplay may have all contributed to her interpretation of this experience. Clybor and Gottlieb suspect that this is likely a combination of the cognitive processes of thinking and reflecting on play, but also the affective experience of play within the game's rules and procedures, including the social experience of play with classmates, which involved gossip, laughter, and personal stories. During the play sessions Danica's behavior was especially animated, as she threw her hands in the air, swung backwards in her seat, and even held up different game cards to the camera recording their play.

In the moment, Clybor wondered whether, with more reflection, students like Danica might draw upon their affective experiences to explore how historically-situated structures, systems, and rules impact behavior and perspectives. Indeed, after Danica responded, several other students mentioned the impact of the game on their behavior. For example, according to Larry: "Aside from teaching you how, giving you a simulation of how the *Mishneh Torah* was really used in real life, or the teachings from it, it also, the game itself helps to develop skills that are useful later in life, like critical decision making, and prioritizing things." Larry had initially argued that the gameplay had limited value as a teaching tool, but here, perhaps responding to Danica, he is pointing out that the game encouraged him to use important skills such as decision-making and prioritizing (in this case player versus group incentives). Looking back at the data, Clybor realized that the curriculum might encourage students such as Larry to consider the skills of decision-making and prioritizing – but in an historically contextualized way, as opposed to such skills understood outside of such historical context. Could we engage students in considering how decision-making might be impacted by the social structures, values, and norms of a particular time and place? How might decision-making in twenty-first century northeastern United States be different than decision-making in twelfth century Fustat? How might decision-making regarding communal responsibility, interdependency, and cooperation have been different in medieval Fustat than in contemporary New Jersey? By considering such context and questions, perhaps Larry could engage directly with presentism.

After Clybor discussed his observations with Gottlieb, one of the conclusions he came to was that he needed to loosen his plans for developing his lessons. While designing a curriculum was still his primary objective from this project, he realized that he did not fully understand what was resonating with the students. He had wanted students to deepen their retention of historical content by reinforcing that content through game play; instead he began wondering how he could encourage them to draw deeper connections between their own affective play experiences and their perceived experience of historical context. They were role-playing the experience of living within the legal and sociocultural systems that inspired the design of the game's mechanics and rules. Moving forward, Clybor would therefore emphasize the *Mishneh Torah* text and de-emphasize the broader historical context by cutting the secondary source article and shortening the lecture. This allowed us to observe with greater flexibility how students were responding to and learning from the game, with an eye towards designing future curricula around these emergent learning experiences.

In 2019, we shifted over to using the legal reasoning party game *Order in the Court*, in which players craft stories to the scenarios that might have led to the origin of a particular law in the *Mishneh Torah*. It is usually played for humor – to see who can create the most entertaining stories. The "judge" position rotates. When players are curious, the actual explanations for the rulings and the laws on which they were derived are provided on the backside of the cards. This time, Clybor designed his classes with less structure and less emphasis on the broader historical context of the Fatimid Caliphate. This class was larger than the previous group, including 15 students, six boys and nine girls, again ranging from 14 to 15 years old.

The first day of class was focused primarily on a discussion of the *Mishneh Torah* excerpts, followed by one day of play, and (after a last-minute change in his school's schedule) a shortened second day of play followed by a quick 20-minute discussion. Finally, instead of including the play sessions as an integrated part of his final unit on the Middle Ages, he scheduled the game for the week after the assessment. In part this was due to timing – he had an extra week of class before the academic year ended – but he also wanted to think more creatively about the types of assessments that he might be able to develop by first observing the students' play.

During their game play, Clybor again noticed that the students were using their reasoning skills to draw upon the *Mishneh Torah*, this time to better situate their rulings in what they imagined to be its "authentic" historical and legal context. The students' efforts to simulate the Maimonides reading was especially strong in one group, with heavy doses of showboating, where the boys seemed eager to win the attention of the girls. In other words, the internal social dynamics of the groups appeared to provide intrinsic motivation to better instrumentalize the class materials. Whatever their underlying motivations, the students only rarely (and at Clybor's behest) read the provided explanations on the backsides of the cards at the end of their turn. They seemed much more likely to incorporate previous information they had already learned "on the fly," including both the Maimonides excerpts and other texts. For example, students in two different groups attempted to simulate the rhetoric of biblical stories and oral myths they had studied in Clybor's class earlier that year.

During the discussion, Clybor followed up on these observations and asked the students whether it had helped them to read the excerpts from Maimonides. Most of the students agreed, and were able to supply specific instances in which they drew upon the excerpts to better simulate legal reasoning or better situate their reasoning in its historical context, at least to the extent that they understood it. Rachel summarized, "You can compare it to the kinds of rulings that happen, or [Maimonides'] general idea of the style of writing." Josh later added, "You could also incorporate other laws, other than the one that was being [used] in the ruling." When Clybor asked if Josh could provide an example, he responded: "Yeah! There was a ruling about how your possessions would take priority over a teacher's possessions. So when I was explaining it I tried to make it sound like you were more knowledgeable than the teacher because there's that thing about how you should return something unless the other person is wiser than the teacher." On the other hand, none of the students offered specific examples of how they applied (or could have applied) content from the (now abbreviated) historical context lecture about the Fatimid Caliphate. When Clybor asked them about it directly, two of the students noted that it was important information to know, but similar to the 2018 group they were unable to provide specific examples of how or why it was important to know. The students also seemed to pick up, at least intuitively, on the importance of simulation as a means of using their historical thinking skills. For example, when Clybor asked them what a "fair assessment" for the game might look like, Katrin suggested: "What do you think, socially, is happening in the period, and how does this impact the rules you were seeing?" Several students agreed that contextualizing the rulings could be a useful exercise for a test. Others suggested that a fair test would ask them to do exactly what they had done in the game, namely to hypothesize situations that may have led to the ruling, but to do so more "academically" by writing out their answer, supplying contextual evidence, and incorporating primary sources such as Maimonides.

While reviewing their gameplay, Clybor noted that similar to the 2018 class the additional materials that seemed to matter most to the students were those that aligned more closely to the procedures simulated in gameplay, perhaps because they provided a gameplay advantage. Because some of the students were demonstrating competitive prowess in the game by making strongly constructed legally reasoned stories, Clybor suggested to Gottlieb that moving forward, we spend more time advancing the class as a whole with additional readings they could draw upon, and more sample turns and cases. We expand on this idea in greater detail in the reflections section below.

2020 was a different year for many reasons. The new standalone expansion to the strategy game, *New Harvest*, was close to release, which meant that Gottlieb's team had an opportunity to playtest it with Clybor's students prior to completing its design. They would be able to make adjustments to the game from what they learned. What might arise from using a not-yet-finished game in the classroom, and how might that influence our work designing curriculum with the series? Our third year was also different in the classroom. Clybor was no longer teaching the ninth-grade ancient and medieval world history class, and opted instead to recruit volunteers and run the sessions shortly after winter break. He found four senior volunteers: Cindy, Daniel, and Zach were enrolled in his video games senior elective, and Frank was conducting his senior capstone research project on the educational uses of *Dungeons & Dragons* in middle school.

The play sessions ran across several weeks from February through early March. Because the sessions were conducted with a prototype early build of *New Harvest* that did not include illustrations, Clybor first had the group play the original *Lost & Found* to help them understand how it might look. The next two play sessions were conducted with the *New Harvest* prototype. The final discussion was cancelled due to the school closing in response to the COVID-19 pandemic outbreak. Given the voluntary nature of the play session, Clybor was unable to deliver an introductory lecture or assign outside reading materials. Instead, Clybor and Gottlieb built upon the open-ended approach to lesson planning they had employed in 2019 so that it focused less on what the students were learning in terms of content and more on the types of interactions and behaviors they were exhibiting.

By dint of how the group was chosen, namely for their interest in games and game design, this group expressed more curiosity about the design process than earlier classes. They were also older, which meant that their suppositions and questions were relatively more sophisticated than previous groups. For these reasons, and unlike previous sessions, Clybor explained the project to them in greater detail before the play sessions began, and instead of providing historical context offered them more direct information about the game itself. As a group, the students seemed to take quite seriously their role as "play testers," a role not afforded to the earlier groups because the games were already published. Throughout their play sessions, they repeatedly analyzed the logic behind game mechanics and drew connections between design decisions and the historical processes that the game simulated. One striking example occurred while the students discussed their plans to complete one of the game's "communal responsibilities," building a mosque. When Frank decided that his character, the stone mason, would complete his "Hajj" (pilgrimage to Mecca) family responsibility before the mosque's completion, the group began to suppose how this might work, both in terms of the game and in terms of the simulated game world:

Frank: Ok . . . I'm going to pay all of [the communal responsibility], and . . .

Cindy: Finish your family responsibility?

Frank: Finish my family responsibility. (*Looks at card and misreads it*) My heritage.

Zach: You mean Hajj?

Frank: (*Correcting himself*) The Hajj . . .

Zach: (*Interrupts*) It's a pilgrimage.
(*Group discussion continues*)

Frank: (*Reading card*) Player cannot contribute to crises and disasters until the end of their next turn.

Cindy: All can't?

Daniel: No, [Frank] can't!

Zach: (*Gasps*) Because you're off in Mecca! (*In a motherly voice*) Have fun in Mecca, sweetie!
(*The game continues and* Frank *takes his next turn*)

Frank: "While I'm away on my pilgrimage I can still pay for [family and community responsibilities] right? . . . I'm just immune to disasters and crises."

Daniel: "Well you are immune, but the community isn't. And if you come back and the community is dead . . . you're in a bit of trouble."

Frank: "But I can still pay for a mosque and stuff."

Zach (*laughing*): "Our mason [Frank] is gonna pick up a boulder out in the desert and chuck it! That would be a *problem* more than it would *help* build a mosque!"

When the conversation shifted to funding the "doctor" community responsibility first, to make the mosque cost less to fund, Clybor asked the group why they thought a doctor would have that effect:

Cindy: I don't know . . .

Zach (*interrupting*): Well if our mason is chucking boulders from miles away, I think we've got our answer!

Here, and at several other points during their play sessions, the students are demonstrating a creative levity while making strong connections between game rules and the enacting of Islamic religious and legal expectations in the twelfth century in Fustat. At other times, their tendency to rationalize game play in terms of historical phenomena led them to over-attribute certain game rules and mechanics that were necessary abstractions from a design perspective – often due to playtime constraints (see Gottlieb and Schreiber 2020a and 2020b). At one point, they began comparing the cost of building a mosque in *New Harvest* to the cost of building a synagogue in *Lost & Found*, and drew spurious conclusions about the cultures and socio-economic status of Jewish and Muslim communities. In this instance and every other, they did not once express the possibility that certain rules or design decisions might not be accurate reflections of the historical past, nor did they do so at any other time throughout their three sessions of play. Gilbert noted what appears to be a similar phenomenon in her study of her use of *Assassin's Creed* with high school history students:

> students perceived so many positives in their emotional engagement with Assassin's Creed that they often uncritically trusted that their gameplay experiences translated to real insight about the lived experiences of people in the past. Even as they theorized about the historical accuracy of Assassin's Creed, they often did so in a way that evidenced a great deal of trust in Ubisoft's game designers.[23]

Gilbert also points to Lynch, Mallon, and Connolly, who:

> [F]ound that students improved their knowledge of the historical event but benefitted from debriefing to clarify which game characters were historical figures and which were fictional. The researchers concluded that there is an 'absolute necessity for post-game reflective discussions to take place in order to disentangle factual and fictional elements and complement the learning experience.'[24]

Similarly, Gottlieb had found that in training educators to use mobile augmented reality games for teaching history, discussion following play was necessary to disentangle historical fiction and fact within a situated documentary. This was key even when distinguishing markers were placed in the game to differentiate moments of historical fiction.[25]

Perhaps the students' emotional engagement was the cause of their misattribution in our *Lost & Found* sessions, or perhaps their self-understanding as playtesters led them to exaggerate the particular level of historical fidelity available to the game design process (*Lost & Found* has high fidelity on legal and material culture and more abstraction of economic systems in order to allow for

---

[23] Gilbert, "Assassin's Creed Reminds Us That History Is Human Experience," 12.
[24] Gilbert, "Assassin's Creed Reminds Us That History Is Human Experience," 5; Cf., R. Lynch, Bride Mallon, and C. Connolly, "The Pedagogical Application of Alternate Reality Games: Using Game-Based Learning to Revisit History," *Int. J. Game Based Learn* 5 (2015): 35, https://doi.org/10.4018/ijgbl.2015040102.
[25] Owen Gottlieb, "Who Really Said What? Mobile Historical Situated Documentary as Liminal Learning Space," *gamevironments*, no. 5 (December 29, 2016): 237–57.

play within the time of a class period).[26] Whatever the reason, we were able to catch these misattributions only because Clybor was in direct conversation with Gottlieb, the game's co-designer, and therefore had intimate knowledge of the design process. Gottlieb knew that the decision regarding the cost of the mosque was made primarily for game play as opposed to specific economic models and even went back and checked his hunch with Ian Schreiber, his collaborator and core mechanics designer, and confirmed this to be the case.

During our conversations, Clybor raised the issue of this being a problem of media literacy and Gottlieb agreed, having written previously on teaching about the constructed nature of historical narratives through the use of historical fiction in games.[27] Gottlieb and Schreiber had also, more recently, published design research regarding such decision-making while designing history games, noting that the level of model fidelity in the *Lost & Found* series was often bounded by the target play time – a game using a high-fidelity economic model of Fustat in the twelfth century would take many hours to play.[28]

Clybor suggested, and Gottlieb readily agreed, that part of the curriculum moving forward, and perhaps for other history games, should include opportunities for students to identify and critically engage the boundaries between the historical research on which games are based and other types of designer intentions, such as making games engaging or fitting within a certain playtime constraint. Could we explore disentangling facts from game design decisions? Central to historical thinking is the ability to engage, analyze, appraise, and interpret different representations of the historical past from a broad range of sources, and much of what students learn about history today often comes from popular media. Understanding game design thus seems essential to understanding the possibilities and limitations of historical representation in games. Moving forward with the curriculum design, we plan to attend to the importance of media literacy in general, and game-design literacy in particular, as part of using game and other historical fictions and believe this is a key opportunity for developing historical thinking.

---

26 See: Owen Gottlieb and Ian Schreiber, "Lost & Found: New Harvest," *Initiative in Religion, Culture, and Policy, MAGIC Spell Studios*, January 1, 2020, https://scholarworks.rit.edu/other/947.
27 Gottlieb, "Who Really Said What?" 2016.
28 See: Owen Gottlieb and Ian Schreiber, "Designing Analog Learning Games: Genre Affordances, Limitations, and Multi-Game Approaches," in *Rerolling Boardgames*, ed. Esther MacCallum-Steward and Douglas Brown (McFarland Press, 2020), 195–211; Owen Gottlieb and Ian Schreiber, "Acts of Meaning, Resource Diagrams, and Essential Learning Behaviors: The Design Evolution of Lost & Found," *International Journal of Designs for Learning* 11, no. 1 (February 5, 2020): 151–64, https://doi.org/10.14434/ijdl.v11i1.24100.

Reflections, Curricular Design Decisions, and Looking Ahead

Over the three years, while there were numerous design decisions that we made over the course of exploring and iterating our curricular approaches, three broader sets of design decisions crystallized for us from our observations and reflections. During the first sessions in 2018, students appeared to be engaging with their role in the game and the procedures they had to enact during game play. We theorized that a shift from emphasis on content synthesis to an historical empathy approach might take best advantage of student affect, engagement, and caring. This would mean de-emphasizing broader lectures and textbook readings on the period, and instead shifting to a greater focus on material that would specifically leverage gameplay (in this case, the primary *Mishneh Torah* legal text). In so doing, and with guided reflection, we would hope this focus could better facilitate historical thinking as students link their game experiences, especially their cognitive and affective responses to game mechanics and systems, back to the historical material. As our thinking moved in this direction, and as we headed into the 2019 iteration, Clybor shortened the background lecture and increased time spent on the *Mishneh Torah* text.

When analyzing our 2019 iteration in preparation for 2020, we noted that certain students demonstrated engagement in competition through skill deployment, including student argumentation and reasoning. Clybor suggested we enhance relevant skill development across the class prior to deploying the game. Although shifts in Clybor's teaching load and the outbreak of the pandemic prevented us from implementing this approach, it resonates with how game design theorists deploy Csikszentmihalyi's work on Flow theory: in order to get deeply absorbed in performance in an activity while performing at a high level, one must have a base level of skill and receive feedback on that skill deployment.[29] In the case of *Order in the Court*, the legal reasoning game, this suggested providing additional and expanded scaffolded example cases to practice the process of building a reasoned case prior to competitive play, or perhaps even between sessions. *Order in the Court* comes with an example case in the rule book, but Clybor suggested more in-depth and repeated practice, ideally with primary source documents. We believe we can better take advantage of engagement across more of the class by raising students' base-level historical thinking skills to improve their gameplay, thereby developing and enhancing their ability to compete. With

---

29 Mihaly Csikszentmihalyi, *Flow: The Psychology of Optimal Experience*, 1st HarperPerennial ed. (New York: HarperPerennial, 1991).

incentives to use the material in play, the students should also retain the material better. We would also expect to see improvements in the quality of their legal reasoning in a historical context. We would need to balance their enhanced skill performance and competition with the need to maintain spontaneity, humor, and playfulness. In the judging role, players can still select for humor, and so based on the playtest with undergraduates, we suspect the high school groups will moderate the competition with humor. If historical thinking is an "unnatural act" for students, silliness certainly is not, especially with a game oriented towards generating humorous answers.

We would need to see how this approach plays out in the classroom. If more scaffolding assists in developing better reasoned legal cases in the context of the historical legal system, it would be a significant advancement for use of the game in the classroom. Boosting perspective taking and simulating period specific, contextualized thinking through the affective experience of operating within a system of game mechanics and rules may also lead to overcoming, or at least recognizing, presentism in a way that would circle back to Endacott and Brooks' dual dimensional understanding of historical empathy.[30] Such an enhanced curriculum could allow for cognitive perspective recognition to reinforce a stronger affective connection while a stronger affective experience in gameplay could reinforce cognitive perspective recognition. Such a recognition of presentism would of course require educator-guided reflection on issues of presentism. To help develop increasing understanding of the specific milieu, the educator can also leverage the game's own "explanation" sides of the card as a reveal by reminding students to turn over the "explanation" at the end of each turn. Each round then can advance understanding of the particular historical context, which should also assist in pointing out the risks of presentism.

By 2020, the third area of design shift for us was towards media literacy, and specifically in this case, literacy regarding game design. Through a better understanding of how designers make choices in their representations of the historical past, students may be able to directly apply historical thinking and historical thinking skills to analysing game environments. Games for which there is access to designer interviews, publications, or statements could be key extra-textual sources. In the case of *Lost & Found*, such material already exists and can be leveraged by educators. For example, students could be assigned the designer article: "Acts of Meaning, Resource Diagrams, and Essential Learning Behaviors:

---

[30] Endacott and Brooks, "An Updated Theoretical and Practical Model for Promoting Historical Empathy," 2013, 41–58.

The Design Evolution of *Lost & Found*."[31] Alongside an analysis of the primary source material, the *Mishneh Torah*, educators could engage students in reflection about historical representations and how game designer decisions impact choices in the portrayal of history, economic systems, and cultural milieu. Such decisions could be further used to analyze how historical narratives are constructed more broadly, something Gottlieb has explored in a mobile phone GPS "situated" documentary.[32] This approach could further leverage research and scholarship in teaching history with other media such as Marcus, Metzger, Paxton, and Stoddard's work in teaching history with cinema.[33]

In terms of future research and design, we are planning to use these three broader design decisions to orient the classroom curriculum. From a research perspective, we would test the theories, using instruments such as pre-and post-tests, semi-structured interviews, analysis of talk practices and artifacts developed by students. From a design perspective, we would iterate the curriculum, working towards more refined lesson plans which we could share with the broader community via the *Lost & Found* website so that other history teachers can benefit from our explorations. Our hope is that through sharing this design case and exploration that other designers and educators may be able to benefit from the steps we have taken thus far, perhaps leveraging more media literacy, expanded targeted skill scaffolding, and taking advantage of engagement for focus on historical empathy – both cognitive and affective. We believe games as a medium offer some particular affordances for teaching history, such as active role play, modelling and analyzing procedural social and economic systems and emulating group or community dynamics. We are excited to be a part of this growing set of practices of games in the history classroom and hope that our explorations help expand and deepen those practices.

Bibliography

Barton, Keith C., and Linda S. Levstik. *Teaching History for the Common Good*. New York: Routledge, 2004. https://doi.org/10.4324/9781410610508.

Boling, Elizabeth. "The Need for Design Cases: Disseminating Design Knowledge." *International Journal of Designs for Learning* 1, no. 1 (2010). https://doi.org/10.14434/ijdl.v1i1.919.

---

[31] Gottlieb and Schreiber, "Acts of Meaning, Resource Diagrams, and Essential Learning Behaviors."
[32] Gottlieb, "Who Really Said What?"
[33] Alan S. Marcus et al., *Teaching History with Film: Strategies for Secondary Social Studies* (Routledge, 2010), https://getit.library.nyu.edu/go/5900661.

Brooks, Sarah. "Historical Empathy in the Social Studies Classroom: A Review of the Literature." *Journal of Social Studies Research* 33, no. 2 (Fall 2009): 213–34.

Csikszentmihalyi, Mihaly. *Flow: The Psychology of Optimal Experience*. 1st HarperPerennial ed. New York: HarperPerennial, 1991.

(DBRC) The Design-Based Research Collective. "Design-Based Research: An Emerging Paradigm for Educational Inquiry." *Educational Researcher* 32, no. 1 (January 1, 2003): 5–8. https://doi.org/10.3102/0013189X032001005.

Endacott, Jason L. "Reconsidering Affective Engagement in Historical Empathy." *Theory & Research in Social Education* 38, no. 1 (January 1, 2010): 6–47. https://doi.org/10.1080/00933104.2010.10473415.

Endacott, Jason L., and Sarah Brooks. "An Updated Theoretical and Practical Model for Promoting Historical Empathy." *Social Studies Research and Practice* 8, no. 1 (2013): 41–58.

Endacott, Jason L., and Sarah Brooks. "Historical Empathy: Perspectives and Responding to the Past." In *The Wiley International Handbook of History Teaching and Learning*, edited by Scott Alan Metzger and Lauren McArthur Harris, 203–25. John Wiley & Sons, 2018. https://onlinelibrary.wiley.com/doi/book/10.1002/9781119100812.

Foster, Stuart. "Using Historical Empathy to Excite Students about the Study of History: Can You Empathize with Neville Chamberlain?" *The Social Studies* 90, no. 1 (January 1, 1999): 18–24. https://doi.org/10.1080/00377999909602386.

Foster, Stuart J., and Elizabeth Anne Yeager. "The Role of Empathy in the Development of Historical Understanding." *International Journal of Social Education* 13, no. 1 (1998): 1–7.

Frantzman, Seth J. "To Pray Where Maimonides Prayed." The Jerusalem Post | JPost.com, February 14, 2017. https://www.jpost.com/diaspora/to-pray-where-maimonides-prayed-481462.

Fullerton, Tracy. *Game Design Workshop: A Playcentric Approach to Creating Innovative Games, Third Edition*. 3 edition. Boca Raton: A K Peters/CRC Press, 2014.

Gee, James Paul. "Stories, Probes, and Games." *Narrative Inquiry* 21, no. 2 (2011): 353–57. https://doi.org/10.1075/ni.21.2.14gee.

Gee, James Paul. *What Video Games Have to Teach Us About Learning and Literacy. Second Edition: Revised and Updated Edition*. 2nd ed. Philadelphia, PA: Palgrave Macmillan, 2007.

Gilbert, Lisa. "'Assassin's Creed Reminds Us That History Is Human Experience': Students' Senses of Empathy While Playing a Narrative Video Game." *Theory & Research in Social Education* 47, no. 1 (January 2, 2019): 108–37. https://doi.org/10.1080/00933104.2018.1560713.

Gottlieb, Owen. "Time Travel, Labour History, and the Null Curriculum: New Design Knowledge for Mobile Augmented Reality History Games." *International Journal of Heritage Studies*, 24, no. 3 (2017): 1–13.

Gottlieb, Owen. "Who Really Said What? Mobile Historical Situated Documentary as Liminal Learning Space." *Gamevironments*, no. 5 (December 29, 2016): 237–57.

Gottlieb, Owen, and Ian Schreiber. "Acts of Meaning, Resource Diagrams, and Essential Learning Behaviors: The Design Evolution of Lost & Found." *International Journal of Designs for Learning* 11, no. 1 (2020): 151–64. https://doi.org/10.14434/ijdl.v11i1.24100.

Gottlieb, Owen, and Ian Schreiber. "Designing Analog Learning Games: Genre Affordances, Limitations and Multi-Game Approaches." In *Rerolling Boardgames: Essays on Themes, Systems, Experiences, and Ideologies*, edited by Douglas Brown and Esther MacCallum-

Stewart, 195–211. McFarland & Company, Inc., 2020. https://scholarworks.rit.edu/article/1900.
Howard, Craig D. "Writing and Rewriting the Instructional Design Case: A View from Two Sides." *International Journal of Designs for Learning* 2, no. 1 (2011). http://scholarworks.dlib.indiana.edu/journals/index.php/ijdl/article/view/1104.
Lévesque, Stéphane. *Thinking Historically: Educating Students for the Twenty-First Century. Thinking Historically: Educating Students for the Twenty-First Century.* Toronto: University of Toronto Press, 2008.
Lynch, R., Bride Mallon, and C. Connolly. "The Pedagogical Application of Alternate Reality Games: Using Game-Based Learning to Revisit History." *Int. J. Game Based Learn.* 5 (2015): 18–38. https://doi.org/10.4018/ijgbl.2015040102.
Marcus, Alan S., Scott Alan Metzger, Richard J. Paxton, and Jeremy D. Stoddard. *Teaching History with Film: Strategies for Secondary Social Studies.* Routledge, 2010. https://getit.library.nyu.edu/go/5900661.
Mills, Geoffrey. *Action Research: A Guide for the Teacher Researcher.* 6th edition. New York, NY: Pearson, 2017.
Nokes, Jeffrey. *Building Students' Historical Literacies: Learning to Read and Reason with Historical Texts and Evidence.* New York: Routledge, 2012.
Seixas, P. "A Model of Historical Thinking." Educational Philosophy and Thinking 49, no. 6 (2015): 1–13. http://dx.doi.org/10.1080/00131857.2015.1101363. NOTE: the publisher and Google Scholar citing of this article only in 2017 is inconsistent with the print edition cited here. The publisher lists a 2017 date and different page numbers, and Google Scholar's citation system, as of February 17, 2022, lists a "review" of the article. Here, we revert to the printed article for clarity of bibliographical tracking.
Smith, Kennon M. "Producing the Rigorous Design Case." *International Journal of Designs for Learning* 1, no. 1 (2010). https://doi.org/10.14434/ijdl.v1i1.917.
Touger, Rabbi Eliyahu. *Rambam Mishneh Torah: Sefer Nezikin.* Brooklyn, NY: Moznaim Publishing, 1997.
VanSledright, Bruce. "From Empathetic Regard to Self-Understanding: Im/Positionality, Empathy, and Historical Contextualizations." In *Historical Empathy and Perspective Taking in the Social Studies*, edited by O. L. Davis Jr., E. A. Yeager, and S. J. Foster, 51–68. Lanham, MD: Rowman & Littlefield Publishers, 2001.
Wineburg, Sam. *Historical Thinking and Other Unnatural Acts: Charting the Future of Teaching the Past.* Critical Perspectives On The Past edition. Philadelphia: Temple University Press, 2002.

Ludography

Attentat 1942. Charles Games, 2017.
Gottlieb, Owen. "Lost & Found: New Harvest." *Initiative in Religion, Culture, and Policy, MAGIC Spell Studios*, January 1, 2020. https://scholarworks.rit.edu/other/947.

Gottlieb, Owen. "Lost & Found: Order in the Court – The Party Game." *Initiative in Religion, Culture, and Policy, MAGIC Spell Studios*, January 1, 2017. https://scholarworks.rit.edu/other/903.

Gottlieb, Owen, Ian Schreiber, and Kelly Murdoch-Kitt. "Lost & Found." *Initiative in Religion, Culture, and Policy, MAGIC Spell Studios*, January 1, 2017. https://scholarworks.rit.edu/other/904.

Svoboda 1945: Liberation. Charles Games, 2021.

Courtnay Konshuh and Frank Klaassen
8 The Renaissance Marriage Game: A Simulation Game for Large Classes

Abstract: This chapter describes the creation and implementation of a large-scale simulation game (30–120 students) based on familial interactions and competition around the arrangement of marriages in the Italian Renaissance. It considers the challenges associated with the delivery of a game of this sort alongside the substantial learning potential offered by this approach. It provides reflection on the use of the game in practice and considers the ways in which it – and similar games – may be deployed more effectively in the future. Ultimately, the chapter makes a case for the use of games as a learning tool and offers a general model for the development of such large-scale games.

Introduction

One of the challenges in a medieval or civilization survey is how to innovate on the traditional mode of teaching sweeping histories of the West. A way of helping students to engage is to focus on a specific event, place or custom, to allow for a more in-depth understanding of a particular aspect of the Middle Ages. Ideally, such focus can also depart from the traditional lecture format and incorporate experiential learning, transforming students from passive receivers of information to active learners who more deliberately encounter and interact with class content. For the Middle Ages and Renaissance in particular, such strategies can help students to access cultures which are temporarily and geographically far removed from their own.[1] Historical gaming allows modern day players or students to engage more directly with the past,[2] creating a kind of escapism where they can abandon contemporary convention in order to follow the "rules" of the past. Games and simulations develop students' critical thinking and ability to synthesize, precisely the goal most of us have when teaching a medieval survey. In particular, a good means of teaching is via a simulation game: "a rule-based, artificial conflict or competition that simulates dynamically

---
[1] Kisha Tracy, "Introduction: Medievalists on the Pedagogical Edge," *Studies in Medieval and Renaissance Teaching* 25 (2017): 7.
[2] Adam Chapman et al., "Introduction: What is Historical Game Studies?" *Rethinking History* 21 (2017): 360.

one or more real-world systems."[3] Through story-telling and decision-making, students can begin to explore how people in the Middle Ages would have acted by being put in the same situations and interacting with others.

It is difficult to explore social phenomena, taking into account economic, social, and cultural factors, in-depth in a survey class. A simulation game can be set up to replicate a village, or a subsection of an entire society, and works even for a large body of students as is often found in a survey course. Emphasis is placed on choice; each student interacts with a simulation of the past and chooses how they would act in order to achieve the set goals. It is precisely with this individual freedom that a narrative-based game provides students where it is seen that "user control over the environment is an important indicator of cognitive gain."[4] This helps students of all backgrounds to put themselves into a past context where they must consider the factors motivating human choice in the past scenario, and develops historical skills of critiquing both past actions and modern representations of these. It is to these ends that we created the Renaissance Marriage Simulation, which we further developed (and gamified) into a Simulation Game.

The Renaissance Marriage Simulation Game is situated in a fictional Italian town and simulates the process of finding godparents and subsequently marriage partners or other suitable positions for one's children. Families work with varying financial and social resources and children of varying numbers, sexes, characteristics, and personalities. They have to quickly close deals that will best benefit their family in a highly competitive, rumor ridden, and potentially violent marketplace. Unlike most board games which are meant for groups of eight or less, this game can be played in very large survey classes of more than 100 students as well as moderately sized classes of 25 or 30. Actual game-play takes about two hours, although time for introducing the game and debriefing afterwards are both recommended, pushing the required time closer to three hours. It is noisy, tumultuous, and unpredictable and has inspired a high level of student engagement described in one review as a "fire of energy." One student review describes it as having an atmosphere of "havoc and panic" forcing families to "scheme and connive." Another student referred to it in an anonymous review as "a mosh-pit, free-for-all episode of the Bachelorette." In short, it has many valuable and genuinely unusual qualities, but we are still working to get it right.

---

[3] Jeremiah McCall, "Navigating the Problem Space: The Medium of Simulation Games in the Teaching of History," *The History Teacher* 46 (2012): 9.

[4] Sean Gouglas et al., "Abort, Retry, Pass, Fail: Games as Teaching Tools," in *Pastplay: Teaching and Learning History with Technology*, ed. Kevin Kee (Ann Arbor, MI: University of Michigan Press, 2014), 129.

Creating a game is a little like writing an article or book in the sense that it is never perfect. Instead, the development process simply has to be arbitrarily terminated at some point. But unlike books, games can be enjoyed in their various iterations, and unlike commercial games, educational games can be tinkered with . . . endlessly. The Renaissance Marriage Game has been in a process of evolution for nearly 20 years, having begun as a classroom simulation developed by Frank Klaassen. The most dramatic process of development began five years ago as we transformed it into a game and then struggled to find a formulation that included the engaging and rewarding mechanisms of gameplay, retained its modular and expandable nature, but found it was also uncomplicated enough to make classroom use manageable. We are not there yet. But these qualities have made it worth coming back to numerous times.

This article thus offers two principal things. It introduces readers to a game model which works well for large classes. This makes it quite unusual and potentially very useful for others as they seek to develop games. This article also plots a development process, in particular our struggles in balancing what is perhaps the core tension of a successful game: a balance between interesting complexity (that allows for multiple strategies), understandable simplicity (that makes a game reasonably easy to learn and run), and engaging mechanics that draw players in. To put it another way, we hope it will save others from the mistakes we have made; in particular, straying too far into the quagmire of complexity is to be avoided at all costs!

In a broader sense, we also hope this article will encourage readers who have not done so to consider developing games for classroom use and also to take the risk of using classroom play as part of the development process.[5] Despite the fact that we have never gotten it right, and have taken some genuine missteps, the Renaissance Marriage Simulation Game has made for a lot of fun and has been a valuable element in our teaching, an experience that students remember and carry with them.

---

[5] In his set of practical guidelines, Jeremiah McCall recommends risk-taking in designing simulation games: Jeremiah McCall, "Simulation Games and the Study of the Past: Classroom Guidelines," in *Pastplay: Teaching and Learning History with Technology*, ed. Kevin Kee (Ann Arbor, MI: University of Michigan Press, 2014): 228–53.

Successes and Takeaways

As this paper seeks to provide practical advice on developing a modular simulation game we will begin with our general conclusions. Evidence for the conclusions follow below.
- Games such as this are valuable ways of developing *esprit de corps* within large classes.
- Don't be too quick to try to smooth out the rough edges of a game. Inefficiencies or bottlenecks may actually add tension and be valuable elements in a game.
- Don't be afraid of a little chaos, particularly if the game is meant to imitate real life.
- Don't be afraid to test out games in the classroom. Although there is a percentage of students who genuinely don't like games, only a few were ever vocal about it. Most students are willing to engage and may give valuable feedback. This also seems to increase engagement and critical historical evaluation of the game, and game-shy students are more receptive of games when they are encouraged to critique them as representations of history.[6]
- Be careful not to make your games too complicated.
- A modular-team system makes it possible to run a single game in a large class.
- Non-engagement was relatively low (perhaps 5%).
- Working in teams not only helps to mitigate the need to explain the rules – students learn by doing and any blunders they make are an important part of the learning process.

Basic Game Elements

The basic elements of the game have not changed a great deal so let us begin by describing them. At the beginning of the game groups of players of two to five people are given a description of their family and a sign with their family name on it to put on their home desk. The family description includes both hard and soft elements. There are hard limits such as what they can spend without going into debt. Some details are more negotiable such as the size of dowry they should expect to accompany a wife of their son. There are also a range of soft or anecdotal elements such as the family story, reputation and character as well as those of the children. The following is an example of one of the family descriptions.

---

6 McCall, "Navigating the Problem Space," 24.

Table 8.1: The Nardi Family.

Family:	Dante and Elanora Nardi
Status:	Middle
Disposable wealth:	fl. 450,000
Minimum dowry acceptable for marriage with son (without shame):	fl. 125,000
Daughters:	**Beatrice** – very pious **Paula** – very pious, decidedly not interested in marriage
Sons:	**Taddeo** – good-natured but with a bad temper
Family History and Reputation:	Dante has held important administrative posts in the city government but the family has fallen on bad times recently in business. The family income has been substantially reduced. It is known as well that the father's brother is quite mad and so there are concerns that mental illness may run in the family.

The families are grouped into three status levels (high-medium-low). The numbers of such families used in any game can be easily varied depending upon the size of the class. We have played with as few as ten and as many as 20.

In addition to the families, we have also included some wild-card characters: an Archbishop, the abbot of a Syneisactic Monastery, and the Confraternity of the Blessed Mary Magdalene. On occasion the Monastery and the Confraternity have been played by the instructor. The Monastery seeks both monks and nuns and expects cash payments in order to accept them. The Confraternity provides dowries for worthy girls from less privileged families. Those who make cash donations become voting members able to decide on whether a particular young woman should receive help. The Archbishop has been a consistent and highly entertaining presence in the game. He is described as follows and, as one might expect, a student (or group of students) with a flair for the dramatic is usually the best choice to play this role.

The game is conducted in a large room with each family having a home location to receive guests. There are two principal stages in game play: finding godparents and negotiating marriages or other positions. Each of these have typically been 50 minutes in length. Laws of consanguinity will prevent marrying one's children to the children of their godparents, so they must be chosen with careful attention to status and also potential future marriage prospects. Being a godparent brings honor as does getting a good one for your child(ren). Godparents and

Table 8.2: Archbishop Armando.

Archbishop Armando	Although there were many dedicated, indeed holy, churchmen in the period, Archbishop Armando is burdened with no particular dedication to anything except money and power. He is still paying off the massive bribes he had to pay to get his position so he is cash poor, but he is rich in the opportunities he can offer and needs to take full advantage of this situation. He can expect to receive substantial bribes in return for securing church offices. These offices bring high status to the family that gets them and in turn the family can expect to benefit from their son's position (e.g. through political influence and other offices for other family members). He can spread rumors without fear of reprisal particularly if he has some "incentive." Offices that he can "help" to acquire are: – one Bishopric (a very high-status position); – two positions as Papal Secretary (a moderately high-status position); and – four priestly benefices (reasonably respectable church incomes which will give sons the opportunity to take university training and to build ecclesiastical careers). Naturally, those who take these positions cannot marry.

marriage partners are chosen to get the greatest possible advantages in status, honor, and wealth as possible. Families also may make contributions to the monastery, church, or the town to cement their position or gain honor.

A final destabilizing principle is the option to spread rumor or respond violently to affronts to honor. During the course of the game, rumors may be spread against other families and members of other families may be assassinated. The outcome of these actions is determined by a roll of the dice and may rebound upon the instigator. The Archbishop (assuming he wishes to do so) will be successful in any rumors he spreads. The rumours bring dishonor on the families they target and may interrupt negotiations for marriage or offices.

The game is thus complex, including a mix of soft, negotiable, and hard elements. The timeline is tight and the possibility of descending into bribery, rumor mongering, or violence is ever present. There is also a fairly significant potential for role-playing although not all the characters have quite the dramatic qualities of the Archbishop. A final aspect of the game which reflects real life is that some families are significantly better off than others. This may be a matter of having only modest resources and four daughters. Families may also be burdened with poor reputations.

Game Development

In its first incarnation as a role-playing simulation, the game was reasonably successful. Students engaged with significant enthusiasm and it was thus worth repeating in numerous classes over the years. It formed the basis for useful discussions about social history and served as a nice break from lectures. Perhaps just as critically, students got to know each other. Prior to the game, classes were commonly quiet as they assembled with students sitting in silence or engaging in muted discussions. Following the game it was often difficult to bring the class to order for a lecture. The pedagogical value of being part of a cohort is well established and so it contributed significantly to the experience of the class. It also gave the instructor a chance to get to know some of the students, which is quite difficult in groups of 50 or more.

Despite these successes there were some ongoing challenges. It was not possible to provoke the well-known dowry inflation that characterized the period. This should have added significant anxiety and challenge to the game. Instead, students negotiated marriages for amounts often well below market value because they were worried about the short timeline. They then dumped their remaining resources into charitable donations. This was an entirely reasonable strategy within the game, but (as fun as they were) these initial iterations did not accurately represent even this very basic aspect of the marriage market. In addition, students rarely took advantage of the options to spread rumors and never of the option for violent attack. Finally, assessing a winner was quite difficult. It fell to the instructor to informally choose families who had stood out for their willingness to engage, but it was very hard to assess their strategies and actions because it was impossible to see everything that was going on.

Our decision to gamify the simulation was motivated by a desire to address these issues. A system of progress, like levels or points, can be a pedagogical tool to correct and reward appropriate game strategies, which in turn leads to greater engagement.[7] We settled on a point system in which families would lose points for accepting a lower than market value dowry or for marrying below their status but would gain "honor points" for high dowries or high-status marriages. Charitable donations, for example, would also bring them "piety points." In so doing, we also hoped to remove the instructor from the position of judge and to make winning a matter of points.

---

7 Rowan Tulloch, "Reconceptualising Gamification: Play and Pedagogy," *Digital Culture & Education* 6, no. 4 (2014): 325.

We adapted the Florentine *Ricordanze / libri di famiglia*[8] so each family could record their actions. *Ricordanze* were merchant-family record books, almost diaries, which recorded both financial accounts and family events, such as betrothals and marriages. This gave students a game tracker, was useful for monitoring their progress and engagement (even attendance), and was immersive besides. We also used it to verify transactions and their legality in disputes, of which there were many, and ultimately to determine final scores.

By some measures this was fabulously successful. Student engagement was dramatically improved. The competition in the marriage marketplace was decidedly higher and more frantic. The use of rumor and even violence increased noticeably (and at times the violence actually got out of hand). In one game a truly evil Archbishop cyclically took bribes for arranging appointments and then promptly had the person she had appointed assassinated so that she could take more bribes for the same position. The success could also be measured with a noise meter. Even as a simulation we had sometimes disturbed classes in adjacent classrooms, but with these changes noise became a serious problem.

Once again, our successes were tempered by failures. We had made one of the most common errors in game development by getting carried away with complex mechanics. First, we decided to have a double system of honor and piety points to recognize different sorts of families and family strategies. Honor was associated more with status and civic actions, piety with acts of charity. Second, we also found that our game reflected social realities too closely. It was all too easy for the wealthy to gain more honor and piety and thereby to win the game. In order to compensate for this, we introduced a system of handicaps which only made the game more complex. Even after multiple iterations of the game we are only marginally closer to making the game fair and something that any family can win. We would have had to play-test the game scores of times in a controlled setting in order to come up with something workable.

We also decided these points should be tallied in real-time so that students would know who was winning, thereby increasing tension. In early iterations students had to register their interactions with a notary (the instructor) who would tally the resulting honor and piety points and keep a running total. This was cumbersome and there was often a long line of students waiting to have their deals notarized. In order to compensate for this we attempted to create a real-time points calculator in a spreadsheet but we found we were very much at

---

[8] Julius Kirshner, *Marriage, Dowry and Citizenship in Late Medieval and Renaissance Italy* (Toronto: University of Toronto Press, 2015), 5.

the mercy of the technology. The programming for a dependable system would not have been that complicated but it would have been time consuming; requiring someone from IT to be on hand is not feasible for multiple iterations (or for new lecturers learning this game). More critically, it was not a particularly challenging project and so there was no value in it for a student or grad student from computer science unless they were to be well compensated and we did not have the financial resources for that.

A final version of the game employed tokens in lieu of a mechanical system of point taking. We also simplified the *ricordanze* process with a form that included checkboxes to make things as easy as possible. The idea was that the honor and piety points would be tallied at the middle and end of the game. This solved some of the problems but involved a huge amount of preparation time. It also remained overly complicated not least because we retained the division of piety and honor points.

This highlights a final issue already alluded to which is the direct correlation between game complexity and instructor over-work. The fact that this has been a shared project for many years now has certainly reduced the required preparation time, but it remains that it is much easier to prepare lectures for the 150–180 minutes of class-time this game replaces. We are now wiser and working towards a simplified version, one which will demand somewhat less work for the instructor.

A Few Key Successes

All of this discussion of our efforts to deal with what went wrong "under the hood" runs the risk of misrepresenting student experiences of the game and its impact on learning and the learning environment. It is important to re-emphasize the successes we listed at the start of this section and to emphasize that the gamified version drove student engagement up considerably. The combination of role-playing and an explicit points system was highly successful. No students questioned this combination or the overall conceit of the game, but rather suggested tweaks to the system.

The impact on the classroom social environment was very positive. A significant number of students commented on how much they appreciated getting to know their fellow students and one suggested the game should be run early in the course to improve the overall experience of the course by promoting esprit de corps early on. Of course, this does not only improve the class atmosphere; students work on their teamwork and communication skills by working in this high-stress group environment.⁹ Effective teamwork is required to designate roles for each player to avoid duplicating each other's actions. One team found several husbands for their daughter; the game became unwinnable for them after incurring the ire of their ex-potential in-laws. Students share and listen to theories and ideas, and we often heard heated debates as students discussed the rules, possible gains, morality of a proposed plan, or whether that "would actually have happened." They go through at least two stages of project management by making a plan and putting it into action, hopefully gaining excellent godparents who help and do not hinder their marriage prospects. This not only promotes teamwork but also their social science analysis skills. Additionally, students love moving around the classroom[10] and movement-based learning not only benefits small children, but also adult learners.[11]

A few other successes are also worth emphasizing. The fact that students did not read the rules properly in advance or that they were too complex is a matter worth attending to, but it was not a purely negative factor. The students learned the rules by playing the game and learned about the historical process at the same time.[12] Panic about not knowing what was going on or awareness of the tight time constraints palpably increased the fervor of the gaming process. A fellow educational game enthusiast, our colleague Ben Hoy, sat in on one of the early gamified iterations and commented that it was chaos but chaos that worked. We expressed concern about the line-up for getting the points counted by the instructor. He suggested (and has written about this factor elsewhere) that the stress of having to stand in line might actually be valuable for the game.[13] Our efforts to try to make a spreadsheet to make this faster may actually have detracted from the game by reducing time constraints. In short, as one develops a game it is critical to recognize the complexities of the gaming experience. Efficiency and clear comprehension of the system by the players are not necessarily positive elements. A little chaos can be a good thing and it may be best to embrace it.

---

9 Osvaldo Jiménez, "Leveraging the Social Aspect of Educational Games," *Theory Into Practice* 54, no. 2 (2015): 103.
10 Wendy Rouse, "Lessons Learned While Escaping From a Zombie: Designing a Breakout EDU Game," *The History Teacher* 50, no. 4 (2017): 554.
11 Hildi Nicksic et al., "Move, Think, Learn: Incorporating Physical Activity into the College Classroom," *International Journal of Teaching and Learning in Higher Education* 32, no. 3 (202): 532; Christina Heckman, "Playing the Game: Collaborative Project-Based Learning in the Medieval Literature Classroom," *Studies in Medieval and Renaissance Teaching* 28 (2021): 19.
12 Rowan Tulloch, "Reconceptualising Gamification," 322; Benjamin Hoy, "Teaching History With Custom-Built Board Games," *Simulation and Gaming* 49 (2018): 2.
13 Benjamin Hoy, "Teaching History," 10–11.

Students also enjoyed the game and remained enthusiastic about it despite what we regarded as mechanical or procedural problems. Part of this was simply having a break from lectures, getting to know their fellow students, and the fantasy of role playing. We also explicitly asked the students to reflect on the game mechanics and to provide feedback or built in short assignments in which students were asked to reflect on the extent to which the game reflected social realities or to raise questions about dynamics in the game and their relationship to real social dynamics.[14] As this article demonstrates, this was valuable to us as we developed the game, but more critically, it also seems to have improved student experience and learning. By being quite open with our students that the game was very much in development, students were part of that process and many embraced it enthusiastically, critically engaging with our representation of history.[15] This no doubt helped students to be more forgiving as we figured out how to do it and to enjoy the aspects of the game that did work. It also allowed any failures of the game to be part of the learning process, ways that the game did not represent the social realities discussed in the lectures and readings.

Notes on the Modular and Team Model

The first iterations of the marriage game were done in a large survey class with an average enrolment of 100–120 students. There were 18 families, the archbishop, and the monastery all in teams of five or so. It was quite easy to scale the simulation down for a small college class of 30–35 students. Families were kept to a minimum of three players; in case some students did not attend class and the family would not be represented by a single player. We reduced the number of families from 18 to 10 or 11, which was still a significant enough range of starting positions and possibilities for godparents and marriage.

In general, when teams were large, it became possible for people to not participate, which was not ideal. On the other hand, when they were too small, it was often difficult to manage all the necessary business which includes staying in the home to receive visitors, seeking information from the instructor, spying, or going out to negotiate with other families. Teams of three or four seems ideal, and this size also allows for non-attendance by one member.

---

14 Jiménez, "Leveraging," 103.
15 McCall, "Navigating the Problem Space," 21–23.

Qualitative Feedback: The Classroom surveys

Student feedback was generous and mostly extremely helpful. Based on observations of the classroom, in each iteration of the simulation roughly 95% of students attending were interested and worked with their groups to find good matches for their children. This was easy to judge because if a student did not participate, their group wrote it up in their records (and we could see any stationary student not contributing to the chaos). It must be admitted that writing up their family's situation was one of a series of weekly "briefs" that required low-stakes assignments, but nonetheless students were very happy to describe their strategies, any problems with game mechanics, and suggestions for the future. Very few of these briefs focused on the existing problems we have noted above, and rather focused on cosmetic suggestions, elements of perceived fairness, or creative ideas about how the game could be developed in the future.

Most students did not find it difficult at all to write engaged responses about their game experience, and many responses showed a high level of immersement. There was a high level of identification with the families. The Medicis were almost universally loathed or envied. They were rude and walked around like they owned the classroom, offering their powers to the highest bidders: "I also learned that the Medici inevitably act like the Medici. Using their unparalleled wealth and influence, they began to manipulate other families to serve their own purposes." One of the students who had played the Archbishop described finding "creative strategies to convince, manipulate, and destroy families to work to our benefit. It was terrible and glorious!" The poor families were cautious and approached the richer families carefully. Those families were also more likely to ask us for assistance understanding the rules or suggestions on how to deal with their children. Some were angry about their family's starting parameters, but responded well to the assertion that this game, like life in the Renaissance, was not fair.

Almost all the students referred to "their" sons and daughters and discussed them as though they were real children, even showing emotion for their fictitious children. One student lamented "if given time we would have retaliated but the assassination [of their daughter] came as a shock and we were unable to respond." Another interesting factor was that such incidents as assassinated children could lead to sanguine responses ("she was married by that time, so she wasn't our problem anymore"), or to emotional retaliation which was unlikely to help them succeed in the game.

Many of the smaller suggestions came from this context – students sought ways to make the game even more immersive. Such suggestions focused not on game mechanics, but aesthetics. They wanted, for example, to have a sign with a coat of arms or some sort of symbol representing their family. They wanted individual names within their families, and name tags so they could advertise their identities to others. These suggestions could be implemented piecemeal over time.

Many of the complaints derived from students "not playing according to the rules" and the students desired either 1) that they had better understood the rules prior to playing, or 2) that there had been more oversight so that other students could not "cheat." The complexity of the rules came up in many student responses. A very common complaint was that they would have played differently from the start had they understood the rules properly; however, most who made this complaint acknowledged that they could have read the rules in advance and this might have helped. Our impression was that most students did not read the rules in advance, and this did not detract from the gaming experience; on the contrary, learning by playing is exactly what made this active learning experience so effective. Several students even remarked that better preparation probably would not have helped, because "the activity required experience to fully understand."

Many students found loopholes in our rules or exploited each other's lack of understanding of the rules. Any historical inaccuracies resulting from our loopholes need not be viewed as deficiencies; when students note these errors, they critique our representation of history.[16] Students were of course unhappy to have been taken advantage of, but in class discussion afterwards they often came to see such situations as reflecting genuine problems that would have been present in the Renaissance. For example, one student described at length how her family had arranged a marriage with another family and even paid them the dowry, only to find their daughter had been assassinated before they could get the marriage recorded. The other family, who this student suspected was responsible for the assassination, refused to return the dowry and even found a witness willing to lie and say they had seen the negotiation and no dowry had been paid. This student was quite upset that there was no way to bring this family to justice and suggested there be more moderators to prevent this situation; however, when we discussed this in class it was agreed that unless these arrangements were properly witnessed, there would have been room for exactly this sort of treachery in the sixteenth century. Interestingly, this same student then went on to use the same trick against a different family to recoup their losses.

---

16 McCall, "Navigating the Problem Space," 21.

Finally, we had some genuinely creative ideas. Students suggested incorporating more complicated rules, to allow for witch trials and other legal proceedings, or the incorporation of the plague. Other suggestions focused on how to improve mechanics. In the year where we used Google sheets and forms to record marriages, one student spent the weekend after the simulation with the source and edited it so that it would function better next time. When the simulation was held over subsequent years, some students volunteered to act as moderators (or to play again).

One big takeaway, which a significant number of students pointed out and which was very clear to us, was that the class dynamic vastly improved as a result of the simulation. Many students had interacted quite closely with their groups, and in the iterations which were done over three one-hour sessions, some even arranged to speak outside of class to plan their strategy. Each student interacted with many members of other families, and since the timeline was short and they were protected by the relative anonymity of their Italian names, they were much more open about talking to other students they had never seen before. Some formed impromptu alliances with other families or did each other favors. In many classes, one family (often the Medicis but not exclusively) was perceived as acting unfairly, and was targeted by many families, often working together covertly. The archbishop's character influenced the game as well; in some cases a particularly engaged archbishop induced families to conspire against each other, or found ways to help the poorer families find spouses for their children. Particularly in the large lecture, the openness with which students interacted was noticeable. Seating patterns shifted after the simulation and students could be seen working together more closely and sharing notes or forming study groups. Generally, we held the simulation towards the end of the term, but moving it forward might be helpful for student learning across the semester.

In general, the complaints about how the game functioned were minor, and did not significantly impact the student experience. Instead of reading or understanding the rules in advance, students learned as they played, and this is how they came to understand sixteenth century marriage dynamics. Feedback was overwhelmingly positive, and many students wanted to play again, or brought up the simulation as the "best part of the course" in semester evaluations. Some students even reported that family and friends would also be interested in playing, which we found especially gratifying; the simulation was effective enough that they sought to share their learning experience with others. Problems with the game were and continue to be more of a problem for those running the simulation than those playing it.

Possible Next Steps

It may be useful to conclude by indicating where we plan to go next with this simulation game. The key problem we see with the game as it stands is the overly complex point/handicap system. Although this was meant to infuse mechanical subtlety into the game, it simply confused things. It did not make it easier to assess a winner since (as some students observed) the handicap system was pretty ragged. The fact that we expand and contract the game depending on class size also made it impossible for us to assess whether our point handicaps were fair (only many iterations of a stable version of the game would make this possible). Finally, we wanted to address the perceived unfairness of the game. Some students did appreciate the "life's-not-fair" quality of the game but it remains that it did affect some student's enthusiasm. While there is good evidence to suggest that unfair games can be valuable in learning[17] we felt that student engagement for some dropped over the course of two class periods. Moreover, the Renaissance recognized and celebrated the ability of an individual to rise above adversity and even fail heroically. We would like very much to have a game that allows such a person to win.

We think we might have the solution.

In the next iteration of the game every family will begin with ten honor cards and the family with the most at the end of the game will win. Families will lose three cards for each child who remains unmarried or without an office at the end of the game. They will lose honor cards for accepting less than recommended dowries, socially blemished spouses for their children, or one from lower status. Conversely, they will gain cards from achieving higher than expected dowries or spouses of higher social status. They may also purchase honor through public acts of charity and these will be prorated to status, making charity more expensive for the wealthier families. This system will put each family on more of a level playing field. It will not entirely address the perceived unfairness, but should help to mitigate it. It will certainly radically simplify the point system and the resulting confusion among students. It will also make it considerably easier for the instructor to print and run the game.

We have also been considering two further options.

First, the social mechanics of games like Cards Against Humanity, Apples to Apples, or Snake Oil would be entirely appropriate ways of assessing a winner in our game. Honor, after all, is socially defined. It would be impractical to have a voting system involving all the families at the end of the game because

---

[17] Hoy, "Teaching History," 11–12.

it would be far too time consuming. More critically, one of the great virtues of the game is the way in which it drives families to be coldly calculating, manipulative, and even brutal. We certainly would not want to dampen these aspects of the game. This being said, it would be possible to resort to voting in the case of a tie.

Second, we are considering a randomized system for establishing family make-up. Every family would randomly draw an identity card (family name, history, wealth, status, expected dowry, etc.). They would also draw five other cards from a separate pile which would include a variety of children (described by sex, inclination, reputation, etc.) as well as other conditions such as business windfalls (allowing for some families to have fewer children and others more). The advantage to this approach is that the unfairness would be explicitly a matter of raw chance. The disadvantage would be that it would be less possible for us to provide the more balanced forms of unfairness in our family descriptions. Some families would almost certainly have extremely difficult configurations.

What all of our possible solutions are really aiming for is a reduction of preparation and monitoring workload for the lecturers running the game. Any problems and solutions, while they might occupy our thoughts, are ultimately not very important to the student learning experience. The game is immersive and fun, creates or strengthens a good class atmosphere, and regardless of our changes students consistently report that it was their favorite part of the class. In a large survey where it is often difficult to develop any sort of camaraderie, the game helps students to connect with each other and engage more with the content of the course. Our main takeaway is not about any details of how to run it, but that we should continue to run it! Our suggestion for our readers is to experiment yourselves!

Bibliography

Chapman, Adam, Anna Foka, and Jonathan Westin. "Introduction: What is Historical Game Studies?" *Rethinking History* 21 (2017): 358–71.
Gouglas, Sean, Mihaela Ilovan, Shannon Lucky, and Silvia Russell. "Abort, Retry, Pass, Fail: Games as Teaching Tools." In *Pastplay: Teaching and Learning History with Technology*, edited by Kevin Kee, 121–38. Ann Arbor, MI: University of Michigan Press, 2014.
Heckman, Christina. "Playing the Game: Collaborative Project-Based Learning in the Medieval Literature Classroom." *Studies in Medieval and Renaissance Teaching* 28 (2021): 7–33.
Hoy, Benjamin. "Teaching History With Custom-Built Board Games." *Simulation and Gaming* 49 (2018): 1–19.
Jiménez, Osvaldo. "Leveraging the Social Aspect of Educational Games." *Theory Into Practice* 54, no. 2 (2015): 101–108.

Kirshner, Julius. *Marriage, Dowry and Citizenship in Late Medieval and Renaissance Italy.* Toronto: University of Toronto Press, 2015.

McCall, Jeremiah. "Navigating the Problem Space: The Medium of Simulation Games in the Teaching of History." *The History Teacher* 46 (2012): 9–28.

McCall, Jeremiah. "Simulation Games and the Study of the Past: Classroom Guidelines." In *Pastplay: Teaching and Learning History with Technology*, edited by Kevin Kee, 228–53. Ann Arbor, MI: University of Michigan Press, 2014.

Nicksic, Hildi, Suzanne Lindt, and Stacia Miller. "Move, Think, Learn: Incorporating Physical Activity into the College Classroom." *International Journal of Teaching and Learning in Higher Education* 32, no. 3 (202): 528–535.

Tracy, Kisha. "Introduction: Medievalists on the Pedagogical Edge." *Studies in Medieval and Renaissance Teaching* 25 (2017): 7–9.

Tulloch, Rowan. "Reconceptualising Gamification: Play and Pedagogy." *Digital Culture & Education* 6, no. 4 (2014): 317–33.

Rouse, Wendy. "Lessons Learned While Escaping From a Zombie: Designing a Breakout EDU Game." *The History Teacher* 50, no. 4 (2017): 553–564.

Part IV: **User Modification as Learning Practice**

Erik Champion, Terhi Nurmikko-Fuller and Katrina Grant

9 Alchemy and Archives, Swords, Spells, and Castles: Medieval-modding *Skyrim*

Abstract: *Elder Scrolls V: Skyrim*[1] has great potential as a teaching and learning tool. The world of Skyrim, although sometimes labelled pseudo-medieval,[2] can aim for a level of historical accuracy comparable to many scholarly digital 3D reconstruction projects. These types of projects are now widely accepted as a vehicle for a new way of thinking about old topics, and as a valuable prompt for engaging students. The advantage of using *Skyrim* is that the historically informed mods[3] can be combined with sophisticated game mechanics to immerse and inspire students in procedural, contestable, and reconfigurable simulations. Through playful exploration, students can investigate the game world and engage with both the historically-informed and fantastical elements. But they can also become designers, and investigate historical developments through the creation of new assets, modified game mechanics, and social storytelling. Designing simulations is a further learning experience and Skyrim's Creation Kit is thus also a pedagogical tool.

In this chapter we will explore ways in which *Skyrim* can be used and modified to explain, through play, three related aspects of medieval society: culture, architecture, and landscape. We will then discuss its modding capability, and conclude with some suggestions for how future Elder Scrolls games and mods could be leveraged as teaching and learning tools.

Introduction

Elder Scrolls V: Skyrim[4] was released in 2011 and has won over 200 gaming awards.[5] *Skyrim*'s narrative and design overlap with many generic medieval

---

[1] We will use *Skyrim* (italicized) to refer to the game itself and disambiguate it from Skyrim (non-italicized) to refer to the geographical location within the fictional universe.
[2] Alexander Von Lünen, Katherine J. Lewis, Benjamin Litherland, and Pat Cullum, *Historia Ludens: The Playing Historian* (New York, USA: Routledge, 2019).
[3] Mods or modifications are player-produced alterations to the game that can affect the objects or the behaviours entities in the game.
[4] *Skyrim* (Bethesda Game Studios, 2011).
[5] "The Elder Scrolls Official website," accessed April 29, 2021, https://elderscrolls.bethesda.net/skyrim/.

tropes (swords, spells, knights, dragons, literary archives, alchemy, cultists, beggars, and castles). But to what extent can it simulate a more historically-informed medieval environment? One reason for *Skyrim*'s enduring popularity is that it offers players and designers the opportunity to modify the game (a practice usually referred to as modding) and change everything from quest lines, characters, weather, objects, and more. This means the game can be endlessly varied. It also offers the opportunity for researchers and medieval specialists to leverage the sophisticated game editor and editing assets to create engaging teaching materials.

Games come in different shapes, sizes, aims, and categories. They can be categorized by the tangible aspects of necessary equipment (a football, a chessboard, a console); by the number of players (a team, a pair of adversaries, a single-player); or the aim (score point, strategize, quest-based problem solving). Even if focusing exclusively on games that are single-player in the digital medium, we can easily differentiate between games such as *Solitaire* (a strategy game with a clear objective and rules, but a degree of undeterminable luck in the way the cards land), *Pokémon Go!* (combining social aspects with a predominantly single-player experience and a real-world dependency),[6] and *Skyrim* (an open-world game with a complex but unfixed narrative, quests of various significance, and a variety of goals that can be followed or ignored).

The value of games and gaming as pedagogical tools is well-established. They have been demonstrated to improve retention rates,[7] and to reduce student drop-out numbers and increase motivation (at least for Computer Science courses).[8] They are also used as complementary modes of assessment.[9] A large, sprawling and fantasy-driven game-world like *Skyrim* may seem more challenging to use for teaching but, as we will argue, it is these very qualities that can offer students a context for engaging with, evaluating, critiquing, and visualizing Medieval Studies.

---

6 David De Roure, J. A. Hendler, D. James, T. Nurmikko-Fuller, M. Van Kleek, and P. Willcox, "Towards a Cyber Physical Web Science: A Social Machines Perspective on Pokémon GO!," in *Proceedings of the 10th ACM Conference on Web Science, Boston, MA, USA, 30 June – 3 July 2019* (New York, NY: ACM, 2019), 65–69.
7 Stan Kurkovsky, "Engaging students through mobile game development," *ACM SIGCSE Bulletin* 41, no. 1 (2009): 44–48.
8 Briana B. Morrison and Jon A. Preston, "Engagement: Gaming throughout the curriculum," In *ACM SIGCSE Bulletin* 41, no. 1 (2009): 342–346.
9 B. P. Nunes, T. Nurmikko-Fuller, G. Rabello Lopes, S. W. M. Siqueira, G. H. B. De Campos, and M. A. Casanova, "Treasure Explorers–A Game as a Diagnostic Assessment Tool," in *Proceedings of the 16th International Conference on Advanced Learning Technologies (ICALT), Austin, TX, USA, 25 July – 28 July 2016* (Piscataway: IEEE, 2016), 217–221.

The suspension of disbelief necessary for playing the game enables the students to immerse themselves not in a relatively static rendition that has the aim of being historically or archaeologically accurate (such as a 3D reconstruction in a museum), but in a world that, despite the artistic license, historical tropes, and composite landscapes, will also offer the player an opportunity to empathize and embody the perspective of those people who lived in Medieval Europe. How might this role-playing enable the player to learn about culture (not just Skyrim's cultures, but also about the cultures of Medieval Europe), if not directly, then through critical evaluation of the game, its settings, and narrative arcs?

Background to the Game and Parallels with Medieval Europe

Game Narrative

The game begins with an unlikely hero clad in rags sitting at the back of a horse-drawn cart. The scene is set: an intermingling of coniferous and deciduous woodland, the unpaved road, the undulating terrain. The clothes, armor, and fur cloaks of the non-playable characters (NPCs), the stone and wood architecture of the road and city, and the cart itself suggest a pre-Industrial time: we feel we are in a generic variant of Medieval Europe.

Within moments, the protagonist (players can choose a female or male character) must escape an unjust execution at the hands of the Imperials, a group dressed in an aesthetic reminiscent of Imperial Rome. She is not saved by a valiant champion, or her own guile, but by the ensuing chaos brought on by an unprecedented dragon attack.[10] Having survived this initial attack at Helgen, she proceeds to complete several challenges and tasks, discovers herself to be the Dragonborn, and rises through the social ranks to become a high-ranking member of society. The main narrative is a complex network of 20 main quests (classified as frame stories by narratologists). These quests are enriched by additional, task-based, optional quests, either prompted by built-in game-flow or stumbled upon accidentally.

---

10 Players can choose from male or female gender, and a variety of human or humanoid animal players, corresponding to any of the races that are present in the fictional world of Tamriel.

The richness and flexibility of the *fabula* (a term coined for formalist analysis referring to the fundamental basics that make up the raw material of the narrative)[11] and the open (free-roaming) world enables and supports a vast array of possible *syuzhet* manifestations (the events within the story do not need to unfold in an absolute, preordained order). Consistency and repetition occur mostly at the granularity of the settings of the largely static but scenic landscape, and in the behavior and dialogs of non-player characters (NPCs).

Certain locations contain self-contained quests that have little impact (often limited to level-appropriate loot) on the overall narrative and can be played at any time. *Skyrim* brings to life a fictional universe replete with multiple historical and mythological timelines, a variety of races and species, distinctive urban settings, architectural styles, and extensive, climate and season-affected landscapes. It immerses the player in a world which parallels the ethnic and cultural diversity of Medieval Europe. The options for engagement with teaching range from moments of almost faithful re-enactment of known historical cultures and customs to discursive explorations on themes and concepts of neo-medievalism and the way in which historical tropes are represented through fictional narratives.

Parallels in Customs

The dominant race in Skyrim are the Nords and they find their equivalent in the Viking cultures of Scandinavia; Nord names have a distinctly northern European feel, sounding Scandinavian or Anglo-Saxon (for example Sven, or Ragnar the Red of the eponymous song sung in Skyrim's taverns, namesake of Ragnar Lodbrok). The main narrative implies a strong bias in favor of one group above all others: the concept art for Skyrim has consistently depicted the protagonist as a male Nord (though players can choose to play a character from a range of races and from two genders), supporting the suggestion that they, above all others, are at the heart of the game.

The architecture and attire of a group called the Skaal, who live on an island off the coast of Skyrim, echo the Indigenous Saami of Northern Europe. Their first names, as with the Nords, have a distinctively pre-Christian Nordic sound, for example, the name of the NPC Frea seems derived from the Norse goddess Freyja. Second names or surnames capture idiosyncratic personality features, such as Fanari Strong-Voice, an outspoken NPC. The Nords have similar names

---

11 Vladimir Propp, *Morphology of the Folktale*, 2nd edition (Austin: University of Texas Press, 1968).

(for example Temba Wide-Arm[12]) promoting a sense of a cultural or ancestral connection between the two groups. These names continue the Scandinavian theme and are reminiscent of names of Viking leaders and the (legendary and historical) kings of Sweden, Norway, and Denmark (such as Ivar the Boneless, Björn Ironside, Harald Bluetooth).

One of the other races that the player most frequently encounters are the Imperials, who are the most powerful and dominant race in Tamriel. They share clear similarities with the nations of the Mediterranean and individual NPCs have Latin names: Cicero and General Tullius, both of whom may be named after Marcus Tullius Cicero, a Roman lawyer, poet and orator. Their military attire seems based on the Roman centurions, and their name and place in the society reflect on the spread and power of the Roman Empire.

The naming conventions of the Bretons appear to reflect Brittany in France. Breton names such as Amaund have a phonetic similarity to French names such as Armand, and female names such as Delphine, Mirabelle, and Colette have French origins, though they are otherwise not especially "French" in their culture. The Redguards and the Alik'r (who hail from the warmer, desert climes) wear distinctive clothes and headdresses reminiscent of traditional Arabian keffiyehs and carry distinctive, curved, scimitar swords that would not look out of place in the hands of a warrior of the Ottoman Empire. Redguard names such as Nazir, Talib, and Nazeem are Arabic male given names.

The parallels with Medieval Europe are apparent, as the denizens of Skyrim are a rich collection of intermixing groups, both ancient and contemporary. Here are echoes of Medieval Europe, a cluster of diverse nascent nation groups (many of them claiming some connection to the Roman Empire) trading and exchanging both material goods and ideas across Europe.[13] Although the races and their roles in the game are historically inspired rather than factual, they and the way that the player engages with them offer a useful point for examination by students. For example, the relatively diverse mix of peoples represented throughout the different towns and cities could offer a starting point for discussing

---

12 This NCP's name is one of many so-called "Easter eggs" embedded into *Skyrim*. They are seemingly arbitrary details, which require the player to know additional information about the science fiction and fantasy subculture beyond that of the game fabula. In this case, the NCP character name is a reference to an episode of the *StarTrek Next Generation* TV-series (namely Season 5, episode 2), where Captain Jean-Luc Picard recounts a reduced and simplified narrative of the Epic of Gilgameš.
13 Rowin J. van Lanen, Esther Jansma, Jan van Doesburg, and Bert J. Groenewoudt, "Roman and early-medieval long-distance transport routes in north-western Europe: modelling frequent-travel zones using a dendro archaeological approach," *Journal of Archaeological Science* 73 (2016): 120–137.

the diversity of global exchange in the medieval period, and a reflection on how that diversity has or has not been represented in earlier research and popular culture.

Linguistic Parallels

Despite the social and racial diversity, Skyrim is remarkably homogeneous linguistically. A total of 15 languages have been defined as part of the Elder Scrolls saga, but only two manifest as spoken languages, with a third (Daedric) surviving as an alphabet only.[14] The first of the spoken languages, Tamrielic, is the *lingua franca* or the common language of Skyrim, spoken by the player and all NPCs alike (throughout the game, Tamrielic is modern English).

The other language is Dovahzul, the Dragon Tongue, and the most defining characteristic of the main protagonist. This language is spoken only by a select few with skill (the Greybeards, Jarl Ulfric Stormcloak, high-level draugr, and the Dragon Priests), but they are few in number and all have positions of great prestige and power. None of the inhabitants of the urban centers, for example, exhibit any knowledge of the tongue. In this regard, it is reminiscent of the role of Latin in Medieval Europe, a language spoken by the intelligentsia, but no longer surviving as spoken language among the masses.

Although it is not often considered in this way, Skyrim is a simulation repository of real and imagined languages. Some modding projects are already adding different languages, or replacing the dominant gameplay language of English, such as the Project Caelifinis, which transforms all player dialogue, quest objectives, spells, items, journal entries, effects, actions, locations, and names into Latin.[15]

Religious Parallels

A recurring theme of the religions of Skyrim is Talos, a Christ-like figure who was born human but transcended upon death to a divine status. In stark contrast to Medieval Europe however, where Christianity was asserting its absolute dominance over myriad pagan belief systems, in Skyrim, the worship of Talos

---

14 "The Elder Scrolls Wiki," accessed April 29, 2021, http://elderscrolls.wikia.com/wiki/The_Elder_Scrolls_Wiki.
15 "Project Caelifinis," accessed April 29, 2021, https://www.nexusmods.com/skyrimspecialedition/mods/27433?tab=description.

is banned, and he is removed from the common pantheon. A more tangible parallel is through the Greybeards, who although not explicitly identified as a religious community live a monastic lifestyle of an isolated communal single-sex environment, where personal property and earthly pursuits have been renounced in favor of quiet contemplation. Their knowledge of Dovahzul further adds parallels to monks of Medieval England, diligently replicating Latin inscriptions.

Culinary Customs

Of the various foods and drinks available in Skyrim, bread, beer, cheese, pies and sweet rolls mirror the culinary traditions of Medieval Europe. So too do apples and cabbages, which would have been available, and even the horker (walrus-type animals that have an additional tusk), if we can suspend our disbelief long enough to equate the horker stew with medieval practices of eating seals. One noticeable discrepancy is the presence of the potato: this now ubiquitous vegetable was not brought to Europe until the end of the sixteenth century and didn't become popular among the masses until the nineteenth century.

Books

Before the invention of the Gutenberg Press at around 1440, European literary materials were exclusively hand-written and copied. This absence of industrial-scale printing is evident in Skyrim, where books are the exclusive means of conveying textual materials, some of which are highly valued and rare.

The official game guide specifies that there are five types of written material in Skyrim: Skills Books (90 distinct ones), Spell Tomes, Functional Books, Common Books (there are a total of 215 different ones), as well as Notes and Journals.[16] There are, however, also 12 unique pieces of parchment, which reveal the location of treasure, and businesses keep track of their revenue using ledgers (as well as large number of parchment rolls which cannot be read). Central to the game narrative are the carved walls scattered across Skyrim that hold the script from which the Dragonborn learns each Shout (World Walls). For the exception of Common Books, each type of written document is significant to gameplay, either skills-enhancing or involved in a quest. Whilst the finer details of

---

16 David Hodgson and Steve Stratton, *The Elder Scrolls V: Skyrim Official Game Guide* (London: Zenimax Europe Ltd., 2011), ff 60.

medieval art, craft, and calligraphy are not clearly conveyed in the books of Skyrim, the importance, prestige, and rarity of the written word can be communicated. The only exception, arguably, is the ubiquity of books with most inhabited residences in Skyrim containing bookcases.

Myth, Fantasy, and Belief

Many aspects of *Skyrim's* fictional universe are not dissimilar to Medieval Europe in terms of the rules of physics and natural sciences, architecture, social order, and level of technological development. Deviations from reality occur in the form of ubiquitous magic, mythical beings (spriggans, ice wraiths, giants), and the presence of prehistoric beasts (mammoths, sabercats, cave bears), and the reinterpretations of existing animals such as skeevers (giant rats) and the aforementioned horkers.

Other creatures that are mythical to us but were widely believed in (and thus formed part of people's lived experience of reality) during the medieval period include vampires, werewolves and werebears, draugrs (a type of Old Norse zombie), and giants.[17] In theory, even these fantastical elements might offer a window into a world where the belief systems and people's imaginative engagement with the world around them was markedly different to our current period.

Skyrim and Neo-Medievalism

Several scholars have already pointed to the neo-medieval aspects inherent in *Skyrim*'s game design, from the characters and costume to the architecture and landscape. All draw on both real and fantastical ideas of medieval Europe. Victoria Cooper's in-depth study of the game looks at the intersection of medievalist fantasy, politics, and whiteness.[18] She traces the origins of the vision of medieval Europe presented in *Skyrim* to the nineteenth century revival of interest

---

[17] Aðalheiður Guðmundsdóttir, "The werewolf in medieval Icelandic literature," *The Journal of English and Germanic Philology* 106, no. 3 (2007): 277–303; Susan Small, "The Medieval Werewolf Model of Reading Skin," in *Reading Skin in Medieval Literature and Culture*, ed. Katie L. Walter (Palgrave Macmillan, New York, 2013), 81–97; and Nora K. Chadwick, "Norse Ghosts (a Study in the Draugr and the Haugbúi)," *Folklore* 57, no. 2 (1946): 50–65.

[18] Victoria Elizabeth Cooper, "Fantasies of the North: Medievalism and Identity in Skyrim" (PhD diss., University of Leeds, 2016), http://etheses.whiterose.ac.uk/16875/.

in Norse sagas and she links this with a growing British nationalism. It was not just Britain that "invented" an ideal of this period; Anders Andrén points out the term "Middle Ages" was introduced by a Norwegian historian Ludvig Holberg in the eighteenth century to refer to the period from the eleventh to the early sixteenth century, and then in the nineteenth century the "Viking Age" was conceptualized as the heroic and glorious era preceding this.[19] Much of our vision of the medieval period is based on this period of rediscovery and its particular vision of the past. While scholars like Cooper rightly point to the depictions of the medieval period in *Skyrim* as "reinscribing of myths of white history and white nostalgia,"[20] there are also elements of the game world that seek to understand a lost world and landscape, albeit filtered through a largely nineteenth- and early twentieth-century aesthetic. As such, engagement with *Skyrim* can prompt discussions of how we reimagine the past, and how modern values and ideology can colour these reconstructions.

The Experience of Medieval Architecture and Urban Settings in Skyrim

Digital reconstruction projects, both urban-architectural settings and lost landscapes, have become more popular in recent years.[21] For example, the Virtual Angkor project uses a game engine to create an immersive space with the aim of creating an "engaging mode of conveying complex and dynamic information to the public."[22] The goal of these reconstructions is a combination of traditional research questions and an emerging interest in driving broader engagement in medieval and earlier history by offering rich immersive environments in place of static, technical reconstructions that had tended to focus only on specific monuments.

One of the key aspects of *Skyrim* that makes it immersive and engaging for players is the rich and varied terrain and architectural settings through which

---

19 A. Andrén, "Medieval and Neo-Medieval Buildings in Scandinavia," in *Manufacturing Middle Ages: Entangled History of Medievalism in Nineteenth-Century Europe*, ed. Patrick J. Geary and Gábor Klaniczay (Leiden: Brill, 2013), 139–159.
20 Cooper, "Fantasies of the North."
21 "Virtual Angkor," accessed April 29, 2021, https://www.virtualangkor.com/about-1; "Virtual Rome" accessed April 29, 2021, https://research.reading.ac.uk/virtualrome/.
22 T. Chandler, B. McKee, E. Wilson, M. Yeates, and M. Polkinghorne, "A New Model of Angkor Wat: Simulated Reconstruction as a Methodology for Analysis and Public Engagement," *Australian and New Zealand Journal of Art* 17, no. 2 (2017): 182–3.

players move as they pursue quests and explore the gaming landscape. One of the greatest challenges for students and researchers alike is to understand the embodied experience of the places where historic events and daily life unfolded. Although *Skyrim* was not designed as a project focused on historic accuracy, nor even based on a quasi-reconstruction of real historic places (as in the *Assassin's Creed* franchise), it does offer a useful starting point for understanding the landscapes and towns of Europe in the medieval period.

As with the naming and culture of the Nords, the design of the architecture and landscape of Skyrim draws upon the general appearance of Northern European architecture and landscape. Very little remains of the urban settings from those periods, generally only stand-alone buildings exist, set within more modern towns and cities. Certain types of buildings are also less likely to exist. The mainly timber vernacular buildings like houses and inns that characterized the built environment of the Nordic region and Scandinavia mostly have not survived. Even large-scale buildings like castles and manor houses have usually been substantially renovated.[23] The urban and architectural settings of Skyrim vary from ruins from at least two pre- or early-Nord civilizations (one being the Dwemer and the other being the ruins where the Draugr are found) to lone farmhouses, small towns, and larger cities. Within the original setting of the game the architectural style seems to draw on several different sources, both original medieval period constructions, later idealized versions of neo-medieval architecture from the nineteenth and early twentieth century, and twentieth-century historic reconstructions of buildings based on archaeological research.

The main building materials are wood and heavy dark masonry and although the game design does not attempt to replicate a specific place or time the overall architectural style depicted in the game is arguably Northern European, with many elements that are drawn directly from the historic architecture of the Scandinavian and Nordic countries. The multi-storey timber construction buildings such as Jarl's Longhouse in Winterhold[24] and the Temple of Kynareth in Whiterun are timber with a thatch or wooden roof, with each level having its own sharply sloped roof (to prevent snow gathering presumably).[25] The central internal space of the Longhouse, the audience hall, projects up through two stories, creating the sense of a lofty, ceremonial space. This design echoes buildings from places like medieval Norway, such as the stave churches (the oldest surviving of these is c. 1500 AD

---

[23] Andrén, "Medieval and Neo-Medieval Buildings in Scandinavia," 139–159.
[24] "Jarl's Longhouse Winterhold," accessed April 29, 2021, https://elderscrolls.fandom.com/wiki/Jarl%27s_Longhouse_(Winterhold).
[25] "Temple of Kynareth," accessed April 29, 2021, https://elderscrolls.fandom.com/wiki/Temple_of_Kynareth_(Skyrim).

but they represent a style dating back to at least the eleventh century).[26] Likewise, the base for the Companions in Whiterun, called Jorrvaskar,[27] is clearly based on Viking longhouses, such as the one recreated at Lofotr Viking Museum in Norway, including the roof shaped like a ship's hull, and the central and sunken hearth surrounded by raised wooden platforms.[28]

The masonry buildings in Skyrim tend to be either those found in the most well-established cities, such as the Solitude, the capital of Skyrim, and older buildings, often partially ruined and repurposed, such as guard towers or the apparently "ancient" castle of High Hrothgar. The style of these buildings is harder to pin to a specific period. Some manors and palaces in Solitude seem to present a masonry version of the more authentic wooden constructions of other towns, with high pitched roofs. Other buildings, such as the Blue Palace and the Bard's College, are more like a version of Romanesque or even Pre-Romanesque architecture that characterized much building across Europe following the decline of the Roman Empire. These buildings incorporated classical elements from ancient Roman architecture as well as elements of Byzantine style, reflecting the Roman Empire's shift to the east in its latter years, these two styles then incorporating local architectural traditions. These styles are generally characterized by larger massing, thicker walls, squatter columns and piers, large towers, and the use of stone undressed by marble. The Bard's College includes low arches at the base, supported by thick pillars, above this the main windows composed of two high narrow archways topped by a small roundel, with rich tracery (echoing elements of the famous Venetian Gothic window). Both the College and the Blue Palace include towers and the palace a small central dome.

Although *Skyrim* does not attempt to faithfully recreate a specific historic time or place, it still offers opportunities for immersive engagement with a built environment that does convey some sense of the medieval period. Buildings and cities have logical layouts, with interior spaces corresponding to external ones, buildings tending to be mostly interactive with players able to traverse stairs, clamber over balconies, and inspect details up close. Even the more fantastical elements were grounded in what one of the designers called "epic reality," meaning that the game world as whole should seem real and logical and

---

26 Evgeny Khodakovsky and Siri Skjold Lexau, *Historic Wooden Architecture in Europe and Russia: Evidence, Study and Restoration* (Birkhäuser: Basel, 2017).
27 "Jorrvaskr," accessed April 29, 2021, https://elderscrolls.fandom.com/wiki/Jorrvaskr.
28 Kevin Moberly and Brent Moberly, "There is No Word for Work in the Dragon Tongue," *The Year's Work in Medievalism* 28 (2013); S. Wickler and G. Nilsen, "Iron Age Boathouses In Arctic Norway Viewed As Multifunctional Expressions Of Maritime Cultural Heritage," *WIT Transactions on The Built Environment* 79 (2005).

the fantasy elements a logical extension of this.[29] They can even interact with the objects in the game, collecting plates and dishes to inspect up close (even though there is little point to this in the game play) and eating food left out in the feasting halls. In doing so the game offers an opportunity to think about these places as lived in and experienced. Educators already use features such as Google Earth and Google Cardboard to give students a sense of the urban setting of buildings and their scale,[30] and *Skyrim* offers an opportunity to do likewise and move away from simple 2D representations of places, which are often hard to comprehend for non-experts.

In a recent study of Viking architecture and society, Marianna Eriksen argues that to understand the society more fully, as more than just ferocious warriors and raiders, it is essential to "embed them within a physical, architectural frame that not only significantly shaped their movements, thoughts and actions, but that was part of them."[31] Perhaps *Skyrim* can offer this to students, in the same way that the popular reconstructions and re-enactments of historic life also do at many museum sites, but with greater global accessibility.

The focus on building types and societies from Scandinavia and other Nordic countries also offers an insight into a style of architecture less well-known globally than the Central European (mostly English and French) style of medieval architecture. Even the points of fantasy and idealism offer useful points for discussion of the idealism and revival of medieval style. The various architectural styles found in the game were all subject to "revivals" in the nineteenth and twentieth centuries. This means that the Romanesque and even medieval Nordic architectural styles are often experienced today through revival buildings or full reconstructions.[32] A study of *Skyrim*'s medieval fantasies by Victoria Cooper points out that although the settings "are fantastical, they are frequently visually grounded in material culture and romantic-yet-recognisable landscapes that create some verisimilitude."[33] This offers a useful point of discussion of styles of medieval architectural revival and the ways in which our historical understanding of the past is filtered through depictions in popular culture.

---

29 Kevin Ohannessian, "How To Create A World: Skyrim's Director On Building A Never-Ending Fantasy," *Fast Company*, November 11, 2011, https://www.fastcompany.com/1794290/how-create-world-skyrims-director-building-never-ending-fantasy, accessed April 28, 2021.

30 Elizabeth Capello, "Virtual Reality in the Art History Classroom," *Art History Teaching Resources*, March 15, 2017, accessed April 29, 2021, https://arthistoryteachingresources.org/2017/03/virtual-reality-in-the-art-history-classroom/.

31 Marianne Hem Eriksen, *Architecture, Society, and Ritual in Viking Age Scandinavia: Doors, Dwellings, and Domestic Space* (Cambridge: Cambridge University Press, 2019).

32 Andrén, "Medieval and Neo-Medieval Buildings in Scandinavia,"139–159.

33 Cooper, "Fantasies of the North."

Most of the current mods for architectural elements have been focused on increasing the resolution and improving the appearance of the built fabric (especially updating it for 2K and 4K displays).[34] However, the fact that the game allows players to build and construct their own dwellings means that there is potential for the creation of new buildings. Most existing mods currently add more fantastical elements, like a skyscraper for Falkreath,[35] but others offer the opportunities to add cathedrals (Figure 9.1) which are dedicated to in-game deities but are clearly based on historic Romanesque and Gothic and even Byzantine examples.[36] There is clearly potential to add more varied architecture in the general style of Skyrim, which could include more faithful reconstructions of extant or well-documented buildings. These could then be experienced in the game, and give students and players a sense of scale, and the sensation of moving through and immersing oneself in the space.

Figure 9.1: A Skyrim Cathedral Mod. Courtesy of Pierrick.[37]

---

34 "Mods for architectural elements," accessed April 29, 2021, https://www.nexusmods.com/skyrim/mods/79746.
35 "Mods for buildings," accessed April 29, 2021, https://www.nexusmods.com/skyrim/mods/28501.
36 "Mods for cathedrals," accessed April 29, 2021, https://www.nexusmods.com/skyrim/mods/73948.
37 "Skyrim Cathedral," accessed April 29, 2021, https://www.nexusmods.com/skyrim/mods/73948.

The Medieval Landscape Settings

The sources for the landscape of *Skyrim* seem to be a mix of real natural environments and idealized visions of landscape from art. The mountains, tundra, and forests all draw on the real existing landscapes of Northern Europe, especially those of the Nordic countries. The artistic sources tend not to be medieval art itself (where landscape was generally abstracted, stylized, and secondary to human action), but rather the visions of wild and semi-wild nature created in landscape painting from the sixteenth century onward.

The visions of idealized landscape in the paintings of Paul Bril (1554–1626), with their jagged sharp mountains and trees clinging to rocky outcrops, are perhaps the earliest version of this ideal of landscape that was developed over the following centuries.[38] There appears to be a particularly clear link with the visions of sublime nature conjured in the art of late eighteenth and early nineteenth-century Romantic painters like Casper David Friedrich (1774–1840). In his paintings human figures venture into remote and often harsh landscapes, and appear overwhelmed by the terrifying spectre of soaring mountains and dense forests. Friedrich was influenced by ideas of the sublime (most famously described by Edmund Burke in his *A Philosophical Enquiry into the Origin of Our Ideas of the Sublime and Beautiful* published in 1757). Burke's ideas and their pictorial realization in the art of painters like Friedrich aimed to find that balancing point between terror and beauty and to explore the ways in which the sense of sublime was roused by things "dark, uncertain, confused," such as a fog obscuring a vast landscape, or precipitous mountain face.[39] This correlation has been noted by fans who have pointed to the "epicness" of the landscapes, the use of giant natural features, and the way that the architecture blends into the natural landscape around it.[40]

Others have pointed to the way that the Skyrim landscape plays to Immanuel Kant's (1724–1804) idea that the displeasure of fear of the unknown is simultaneously a pleasure, because "the sight of them becomes all the more attractive the more fearful it is, provided we are in a safe place,"[41] and the relationship

---

[38] Francesca Cappelletti, *Paul Bril e la pittura di paesaggio a Roma, 1580 – 1630* (Turnhout: Brepols, 2006).
[39] Joseph Leo Koerner, *Caspar David Friedrich and the Subject of Landscape* (London: Reaktion Books, 2009).
[40] "Friedrich Romanticism and Games," accessed April 29, 2021, http://howtonotsuckatgamedesign.com/2016/02/friedrich-romanticism-and-games/.
[41] "Kant's ideas and landscape," accessed April 29, 2021, unpaginated, http://joannaetaylor.blogspot.com/2012/12/the-modern-sublime-gaming-and-romantic.html.

between humans and the harsh natural landscape. The landscapes the players move through are essentially composites of visual tropes designed to evoke a fantasy of northern European landscapes in a pre-industrial period. So, although Skyrim's landscapes don't specifically place the player in a version of a medieval landscape, they do offer an experience of landscape vastly different to that many of us now have.

Immersion in Natural Landscapes

Many of the existing mods for *Skyrim* that focus on the landscape appear to be designed to enhance the immersive quality of the game. Mods include "Logical Grass," which will add more grass and wild foliage,[42] "Real Clouds," which adds "pseudo-volumetric clouds,"[43] or, "Summer Skyrim," where players can experience seasonal change.[44]

Unlike our typical modern-day experience of nature, where we often travel from urban centers to protected pockets of natural or wild landscape, in *Skyrim* the forests, plateaus, tundra, wide-flowing rivers, and snowy peaks are the norm. As players move through questlines they spend hours of time walking or running through the natural landscape. Human traces in the landscape are never difficult to find, whether occupied caves, abandoned buildings, rough roads, and signposts. Yet the presence of wild and untamed nature is always close by, the threat of attack by animals is constant, and it is easy to find oneself lost and have to backtrack and restart in order to find undiscovered places (once a place has been discovered the player can fast travel there and back, reducing the need for wayfinding).

Although not technically medieval, and actually based on a much more recent fantasy of the wild landscapes of Northern Europe, *Skyrim* does offer the opportunity for immersion in a vast landscape that is otherwise difficult to replicate. There is potential for modding the flora and fauna, and even the farming practices. One mod offers an alternative to the combative, exploration quest

---

[42] "Mods for foliage," accessed April 29, 2021, https://www.nexusmods.com/skyrim/mods/65215/.
[43] "Mods for clouds," accessed April 29, 2021, https://www.nexusmods.com/skyrim/mods/39450.
[44] "Mods for seasonal change," accessed April 29, 2021, https://www.nexusmods.com/skyrim/mods/22300.

line with an opportunity to set up as a farmer instead.[45] This immersion in the time and place is not dissimilar to the effect being sought by various digital heritage researchers.[46]

Extending Skyrim Via Modding

Skyrim has been around since 2011 in various versions, on Windows PCs (with a 2018 version for VR headsets), Xbox One, PlayStation 4 (and PS4VR), Nintendo Switch, and most recently PlayStation 5. Its long life has been aided by its content ecosystem of mods and modders and the sheer number, scale, and variety of the mods; it is one of the most modded games of all time.[47] Modders have created everything from tiny tweaks to silly memes to entirely new campaigns for *Skyrim* since its release in 2011.[48] One of the authors of this paper, Erik Champion, has suggested how *Skyrim* mods could be developed for the GLAM (Galleries, Libraries, Archives, and Museums) sector published on various aspects of digital gaming in general and modding culture in the context of *Skyrim* in particular for over a decade.[49]

Almost any content in the game can be modified, deleted, or replaced (Figure 9.2). *Skyrim* can host virtual recreations, the player can control the avatar, and issue voice commands recognized by the game. NPCs can be easily reprogrammed to share stories. There are 18 eighteen skills shared equally across Magic, Combat, and Stealth, and each of these skills is available for modding.

---

[45] "Mod for farmer lifestyle," accessed April 29, 2021, https://www.pcgamesn.com/the-elder-scrolls-v-skyrim/mod-stardew-valley.
[46] Kit Devine, "Sense of Place: The phenomenology of virtual heritage place" (paper presented at the 21st International Conference Information Visualisation (IV), 2017); Jessie Rogers, Marc Aurel Schnabel, and Tane Moleta, "Digital Design Ecology to Generate a Speculative Virtual Environment with New Relativity Laws," *Communications in Computer and Information Science (CCIS)* 1028 (2019): 120–133.
[47] There have been over 65,000 submissions on Nexus Mods and 28,000 in the Steam Workshop.
[48] Christopher Livingston, Diana Papiz, Jody Macgregor, and Lauren Morton, "The Best Skyrim Mods," *PCGamer*, February 25, 2021, 2021, https://www.pcgamer.com/au/best-skyrim-mods/.
[49] Erik Champion, "Heritage Role Playing-History as an Interactive Digital Game" (paper presented at the Interactive Entertainment (IE2004), Sydney, Australia, 2004); Erik Champion, "Ludic Literature: Evaluating Skyrim for Humanities Modding" (paper presented at the Digital Humanities Congress, 2014).

Figure 9.2: A Skyrim Mod (courtesy of Jack Chapman).

This means the game can be modded to focus on trading, praying, conversing, gaining followers, healing, and so on, not just violence and magic.

The nexusmods website list at least 23 assets and environments linked specifically to medieval history.[50] There are a huge number of fantasy medieval castles and swords on the nexusmods website, including a Knights of the Garter mod.[51] Narratives in the style of Icelandic Saga books already exist in *Skyrim* although they don't appear to affect gameplay, but they suggest a possible avenue for future modding.[52] *Skyrim*'s modding tool, the Creation Kit,[53] can also import 3D models from Sketchfab.[54] There is an existing Skyrim section on Sketchfab where custom *Skyrim* 3D models can be bought or downloaded for free, but

---

50 As at March 26, 2021. As an aside many of these actually seek to add in more traditionally recognized medieval era clothing, armor, and weapons, such as those found in depictions of French, English, and crusader knights, rather than Northern Europe and Scandinavia.
51 "Mods for Kings of the Garter," accessed April 29, 2021, https://www.nexusmods.com/skyrim/mods/57489/. This mod adds a multitude of crusader armor (even crusader dragon shouts).
52 "Icelandic sagas," accessed April 29, 2021, https://steamcommunity.com/sharedfiles/filedetails/?id=130244719.
53 "The Creation Kit," accessed April 29, 2021, https://www.creationkit.com/.
54 "Sketchfab," accessed April 29, 2021, https://sketchfab.com/. Sketchfab converts 3D models (from 3D programs or from photogrammetry) and adds a JavaScript layer and formats that allow 3D models to run on the web, in VR head-mounted displays, or even via Twitter and Facebook.

another obvious use of this capability is to bring in some of the ever-increasing number of cultural heritage objects being made available on Sketchfab.[55]

The 3D models (meshes) do not have to be created from scratch but can be built in software such as 3D Studio Max, Blender, Maya, and a range of other 3D modelling tools and imported as .OBJ or .3DS format to the Creation Kit. It may also be possible to use Blender with SketchUp to create architectural models for *Skyrim*. An archived online reddit post explains that there are many more medieval related assets (and even scripting mods) than are found via a "medieval" search on the *Skyrim* mod websites.[56] There are also fix-it mods that allow players to add new roles, such as a bard with their own instrument, and that can create more realistic conversations between the NPCs.[57]

Modding Time

Although not specifically connected to the medieval tropes of the game, modding *Skyrim* can produce interesting morality tales and narratives involving time travel.[58] For example, the abandoned and mysterious Dwemer cities mentioned above have become the settings for historical mysteries designed by modders. One such mod, The Forgotten City (Nexus Mods 2021) requires the player to master time travel to solve the non-linear murder mystery and resolve ethical dilemmas. It was later developed into a standalone game of the same name in which 26 people in an ancient Roman city live inside a time loop.[59] Although

---

[55] "Sketchfab for Skyrim," accessed April 29, 2021, https://sketchfab.com/tags/skyrim; "Sketchfab for cultural heritage," accessed April 29, 2021, https://sketchfab.com/tags/cultural-heritage. There is a huge variety of mods, including Medieval clothing, landscape, architecture, and weaponry, to choose from.
[56] "[Guide] Going Medieval: High Middle Ages in Skyrim" [online forum], Reddit, accessed April 29, 2021, https://www.reddit.com/r/skyrimmods/comments/43pe07/guide_going_medieval_high_middle_ages_in_skyrim/.
[57] Zoe Delahunty-Light and Cian Maher, "Remember Skyrim's Radiant AI? It's Got the Potential to Revolutionise RPGs," *gamesrader.com*, March 5, 2018, https://www.gamesradar.com/au/remember-skyrims-radiant-ai-its-got-the-potential-to-revolutionise-rpgs/; and Cian Maher, "The story behind the Oblivion mod Terry Pratchett worked on," *EUROGAMER*, January 31, 2019, accessed April 29, 2019.
[58] The Papyrus script can control how quickly time has passed, for example.
[59] "The Forgotten City," accessed April 29, 2021, https://forgottencitygame.com/. They must obey the Golden Rule; if anyone breaks the Golden Rule, all die. The player travels back in time to unravel the mystery, each decision and moral choice changes details in the next (otherwise repeating) day.

this narrative is not set in medieval times, the ability to deviate from linear time could also be used to explore counterfactual medieval hypotheses.[60]

Appropriate use of time travel can also help resolve an issue in historical reconstructions: games traditionally increase difficulty power and knowledge as one develops mastery (to reward commitment and to avoid boredom), and the chronological setting of the game typically advances forwards in time. However, we typically (but not always) know more about history as it advances closer to our own time, but there is less chance for interaction, as changing the storyline changes history. One of the authors, Erik Champion, has written about ways digital simulations of history and heritage can be visited, suggesting nine ways to travel to the past and interact with known events and figures.[61]

Modding Actors, Artefacts, Society, and Culture

Medieval roles have specific place-related and people-related behavior, and luckily specific equipment and the NPCs can also be scripted or targeted by script. Erik Champion has written about the ways in which Skyrim and other games with mod editors can be deployed in terms of memes and artefactual desirability.[62] In 2005, he supervised an undergraduate game design class who modded Morrowind (Elder Scrolls: III) to build an Egyptian game level (Figure 9.3),[63] and in 2019, an undergraduate project by Jack Chapman (Figure 9.4) to model the mundane life of the poor.[64] While not specifically medieval, the research these students undertook, and the reasoning they displayed, show the level and scale of self-directed learning possible when students are given a game mod to design.

Libraries and librarians can harbor powerful archives of knowledge and librarians and scholars can be imbued with magical or supernatural (or religious)

---

60 This is already familiar to the player, because even in the vanilla version, Skyrim breaks up the overall environments that are needed to be rendered by teleporting the player from landscapes to internal scenes. In Skyrim mods these teleportation devices (such as doors and gates) can control the pathway and gameplay. The ability to dynamically change time and space allows for historical mods where the player must work out more likely counterfactuals in order to unravel a mystery or progress through the narrative.
61 Champion, "Heritage Role Playing-History as an Interactive Digital Game."
62 Champion, "Heritage Role Playing-History as an Interactive Digital Game."
63 They designed a hybrid Egyptian temple, using created and in-built assets, to teach players how to read Egyptian Hieroglyphs in the temple (in order to gain god-like powers).
64 As Skyrim controls not just skill levels, equipment, and wealth, but also health, in Chapman's mod the player (as Hobo Johnson) has to sneak and steal or otherwise find food and water (as well as sleep adequately) in order to survive.

power and foresight. This allows for the design of a mod that parallels legends, myths, and superstitions of the medieval era. Further, the ability to mod roles and location, race, and role-related behaviors can convey different social, cultural chronological, and regional sensitivities to behaviors, needs, rituals or options. Thus, xenophobia, social roleplay, and the respect given to rituals and roles (such as in the feudal system) can be simulated in mods and explored via gameplay and discussed in classroom settings.[65]

Modding the Landscape

Medieval alchemists believed that all matter was composed of four elements: earth, air, fire, and water, while famous alchemists such as Albertus Magnus were also botanists (some believe he discovered arsenic). Knowing when and where to find suitable ingredients, minerals, and materials would have been essential knowledge. Through Papyrus (the scripting language of *Skyrim's* Creation Kit), the game can control the climate (and weather) as well as change the flora and fauna.

Given *Skyrim* already has a gameplay relationship between the seasons, natural ingredients, potions, and the effect of the potions on the player or the NPCs, medieval mods could tell the history of alchemy, witchcraft, or agriculture. Geologist Jane Robb has, for example, used *Skyrim* to explain geological processes.[66] In the vanilla game, the player can also craft objects, discover precious materials, and mine the landscape. This aspect of gameplay could be extended via a mod to explain the relationships between geology, geography, agriculture, society (social status), and cultural relationships of value, trade, and power.

Future Modding Possibilities

Another area for development is to employ voice recognition with the game. This requires a higher level of expertise in development, but some modders have created mods that can be deployed on the Xbox, using the Kinect Camera and its voice recognition ability to allow players to physically shout commands

---

[65] Champion, "Ludic Literature: Evaluating Skyrim for Humanities Modding."
[66] Jane Robb and Gamespot Staff, "A Sight For Ore Eyes: Examining The Geology Of Skyrim," *Gamespot*, February 15, 2013, accessed April 29, 2021, https://www.gamespot.com/articles/a-sight-for-ore-eyes-examining-the-geology-of-skyrim/1100-6403844/.

Figure 9.3: 2005 Egyptian Temple Game Mod (Morrowind).

Figure 9.4: "Peasantry" 2019 Skyrim Mod (courtesy of Jack Chapman).

of power to the game.[67] Controlling the game by voice could be a greatly engaging way of learning medieval words (and pronunciation), and frees up the player to explore while verbally interacting with the game.

There is some room for improvement. The speed and user-friendliness of the Creation Kit could be improved. High-resolution 3D models and more documentation on how to use the Creation Kit (along with how-to videos, demos, case studies, and free assets) would help scholarly projects and teaching. Ideally, game assets could be easily saved via GitHub or Bitbucket as well as Sketchfab. Newer formats for 3D such as glTF and IIF-3D (if developed in time) could be supported. Another advantage would be the provision of easier methods to dynamically load scripts, textures or 3D models. This would mean that dynamic Linked Open Data and online digital collections could be connected to gameplay, as has already happened with other games such as *Assassin's Creed: Odyssey* (2018).[68] Mods that focus on

---

[67] "The Ultimate Skyrim Spell and Shout voice control," accessed April 29, 2021, https://www.nexusmods.com/skyrimspecialedition/mods/14091.

[68] Kaitlyn Kingsland, Rebekah Munson, and Madeleine Kraft, "Analyzing the Assassins Creed Odyssey Discovery Tour Spatial and Temporal locations of featured static images," *Archaeogaming*, February 26, 2020, accessed April 29, 2021, https://archaeogaming.com/2020/02/26/analyzing-the-assassins-creed-odyssey-discovery-tour-spatial-and-temporal-locations-of-featured-static-images/.

specific aspects of material culture within the game could be developed more specifically to focus on the power and value and insight of the object in question.

In the case of books, a mod could be developed to reward the player for engaging with them: the player is recognized and identified by NPCs based on the type or condition of the books they carry, use and protect. Books could have a condition status, and the player's progress could also be influenced by how well they care for items or are respectful to the NPCs. Additionally, if mod designs could be more easily shared between team members, the process could be re-envisioned as a pedagogical activity. Providing copyright permission for exhibiting mods and as interactive exhibitions at museums and galleries would open up the mods for new audiences through engagement with the GLAM sector.

The rumored next iteration of the game, Elder Scrolls: VI, will be backed by Microsoft, who have acquired Bethesda Studios. Given the new funding, and access to Microsoft technology and education reach (as exemplified by the direction they have taken with Minecraft), the next Elder Scrolls game is likely to show improvements both in the power and flexibility of mods, which in turn may increase their appeal as teaching resources. Rival Ubisoft's *Assassin's Creed* series already allows players to upload pictures, add their own story quests, and explore the game as a non-violent, slightly interactive 3D documentary, with hotspots of information and voice narration. Hopefully, Elder Scrolls VI will offer similar features.

Conclusion

There is clearly a difference between a fantasy world developed as a backdrop for gaming, and the use of a game engine to support an evidence-based, research-led reconstruction. However, the affinities in settings, goals and techniques of *Skyrim* mods, and digital heritage projects demonstrate the possible benefits of modding a rich, well-developed, and easily accessible existing game world like *Skyrim* for engaging students in a richer understanding of the medieval world. The participatory and creative aspects of modding means that students are no longer passive observers, they learn through actively developing historic worlds.

Bibliography

André, Andre. "Medieval and Neo-Medieval Buildings in Scandinavia." *In Manufacturing Middle Ages: Entangled History of Medievalism in Nineteenth-Century Europe*, edited by Patrick Geary and G. Klaniczay, 139–159. Brill: Leiden, 2013.

Cappelletti, Francesca. *Paul Bril e la pittura di paesaggio a Roma, 1580 – 1630*. Turnhout: Brepols, 2006.

Capello, Elizabeth. "Virtual Reality in the Art History Classroom." *Art History Teaching Resources*, March 15, 2017. Accessed April 28, 2021. https://arthistoryteachingresources.org/2017/03/virtual-reality-in-the-art-history-classroom/.

Chadwick, Nora K. "Norse Ghosts (a Study in the Draugr and the Haugbúi)." *Folklore* 57, no. 2 (1946): 50–65.

Champion, Erik. "Heritage Role Playing-History as an Interactive Digital Game." Paper presented at the Interactive Entertainment (IE2004), Sydney, Australia, 2004.

Champion, Erik. "Ludic Literature: Evaluating Skyrim for Humanities Modding." Paper presented at the Digital Humanities Congress, 2014.

Chandler, T., B. McKee, E. Wilson, M. Yeates, and M. Polkinghorne. "A New Model of Angkor Wat: Simulated Reconstruction as a Methodology for Analysis and Public Engagement." *Australian and New Zealand Journal of Art* 17, no. 2 (2017): 182–194.

Cooper, Victoria Elizabeth. "Fantasies of the north: medievalism and identity in Skyrim." PhD diss., University of Leeds, 2016. http://etheses.whiterose.ac.uk/16875/.

Delahunty-Light, Zoe, and Cian Maher. "Remember Skyrim's radiant AI? It's got the potential to revolutionise RPGs." *gamesrader.com* (blog), March 5, 2018. https://www.gamesradar.com/au/remember-skyrims-radiant-ai-its-got-the-potential-to-revolutionise-rpgs/.

De Roure, David, James A. Hendler, Diccon James, Terhi Nurmikko-Fuller, Max Van Kleek, and Pip Willcox. "Towards a Cyber Physical Web Science: A Social Machines Perspective on Pokémon GO!" In *Proceedings of the 10th ACM Conference on Web Science* (Boston, MA, USA, June 30 – July 3), 65–69. New York: ACM, 2019.

Devine, Kit. "Sense of Place: The phenomenology of virtual heritage place." Paper presented at the 21st International Conference Information Visualisation (IV), 2017.

Eriksen, Marianne Hem. *Architecture, Society, and Ritual in Viking Age Scandinavia: Doors, Dwellings, and Domestic Space*. Cambridge: Cambridge University Press, 2019.

Guðmundsdóttir, Aðalheiður. "The werewolf in medieval Icelandic literature." *The Journal of English and Germanic Philology* 106, no. 3 (2007): 277–303.

Hodgson, David, and Steve Stratton. *The Elder Scrolls V: Skyrim Official Game Guide*. London: Zenimax Europe Ltd, 2011.

Khodakovsky, Evgeny, and Siri Skjold Lexau. *Historic Wooden Architecture in Europe and Russia: Evidence, Study and Restoration*. Birkhäuser: Basel, 2017.

Kingsland, Kaitlyn, Rebekah Munson, and Madeleine Kraft. "Analyzing the Assassins Creed Odyssey Discovery Tour Spatial and Temporal locations of featured static images." *Archaeogaming*, February 26, 2020. Accessed April 29, 2021. https://archaeogaming.com/2020/02/26/analyzing-the-assassins-creed-odyssey-discovery-tour-spatial-and-temporal-locations-of-featured-static-images/.

Koerner, Joseph Leo. *Caspar David Friedrich and the Subject of Landscape*. London: Reaktion Books, 2009.

Kurkovsky, Stan. "Engaging students through mobile game development." *ACM SIGCSE Bulletin* 41, no. 1 (2009): 44–48.

Livingston, Christopher, Diana Papiz, Jody Macgregor, and Lauren Morton. "The Best Skyrim Mods." *PCGamer*, February 25, 2021, 2021. Accessed April 29, 2021. https://www.pcgamer.com/au/best-skyrim-mods/.

Maher, Cian. "The story behind the Oblivion mod Terry Pratchett worked on." *EUROGAMER* (blog), January 31, 2019. Accessed 29 April, 2021.https://www.eurogamer.net/the-story-behind-the-oblivion-mod-terry-pratchett-worked-on.

Moberly, Kevin, and Brent Moberly. "There is No Word for Work in the Dragon Tongue." *The Year's Work in Medievalism* 28 (2013): 1–9.

Morrison, Briana B., and Jon A. Preston. "Engagement: Gaming throughout the curriculum." *ACM SIGCSE Bulletin* 41, no. 1 (2009): 342–346.

Nexus Mods. 2021. "The Forgotten City." NEXUSMODS (blog). April 29, 2021. https://www.nexusmods.com/skyrimspecialedition/mods/1179.

Nunes, Bernardo Pereira, Terhi Nurmikko-Fuller, Giseli Rabello Lopes, Sean W. M. Siqueira, Gilda H. B. De Campos, and Marco A. Casanova. "Treasure Explorers–A Game as a Diagnostic Assessment Tool." In 2016 IEEE 16th International Conference on Advanced Learning Technologies (ICALT), 217–221. IEEE, 2016.

Ohannessian, Kevin. "How To Create A World: Skyrim's Director On Building A Never-Ending Fantasy." *Fast Company*, November 11, 2011. Accessed 28 April 2021. https://www.fastcompany.com/1794290/how-create-world-skyrims-director-building-never-ending-fantasy.

Propp, Vladimir. *Morphology of the Folktale*, 2nd edition: Austin: University of Texas Press, 1968.

Reddit. "[Guide] Going Medieval: High Middle Ages in Skyrim." Last Modified April 24, 2021. https://www.reddit.com/r/skyrimmods/comments/43pe07/guide_going_medieval_high_middle_ages_in_skyrim/.

Robb, Jane, and Gamespot Staff. "A Sight For Ore Eyes: Examining The Geology Of Skyrim." *Gamespot* (blog), February 15, 2013. Accessed April 29, 2021. https://www.gamespot.com/articles/a-sight-for-ore-eyes-examining-the-geology-of-skyrim/1100-6403844/.

Rogers, J., M. A. Schnabel, and T. J. Moleta. "Future Virtual Heritage-Techniques." Paper presented at the 2018 3rd Digital Heritage International Congress (DigitalHERITAGE) held jointly with 2018 24th International Conference on Virtual Systems & Multimedia (VSMM), 2018.

Small, Susan. "The Medieval Werewolf Model of Reading Skin." In *Reading Skin in Medieval Literature and Culture*, edited by Katie L. Walter, 81–97. New York: Palgrave Macmillan, 2013.

van Lanen, Rowin J., Esther Jansma, Jan van Doesburg, and Bert J. Groenewoudt. "Roman and early-medieval long-distance transport routes in north-western Europe: modelling frequent-travel zones using a dendro archaeological approach." *Journal of Archaeological Science* 73 (2016): 120–137.

Von Lünen, Alexander, Katherine J. Lewis, Benjamin Litherland, and Pat Cullum. *Historia Ludens: The Playing Historian*. New York: Routledge, 2019.

Wickler, S., and G. Nilsen. "Iron Age Boathouses In Arctic Norway Viewed As Multifunctional Expressions Of Maritime Cultural Heritage." *WIT Transactions on the Built Environment* 79 (2005): 15–23.

Ludography

Skyrim. Bethesda Game Studios, 2011.

Robert Houghton
10 Playing the Investiture Contest: Modding as Historical Debate in the Undergraduate and Postgraduate Classroom

Abstract: This chapter addresses the practical application of user modification as a pedagogical method within an undergraduate module and a taught postgraduate module at the University of Winchester. Through a practical example it demonstrates that tabletop games may provide an effective medium for students to explore historical arguments, to interrogate these arguments, and ultimately to create their own counterarguments and debate through the alteration of the game. In doing so, this chapter engages with a diverse range of pedagogical literature and highlights the potential and pitfalls of the approach. In sum, the chapter makes a case for the use of games as educational tools at the highest levels of history study.

Introduction

In principle, the student led modification of history games has substantial learning and teaching potential. Whether by design or coincidence, the mechanics of any historical game inherently represent the expression of historical models and arguments. These models are by necessity abstract and truncated,[1] but must also be holistic and internally consistent in order for the game to function.[2] They represent a means of historical interaction which is fundamentally different from traditional literary approaches, but which may nevertheless be intellectually and

---

[1] Jeremiah McCall, "Historical Simulations as Problem Spaces: Criticism and Classroom Use," *Journal of Digital Humanities* 1, no. 2 (2012): 43–44, http://journalofdigitalhumanities.org/1-2/historical-simulations-as-problem-spaces-by-jeremiah-mccall/; Adam Chapman, "Is Sid Meier's Civilization History?," *Rethinking History* 17, no. 3 (September 2013): 322–25, https://doi.org/10.1080/13642529.2013.774719; Robert Houghton, "World, Structure and Play: A Framework for Games as Historical Research Outputs, Tools, and Processes," *Práticas Da História* 7 (2018): 37–38.
[2] Andrew B. R. Elliott, "Simulations and Simulacra: History in Video Games," *Práticas Da História* 5 (2017): 29–31; Houghton, "World, Structure and Play," 19.

https://doi.org/10.1515/9783110712032-010

academically rigorous.[3] As playing a game requires interaction with, if not mastery of, its mechanics,[4] playing a historical game demands interaction with its rules and by extension with the arguments which these rules represent.[5] Through critical play and engagement with the relevant primary and secondary sources, the player-historian may recognize these arguments,[6] identify their position within the historiographical tradition, and consider their shortcomings: effectively interrogating these arguments as they would a monograph or academic article.[7] Players may also identify potentially unexpected emergent arguments through unforeseen interaction between mechanics. Ultimately, by changing the rules of a historical game through user modification, the player may create nuances and counterarguments to the position expressed through the original game.[8]

---

3 Adam Chapman, "Affording History: Civilization and the Ecological Approach," in *Playing with the Past: Digital Games and the Simulation of History*, ed. Matthew Kapell and Andrew B. R. Elliott (New York: Bloomsbury Academic, 2013), 324–26; Elliott, "Simulations and Simulacra," 20–21; Houghton, "World, Structure and Play," 17.

4 Jesper Juul, *Half-Real: Video Games between Real Rules and Fictional Worlds* (Cambridge, Mass: MIT Press, 2005), 95–97; Ian Bogost, "The Rhetoric of Video Games," in *The Ecology of Games: Connecting Youth, Games, and Learning*, ed. Katie Salen Tekinbaş, The John D. and Catherine T. Macarthur Foundation Series on Digital Media and Learning (Cambridge, Mass: MIT Press, 2008), 117–40; Ian Bogost, *Persuasive Games: The Expressive Power of Videogames* (Cambridge, Mass.: MIT Press, 2010).

5 Rolfe Daus Peterson, Andrew Justin Miller, and Sean Joseph Fedorko, "The Same River Twice: Exploring Historical Representation and the Value of Simulation in the Total War, Civilization and Patrician Franchises," in *Playing with the Past: Digital Games and the Simulation of History*, ed. Matthew Kapell and Andrew B. R. Elliott (New York: Bloomsbury Academic, 2013), esp. p. 38; Chapman, "Affording History," 61–73; Dawn Spring, "Gaming History: Computer and Video Games as Historical Scholarship," *Rethinking History* 19, no. 2 (2015): 215, https://doi.org/10.1080/13642529.2014.973714; Vinicius Marino Carvalho, "Videogames as Tools for Social Science History," *Historian* 79, no. 4 (2017): 812, https://doi.org/10.1111/hisn.12674; Houghton, "World, Structure and Play," 25–27.

6 Gary King, Robert O Keohane, and Sidney Verba, *Designing Social Inquiry: Scientific Inference in Qualitative Research*, 1994, http://www.dawsonera.com/depp/reader/protected/external/AbstractView/S9781400821211; Harry J. Brown, *Videogames and Education* (Armonk, N.Y.: M.E. Sharpe, 2008), 118; Juan Francisco Jiménez Alcázar, "The Other Possible Past: Simulation of the Middle Ages in Video Games," *Imago Temporis* 5 (2011): 300–301; Peterson, Miller, and Fedorko, "The Same River Twice," esp. p. 38.

7 Andrew McMichael, "PC Games and the Teaching of History," *The History Teacher* 40, no. 2 (February 2007): 203–4; McCall, "Historical Simulations as Problem Spaces," 21; Houghton, "World, Structure and Play," 27–29.

8 Shawn Graham, "Rolling Your Own: On Modding Commercial Games for Educational Goals," in *Pastplay: Teaching and Learning History with Technology*, ed. Kevin Kee (University of Michigan Press, 2014), 226–27, https://doi.org/10.2307/j.ctv65swr0; Kevin Kee and Shawn Graham, "Teaching History in an Age of Pervasive Computing: The Case for Games in the High

In doing so they may demonstrate the same critical thinking developed through undergraduate or even postgraduate history courses,[9] and potentially equal to that of professional scholars.[10]

This potential is largely untapped. While commercial and bespoke games have been used to great effect as introductions to periods and regions, as discussions of historical arguments through their mechanics as tools for exploring popular history, the student led design and modification of such games has been explored much less frequently. There are a growing number of examples of a user modification approach – such as Kee and Graham's successful deployment of *Civilization IV* as the basis for such an exercise[11] – but these remain very much in the minority.

There are several reasons for the limited adoption of computer games in this manner. Game development is time consuming and fully engaging students in the process can easily occupy more time than is typically available in class.[12] The skills required are not obviously compatible with the common skillset of history students (or instructors) and their development may appear at odds with the more traditional content of history classes or their learning goals.[13] The level of study at which this approach is most valuable is also the level at which the use of games is most likely to be derided or rejected outright. Development and modification of games can also prove expensive and the cost of

---

School and Undergraduate Classroom," in *Pastplay: Teaching and Learning History with Technology*, ed. Kevin Kee (University of Michigan Press, 2014), 279, https://doi.org/10.2307/j.ctv65swr0.17; Greg Koebel, "Simulating the Ages of Man: Periodization in Civilization V and Europa Universalis IV," *Loading . . . The Journal of the Canadian Game Studies Association* 10, no. 17 (2017): 72; Houghton, "World, Structure and Play," 27–31.

9 Kee and Graham, "Teaching History in an Age of Pervasive Computing"; A. Martin Wainwright, "Teaching Historical Theory through Video Games," *The History Teacher* 47, no. 4 (2014): 579–612; Stephen Ortega, "Representing the Past: Video Games Challenge to the Historical Narrative," *Syllabus* 4, no. 1 (2015): 1–13.

10 Jeremy Antley, "Going Beyond the Textual in History," *Journal of Digital Humanities* 1, no. 2 (2012), http://journalofdigitalhumanities.org/1-2/going-beyond-the-textual-in-history-by-jeremy-antley/; Carvalho, "Videogames as Tools"; Robert Houghton, "Scholarly History through Digital Games: Pedagogical Practice as Research Method," in *Return to the Interactive Past: The Interplay of Video Games and Histories*, ed. Csilla E. Ariese-Vandemeulebroucke et al. (Sidestone Press, 2021), 137–55.

11 Kee and Graham, "Teaching History in an Age of Pervasive Computing."

12 Jeremiah McCall, "Teaching History With Digital Historical Games: An Introduction to the Field and Best Practices," *Simulation & Gaming* 47, no. 4 (2016): 533, https://doi.org/10.1177/1046878116646693.

13 Carvalho, "Videogames as Tools," 818–89.

resources may make such an approach unviable at many institutions.[14] Perhaps most significantly, computer games almost invariably adopt a "black box" approach to conceal a sizeable portion of their mechanics from the player. This is often a practical necessity, but by withholding a part of the game rules, creators deny players access to an element of the argument presented through the game, thus undermining its utility as a tool for historical analysis and debate.[15] The approach has substantial potential, but is often rejected for its perceived practical constraints.

Board, card, or tabletop games – more simply "physical" or "analogue" games – present a number of advantages over their digital counterparts in this area. In contrast to the "black box" of computer game mechanics, the rules of physical games must be apparent to the players: they must parse these rules in order to play the game.[16] As such, the arguments and logic represented through the mechanics are more accessible and easier to interrogate and modify.[17] Beyond this, physical games require a substantially smaller economic outlay to create and alter than computer games and their modification requires fewer specialist skills.[18] The limitations of the medium can either be easily overcome – access to counters, dice, and other paraphernalia – or have little impact on the use of such a game in the classroom – reproduction costs; modelling complex data.

This chapter demonstrates the practical application of play and modification as historical debate at undergraduate and postgraduate level study. It discusses the development of a bespoke board game titled *The Investiture Contest* and its use within the taught postgraduate module *Church, Society and Conflict in the Medieval West* and the final year undergraduate module *The Middle Ages in Computer Games* at the University of Winchester in the academic year 2019/20. To this end I will:

1) Outline the learning context: the purpose of the game; its place within the two modules; and the core historiographical debates which formed the basis for the game's mechanics.
2) Set out the principles and goals of the design process, highlighting in particular the approaches used to mitigate difficulties with this method.

---

14 Timothy Compeau and Robert MacDougall, "Tecumseh Lies Here: Goals and Challenges for a Pervasive History Game in Progress," in *Pastplay: Teaching and Learning History with Technology*, ed. Kevin Kee (University of Michigan Press, 2014), 101–2, https://doi.org/10.2307/j.ctv65swr0.8; Houghton, "World, Structure and Play," 39.
15 Antley, "Going Beyond the Textual."
16 Antley.
17 Houghton, "World, Structure and Play," 40.
18 Houghton, 40.

3) Present an overview of the game and its interaction with the pertinent history and historiography.
4) Detail the integration of the game within the two modules and consider its learning utility in practice.

Ultimately I will argue that there is substantial educational potential for this approach and suggest possible evolutions of its use in light of this case study.

Learning Context

The game was designed to support two distinct modules. *Church, Society and Conflict in the Medieval West* makes use of traditional teaching and research methods (primary source analysis, historiographical debate, and student led research) to address the changing interaction between the Church and secular rulers in the central Middle Ages. It places a particular emphasis on the causes, events, and consequences of the Investiture Contest c.1073–1122. *The Middle Ages in Computer Games* considers the ways in which games represent the medieval period through the worlds and mechanics their developers create and the narratives these elements may create through player interaction. The course engages with the growing body of literature addressing history in this medium and employs computer games and the communities around them as primary sources.

Within *The Middle Ages in Computer Games*, the game was used early in the course as part of the front loading of theory before the consideration of a series of weekly themes (such as violence, gender and sexuality, and the "Dark Ages") over the remaining nine weeks of the course. The game served as a demonstration of the use of game mechanics as historical argument and the capacity through which modification of these mechanics facilitates an adjustment of the argument. This understanding forms a cornerstone for the analysis of the various themes addressed in the remainder of the course and hence needed to be deployed early in the module. The subject matter of the game was largely coincidental for the purposes of this module: the exercise could easily be run with a game focusing on any period or issue, providing the game allowed the easy exploration and modification of mechanics clearly connected to historical arguments.

The game was used towards the end of the module *Church, Society and Conflict in the Medieval West* after students had engaged with the materials pertaining to the Investiture Contest. It was used as an exercise whereby the students could explore and challenge differing historical arguments through a different medium, hence augmenting their understanding of the previously covered materials and potentially developing new avenues for their research. This module required a game focused on the conflict, although this still allowed for a substantial variety of themes, regions, and approaches. As with *The Middle Ages in Computer Games* this module required a game which allowed exploration and modification of rules connected clearly to historical arguments.

The Investiture Contest was traditionally presented as a bilateral conflict, primarily over the control of Investiture (the appointment of bishops and other clergymen within the Empire), between a reforming Pope and conservative Emperor.[19] However, this narrative has been challenged extensively in recent decades.[20] The cause of this conflict has been disputed and factors other than Investiture have been highlighted.[21] Likewise, the supposed monopoly of the papacy over reform has been challenged with several authors emphasizing the role of the secular magnates,[22] lower orders of society,[23] local clergy,[24] and the imperial faction.[25] The notional supporters of both acted with their own interests in mind: Matilda of Canossa supported Gregory VII wholeheartedly, but her relationship with Urban II was lukewarm, and by the time of Paschal II she was no longer willing

---

19 Louis Marie Olivier Duchesne, ed., *Liber Pontificalis. Texte, introduction et commentaire*, vol. 2 (Paris, 1892); Augustin Fliche, *La Réforme grégorienne: Tome I La formation des idées grégoriennes*, vol. 1, 3 vols., Spicilegium Sacrum Lovaniense (Louvain, 1926), 6; Gerd Tellenbach, *Church, State, and Christian Society at the Time of the Investiture Contest*, trans. R. Bennet (Oxford: Oxford University Press, 1966), 27.
20 For an excellent overview see: Maureen C. Miller, "The Crisis in the Investiture Crisis Narrative," *History Compass* 7, no. 6 (2009): 1570–80, https://doi.org/10.1111/j.1478-0542.2009.00645.x.
21 Maureen C. Miller, *Power and the Holy in the Age of the Investiture Conflict: A Brief History with Documents*, The Bedford Series in History and Culture (Boston: Bedford St. Martins, 2005).
22 John Howe, "The Nobility's Reform of the Medieval Church," *American Historical Review* 93 (April 1988): 317–39; Dorothy F. Glass, *The Sculpture of Reform in North Italy, ca. 1095–1130: History and Patronage of Romanesque Façades* (Farnham: Ashgate, 2010).
23 Amy G. Remensnyder, "Pollution, Purity, and Peace: An Aspect of Social Reform between the Late Tenth Century and 1076," in *The Peace of God: Social Violence and Religious Response in France around the Year 1000*, ed. Thomas Head and Richard Allen Landes (Ithaca, N.Y: Cornell University Press, 1992).
24 Hubertus Sibert, "Kommunikation, Autorität, Recht, Lebensordnung. Das Papsttum und die monastisch-kanonikale Reformbewegung (1046–1124)," in *Vom Umbruch zur Erneuerung?: das 11. und beginnende 12. Jahrhundert: Positionen der Forschung*, ed. Jörg Jarnut and Matthias Wemhoff, MittelalterStudien 13 (München: Fink, 2006), 11–29.
25 Regina Pörtner, "Reichspolitik, Reform und bischöfliche Autonomie: Der Investiturstreit im Spiegel der Gesta Treverorum," *Mediaevistik* 22 (2009): 83–115.

to risk her position on behalf of the imprisoned pope.[26] Welf of Bavaria aligned himself with the interests of the papacy and Matilda against Henry IV, but only as long as this suited his political purposes in Germany and his dynastic territorial ambitions in Italy. The antipope Guibert of Ravenna was traditionally portrayed as the puppet of Henry IV, but was driven by his own personal ideology and political goals.[27] Across Italy bishops, secular magnates, and cities took advantage of the broader conflict to settle their own scores, aligning themselves with whichever faction was convenient and often changing allegiance as the conflict progressed.[28]

A core element of teaching the Investiture Contest is often disabusing students of the simple accounts dominant in generalist literature in favor of more nuanced discussion of the causes and developments of the period. The conflict needs to be understood in the context of broader issues: Church hierarchy and autonomy of Lombard bishops; history of German intervention in Italy; Imperial legacy of Rome; Papal legacy of Rome; overlap of these two legacies; the rise of the Canossan dynasty and issue of Matilda's lands; and the emergence of the Italian city communes. From this foundation students may be introduced to the various historiographical traditions ranging from the older divergence between Italian and German schools and between Catholic and Protestant authors through to more modern perspectives and approaches.

The complex and contested historiography surrounding the Investiture Contest makes it ripe for teaching through games. The production of a game whose mechanics are based on any one of these arguments or historical models provides the opportunity for students to engage with and interrogate these arguments through play. Discrepancies and imbalances within the game rules may be identified through experience during play, allowing students to highlight the shortcomings of the arguments on which these rules are based. Students may then adjust and nuance the game's mechanics to more closely match their understanding of the period and events on the basis of their research and

---

26 Glauco Maria Cantarella, *Pasquale II e il suo tempo*, Nuovo Medioevo 54 (Napoli: Liguori, 1997).
27 Orazio Francabandera, "La Chiesa Ravennate sotto l'arcivescovo Guiberto," in *Le carte ravennati del secolo undicesimo*, ed. Ruggero Benericetti, Studi della Biblioteca Card. Gaetano Cicognani, nuova ser. 13 (Faenza: Biblioteca Cicognani, 2003), vii–xii.
28 I. S Robinson, "The Friendship Network of Gregory VII," *History* 63 (1978): 1–22; I. S Robinson, "The Friendship Circle of Bernold of Constance and the Dissemination of Gregorian Ideas in Late Eleventh-Century Germany," in *Friendship in Medieval Europe*, ed. Julian Haseldine (Stroud: Sutton, 1999), 185–98.

engagement with the historiography: in doing so they effectively engage in academic historical debate through the medium of the game.

Design Principles

Ease of modification was the central design principle for this game. The core pedagogical aim of the exercise was to allow students to engage in historical debate through the medium of game modification and to do so within the time constraints of a single three hour class. To this end, the game was designed with an emphasis on several core characteristics: simplicity of mechanics; speed of play; familiarity of materials and mechanics; and asymmetry of objectives. Conversely, random elements were avoided and playability was not prioritized within the design process.

The game mechanics were designed to be simple and clear. Students must be able to identify the argument presented through the rules of the game and so these rules must present that argument clearly and succinctly.[29] This simplicity also facilitates the modification of the game as students should be able to estimate the impact of any changes they make with relative ease. Further, simple rules for the initial game allows greater freedom for modification: the goal is to represent a skeleton argument which the students may alter to create deeper nuance.

Facilitating swift play was a further central concern for this project. Although there is great academic and pedagogical merit in devoting an entire module to the development and play of historical games, this approach is often impossible to implement within curricula due to time constraints, pedagogical concerns, or departmental and Institutional policy.[30] This particular game was to be used within sessions of no longer than three hours and thus demanded a play time of around half an hour per session to allow discussion and modification. A focus on simple mechanics supported this objective to a substantial degree, but a more concrete end point – a limited turn track for example –formed an arbitrary but necessary conclusion for each cycle of play.

Commonly familiar gaming materials and mechanics were employed to facilitate the accessibility of the game and allow faster play. While it is important

---

[29] McCall, "Teaching History With Digital Historical Games," 533; Jeremiah McCall, "Video Games as Participatory Public History," in *A Companion to Public History*, ed. D. M. Dean, 1 edition (Hoboken, NJ: Wiley, 2018), 407; Houghton, "World, Structure and Play," 35–36.
[30] McCall, "Teaching History With Digital Historical Games," 533.

to avoid generalizations about students' prior gaming experiences, most students can reasonably be assumed to be familiar with pawns, game boards, playing cards, standard dice, and various other paraphernalia – if not from childhood or more recent play, then through popular culture. Most students will also have experience with associated basic mechanics such as counter movement, placement of control markers, or drawing and discarding cards. Building a game based on these familiar components and rules reduces the time necessary for students to interpret the game, allows more intuitive interaction with the arguments represented by these rules, and lowers the potential for frustration amongst students. While other less conventional components or mechanics – such as worker placement, shared resource pools, or deck building – can be very effective methods of representing historical arguments, these materials and mechanics were avoided as they were likely to be unfamiliar to a proportion of students and so lengthen play time and complicate interaction with the arguments represented by the game's rules.

Clear links between the game's components and rules and the situation around the Investiture contest were employed to support student engagement and help to clarify the historical arguments presented through the rules.[31] Maps and names of locations and characters can underline the connection between actions taken within the game and the historical content of the remainder of the module. In a similar fashion, explicit connection between game mechanics and historical mechanisms they are designed to emulate can ground the game in any pertinent historiographical traditions. In concert, clearly embedding the components and rules of the game in its historical theme facilitates the creation of a historical narrative through a collaboration between the players and the developer. In doing so, this design approach supports the interrogation of the narrative and the identification of any emergent arguments.

The mechanics were designed with the core historical arguments in mind – thus asymmetric objectives were provided for the various player characters. Objectives can substantially alter players' behavior and hence providing different objectives for each player allows the discussion of the interaction of these different personalities and goals.[32] For this particular game, the use of asymmetric and compatible objectives was particularly important as one of the core arguments

---

31 McCall, 534–35; Carvalho, "Videogames as Tools," 811–12.
32 Robert Houghton, "If You're Going to Be the King, You'd Better Damn Well Act like the King: Setting Objectives to Encourage Realistic Play in Grand Strategy Computer Games," in *The Middle Ages in Modern Culture: History and Authenticity in Contemporary Medievalism*, ed. Karl Alvestad and Robert Houghton (IBTauris, 2021), 186–210.

set out by the game was that the Investiture Contest was a multifaceted conflict between numerous actors, each of which possessed their own goals.

Conversely, random elements were almost entirely avoided within the game. Randomness can serve an important element within simulations and learning games as a representation of complexity and uncertainty.[33] However, these advantages are undermined in this case by two factors. Firstly, randomness can easily extend play time as players are obliged to calculate the outcomes of unforeseen variables and determine their impact on the game. Secondly, and more significantly, randomness can obscure the mechanics of a game and hence the arguments they represent thus undermining the purpose of the exercise.

Likewise, playability was not a priority. While the entertainment factor of a game (or any form of media) can certainly generate interest in its historical subject matter, this was not the purpose of this game: these were optional modules at higher levels of study and there was little prospect of further increasing students' interest in the subject matter and little pedagogical benefit in doing so. Further, an emphasis on "fun" can undermine the educational potential of a game. As McCall has highlighted, students are often wary of the educational value of games and suspicious of entertainment as education in general.[34] Indeed, one of the most common failings of edutainment games is an overemphasis on entertainment which falls flat.[35] While almost all students reported enjoyment of the exercise, this was coincidental to its purpose.

The Investiture Contest Game

The purpose of the game was to demonstrate two opposing accounts of the Investiture Contest – namely the traditional presentation of a binary struggle between pope and emperor and a more nuanced explanation of shifting and conflicting alliances between key figures – before asking students to modify the game rules in order to better represent their understanding of the period.

The game focused on political influence in northern Italy in the later eleventh century. The full rules are attached as an Appendix after the bibliography,

---

[33] Kevin Schut, "Strategic Simulations and Our Past: The Bias of Computer Games in the Presentation of History," *Games and Culture* 2, no. 3 (2007): 226, https://doi.org/10.1177/1555412007306202.
[34] McCall, "Teaching History With Digital Historical Games," 532–33.
[35] Richard Van Eck, "Digital Game Based Learning: It's Not Just the Digital Native Who Are Rest-Less," *Educause Review* 41 (2006): 16–30.

but in short: players took the role of one of six key figures within the conflict (Emperor Henry IV, Pope Urban II, Antipope Guibert of Ravenna, Countess Matilda of Canossa, Archbishop Arnulf of Milan, and Duke Welf of Bavaria) represented by a colored pawn; they took it in turns to move around the map, placing counters representing their influence in a province, and removing the influence counters placed by their opponents; play ended after six rounds and victory was decided. The game was designed to function with fewer than six players – characters could be omitted or a player could control more than one character – and with more than six players – players could take joint control of a character.

Two divergent arguments about the nature of the Investiture Contest were expressed through the victory conditions of the "basic" and "advanced" versions of the game. The Basic Game set out the traditional presentation of the struggle as a binary conflict between the German Emperor and the Pope. Players were divided into two teams representing Papal and Imperial factions and tasked with exerting greater influence over more of the map than their rivals.

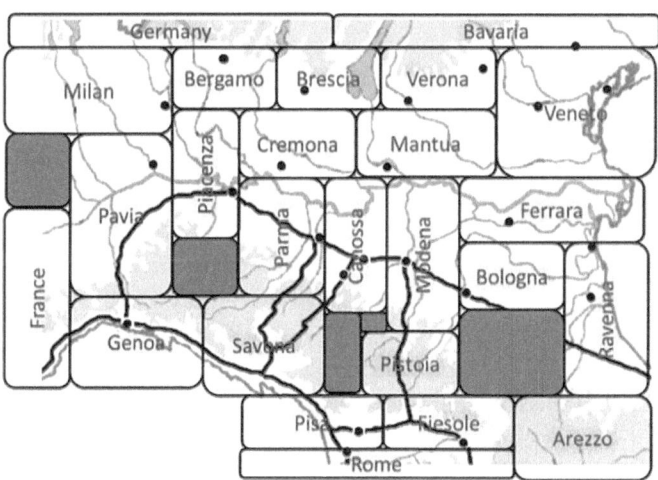

Figure 10.1: *The Investiture Contest* game map.

The Advanced Game presented a more nuanced argument of shifting alliances and goals. Each player was given a different series of four objectives designed to coincide with the recorded behavior and apparent aims of their characters. For example, the Pope was tasked with gaining control over key provinces central to their reform strategy including Rome and the archepiscopal cities of Milan and Ravenna, while Matilda of Canossa was focussed on retaining control of her territories. These objectives were sequential (earlier objectives had to be completed for later objectives to be counted) giving a sense of the priorities for each of these figures. The majority of these objectives were compatible with the goals of other players, but completing these objectives required negotiation and trust between the players and each player's final objective was incompatible with the final objective of at least one other player, allowing the exploration of the complex interactions between these figures.

Beyond the victory conditions, the mechanics of the Basic and Advanced games were identical and represented several other arguments about the politics of the medieval period. For example, the emphasis on movement and the restriction of most actions to the immediate vicinity of the player's pawn is a ludic depiction of the predominance of itinerant rulership within the medieval period. The probable coexistence of influence counters from multiple players within a single province represented the argument that nuanced and overlapping relationship networks existed across the region and that absolute control over an area was an anachronism.

The game was designed around the principles outlined above. The mechanics were kept simple and succinct – the rules of the basic game fit on a side of A4 while a second side of A4 was required to list the objectives for the advanced game. The length of the game was restricted through the round limit. Familiar materials – pawns, counters, and game board – were employed alongside familiar mechanics – turn taking, movement, area control. Mechanics and play were clearly tied to the period and issues through the rulebook, map, and characters. The game contained no random elements beyond turn order being determined by position around the table. Although the Basic Game was relatively balanced (the only differences between the competing sides were starting locations), this was coincidental rather than a deliberate product of the design while the objectives of the Advanced Game were fundamentally imbalanced – an issue raised during the class as outlined below. The game was relatively abstract: although maps and characters were based on reality, details were kept vague and mechanics were kept simple.

Play and Modification

The classroom deployment of the game was a qualified success, although the sessions highlighted a number of considerations for the future development of this approach. Feedback was broadly positive and students typically reported that the game helped them to develop their understanding of the arguments around the conflict and allowed them to think about new ways of exploring historical issues. It must be emphasized that this feedback was solicited from a captive audience and small sample size and should in no way be seen as an endorsement for the commercial viability of the game. Nevertheless, these responses underline the pedagogical utility of the approach. The time taken for each playthrough was roughly 40–45 minutes and this remained the case after multiple playthroughs: it seems that any acceleration of play through familiarity with the rules was countered by more lengthy strategizing and consideration of the implications of the mechanics. Throughout the sessions students engaged with a number of learning activities: interrogation of the game mechanics as historical arguments; identification of emergent arguments; self-driven research; and roleplay as their assigned characters. Beyond this, the behavior of several students highlighted new elements for consideration through this approach by engaging in suboptimal play, objective driven play, and metagame betrayal. Students proposed and developed a range of mods for the game which can be broadly categorized as addressing four key issues: balance, realism, randomness, and playability.

Students were able to identify the arguments set out through the game's mechanics and ultimately to interrogate these mechanics and arguments. Both classes followed the opposing arguments debating the binary or multifaceted nature of the conflict presented by the basic and advanced versions of the game. Interrogation of these arguments was a more difficult prospect, but students generally engaged well with this part of the exercise. Students within the postgraduate class identified the fact that each character was mechanically identical and argued that several of the characters – most notably the emperor Henry IV – were underpowered in comparison to their understanding of the conflict. Students also criticized the objectives of the various characters. Broadly speaking students on the postgraduate course focused their criticism on adherence to historical issues and questioning the logic behind the selection and order of these objectives based on their research into the behavior and goals of these figures. Students on the undergraduate course tended instead to note mechanical discrepancies and imbalances focusing on the translation of arguments into rules rather than the veracity of the arguments themselves. More generally, both groups criticized the abstractions and absences within the game. The absence of key powers including the Sicilian Normans, the Byzantine Empire, and the Italian city communes (especially Venice) were noted and critically discussed by players.

In each class students identified a number of arguments which emerged unexpectedly from the ruleset. Most notably, Canossa was observed as a particularly important province within several playthroughs of the game in both classes. This factor emerged in part because four of the players had an interest in the province to complete their objectives, but also because of the central position of the province and the intervention of players who did not require control of Canossa for their goals, but saw the strategic benefit of challenging other players' control of the area. This was an unintended outcome of the game, but meshes well with dominant historical understandings: Canossa is almost universally accepted as a strategically vital site during the Investiture contest, it was the location (in 1091) of one of the pivotal battles of the conflict, and control over Matilda's lands remained an issue of substantial conflict for decades after her death. Although they were unable to complete it in practice, one group within the undergraduate class observed the possibility of a viable alliance against the Pope amongst all other players which would allow them each to achieve at least their third objective. On this basis, they concluded that if the arguments represented through the rules of the game were accepted then it followed that the ambitions of the Pope were the main obstacle to the resolution of the Investiture Contest.

In an unforeseen and unprompted development, students within the undergraduate class were driven to engage in exploratory research around the characters and events of the Investiture Contest as a means to drive their strategy and ultimately their mods. This research was fairly rudimentary, focusing on Wikipedia and other easily accessible online tools, but represents an important opportunity for the use of games such as this in an educational setting. The impact of this approach here was broadly positive, although a couple of players took their research as a playbook to recreate historical events. This is certainly an interesting approach to the game – and should perhaps have been expected – but was not ideal here as the goal of the exercise was to investigate and develop historical arguments rather than to recreate historical events.

Students in both the postgraduate and undergraduate classes – again without prompting – took a roleplaying approach to their characters and the game. The most consistent example of this is that in both groups players representing Matilda and Welf generally worked together throughout the game. This was in part because of the alignment of their early objectives, but many students reported that they were honoring the marriage alliance between the two figures. In one case, a player in control of Matilda maintained close co-operation with Welf until the final turn of the game, when they suddenly turned against their erstwhile ally, seizing control of two key provinces and completing the last of their objectives. In response to the Welf player's accusations of betrayal and infidelity, the Matilda player countered that this was perfectly fitting with the tumultuous relationship between the two and the irreconcilable breakdown of the marriage. Other examples of roleplay include: the player representing the archbishop of Milan swearing undying allegiance to the emperor as long as the imperial player refrained from interfering within the city and its environs;

vocal, lively, and largely authentic rhetoric being hurled between the players controlling the Pope and Antipope; and an urgent and impassioned plea from the Antipope to the Emperor for help against an alliance of the Pope, Matilda, and Welf. This was not a designed part of the game, but was somewhat anticipated and welcome as a component of the learning experience. In adopting this roleplay driven approach, players moved away from the sometimes cold and logical reasoning applied by historians to the political actors of this period and collectively created an explanation for the conflict which was much more personal and emotional. In doing so, they moved well beyond the rules of the game and created their own argument.

The personal aspects students brought to the game extended beyond roleplaying to incorporate other metagame elements: players brought relationships and experience from outside the game to influence their behavior within the game. At its most basic level this meant that players who were friends tended to act in concert within the game – although there were several exceptions to this trend where close friends engaged in deep and embittered rivalries. Within the classroom, relationships between players often carried over from one game to the next: mutual support in one game tended to form the basis for good relations in the next; dramatic success and perceived competence by one player in the first game led to a wide-ranging alliance against that player in the second; and betrayal of trust was remembered not only by the victim but by the rest of the table in all future games. Again, this was not a designed element of the game, but was anticipated to some extent. These metagame influences moved the focus of the constructed arguments away from the rules and towards players' personal interactions creating a new exploration of the conflict in an unintended, but still valid and useful, manner. Through these play approaches, players created alternative arguments for the behavior of their characters and new explanations for events. In most cases, these approaches were deployed acritically but reflection allowed students to consider the implications of their actions and motivations on the account they created through the game and consider parallels within the period.

On several occasions this focus on roleplay or other metagame considerations led to suboptimal strategic decisions. With the exception of the example of Matildine betrayal highlighted above, the alliances between Matilda and Welf inevitably led both their players to take actions which were counterproductive in pursuing their victory objectives even while they conformed to their roleplay premise. Friendships and grudges likewise led games to progress in unexpected ways inspiring difficult alliances or self-destructive and all-consuming conflicts – which almost inevitably undermined the ability of the involved players to complete their goals. This behavior represents a rejection of the arguments presented through the game's objectives: players undertook actions which did not fit with the historical narrative envisaged in the game's design. Through these acts of counterplay they – deliberately or coincidentally – challenged the games objectives and hence the historical arguments it represented.

After completing the first playthroughs, students proposed a range of modifications to the game. These most frequently included scenario variations which kept the rules of the game almost entirely intact but introduced new elements. Students suggested adjustments to the board including the introduction of more provinces to create a more detailed representation of the region, expansion of the map to incorporate new areas in Central Italy and the rest of the Empire, and rearrangement of existing provinces and impassable areas. Other groups suggested the introduction of new playable characters such as the Doge of Venice, Emperor of Byzantium, or Duke of Apulia and Calabria – figures with an interest in the area and the events of the Investiture Contest. These adjustments represent a relatively simple form of user modification, but nonetheless substantially changed the argument set out through the game's rules. Changing the scope and composition of the board changed the strategic importance of key areas of the map and altered interactions between players, creating new strategies, alliances, and conflicts. In doing so, students created new arguments about the relative importance of the regions of the conflict and set out new explanations for the behavior of key figures. Likewise, the introduction of new characters emphasized some shortcomings of the original game: namely its failure to place the conflict in a broader context. Through this adjustment students created a more nuanced and holistic approach to the issue.

Various groups also proposed adjustments to the board and characters alongside concrete (and sometimes elaborate) changes to the rules. Students within the postgraduate class suggested the inclusion of geographic features such as forests, hills, rivers, and major roads which would obstruct or speed movement around the map. They likewise introduced "home regions" which were easier for particular characters to influence. One group within the undergraduate class modified the abilities of each character. For example, following their identification of the Emperor as underpowered (noted above) this group substantially increased this character's ability to exert influence within his immediate vicinity. Conversely, the Pope was granted improved powers to exert influence at a distance. This somewhat more advanced approach allowed students to create more detailed counters to the arguments posed through the rules of the game. By adapting the map and its associated rules, students created a more complex representation of the practicalities of itinerant rulership and created nuance around the regional loyalties to key figures during the conflict. By changing the rules through which different players exerted influence, students highlighted different approaches to power between the overwhelming force of the Imperial court and host contrasted with the softer but more flexible influence of the Papal curia and Church networks.

Students frequently suggested mods which incorporated random elements. A couple of groups proposed semi-random outcomes for attempts to exert influence making use of several variations of dice driven mechanics to introduce a level of uncertainty around the ability of a player's character to act in a given turn. These approaches ranged from fairly simple – the number of influence counters a player could place in their turn was determined by rolling a die – to rather complicated – players had to roll above a certain number to place an influence counter, with the chance of success influenced by several factors including the influence of other characters, distance from the player's character, and the presence of other characters in the targeted province. Other groups introduced random events chosen by rolling dice and consulting tables or by drawing cards. These events included bad weather, external intervention, and urban uprisings and their impact was translated into the game's mechanics to disrupt or aid the plans of the players. Although random elements such as these had been consciously avoided within the design of the core game and these elements substantially extended play time, these modifications represent important reconfigurations of the arguments posed through the game's rules. Introducing random elements allowed the simulation of events beyond the control of the players, creating a broader, if more abstract, exploration of the Investiture Contest. Moreover, the introduction of these elements changed the behavior of the players. Disruption – or even the threat of disruption – of plans led to a more cautious approach from several players which in turn altered the explanation of the actions taken by the key figures in the conflict.

Conclusion

The deployment of a ludic model of historical debate in practice was broadly successful. Students engaged with key materials and game mechanics, parsed these mechanics for their historical arguments, interrogated these arguments, and ultimately created arguments of their own through user modification. Nevertheless, a handful of issues emerged: the game took longer to play than hoped; there was occasional disconnection between the theory put forth by students and the mechanics they created to represent this theory; and roleplay and metagame activity overrode the arguments suggested through the game's mechanics.

Streamlining play is the most immediate practical concern going forward, but is an issue with several manageable solutions. Students typically spent around 80 to 90 minutes playing through the Basic Game and Advanced Game before beginning their modification of the game which left relatively little time to fully engage in the core activity of the class and hence undermined the impact of the approach. Marco Tibaldini, who supported the undergraduate session, has suggested the removal of the Basic Game from the start of the exercise, noting that students within the undergraduate class were able to grasp the game rules and their implications swiftly and gained no significant benefit from the additional first playthrough. This idea has a great deal of merit as it has the potential to substantially reduce the lead in time before students engage in the modification activity, and this approach will be developed within future iterations of the game. Other simple short term solutions include reducing the number of players or the number of available turns, but in the longer term the mechanics and scope of the game will need to be addressed in order to speed play and provide more time for students to parse and discuss the game and to create mods.

Improving students' ability to translate their historical arguments into game mechanics is a deeper challenge. While students in the postgraduate class composed complex counter arguments on the basis of their knowledge of the various historiographical traditions surrounding the Investiture Contest, they sometimes struggled to conceive these arguments in the form of rules. Conversely, while the undergraduate class were more confident in their creation and adjustment of rules and more fluent in their conversion of arguments into these rules, their arguments tended to be more limited and disjointed from the body of literature. These outcomes were anticipated and in no way represent failures on the part of the students: instead they are consequences of the distinct nature of the two modules. These outcomes underline the importance of integrating the exercise into the broader syllabus and highlight the need to ensure participants are sufficiently familiar with the source material and literature but also with the ludic approach. A potential resolution for this issue is to devote more time to supporting exercises – although this is of course limited by the class schedule and other requirements within the module. Alternatively, and more practically, the modification element of the exercise could be more closely guided. Students could be provided with a specific variation of the game's argument to represent through modification. This would be based on elements of current historical debate, for example: "The city communes played a central role in the Investiture Contest" or "The enmity between Matilda of Canossa and Henry IV was insurmountable." This could be accompanied by a short summary of basic modifications and their implications for the arguments presented by the game. A tighter focus like this would limit students' ability to express their own arguments, but would provide direction within an unfamiliar task.

The influence of metagame elements on player behavior was underestimated in the preparation of the exercise. Roleplay, external knowledge, personal friendships and rivalries, and counterplay created new elements to the arguments presented through the game which, as outlined above, created some interesting and constructive insights for the players. However, the substantial impact of these elements also underlines the limitations of the game rules to dictate player behavior and hence the arguments represented through the game. This is an issue which needs to be considered carefully, but my instinct is that the solution is not to restrict player agency but rather to embrace it. Students should be encouraged to engage closely with their characters and to roleplay not only their strategic goals, but also their personal relationships and personalities insofar as these can be discerned. To this end, it may be advisable to lessen the focus on specific objectives and victory conditions and instead have the players analyze and explain whether their character has succeeded or failed at the end of the game.

The exercise could also be beneficially extended by allowing students to interrogate the arguments set out in each other's modifications. This would, as Marco Tibaldini has suggested, take the form of students playtesting the modded games created by other groups. They would then interrogate the arguments represented by the new ruleset and consider the effectiveness of the altered mechanics in conveying the new argument. There are substantial potential learning benefits to this approach as it allows the exchange of ideas between groups and facilitates broader debate. Further, this method will allow students to experience the impact of player agency on their constructed mechanics, providing them with greater insight into the corporate authorship of the histories presented through games.

A final issue concerns the practicalities of delivering this exercise during the global pandemic. Face to face teaching has been impossible for much of the past academic year and the close proximity required to play the game remains unfeasible at the time of writing. While it is far from ideal, a workable solution here is to move the exercise online and present the game through a browser based tabletop simulator. Various free to use platforms exist which could facilitate this such as *Board Game Arena*, *Roll20*, or *Vassal*. New issues around communication and accessibility will certainly emerge with this shift of medium, but the digital approach mitigates the problems posed by the pandemic and creates the potential to use game modification based learning at a distance. There are other benefits to this approach including most notably a greater ability to introduce new components without the restraints of physical creation or acquisition.

The qualified success of the Investiture Contest game as a learning tool suggests broader applications for the approach. The system could easily be adapted to consider other historical periods or regions when embedded within modules addressing relevant eras and areas. Consideration of other subfields within history may require more thought: games for the debate of warfare are perhaps the most obvious area for further exploration as a massive corpus of commercial games exist which may provide exemplar mechanics, but economic structures can easily provide the basis for the mechanical systems within a game, and role-play elements provide huge potential for the exploration of social interactions and connected issues. Provided the rules fit the arguments, it is entirely possible to deploy a game for the exploration for almost any historical debate. This approach must be used with care, particularly around sensitive historical issues, but it represents a great deal of learning potential.

The development and deployment of the Investiture Contest game has provided a practical demonstration of the utility of user modification as a form of historical debate. Students successfully parsed, interrogated, and modified the arguments represented through the game's rules and in doing so displayed a substantial range of advanced analytical skills. While the format was very far removed from more traditional academic and learning approaches and the history was produced and communicated in a very different manner, this nevertheless represents a valid and constructive approach. There are certainly several issues to be considered in the future, but these do not appear to be insurmountable, even with limited availability of time in classes. The approach must be embedded within the content of the module and students must be able to acquire relevant knowledge of the period, events, and historiography under discussion and also develop an understanding of how games can communicate history: they must be familiar with both the content and the method. However, these parameters apply to any teaching approach. Ultimately all that is required is a greater flexibility in what we see as valid approaches to history and a fundamental change to the academic respect we assign to games.

Appendix: *The Investiture Contest* Game Rules

The Investiture Contest – Basic Game

Introduction

The year is 1088 and the Investiture Contest dominates northern Italy.[36] The emperor Henry IV – supported by the antipope Guibert of Ravenna and archbishop Anselm of Milan – is pitted against the newly elected pope Urban II and his allies countess Matilda of Canossa and her husband duke Welf of Bavaria. Which faction, imperial or papal, can exert the most influence over the fractious region?

Objective

The side which dominates the most provinces wins. Dominate provinces by having the most influence counters on them.

Board and Pieces

The main board consists of 25 provinces each representing a region of Italy or a neighboring kingdom.
The turn track consists of 6 spaces each representing a year.
Each player has a pawn representing their character and their entourage.
Each player has a set of 30 counters representing their characters influence.

Set up

Place a counter on the first space of the turn track.
Place the players' pawns in the following provinces:
    Emperor Henry IV (Yellow): Germany
    Pope Urban II (White): France
    Antipope Guibert of Ravenna (Blue): Ravenna
    Countess Matilda of Canossa (Green): Canossa
    Archbishop Anselm of Milan (Red): Milan
    Duke Welf of Bavaria (Black): Bavaria

---

[36] *The Investiture Contest* (Robert Houghton, 2020).

Play

The Emperor goes first. Play then proceeds clockwise around the table.

Each player's turn consists of a series of actions. On your turn you may take all/any/none of these actions in the following order.

1) Movement: move your pawn into any adjacent province. You may freely move into provinces already occupied by other players.
2) Hold court: place up to four influence counters in the province your pawn occupies or any adjacent provinces.
3) Disrupt opponents: remove up to two counters belonging to other players from the province occupied by your pawn.
4) Despatch envoy: the player may place a single influence counter on any province on the board. This includes the province currently occupied by the player's pawn.

Play then passes to the next player. When play returns to the emperor, move the counter on the turn track on.

End of the game

The game ends at the end of turn 6. Establish which player has the most influence counters in each province. The side with the highest number of provinces under their domination wins.

NB: Although this is a team game, dominance is determined individually. So if Matilda and Welf each have two counters on Canossa, but Henry has three, then Henry is dominant and the province counts for the imperial side.

The Investiture Contest – Advanced Game

Introduction

The Investiture Contest was more complicated than a straightforward clash between emperor and pope and their partisans. Allegiances were fluid and each of the participants had their own goals. There are no fixed factions and each player is free to make and break alliances to complete their objectives.

Objectives

Each player has their own set of objectives. Their success is measured by how many of these they fulfil at the end of the game. For a higher numbered objective to count as complete, all lower numbered objectives must also be completed. i.e. if a player has not completed their first objective, then none of their other objectives counts as complete.

Emperor Henry IV (yellow):
1) Secure your kingdom: Be dominant in Germany
2) Re-establish political networks: Have at least one influence counter in at least twelve provinces
3) Take control of reform: Prevent the Pope from being dominant in Rome
4) Counter the Canossan threat: Prevent Matilda or Welf from being dominant in Canossa

Pope Urban II (white):
1) Exert papal authority: Be dominant in one of Rome, Milan, Ravenna, Germany, France
2) Exert papal authority: Be dominant in two of Rome, Milan, Ravenna, Germany, France
3) Exert papal authority: Be dominant in three of Rome, Milan, Ravenna, Germany, France
4) Exert papal authority: Be dominant in four of Rome, Milan, Ravenna, Germany, France

Antipope Guibert of Ravenna (blue):
1) Secure your seat: Be dominant in Ravenna
2) Reign in suffragans: Be dominant in three of Bologna, Ferrara, Modena, Canossa, Parma, Piacenza
3) Claim the throne of St Peter: Be dominant in Rome
4) Control the archdiocese: Be dominant in five of Bologna, Ferrara, Modena, Canossa, Parma, Piacenza

Countess Matilda of Canossa (green):
1) Retain the mountain fortress: Be dominant in Canossa
2) Protect the Canossan lands: Be dominant in four of Mantua, Modena, Ferrara, Savona, Pistoia, Pisa, Fiesole, Arezzo
3) Expand the Canossan lands: Be dominant in two of Brescia, Verona, Parma, Cremona, Bologna, Genoa

4) Secure the Canossan heritage: Prevent anyone else from achieving their final objectives

Archbishop Anselm of Milan (red):
1) Protect the see of Ambrose: Be dominant in Milan
2) Retain archiepiscopal authority: Be dominant in three of Pavia, Bergamo, Brescia, Cremona, Mantua
3) Counter the threat from Ravenna: Be dominant in Piacenza and Parma
4) Assert primacy: Be dominant in Ravenna or Rome

Duke Welf of Bavaria (black):
1) Retain Bavaria: Be dominant in Bavaria
2) Protect the Matildine lands: You or Matilda must be dominant in at least five of Canossa, Mantua, Modena, Ferrara, Savona, Pistoia, Pisa, Fiesole, Arezzo
3) Drive out the Imperial partisans: The emperor must not be present in more than four of Canossa, Brescia, Verona, Mantua, Modena, Lucca, Florence, Bologna
4) Secure the position of the house in Germany or Italy: Be dominant in Germany or Canossa

Bibliography

Alcázar, Juan Francisco Jiménez. "The Other Possible Past: Simulation of the Middle Ages in Video Games." *Imago Temporis* 5 (2011): 299–340.

Antley, Jeremy. "Going Beyond the Textual in History." *Journal of Digital Humanities* 1, no. 2 (2012). http://journalofdigitalhumanities.org/1-2/going-beyond-the-textual-in-history-by-jeremy-antley/.

Bogost, Ian. *Persuasive Games: The Expressive Power of Videogames*. Cambridge, Mass.: MIT Press, 2010.

Bogost, Ian. "The Rhetoric of Video Games." In *The Ecology of Games: Connecting Youth, Games, and Learning*, edited by Katie Salen Tekinbaş, 117–40. The John D. and Catherine T. Macarthur Foundation Series on Digital Media and Learning. Cambridge, Mass: MIT Press, 2008.

Brown, Harry J. *Videogames and Education*. Armonk, N.Y.: M.E. Sharpe, 2008.

Cantarella, Glauco Maria. *Pasquale II e il suo tempo*. Nuovo Medioevo 54. Napoli: Liguori, 1997.

Carvalho, Vinicius Marino. "Videogames as Tools for Social Science History." *Historian* 79, no. 4 (2017): 794–819. https://doi.org/10.1111/hisn.12674.

Chapman, Adam. "Affording History: Civilization and the Ecological Approach." In *Playing with the Past: Digital Games and the Simulation of History*, edited by Matthew Kapell and Andrew B. R. Elliott, 61–73. New York: Bloomsbury Academic, 2013.

Chapman, Adam. "Is Sid Meier's Civilization History?" *Rethinking History* 17, no. 3 (2013): 312–32. https://doi.org/10.1080/13642529.2013.774719.

Compeau, Timothy, and Robert MacDougall. "Tecumseh Lies Here: Goals and Challenges for a Pervasive History Game in Progress." In *Pastplay: Teaching and Learning History with Technology*, edited by Kevin Kee, 87–108. University of Michigan Press, 2014. https://doi.org/10.2307/j.ctv65swr0.8.

Duchesne, Louis Marie Olivier, ed. *Liber Pontificalis. Texte, introduction et commentaire*. Vol. 2. E. Thorin: Paris, 1892.

Elliott, Andrew B. R. "Simulations and Simulacra: History in Video Games." *Práticas Da História* 5 (2017): 11–41.

Fliche, Augustin. *La Réforme grégorienne: Tome I La formation des idées grégoriennes*. Vol. 1. 3 vols. Spicilegium Sacrum Lovaniense 6. Louvain, 1926.

Francabandera, Orazio. "La Chiesa Ravennate sotto l'arcivescovo Guiberto." In *Le carte ravennati del secolo undicesimo*, edited by Ruggero Benericetti, vii–xii. Studi della Biblioteca Card. Gaetano Cicognani, nuova ser. 13. Faenza: Biblioteca Cicognani, 2003.

Glass, Dorothy F. *The Sculpture of Reform in North Italy, ca. 1095-1130: History and Patronage of Romanesque Façades*. Farnham: Ashgate, 2010.

Graham, Shawn. "Rolling Your Own: On Modding Commercial Games for Educational Goals." In *Pastplay: Teaching and Learning History with Technology*, edited by Kevin Kee, 214–27. University of Michigan Press, 2014. https://doi.org/10.2307/j.ctv65swr0.

Houghton, Robert. "If You're Going to Be the King, You'd Better Damn Well Act like the King: Setting Objectives to Encourage Realistic Play in Grand Strategy Computer Games." In *The Middle Ages in Modern Culture: History and Authenticity in Contemporary Medievalism*, edited by Karl Alvestad and Robert Houghton, 186–210. IBTauris, 2021.

Houghton, Robert. "Scholarly History through Digital Games: Pedagogical Practice as Research Method." In *Return to the Interactive Past: The Interplay of Video Games and Histories*, edited by Csilla E. Ariese-Vandemeulebroucke, Krijn H. J. Boom, Angenitus Arie Andries Mol, and Aris Politopoulos, 137–55. Leiden: Sidestone Press, 2021.

Houghton, Robert. "World, Structure and Play: A Framework for Games as Historical Research Outputs, Tools, and Processes." *Práticas Da História* 7 (2018): 11–43.

Howe, John. "The Nobility's Reform of the Medieval Church." *American Historical Review* 93 (April 1988): 317–39.

Juul, Jesper. *Half-Real: Video Games between Real Rules and Fictional Worlds*. Cambridge, Mass: MIT Press, 2005.

Kee, Kevin, and Shawn Graham. "Teaching History in an Age of Pervasive Computing: The Case for Games in the High School and Undergraduate Classroom." In *Pastplay: Teaching and Learning History with Technology*, edited by Kevin Kee, 270–91. University of Michigan Press, 2014. https://doi.org/10.2307/j.ctv65swr0.17.

King, Gary, Robert O. Keohane, and Sidney Verba. *Designing Social Inquiry: Scientific Inference in Qualitative Research*. 1994. http://www.dawsonera.com/depp/reader/protected/external/AbstractView/S9781400821211.

Koebel, Greg. "Simulating the Ages of Man: Periodization in Civilization V and Europa Universalis IV." *Loading . . . The Journal of the Canadian Game Studies Association* 10, no. 17 (2017): 60–76.

McCall, Jeremiah. "Historical Simulations as Problem Spaces: Criticism and Classroom Use." *Journal of Digital Humanities* 1, no. 2 (2012). http://journalofdigitalhumanities.org/1-2/historical-simulations-as-problem-spaces-by-jeremiah-mccall/.

McCall, Jeremiah. "Teaching History With Digital Historical Games: An Introduction to the Field and Best Practices." *Simulation & Gaming* 47, no. 4 (2016): 517–42. https://doi.org/10.1177/1046878116646693.

McCall, Jeremiah. "Video Games as Participatory Public History." In *A Companion to Public History*, edited by D. M. Dean, 1 edition, 405–16. Hoboken, NJ: Wiley, 2018.

McMichael, Andrew. "PC Games and the Teaching of History." *The History Teacher* 40, no. 2 (February 2007): 203–18.

Miller, Maureen C. *Power and the Holy in the Age of the Investiture Conflict: A Brief History with Documents*. The Bedford Series in History and Culture. Boston: Bedford St. Martins, 2005.

Miller, Maureen C. "The Crisis in the Investiture Crisis Narrative." *History Compass* 7, no. 6 (2009): 1570–80. https://doi.org/10.1111/j.1478-0542.2009.00645.x.

Ortega, Stephen. "Representing the Past: Video Games Challenge to the Historical Narrative." *Syllabus* 4, no. 1 (2015): 1–13.

Peterson, Rolfe Daus, Andrew Justin Miller, and Sean Joseph Fedorko. "The Same River Twice: Exploring Historical Representation and the Value of Simulation in the Total War, Civilization and Patrician Franchises." In *Playing with the Past: Digital Games and the Simulation of History*, edited by Matthew Kapell and Andrew B. R. Elliott, 33–48. New York: Bloomsbury Academic, 2013.

Pörtner, Regina. "Reichspolitik, Reform und bischöfliche Autonomie: Der Investiturstreit im Spiegel der Gesta Treverorum." *Mediaevistik* 22 (2009): 83–115.

Remensnyder, Amy G. "Pollution, Purity, and Peace: An Aspect of Social Reform between the Late Tenth Century and 1076." In *The Peace of God: Social Violence and Religious Response in France around the Year 1000*, edited by Thomas Head and Richard Allen Landes. Ithaca, N.Y: Cornell University Press, 1992.

Robinson, I. S. "The Friendship Circle of Bernold of Constance and the Dissemination of Gregorian Ideas in Late Eleventh-Century Germany." In *Friendship in Medieval Europe*, edited by Julian Haseldine, 185–98. Stroud: Sutton, 1999.

Robinson, I. S. "The Friendship Network of Gregory VII." *History* 63 (1978): 1–22.

Schut, Kevin. "Strategic Simulations and Our Past: The Bias of Computer Games in the Presentation of History." *Games and Culture* 2, no. 3 (2007): 213–35. https://doi.org/10.1177/1555412007306202.

Sibert, Hubertus. "Kommunikation, Autorität, Recht, Lebensordnung. Das Papsttum und die monastisch-kanonikale Reformbewegung (1046-1124)." In *Vom Umbruch zur Erneuerung?: das 11. und beginnende 12. Jahrhundert: Positionen der Forschung*, edited by Jörg Jarnut and Matthias Wemhoff, 11–29. MittelalterStudien 13. München: Fink, 2006.

Spring, Dawn. "Gaming History: Computer and Video Games as Historical Scholarship." *Rethinking History* 19, no. 2 (2015): 207–21. https://doi.org/10.1080/13642529.2014.973714.

Tellenbach, Gerd. *Church, State, and Christian Society at the Time of the Investiture Contest*. Translated by R. Bennet. Oxford: Oxford University Press, 1966.

Van Eck, Richard. "Digital Game Based Learning: It's Not Just the Digital Native Who Are Restless." *Educause Review* 41 (2006): 16–30.

Wainwright, A. Martin. "Teaching Historical Theory through Video Games." *The History Teacher* 47, no. 4 (2014): 579–612.

Ludography

The Investiture Contest. Robert Houghton, 2020.

Frank Klaassen
11 Game Development in a Senior Seminar

Abstract: The pedagogical value of employing games or simulations in the classroom is well established, but less has been written on game development in the classroom. This article discusses the development of two games in the classroom, one (Virtus) in a course on masculinity, the other (Distaff) in a dedicated game-development course. It explores the successes and failures of these two exercises and makes three main arguments. First, it suggests that a dedicated game-development course is much preferable to employing the exercise in the context of another course. Second, it argues that game-development offers a powerful and singular pedagogical dynamic. Students must condense a range of complex historical arguments made by various scholars into a simple, elegant mechanic. This process results in highly critical and comparative readings of scholarly arguments and valuable discussions of the question of historical significance. Finally, the process teaches valuable skills in communication and the practice of public history.

Introduction

In a recent article, Ben Hoy has demonstrated how games about the North American West historically have been used to propagate racist images of indigenous peoples.[1] More critically, he has shown how, in recent years, games have also been used to re-write and overthrow such images. They access a significant demographic of users and can be highly effective ways of communicating responsibly constructed views of the past. Although he does not explicitly say it, the article beautifully illustrates how games can be a critical form of public history. This is how I frame the project of making a game about the Middle Ages in my dedicated fourth-year course "History in Games."

For the last three centuries, the Middle Ages have served as a screen upon which western writers, artists, and scholars have projected their dreams of a better future, told eulogies for a lost past, or illustrated criticisms of injustice, ignorance, and fanaticism. The knight, warrior, peasant, magician, witch, fairy, and princess are all stock figures in shared mythologies and metaphors. So too

---

[1] Benjamin Hoy, "Cardboard Indians: Playing History in the American West," *The Western Historical Quarterly* 49 (2018): 299–324.

are notions of the crusade, quest, witch-hunt, and plague. Since a significant percentage of modern games may be traced directly to the medievalism and world-creation of Tolkien, modern board games are also significant examples of the ways in which the medieval past has tremendous cultural currency. Such co-opting of the past tends to be highly anachronistic and, as contemporary uses by ignorant far-right groups illustrate, may be not only offensive but also genuinely dangerous.[2]

The pedagogical effectiveness of using games in the classroom, either off-the-shelf or custom-built, is well established.[3] This is particularly the case given the current surge of popular interest in board games.[4] Games provide experiential forms of learning, create profound feelings of personal investment that can leverage learning, and, if all else fails, provide a nice break from more the conventional approaches of lectures and seminars. This article pushes one step beyond the simple use of games in the classroom to explore how developing a game that simulates a historical moment or pattern can be a powerful pedagogical tool. It also seeks to provide helpful information on how to organize, run, and defend the offering of such courses.

My observations and conclusions are based upon my experience in having employed simulations and games in the classroom for the last 15 years, and more critically, running two classes in which I worked with a group of senior undergraduates to develop a game. They are not based upon any systematic psychological or sociological analysis.

---

[2] Predating many recent events is Andrew Elliot, *Medievalism, Politics and Mass Media: Appropriating the Middle Ages in the Twenty-First Century* (Cambridge: D.S. Brewer, 2017). Examples of explorations of this topic in the public media and academic publications are too extensive to document here. They span venues from the *Economist* and *The New York Times* to a host of academic organizations. See for example "Medieval Memes: The Far Right's New Fascination with the Middle Ages," *The Economist*, 2017; Paul B. Sturtevant, "Race, Racism, and the Middle Ages: Tearing Down the "Whites Only" Medieval World," *The Public Medievalist*, February 7, 2017, https://www.publicmedievalist.com/race-racism-middle-ages-tearing-whites-medieval-world/; Jennifer Schuessler, "Medieval Scholars Joust with White Nationalists. And One Another," *New York Times*, May 5, 2019.

[3] W. Admiraal et al., "The Concept of Flow in Collaborative Game-Based Learning," *Computers in Human Behavior* 27, no. 3 (2011); S. K. Smith, "Pounding Dice into Musket Balls: Using Wargames to Teach the American Revolution," *The History Teacher* 46, no. 4 (2013); Benjamin Hoy, "Teaching History with Custom-Built Board Games," *Simulation and Gaming* 49, no. 2 (2018); K. Kee et al., "Towards a Theory of Good History through Gaming," *The Canadian Historical Review* 90, no. 2 (2019).

[4] N. B. Sardone and R. Devlin-Scherer, "Let the (Board) Games Begin: Creative Ways to Enhance Teaching and Learning," *The Clearing House* 89, no. 6 (2016).

In both classes discussed here, the students were challenged to create a game that would effectively communicate key aspects of a particular historical moment or context to people who knew nothing about the subject. This is to say, the point of the exercise was not merely to create a game that modelled a historical circumstance, but also a game that entertained and educated. The first game concerned the construction and loss of male honor in the pre-modern world (*Virtus*), the second, the lives and agency of medieval women (*Distaff*).[5] Although I first suggested this classroom project more as an entertaining alternative to regular instruction (for both myself and my students) than as a dedicated form of teaching, I discovered the pedagogical potentials of this approach to be startlingly strong.

In what follows, I will adopt the more pragmatic practice of the sciences and begin with my findings and recommendations. A more prosaic explication and justification follows.

Findings (or How to Convince Others of the Value of a Game-Development Course)

Those who propose a course on making games inevitably have to confront tacit or even openly expressed concerns that that it will not demand the kind of detailed and analytical engagement that we expect from a senior history course, but rather will be narrow in focus, simplistic, and superficial. As tempting as it is to reject such hesitations as nothing but puritanical suspicion of anything fun, these are valid concerns. By definition, a game development course must focus on a narrow set of historical conditions and produce an abstracted, if not simplified, view of the past. However, it is precisely for these reasons that it offers powerful pedagogical and learning opportunities that drive students to confront and explore historical questions in sophisticated ways. This is particularly the case if the students are set the additional challenge of thinking about the game as a form of public history that seeks to engage and educate.

Such a course offers students diverse modes of engagement all of which must be linked to solid research. These include not only work on relating game mechanics to historical realities and the subsequent testing and evaluation of

---

5 Full copies of these games may be found at http://historygames.usask.ca. They may be downloaded and printed for free. At point of writing, professionally printed copies of *Virtus* are still available for purchase on etsy.ca.

those mechanics, but also the creation of representative visual elements, the collection of relevant "flavor texts" from the period, and the articulation of arguments to explicate and justify all of these. It also builds key skills in the exercise of public history, that is, in the synthesis and communication of complex information to a wide public audience in a clear, focused, and engaging form. As any historian knows, the practice of synthesis and summary of secondary sources is far from simple and is a fundamental skill in our discipline.

Two pedagogical dynamics also make this kind of course particularly effective and drive students to probe historical questions in ways that are unusual in conventional seminars. First, having a project with necessarily narrow parameters gives a concrete and fixed goal shared by everyone in the class. This stimulates group discussion and interaction and produces precisely the sort of group learning environment we seek in a seminar and – sadly but realistically – frequently fail to achieve. Second, asking students to create a game as a form of public history stimulates a powerful sense of responsibility among students as they digest the secondary scholarly literature necessary to produce the game. This is particularly the case if they know it may actually be used in teaching and will have their names attached as co-authors. As a result, students have significant motivation for analyzing, comparing, contrasting, and synthesizing their readings and, just as critically, for doing this as a group. In turn, these dynamics open up the possibility for rich reflections and discussions not only about specific theoretical or methodological approaches, but also more broadly about the value and limitations of theoretical models for understanding the past.

Recommendations

The following are my key recommendations for using the creation of a game as a way of teaching about the Middle Ages.
- Make a dedicated course that focuses on developing a game rather than attempting to include game-making as a project within an existing course. This will assure student buy-in and allow you more leeway in formulating an effective course.
- Cut the amount of reading material you would normally use in a seminar in half.
- Have a clear idea of the basic mechanics you wish to employ prior to the course. Although you will modify that mechanic based on student input, a 10–13 week class does not provide sufficient time for extended discussion of various kinds of mechanics.

- As a group, have the students create and maintain a list of the key messages they wish to communicate and a single key theme. This will allow you to keep the game from becoming too complicated and also keep the message of the game clear.
- Have the students write a "Developers' Intention Statement." This will be useful to focus their efforts on their theme and messages, and also be useful for subsequent use of the game in classes.
- Have students evaluate the game they have created once it is done in light of their knowledge of the field.
- Emphasize to the students that this is an exercise in public history. This both identifies the non-academic skills that it provides (synthesis, writing, communication, and so forth) but also keeps them focussed on the responsibilities that being a public historian entails.
- Keep the game simple in terms of the number cards or parts. This will make creating copies for testing and producing a professionally printed copy much easier and less expensive.
- Refrain from making it too complicated. Balance engaging complexity against elegant simplicity.
- If you need to justify the development of such a course to your department, you may wish to argue, in addition to the pedagogical benefits mentioned in this article, that card games are an inexpensive form of public history that employs all the same skill sets as developing a museum exhibit, documentary, or website but is a project that can be accomplished within a single course.
- Make use of such websites as playingcards.io and Roll20 for game development. It is possible to play games on these sites virtually, but also relatively easy to upload and modify various versions of the game as it is developed.
- Be aware of potential intellectual property implications in subsequent publication of the game.

Background (*Virtus*)

I first attempted producing a game as part of a class in a senior seminar on Masculinity and Gender. I had a rough idea of the mechanic we would use prior to the start of the course but it was not fully developed. I reduced the number of readings to accommodate the extra work and developed a system for keeping track of individual students' contributions to the game outside of class. I set aside time for game development in every class session. We started by trying out games that had similar mechanics and eventually used the time for discussing game mechanics and talking about our developing game. Students made short presentations on how their research could contribute to the game.

The result was startlingly successful. In significant measure this was due to having an unusually lucky combination of students in the class who had a background in medieval literature, history, and art as well as a few accomplished artists. By the end of the class we had a more or less workable (and quite attractive) beta version. Excited by the quality of what we had accomplished, I began to consider making a copy that we might sell privately to a few other academics and friends and that I could use in teaching. The students agreed that any profits would go to the University's Museum of Antiquities for student programming. I then found some funds for a group of students to develop this into a professionally printed version that I could use in my undergraduate classes and, perhaps, other people might be interested in buying. The demand for the game was unexpectedly high and we ended up printing 400 copies!

Needless to say, I had no intention of doing anything like this when I proposed the group project, but its limited commercial success is not the real story here. Let me focus instead on the pedagogical successes and failures of this project, starting with the former.

For the most part student responses to the project and the pedagogical results were strong. About one third of the class were tremendously enthusiastic, many of them dedicated board game players. A second third of the class had less experience with games and did not play board games regularly, but they were still quite interested in the idea. I'll talk about the final third below, but in general, having two thirds of the class reasonably enthusiastic about the idea was not a bad level of student engagement. The fact that developing the game afterwards provided a selected group of students with paid work and an interesting entry for their CVs was also a positive outcome. But let me focus on the classroom.

The effect on the pedagogical environment of the class was largely quite positive. The game allowed us to reflect on theoretical models in a very concrete way. For example, it gave tangible and experiential dimensions to the theory that men can build honor but women could only maintain it. Similarly, we had to examine the idea that there were different kinds of masculinities, propose how we would classify them, and delimit what was specific to these groups and what was shared by all pre-modern men. All of these ended up being reflected in concrete ways in the game. Following Ben Hoy's suggestion we also discussed the ways in which our game failed to represent historical realities or emphasized some at the expense of others.[6] All of this was quite positive.

---

6 Hoy, "Teaching History with Custom-Built Board Games."

The game also prompted some very interesting discussions. One student brought up the question of how a game about women would be different. The game we produced is very much a melodrama. It encompasses very real tragedy and struggle, but is also quite humorous, not least because many of the scenarios on the cards are full of unreflective masculine bravado. In comparison, what would the literary form of a game about women be? A David and Goliath myth, a tragedy, or an epic? So, on the one hand making the game led to a student-driven reflection on the historical differences between the lives of men and women in the Middle Ages. On the other, it led into a discussion of Hayden White and the extent to which history is literary.

The failures of this class were also useful in the long run. Perhaps a third of the students were unenthusiastic. The simple reality is that some people hate playing games. Although I think the project was entirely defensible in pedagogical terms, this fact suggested to me that a dedicated game course would be a better approach since it would pre-select enthusiastic students or at least students who knew what the course would be like. In an age when many instructors live or die based on student evaluations, this is worth keeping in mind.

Another unrelated lesson I learned from this first attempt had to do with the game itself. As a game, *Virtus* was a little long and somewhat complicated which forced us to develop a simplified version of the game afterwards that could be used in shorter classes. More critically, because it uses a deck of 235 cards, it was very time consuming to produce decks for testing and expensive to print. In short, a simpler game would have made the course easier to run.

On balance, however, the experience convinced me that the model would work, and I had a clearer sense of what I needed to do. The next game would need fewer cards and have a shorter play period. I would create a dedicated game-creation course. And we'd build a game about women to try to answer the questions the first game prompted.

The Game-development Course (*Distaff*)

Setting up the Course

Like all of our senior seminars, "History in Games" was limited to nine students. The complexities of the course would make it difficult to run with more than 12. It attracted roughly equal numbers of men and women. Unlike the previous course in which I introduced a group game-development project only in the details of the syllabus, the students in this class knew the course would involve games and game development when they selected it and were uniformly interested in the project or genuinely enthusiastic. I suspect that the topic of medieval women might not have been one they would have chosen themselves, being neither glamorous nor trendy.

Even our relatively long 13-week term (39 contact hours) does not provide a great deal of time for this project, and the best one can manage is to produce a workable beta version. In fact, reaching this modest goal demanded that I make some decisions ahead of time about basic mechanics and theme. This required considerable preparation on my part, prior even to setting up the syllabus, including buying and testing off-the-shelf games and consulting with my dedicated gamer friends (Ben Hoy deserves particular thanks) about possible base mechanics.

I ultimately decided the best form for a game about medieval women would be a deck-building game involving competition over limited resources and having two kinds of win conditions: one which would be unusual but would teach about singular pre-modern women, and one which would be entirely conventional (i.e., building resources prior to marriage, marriage itself, and finally producing a male heir).

Some students initially felt a little disappointed not to have greater input on these more general constructs, but my ideas were fairly open-ended. More critically, the huge variety of finer mechanics within the broader game-type I had chosen offered no end of room for their input. I don't think anyone felt excluded from the development process as a result, certainly not after the first few weeks when they realized how complicated the process was going to be.

A second adjustment was also required due to time constraints. I reduced the readings to about half of what I would expect in a regular seminar and made all the research assignments focussed directly on the game. Having decided on a rough mechanic I was able to make assignments and choose readings accordingly. I set up the readings and seminar discussions to run through most of the term, but weighted the readings more heavily to the first part of the term. I also began with more general foundational readings (i.e., peasant women, town women, or noble women) and reserved readings of more specific topics such as "prostitution" for later in the term.

In their independent research projects, students were asked to choose a singular pre-modern woman as the focus of their paper or research presentation (for example, Christine de Pisan, Marjory Kempe, or Joan of Arc). We would build these women into the game. Their research was to be focussed on the ways in which the woman in question was singular among women, but also on the ways in which she shared the conditions faced by all women. Finally, based on their research, students were asked to make a range of concrete suggestions for game mechanics or elements that might be included in the game (for example, visual elements or quotations). These could be specific, relating to the woman they had researched, or more general. A final short assignment (in lieu of a final exam) required the students to evaluate the successes and limitations of the game we had produced.

The hardest part of doing group projects in the classroom is to overcome student concern that their grades may be dragged down by others or that they will put in more work than others and that this fact will not be duly compensated. In this class, seminar participation, the research report and presentation, and the final evaluation of the game were all individually graded. However, developing the game also required a considerable range of other kinds of contributions including artistic or design work, investigating other games for useful mechanics, testing the game themselves, arranging tests by their friends, or producing test decks. This could involve a considerable amount of time. On average students had to contribute 15–20 hours outside of class time. This was not at all unreasonable in lieu of the considerable amount of reading I had removed, but it had to be recognized in the grade.

To keep track of their contributions I created a folder of individual timesheets where students could list their various contributions, the number of hours they had taken, and a running total of their hours. All sheets were publicly accessible to all students and I encouraged them to keep track of where they stood in relation to others. In addition to encouraging equal contributions, this also meant there was a built-in pressure for students to present their time contributions fairly and accurately. My model for grading this contribution (separate from seminar participation which was solely focussed on classroom discussions) was that everyone with an approximately average contribution would receive a strong grade (in Canadian terms 80% – roughly the minimum expectation for admission to graduate study). Students contributing less or more would have grades adjusted accordingly.

Game Mechanics and Need for a Thematic Focus

Games are a form of public history. In emphasizing this function in the introduction to this paper and in my game development course I have already made a decision about where my priorities lie in developing game mechanics. This is to say, I have decided that the game must help players better understand the historical realities and, in particular, that players should be able to connect their experience of the game to those realities (i.e., they will know more about the Middle Ages having played the game). The most useful model I have found for developing games as public history derives from techniques used in curating museum exhibits.[7]

An effective museum exhibit explores a single theme. Each element in the exhibit should refer back to that theme and provide an elaboration upon it. An exhibit should also have no more than three core messages it seeks to communicate. In the absence of such concerted efforts at focusing the message, the viewer gets lost in the details. The same applies in games where it is easy for a player to forget the historical context and to focus purely on winning or on scattered details like roles, titles, or clothing. More critically, it is easy to lose focus when developing a game as one thinks of all the possible ways to reflect the complexities of the past. The result is the gaming equivalent of a paper full of interesting details but lacking a discernible thesis. This may also negatively affect the game in another way.

As we worked through the readings, the desire to add additional levels of complexity to the game every time we encountered an interesting idea was almost irresistible. Naturally, some complexity is very much desirable, but at the same time, it is essential to have some way of deciding what to include and what not. In order to facilitate this, I worked with the students to decide on and maintain a short list of the key messages they wished to communicate in the game. These had to be expressed in a single sentence and, ideally, prioritized. We returned to this list each week after we had discussed the readings.

By the end of the course, we were able to distil these key messages down to three, all of them connected to our overall theme, which we expressed as a question. The result was as follows:

Theme	Where and to what extent did medieval women have independent agency?
Key messages:	1. Many of the restrictions on women's lives applied to all women (for example, regulation of their sexual lives, general lack of authority, relegation to reproductive roles, or being subject to a man, usually a father or husband).
	2. Women's agency tended to be opportunistic. Their attempts to seize opportunities were often risky and took place in an "economy of makeshift."
	3. Although some medieval women did remarkable things, most women did not have the opportunity or ability to do more than conform to conventional goals.

---

[7] A brief and useful discussion on curating museum exhibits may be found online: Texas Historical Commission, "Exhibit Design and Development Workbook" (Austin 2015), https://www.thc.texas.gov/public/upload/publications/2015%20LR%20Museum%20Services%20Exhibit%20Development%20Workbook%20with%20Introduction.pdf.

Although it took three months to arrive at this level of focus (and I'm now editing this a little), having a working list like this allowed us to make decisions as we developed the game.

This process had two other benefits. First, being self-conscious about our intended messaging led to more focussed and analytical reading and more effective and interesting discussions. Second, it also made it much easier to write an effective intention statement at the end of the course. This was useful as a kind of summation of what we had accomplished. More critically, it also provided a key element in the presentation of our game to subsequent players. It was like the introductory panel in a museum exhibit, giving them a better appreciation for the game, its virtues, and its limitations.

Game Development

In the first day of the course, I described the rough outlines of the game mechanic I expected to use, explaining how we did not have enough time to open that up for discussion. I asked students to suggest off-the-shelf games that they thought might provide interesting or useful mechanics within the parameters I had suggested. When I developed *Virtus* I brought in one myself, but in the case of *Distaff* the students had a range of their own suggestions, which gave us a very rich set of ideas to draw upon. Some of these were discussed in class but I also set this up as the first out-of-class activity that could be added to their game-development time sheet.

The multiple ways of engaging with the course meant that it was not necessary for everyone to participate in this and many did not. For example, I knew that later in the course, some students would work on visual or other elements. So everyone could focus on their areas of interest. In the process of developing both *Virtus* and *Distaff* a clear sub-group of people with a fascination for game mechanics quickly presented themselves. So this smaller group reviewed and play-tested other games for useful approaches, taking due credit on their time sheets. In my role as head developer it was critical for me to participate, and these sessions proved particularly useful for me since I am not a dedicated gamer.[8] The students in this group then reported back to the class on approaches we had discovered in these other games that might be useful, interesting, or effective.

---

[8] Another useful resource is Geoffrey Engelstein and Isaac Shalev, *Building Blocks of Tabletop Game Design: An Encyclopedia of Mechanisms* (New York: CRC Press 2020).

Over the next few weeks we combined the broad conceptualization of the game I had provided at the start, with ideas from these other games, and with ideas prompted by course readings. Eventually, when students began presenting on their research, we also selected ideas that they offered. As student knowledge of the field deepened, we also had an increasingly clear sense of the messages we wanted to communicate. Within a few weeks we had developed a basic working model of a game.

Due to time constraints it was critical to be expeditious in producing a working model of the game that allowed us to test the mechanics of play even though we had filled in very few historical details. We were at that stage within three or four weeks. Once again, those interested in game mechanics in their own right play-tested these early versions and provided feedback to the class. We also took time in class to test and discuss them.

Even within the narrower parameters I had initially suggested we had an almost dizzying set of mechanics and ideas to choose from. In addition, a range of different general approaches were possible. For example, more dedicated game players might wish to have mechanics that emphasize logic, skill, or make possible a variety of strategic approaches. On the other hand, games involving higher levels of raw chance might be more appropriate reflections of a past in which class or gender systems radically predetermined the shape of people's lives. Just as critically, historical games can communicate ideas about the past in a variety of ways. For example, almost every card in *Virtus* contains a real or at least credible historical scenario (for example, Congratulations! You are born a man. You bring honor to your family. One honor point). By comparison, *Distaff* communicated specific historical ideas through the mechanics or win conditions (for example, winning the game by having all the peculiar qualifications of Joan of Arc or Christine de Pisan). Visual details or quotations can also provide considerable historical depth. Colors and symbols to make the uses of cards immediately obvious can be carefully inflected to reflect the period.

Deciding between these diverse potential approaches gave us more than enough to do and students did not feel excluded from the development process even if they had initially felt that way. In fact, as the possibilities multiplied it became necessary to find our way through a set of otherwise unrealistic ambitions. There is a key balance that must be achieved between complex and subtle verisimilitude on the one hand and the elegant simplicity of an engaging game mechanic on the other. Here having developed a set of key messages that we wished to communicate was central to helping me guide the process of achieving greater simplicity and focus. I found it is easier to politely but firmly exclude unnecessarily complicated ideas suggested by students by referring back to the goals that we set as a group. Continual testing will also help to achieve this balance as well as evaluating suggestions in light of the interests and talents of the students. If the class has three art historians, for example, a particular focus on visual content is more advisable.

There is no escaping the fact that at this stage there is a significant level of indeterminacy in the process. But a few observations may be useful to guide the process. First, as Ben Hoy has demonstrated, it is not a disaster if the game is unfair or if people lose, so long as players are not thereby excluded from a game that goes on for another hour.[9] Second, the process of game development will always tend towards increasing complexity. If unchecked, it will render a game increasingly difficult to learn if not unplayable. Third, it is better to have a game with fewer pieces (e.g., 70 versus 300 cards) and with a relatively shorter playing time. This makes testing much easier. It also will make it much easier to produce and use a game subsequently for teaching. Fourth, you may have to say repeatedly that you can never perfectly reflect human life. Games can only focus on a particular historical dynamic. Finally (and in response to concerns about leaving things out) you can reiterate that a game can be useful for understanding the past precisely because it is a partial view, particularly if players are encouraged to reflect on this through the intention statement.

Pedagogical Wins

Making a game can be a lot of fun, and that is as good a reason as any to do it. But as educators our fundamental concern is to facilitate learning. Here I can be far less equivocal about the process of game development. A game development course offers significant pedagogical opportunities, particularly if the project is framed as work of public history.

One of the things that made the course successful was the excitement around creating a game. Even in our first discussion of readings for producing *Distaff*, it was difficult to keep the focus on the content of the readings rather than how we might use an idea they proposed in the game. In order to do my job I had to work hard to steer students back to the articles to ensure they had understood them and to model critical reading. However, my initial ambivalence for the almost obsessive impulse to focus on game mechanics eventually dissolved as I realized how positive this was if properly leveraged. It drove students to do exactly what we, as instructors, want them to do, i.e., to read,

---

[9] Hoy, "Teaching History with Custom-Built Board Games."

extract, summarize, and apply ideas from secondary sources. It also made the historical realities of topics like medieval peasant women immediately and powerfully relevant to them. How often does that happen?

One of the positive manifestations of this high level of engagement was that students quickly started to read the articles more critically. If one article suggested a historical dynamic they found promising, students looked for evidence of that idea in other articles, or they compared it to articles where the author took a slightly different approach. For example, quite without my prompting they compared Judith Bennet's theory that adolescent women had a short period of increased agency in adolescence to cases involving women from other classes and in countries other than England. They did this because this offered a potential mechanism that they could build into the game. The same thing happened as we considered the various theories concerning the impact of exogamous shocks such as plague or famine on women's agency. In that case they had to decide on the theory that they found more convincing, understanding that it was not perfect or universally supported. In short, the need to establish an abstracted set of mechanics drove them to think more critically and systematically about secondary readings. Rather than cajoling students into these sorts of critical comparisons as one typically has to do in a seminar, they did it almost entirely on their own and for their own reasons.

The requirements that we produce a game representative of women's lives also led to interesting dialogues, particularly a very rich discussion about prostitution. One student made the observation that prostitution involved such a tiny proportion of the population of women that perhaps we should leave it out of the game altogether. Another student responded that, although the percentage of women involved was small, the numbers of men who used their services was significantly larger. In short, prostitutes were socially significant. Another added that this was like noble women, who we also had in the game, and whose social significance did not lie in their numbers. Yet another student pointed out that another article had talked about how some women in the laboring classes had to resort temporarily to prostitution if things got bad. Even if they did not have to do it, it was certainly a threat that lower class women felt. If they lost key social supports (mostly from men) they might have to resort to prostitution simply to survive. In short, the demands of the game gave students a high level of motivation to critically think through the various aspects of what makes something historically significant.

Let me give one final example where the class essentially taught itself.

We eventually established that our overall theme in the game was women's agency, although this did not happen until around the middle of the course. We had implicitly done this much earlier by making highly influential women with a high degree of individual agency into "win conditions" (i.e., you could win the game by being like Veronica Franco or Julian of Norwich). At the start of one class a student spoke out – again entirely without my prompting – saying he had a comment or question. All this focus on agency seemed to him a problem. Agency does not make people happy. Why would we make this a "win condition"? Franco certainly had a high level of personal agency, but look how she died! This led to a larger reflection on how medieval women would have been very unlikely to have talked about their own lives in this way. In turn, this led to reflections on how our focus on agency was, in fact, a modern concern prompted by the concerns of modern women's historians and, more broadly, of second wave feminism. Although it was I who directed the end of that conversation to historiography, when I did it, I was only giving shape to arguments that the students had articulated essentially on their own.

I have connected these very insightful and critical discussions of women's history and of the discipline of history in general to the project-driven nature of the course and its requirement that the game be systematically representative of the pre-modern period. In this context, the subtle differences among historians became quite important to students who otherwise simply would not have noticed them. Part of the motivation for arriving at a game that accurately represents if not the past at least what historians had said about the past was also the fact that the students were required not only to learn, but also to take up the role of educators. By emphasizing that this was to be used as an educational tool, or more broadly, to introduce an interested public to the lives of medieval women, students were imbued with a significant sense of responsibility that they simply would not have had in preparing a conventional seminar or paper.

Testing, Rules, and Final Production

I have already talked about the importance of engaging in rounds of testing as part of the development process. Towards the end of the course this became critical for fine-tuning the game. It was also becoming increasingly apparent that I would seek to develop *Distaff* for use in undergraduate teaching and possibly also to have it professionally printed and made available for sale (I have since employed both *Virtus* and *Distaff* in first- and second-year classes and have found them both useful and engaging breaks from lectures). So let me conclude with a few observations about testing and final production.

Students were asked at this point to conduct tests with friends, allowing them to figure out the game, timing the average length of play, keeping an eye out for inconsistencies or lack of clarity in the cards, and assessing player's enjoyment and learning. Multiple rounds of play made clear the usual length of play and allowed us to adjust the game accordingly. We were aiming for a game that could be introduced, played, and debriefed in a 70-minute class. We found we had to shorten game play because we discovered (unsurprisingly) that the student developers could complete a game much more quickly than those playing it for the first time. More critically, we sought to assure that it communicated our theme and key messages but also that the rules and instructions were clear.

I have mentioned the value in having a game with fewer elements for testing. Having a mere 70 cards (*Distaff*) as opposed to 235 cards (*Virtus*) made the simple physical requirements of reproducing test decks considerably less onerous. A smaller deck will also dramatically reduce the costs of printing. There are commercial web sites that allow you to upload card images and have decks professionally printed. Proper cardstock makes cards fully opaque, easy to shuffle, and much more pleasant to play with. Many of these operate out of China, but it is worthwhile seeking out local printers as well, asking them to match the pricing. We have made available our decks online for free download (historygames.usask.ca) on the same model as *Cards Against Humanity*. This has not, so far as we can tell, reduced the number of professionally printed copies we have sold.

Another alternative to printing cards for testing is to use sites such as Roll20 and playingcards.io for virtual testing. During COVID lockdown when I taught all my classes virtually, I successfully used the latter for virtual game play in my classes. It would also be useful for game testing, particularly playingcards.io which allows you to upload a spreadsheet file (.csv) with all the deck information in it. This would be quick to edit in a spreadsheet, although it does not offer much sophistication in design.

If you have access to a 3D printer, numerous figurines or other kinds of playing pieces may be found on sites such as thingiverse.com that provide free 3D vectors. It may, however, be easier to pillage your local dollar store for tokens.

Rules of play are tricky to write and to communicate but are critical. Refer to historygames.usask.ca for examples you may wish to follow. We have opted for a particular format with major headings: 1. Number of Players and Set Up; 2. Win Conditions; 3. Types of Cards; 4. Order of Play; and 5. Special Conditions or Mechanics. I have also produced short instruction videos for introducing games in the classroom in order to assure efficient use of time. In general, however, I have found that introducing a game in person usually works better.

In addition to rules, the intention statement is a valuable element in using a game in a classroom. It helps students to better appreciate the game in relation to its historical basis and I have typically used it as required reading for the class in which we play a game. In particular, it facilitates discussion of both the game's virtues and also its limitations.

Caveat Regarding Intellectual Property

A key issue that should not be overlooked is intellectual property. The students will have some partial level of legal right to the game you have made together which may limit what you can do with it. My university's copyright specialists advised me that it was sufficient for me to openly discuss the question of copyright in class. Should you decide that you wish to have a game professionally printed for sale, or think this might happen, it is best to have that discussion both with your institution's lawyers and subsequently with the students.

In my case, I promised students that in the unlikely case that the game became a runaway bestseller, making tens of thousands of dollars, that they would have shares in the profits, although anyone who participated in developing and producing the game after the course was over would naturally take a larger share. However, in the far more likely scenario that it returned quite modest profits in the range of a few thousand dollars, such funds would be turned over to our university's Museum of Antiquities to support student programming. I also proposed that the game be made available online for free download. As it turned out, *Virtus* did return some quite modest profits, so the discussion was worthwhile. The benefit of being able to claim co-authorship on their CVs was probably just as valuable as any small cash return they might have had.

Bibliography

Admiraal, W., J. Huizenga, S. Akkerman, and G. ten Dam. "The Concept of Flow in Collaborative Game-Based Learning." *Computers in Human Behavior* 27, no. 3 (2011): 1185–94.
Commission, Texas Historical. "Exhibit Design and Development Workbook." Austin, 2015.
Elliot, Andrew. *Medievalism, Politics and Mass Media: Appropriating the Middle Ages in the Twenty-First Century*. Cambridge: D.S. Brewer, 2017.
Engelstein, Geoffrey, and Isaac Shalev. *Building Blocks of Tabletop Game Design: An Encyclopedia of Mechanisms*. New York: CRC Press 2020.

Hoy, Benjamin. "Cardboard Indians: Playing History in the American West." *The Western Historical Quarterly* 49, Autumn 2018 (2018): 299–324.

Hoy, Benjamin. "Teaching History with Custom-Built Board Games." *Simulation and Gaming* 49 no. 2 (2018): 115–33.

Kee, K., S. Graham, P. Dunae, J. Lutz, A. Large, M. Blondeau, and M. Clare. "Towards a Theory of Good History through Gaming." *The Canadian Historical Review* 90, no. 2 (2019): 303–26.

"Medieval Memes: The Far Right's New Fascination with the Middle Ages." *The Economist*, 2017.

Sardone, N. B., and R. Devlin-Scherer. "Let the (Board) Games Begin: Creative Ways to Enhance Teaching and Learning." *The Clearing House* 89, no. 6 (2016): 215–22.

Schuessler, Jennifer. "Medieval Scholars Joust with White Nationalists. And One Another." *New York Times*, May 5, 2019, 1.

Smith, S. K. "Pounding Dice into Musket Balls: Using Wargames to Teach the American Revolution." *The History Teacher* 46, no. 4 (2013): 561–76.

Sturtevant, Paul B. "Race, Racism, and the Middle Ages: Tearing Down the "Whites Only" Medieval World." https://www.publicmedievalist.com/race-racism-middle-ages-tearing-whites-medieval-world/.

Part V: **Games beyond the Classroom**

Mariana López, Marques Hardin and Wenqi Wan

12 *The Soundscapes of the York Mystery Plays*: Playing with Medieval Sonic Histories

Abstract: The *York Mystery Plays* are a series of plays that were performed from the fourteenth to the sixteenth century in the streets of York (UK) using wagons specifically constructed for the occasion. The "sound" of the *York Mystery Plays* is as crucial to their history as the visual aspects linked to staging. However, aspects on acoustics and soundscapes are often difficult to convey to non-specialist audiences. The present chapter discusses how strategies found in digital games and simulations have been combined with specialist knowledge on acoustical heritage, soundscape recreation, and medieval drama to create the online interface *The Soundscapes of the York Mystery Plays*. Users are able to combine dialogue and music with acoustical data as well as add sound effects linked to the history of the medieval city of York to create their own experience of the plays, allowing them to listen to what the plays could have sounded like, while also assessing how those experiences are still relevant to modern organizers and performers by accessing bespoke interviews. The interface also explores how digital gaming and simulation experiences can help overcome the ethical challenges of presenting one version of the sounds of the past, by introducing multiple possible acoustical experiences, which present the rich array of possible sonic histories linked to the *York Mystery Plays*.

Introduction

Sensory history, that is, the study of the senses in past cultures, is far from new.[1] Similarly, acoustical heritage involving the on-site measurement of heritage sites and the utilization of computer models, is a well-researched area.[2] In

---

[1] Mark Smith, *Sensory History* (Oxford: Bloomsbury, 2007).
[2] For early work on the subject see Z. Karabiber, "A New Approach to an ancient subject: CAHRISMA project" (paper presented at the Seventh International Congress on Sound and Vibration, August 1, 2000); Martin Lisa Nielsen et al., "Acoustical computer simulations of the

---

Acknowledgements: The authors wish to thank everyone who contributed oral histories to the project as well as everyone who participated in surveys to provide feedback.

https://doi.org/10.1515/9783110712032-012

acoustical heritage work, researchers define sound source and receiver (listener) combinations, which allow the measurement or rendition of impulse responses (IRs). Impulse Responses represent how space modifies sound in that specific source-receiver combination and allow the calculation of acoustical parameters that contribute to our understanding of sound decay, music clarity, speech intelligibility, and sound envelopment, among others.[3] Furthermore, when IRs are convolved with dry recordings (that is, recordings with no spatial information), to produce auralisations, we can hear what those recordings would have sounded like in the site being studied, opening up the potential for listening to acoustical heritage rather than just studying numerical data.

Acoustical heritage techniques are incredibly valuable in heritage studies and in relation to sensory history, but they need to be paired up with a clear acknowledgement of the cultural specificity of sensorial experiences.[4] We can study those sensorial experiences, but we will never be able to fully recreate them as we do not share the same experiences as past societies, and all recreations we produce are inevitably affected by our own cultural frameworks.[5] Furthermore, acoustical measurements and computer models are affected, as all methods are, by the assumptions made by researchers. Said assumptions

---

ancient Roman theatres," *Proceedings of the ERATO Project Symposium* (2006): 20–36; Jens Holger Rindel and Martin Lisa Nielsen, "The ERATO Project and its contribution to our understanding of the acoustics of ancient Greek and Roman theatres," *Proceedings of the ERATO Project Symposium* (2006): 1–10; R.S. Shankland, "Acoustics of Greek theatres," *Physics Today* 26 (1973): 30–35; Z. Yuksel, C. Binan, and R. Unver, "A research project in the intersection of architectural conservation and virtual reality: CAHRISMA," *Nineteenth International Symposium CIPA* (2003).

3 The literature on acoustic parameters is extensive, some texts of importance are: M. Barron and A. Marshall, "Spatial impression due to Early Lateral Reflections in Concert Halls: the derivation of a physical measure," *Journal of Sound and Vibration* 77, no. 2 (1981): 211–32; Leo Beranek, *Music, Acoustics and Architecture* (New York and London: John Wiley & Sons.Inc, 1962); Leo Beranek, *Concert and Opera Halls: how they sound* (New York: Acoustical Society of America, 1996); *ISO 3382–1. Acoustics—Measurement of Room Acoustic Parameters. Part 1: Performance Rooms* (Geneva: International Organization for Standardization, 2009); T. Okano, L. Beranek, and T. Hidaka, "Relations among interaural cross-correlation coefficient ($IACC_E$), lateral fraction (LF_E), and apparent source width (ASW) in concert halls," *Journal of the Acoustical Society of America* 104, no. 1 (1998): 119–31; G. Soulodre and J. Bradley, "Subjective evaluation of new room acoustic measurements," *Journal of Acoustical Society of America* 98 (1995): 294–301.

4 Constance Classen, "Foundations for an Anthropology of the Senses," *International Social Science Journal* 49 (1997): 401–12; Yannis Hamilakis, *Archaeology and the Senses: Human Experience, Memory, and Affect* (New York: Cambridge University Press, 2013); Smith, *Sensory History*.

5 Tony Bennett, *The Birth of the Museum: History, Theory, Politics* (London: Routledge, 1995).

include what sites are deemed worthy of study, the choice of source and receiver positions, and surface materials selected. Therefore, the rigor of acoustical work needs to be accompanied by a deep historical understanding as well as an acknowledgement that every and any aural recreation is just one possible version of the past.

When presenting digital heritage recreations relying on auditory experiences (and also when working on visual heritage), there is a tendency to present one version of the past. When used in the context of, for example, a museum visit, it could end up being considered as a definitive interpretation of what past cultures heard. Rather than encouraging the questioning of historical digital recreations, their use can in-fact crystallize a particular interpretation of the past, one which is invariably partial (because it can only be that way) and is necessarily the result of curatorial practice.[6] As indicated by O'Neill and O'Sullivan,[7] by presenting experiences unreflexively, we risk new interpretations of the past being based on them, and potentially facilitate a lack of questioning concerning their validity.

In this chapter, the authors consider gaming experiences and simulations as a gateway to explore the presentation of the multiplicity of possible sonic histories, as well as an opportunity to disseminate acoustical heritage and historical soundscapes, through a playful and engaging approach. *The Soundscapes of the York Mystery Plays* is an interactive web-based experience that explores how acoustic research linked to the medieval drama cycle the *York Mystery Plays* can be made available to wide audiences, providing creative ways of engaging with sonic histories.[8] The interface sought to explore solutions to the ethical challenges of presenting one fixed version of a sensorial past, and instead worked on providing a more transparent experience, while also allowing users to engage playfully with the sounds of medieval York. Although the present chapter is focused on this particular interactive experience, the theoretical framework provided, the design strategies explored and the lessons learnt are applicable to the wider fields of historical games, acoustical heritage, and sensory history.

---

6 Mariana Lopez, "Heritage Soundscapes: contexts and ethics of curatorial expression," in *The St. Thomas Way and the Medieval March of Wales: Exploring place, heritage, pilgrimage*, ed. Catherine A.M. Clarke (Leeds: Arc Humanities Press, 2020), 103–20.
7 Brendan O'Neill and Aidan O'Sullivan, "Experimental archaeology and re-experiencing the senses of the medieval world," in *Routledge Handbook of Sensory Archaeology*, ed. Robin Skeates and Jo Day (Oxon: Routledge 2020), 458.
8 Mariana Lopez, Marques Hardin, and Wenqi Wan, *The Soundscapes of the York Mystery Plays*, accessed April 6, 2021, http://soundscapesyorkmysteryplays.com/interface/.

The chapter starts by introducing readers to a brief history of the *York Mystery Plays*, focusing on sonic and acoustic considerations, before moving on to explore the need for developing interactive and transparent sound heritage experiences. An exploration of historical games and simulations is then included, before evaluating *The Soundscapes of the York Mystery Plays* experience in detail. The chapter concludes with a summary of the lessons learnt and a reflection on the future of the field.

The *York Mystery Plays*: A Very Brief History and Sonic Considerations

The *York Mystery Plays* are a series of plays that were performed in the city of York (UK) from the fourteenth to the sixteenth century in connection to the Corpus Christi feast. They had a religious subject matter, were organized by the City Council, and each play was performed by a crafts guild using a wagon that was specifically constructed or adapted for the occasion.[9] The wagons were handled through the streets of York and stopped at predetermined street spaces to perform for an audience. Audiences are thought to have been a mix of standing audiences, watching the plays for free, as well as seated, paying audiences, watching from scaffolds arranged for the occasion.[10] In addition to speech, the plays included both monophonic and polyphonic music.[11]

---

[9] A. Johnston and M. Dorrell, "The Doomsday pageant of the York mercers, 1433," *Leeds Studies in English*, New Series V (1971): 11–35; A. Johnston and M. Dorrell, "The York mercers and their pageant of Doomsday, 1433–1526," *Leeds Studies in English*, New Series VI (1973): 10–35; A. Johnston and M. Rogerson eds., *Records of Early English Drama: York* (REED) (Toronto: University of Toronto Press, 1979); P. Meredith, "Development of the York Mercers' Pageant Waggon," *Medieval English Theatre* 1 (1979): 5–18.

[10] D. Crouch, "Paying to see the play: the stationholders on the route of The York Corpus Christi Play in the fifteenth century" *Medieval English Theatre* 13 (1991): 64–111; A. Johnston and M. Rogerson, *REED;* P. Meredith, "The fifteenth century audience of the York Corpus Christi Play: Records and Speculation," in *'Divers toyes mengled': Essays on Medieval and Renaissance Culture in Honour of Andre Lascombes*, ed. M. Bitot, R. Mullini, and P Happé (Tours: Université François Rabelais, 1996), 101–11; M. Walsh, "High places and travelling scenes: some observations on the staging of the York Cycle," *Early Theatre* 3, no. 1 (2000): 137–54.

[11] Richard Rastall, *Six Songs from the York Mystery Plays 'The Assumption of the Virgin'* (Devon: Antico Edition, 1984); Richard Rastall, "Heaven: The Musical Repertory," in *The Iconography of Heaven*, ed. C. Davidson (Kalamazoo: Medieval Institute Publications, 1994), 162–96; Richard Rastall, *The Heaven Singing: Music in Early English Religious Drama I*

The many unknowns regarding the staging of the *York Mystery Plays* have been discussed in previous publications, although the remaining documents of the period, modern performance practices, and similar performance traditions in continental Europe have helped further our understanding.[12] It is these unknowns surrounding the performances that inspired the interface design of *The Soundscapes of the York Mystery Plays*, exploring how digital representations of the past can express the myriad possible interpretations of medieval drama and its associated sonic histories, thus providing transparency on our inability to reach a definitive, neatly organized version of historical events.

Previous work by López explored the importance of the acoustics of the performance settings of the *York Mystery Plays*, in terms of speech intelligibility and musical items, alongside its relationship to the importance of delivering the Christian message to lay audiences.[13] Such studies added an experimental and sensorial angle to previous work by Rastall on the music of the *York Mystery Plays*,[14] and by King,[15] who reflected on the importance of hearing over seeing in the plays through a careful analysis of the text.

(Cambridge: D.S. Brewer, 1996); Richard Rastall, *Minstrels Playing: Music in Early English Religious Drama II* (Cambridge: D.S. Brewer, 2001).

12 Richard Beadle and Pamela King, *York Mystery Plays: a selection in modern spelling* (Oxford: Oxford University Press, 1995); R. Blasting, "The pageant wagon as iconic site in the York Cycle," *Early Theatre* 3, no. 1 (2000): 127–36; A. Johnston and M. Rogerson, *REED*; J. McKinnell, "The medieval pageant wagons at York: their orientation and height," *Early Theatre* 3, no. 1 (2000): 79–104; A. Nelson, "Easter week pageants in Valladolid and Medina del Campo," *Medieval English Theatre* 1 (1979): 62–70; Margaret Rogerson, "Raging in the streets of medieval York," *Early Theatre* 3, no. 1 (2000): 105–25; M. Twycross, "The Flemish *Ommegang* and its pageant cars," *Medieval English Theatre* 2 (1980): 15–41; Walsh, "High places and travelling scenes."

13 Mariana Lopez, Sandra Pauletto and Gavin Kearney, "The application of impulse response measurement techniques to the study of the acoustics of Stonegate, a performance space used in medieval English drama," in *Acta Acustica united with Acustica* 99, no. 1 (2013): 98–108; Mariana Lopez, "Objective evaluation of a simulation of the acoustics of a medieval urban space used for dramatic performances," *Applied Acoustics* 88 (2015): 38–43; Mariana Lopez, "Using multiple computer models to study the acoustics of a sixteenth-century performance space," *Applied Acoustics* 94 (2015): 14–19; Mariana Lopez, "An acoustical approach to the study of the wagons of the York Mystery Plays: structure and orientation," *Early Theatre* (2015): 11–36; Mariana Lopez, "The York Mystery Plays: Exploring Sound and Hearing in Medieval Vernacular Drama," in *Sensory Perception in the Medieval West*, ed. S. Thomson and M. Bintley (Turnhout: Brepols, 2016), 53–73.

14 Rastall, *Six Songs from the York Mystery Plays*; Rastall, "Heaven: The musical repertory"; Rastall, *The Heaven Singing*.

15 Pamela King, "Seeing and hearing: looking and listening," *Early Theatre* 3, no. 1 (2000): 155–66.

The acoustical work included in the interactive interface is the result of previous work by the first author,[16] which involved the exploration of a multiplicity of performance scenarios and a detailed study on the impact said scenarios would have had on the acoustics of the performance spaces and the experience of the performances. The acoustical scenarios developed included the simulation of one of the streets used for performances in the sixteenth century (Stonegate, in central York), along with two different wagon structures: one being closed on three sides (referred to here as a closed wagon, featuring two height levels: the lower representing the Earth, with the one above, Heaven) and the other open on all sides with the roof supported by four columns (referred to here as an open wagon). The scenarios developed enable these wagon structures to be oriented either towards the side of the street (side-on) or the end of the street (front-on), and also capture a variety of performer and audience positions.

The studies resulted in a large amount of data, as well as auralisations, allowing us to hear the impact of those acoustical settings on recorded speech and musical extracts from the *York Mystery Plays*. It was the desire to bring these aural renditions, exemplifying a wide range of options on what the past settings of the performances might have sounded like, to wider audiences that inspired the creation of the interface *The Soundscapes of the York Mystery Plays*.

Although acoustics would have had a huge impact on the performance and reception of the plays, the myriad sounds occurring simultaneous to the performances would have been equally influential. The soundscapes would have included sounds that were part of the narrative, such as speech, music, and sound effects; sounds that were a result of the performance but not part of the narrative, such as the wagon wheels and the audience; and sounds that were completely independent from the performance, such as those related to weather conditions and the animals found in the medieval city of York.[17] It is worth reflecting that the sonic experiences of performers and audiences would have been influenced

---

16 Lopez, Pauletto, and Kearney, "The application of impulse response measurement techniques to the study of the acoustics of Stonegate"; Lopez, "Objective evaluation of a simulation of the acoustics of a medieval urban space used for dramatic performances"; Lopez, "Using multiple computer models to study the acoustics of a sixteenth-century performance space"; Lopez, "An acoustical approach to the study of the wagons of the York Mystery Plays"; Lopez, "The York Mystery Plays."
17 C. Davidson, *Corpus Christi Play at York: a context for religious drama* (New York: AMS Press, 2013); Pamela King, "Poetics and beyond: noisy bodies and aural variations in medieval English outdoor performance" (paper presented at the 14th Triennial Colloquium of the Société Internationale pur l'etude du Théâtre Médiéval, Poznań, July 25, 2013); Lopez, "The York Mystery Plays."

by all these sounds combined, and even those external to the performance still contributed to the full auditory experience.

The Soundscapes of the York Mystery Plays brings together the results of acoustical studies and soundscape considerations, combined with aspects of gaming and historical simulations to present the rich array of possible sonic histories to users through a novel interface.

On Sound Installations, Interactive Interfaces, and Sonic Histories

The dissemination of acoustical heritage research in an engaging and transparent manner to non-experts has received limited attention.[18] By transparent, we refer to an acknowledgement of the unknowns linked to acoustical work in the field, as well as the curatorial effort involved in its presentation to the public. The unknowns are linked firstly to the way history is reconstructed often from fragmented sources, and that several interpretations are therefore possible, but they also link to the fact that acoustical measurements and computer modelling have their own limitations, as derived from the acoustical theories employed, the positioning of sound sources and listeners, and the determined acoustical properties of materials, which all require careful consideration.[19]

The lack of research in this field is curious, as its counterpart, visual representations in archaeology, has received considerable attention in terms of the ethics of presentation.[20] Furthermore, the potential of playing with historical soundscapes and acoustics research has also been underexplored, with studies

---

18 Lopez, "Heritage soundscapes."
19 Lidia Álvarez-Morales, Mariana Lopez, and Angel Álvarez-Corbacho, "The acoustic environment of York Minster's Chapter House," *Acoustics* 2, no. 1 (2020): 13–36; Michael Vorländer, "Computer simulations in room acoustics: Concepts and uncertainties," *Journal of Acoustical Society of America* 133 (2013): 1203–13.
20 H. Denard, *The London Charter: for the computer-based visualisation of cultural heritage* (King's College London, 2009); K. Giles, A. Masinton and G. Arnott, "Visualising The Guild Chapel, Stratford-upon-Avon: digital models as research tools in buildings archaeology," *Internet Archaeology* 32 (2012), accessed April 6, 2021, https://doi.org/10.11141/ia.32.1; P. Miller and J. Richards, "The good, the bad, and the downright misleading: archaeological adoption of computer visualization," in *Proceedings of the 22nd CAA Conference*, ed. J. Huggest and N. Ryan (Oxford: ArchaeoPress, 1995), 19–22.

around visual elements of archaeology in games being much more prominent.[21] An exception to this is Álvarez-Morales and Cáceres Muñoz's pilot *Cathedral's Treasures*, which explores the presentation of research on the York Minster's *Chapter House* acoustics to children through a simple Unity game.[22] Furthermore, López has explored transparency of results presentation through sound installations based on the *York Mystery Plays*.[23]

The Soundscapes of the York Mystery Plays project sought to increase engagement with acoustical research, while also providing a playful and interactive experience. The aim was to bring to the forefront the multiplicity of possible scenarios linked to performances and the impact of the different scenarios on the acoustical experience. The interface was designed to place the listening experience in the user's hands by providing different layers of control, in which different acoustical settings could be explored and different soundscape elements could be added and mixed, while also exploring the different factors involved in the aural experiences of medieval drama. Furthermore, the interface provided a means to connect the present and the past, through a series of newly recorded oral histories focused on performers and organizers of the *York Mystery Plays* in modern times. The oral histories sought to demonstrate that the *York Mystery Plays* are part of living heritage, and our knowledge of the past informs modern performances, which in turn shed light on possible past practices.

Playful Approaches to History

The Soundscapes of the York Mystery Plays explored the design of an interactive website for the simulation and exploration of acoustical settings and soundscapes linked to the performance of the *York Mystery Plays*, allowing the user to play with the sounds from the past, and acknowledge that there is not one version of what the past might have sounded like, but a multiplicity of options that are worth exploring.

---

21 Andrew Reinhard, *Archaeogaming: An introduction to archaeology in and of video games* (Berghahn Books: 2018).

22 Lidia Álvarez-Morales and Alvaro Cáceres Muñoz, *Cathedral's Treasures*, accessed April 6, 2021, https://alvarocaceresmunoz.itch.io/cathedrals-treasures.

23 Mariana Lopez, "Giving History a Voice," in *The Cambridge Companion to Music in Digital Culture*, ed. Nicholas Cook, Monique Ingalls, and David Trippett (Cambridge: Cambridge University Press, 2019); Mariana Lopez, *Heritage Soundscapes*.

The exploration of digital games as opportunities to reflect on the past is not a new phenomenon,[24] but it is the focus on acoustical heritage and soundscapes, rather than visual elements, or political and economic simulations, that make this interface unique.

The Soundscapes of the York Mystery Plays interface borrows elements of its visual design as well as some of the interaction mechanics from the field of digital games, more specifically role-playing (RPG) and strategy games, such as *The Elder Scrolls* series[25] and *Age of Empires*.[26] However, *The Soundscapes of the York Mystery Plays* is not a game in itself, as it has no goals, there is not a problem or challenge that needs solving, and there are no rewards in the form of points or trophies for those using it.[27] Therefore, even though it simulates the past and allows for different routes to be taken in the search for alternative outcomes (in this case, sonic outcomes), it is not a historical simulation game, such as those analyzed by McCall.[28] Restated succinctly, it is a historical simulation but not a historical simulation game.

Whereas linear sound recreations would present one version of the past, the non-linear nature of digital videogames and interfaces allows for the exploration of different possibilities. The interactive environment, as pointed out by Holdenried and Trépanier, lends itself to experimentation of multiple scenarios.[29] *The Soundscapes of the York Mystery Plays* therefore addresses the issue highlighted by Elliott and Kapell,[30] who note how the user is limited to those facts or details selected by the designer. Although the interface also presents the choices made by the research and design team, the multiplicity of possible sonic experiences it facilitates are far greater than could be achieved through a

---

24 Andrew B. R Elliott and Matthew Wilhelm Kapell, eds., *Playing with the Past: digital games and the simulation of history* (London: Bloomsbury, 2013); Jeremiah McCall, *Gaming the Past: Using video games to teach secondary school history* (Routledge, 2011); Reinhard, *Archaeogaming*.
25 *The Elder Scrolls* (Bethesda Game Studios, 2014).
26 *Age of Empires* (Ensemble Studios, 1997).
27 Katie Salen and Eric Zimmerman, *Rules of Play: Game Design Fundamentals* (MIT Press, 2003), 80.
28 McCall, *Gaming the Past*.
29 Joshua Holdenried and Nicolas Trépanier, "Dominance and the Aztec Empire: representations in *Age of Empires II* and *Medieval II: Total War*," in *Playing with the Past: digital games and the simulation of history*, ed. Andrew B. R. Elliott and Matthew Wilhelm Kapell (London: Bloomsbury, 2013), 107–20.
30 Andrew B. R. Elliott and Matthew Wilhelm Kapell, "Introduction: To Build a Past that Will "Stand the Test of Time": Discovering Historical Facts, Assembling Historical Narratives," in *Playing with the Past: digital games and the simulation of history*, ed. Andrew B.R. Elliott and Matthew Wilhelm Kapell (London: Bloomsbury, 2013), 6.

set version of a historical game with a single sonic simulation, or a defined soundscape in a historical film.

The Soundscapes of the York Mystery Plays subscribes to the belief in the importance of games as outputs of research as well as tools to encourage debate and analysis, as proposed and reflected on by Houghton.[31] Digital games were explored in this project due to their potential to communicate historical data, which in turn could be used by others in the field of history to inform their work. For instance, those exploring the performance of medieval drama but without a background in acoustics and soundscapes. In this way, similarly to what is presented by Houghton, while the interface is the outcome of research in the field of historical acoustics it also acts as a tool supporting those wanting to study the plays sonically.[32] *The Soundscapes of the York Mystery Plays* project brings to the forefront the uncertainty of historical acoustics and of historical research in general. It reveals the gaps in studies and welcomes uncertainty. As a result, it allows the dissemination of acoustical heritage but also invites scholars to use the tool as a means of rediscovering and rethinking the performances overall. Interactive interfaces and digital games can be seen therefore as vehicles for the exploration of historical uncertainty and the curatorial work involved in historical research.

The Soundscapes of the York Mystery Plays can additionally be linked back to work on procedural rhetoric and persuasive games,[33] as the interface is built to allow for reflection and acknowledgement of the curation process behind the presentation of sonic histories, while demonstrating the myriad possible scenarios suggested by historical and acoustical research. The aural past cannot be fixed, the details will never be truly known. The interface hopes to encourage users to question their knowledge and beliefs about history, its curation, acoustical heritage, and the Mystery Plays overall. The processes facilitated by the interface are determined by the argument being put forward: that acoustical history is not a unified, linear history, but is instead dependent on a myriad of factors, although such unknowns should not stop us from considering its crucial value for medieval studies.

The interface here presented, at its core, and in relation to Lefebvre's discussions on space as a social product,[34] articulates a response to existing perspectives

---

31 Robert Houghton, "World, Structure and Play: A Framework for Games as Historical Research Outputs, Tools, and Processes," *Práticas da História* 7 (2018): 11–43.
32 Houghton, "World, Structure and Play."
33 Ian Bogost, *Persuasive Games: The Expressive Power of Videogames* (MIT Press, 2007).
34 Henri Lefebvre, *The Production of Space*, trans. Donald Nicholson-Smith (Oxford: Blackwell Publishing, 1974).

surrounding medieval drama and acoustics in relation to their performance space. Studies on acoustical heritage focused on pre-seventeenth century drama have favored the study of performances that are conducted within fixed and, often, impressive structures, such as those utilized in Greek, Roman and Elizabethan drama, with medieval acoustical studies often centered around places of worship.[35] Preconceptions on the performances of medieval drama and their performance spaces, based on their use of outdoor settings and temporary structures, have determined them unworthy of acoustical studies, and so resulted in a significant gap in our knowledge of the impact of acoustical settings on the performances. The street space can, therefore, be reclaimed as being worthy of study, with its own unique acoustical settings and a domain in which every day life was mixed with dramatic performances. That is, the "worthiness" of spaces is expanded to include the interaction between performance and everyday spaces. Researchers' self-imposed restrictions and subsequently biased work on historical acoustics has unnecessarily restricted our appreciation of the importance of acoustics for medieval outdoor drama, a restriction that this project seeks to rectify.

The interactive interface here presented takes the first step towards disseminating the value of outdoors acoustical settings for medieval drama, employing digital technologies for audio recreations and non-linear interactive experiences. As a result, it helps to catalyze conversations around the use of space and its implications for sonic histories.

Designing the Interactive Experience

In the initial stage of the design, different online interactive interfaces were explored as sources of inspiration, including those mixing a combination of sounds selected from a pool of choices by the user for the purposes of relaxation and meditation.[36] Such interfaces had simple controls and minimalistic designs, making them easy to use. Additionally, they allowed multiple, concurrent sounds to be active at once and demonstrated the robustness of standard web development tools like HTML5, CSS3, and JavaScript for interactivity and audio playback.

The research team decided that users would be given the option to hear extracts from three of the *York Mystery Plays*: *The Resurrection*, *Pentecost*, and *The*

---

[35] Lopez, Pauletto, and Kearney, "The application of impulse response measurement techniques to the study of the acoustics of Stonegate"; Lopez, "Objective evaluation of a simulation of the acoustics of a medieval urban space used for dramatic performances."
[36] See "Defonic," accessed March 11, 2021, http://defonic.com.

Assumption of the Virgin. They would have the flexibility to alternate between plays and also select different acoustical settings for each of the performances. In addition to this, users would be able to add other sounds to the experience, and so build their own soundscapes. The sounds available encapsulated three types: sounds that were part of the performance and the narrative of the plays, such as speech and music; sounds resulting from the performance event but not part of the narrative, such as the wheels of the wagons and the audience reactions; and sounds external to the performance, such as animal sounds, weather conditions, and church bells.[37]

Newly recorded commentaries from contributors in modern productions served as oral histories, providing greater context to the sound elements and their impact on the performance. The oral histories were then incorporated into the interface, providing the user with further insights into the importance of particular sounds, while highlighting concurrently the value of modern recreations in historical research: serving the purpose of understanding the past, while placing the Mystery Plays within a continuum that connects medieval performers, organizers and audiences, with contemporary ones.

At the core of the design strategy for the interface was the desire to convey historical knowledge on acoustical heritage and the multiplicity of possible interpretations. This resonates with work by Holter, Muth, and Schwesinger,[38] who reflected on how investigations on the acoustics of public assemblies in Late Republican Rome could be studied through different possible scenarios based on evidence and allowing comparisons, but a definite recreation could not be reached. Nevertheless, it was also considered important to convey these experiences without overcrowding the interface with lengthy textual extracts that were unlikely to be read extensively by users.

First Stage

The selection and rendering of the acoustical simulations were crucial to determine what the interface needed to facilitate. The audio recordings of the extracts from the plays were selected from the collection of recordings owned by the first author, and once the acoustical settings were selected, the recordings

---

37 Davidson, *Corpus Christi Play at York*; King, *Poetics and beyond*; Lopez, *The York Mystery Plays*.
38 Erika Holter, Susanne Muth, and Sebastian Schwesinger, "Sounding out public space in Late Republican Rome," in *Sound and the ancient senses*, ed. Shane Butler and Sarah Nooter (Oxon: Routledge, 2019), 44–60.

were convolved with the corresponding impulse responses to generate the auralised files. Seven acoustical variations of the performance audio for each play were selected (see Table 12.1).

Table 12.1: Different acoustical settings available for the different plays.

Settings	The Resurrection	Pentecost	The Assumption of the Virgin
Street space with no wagon, performers, and one listener	✓	✓	✗
Performers on closed side-on wagon (Earth), and one listener at street level	✓	✗	✓
Performers on closed front-on wagon (Earth), and one listener at street level	✓	✗	✓
Performers on closed side-on wagon (Earth), with audiences both standing and seated, but listeners positioned at mid-level scaffolding	✓	✗	✗
Performers on closed front-on wagon (Earth), with audiences both standing and seated, but listeners positioned at mid-level scaffolding	✓	✗	✗
Performers on open side-on wagon, and one listener at street level	✓	✗	✗
Performers on open front-on wagon, and one listener at street level	✓	✗	✗
Performers at street level in front of closed front-on wagon, and one listener at street level	✗	✓	✗
Performers at street level in front of closed front-on wagon, with audiences both standing and seated, but listeners positioned at mid-level scaffolding	✗	✓	✗
Performers at street level in front of closed side-on wagon, and one listener at street level	✗	✓	✗
Performers at street level in front of closed side-on wagon, with audiences both standing and seated, but listeners positioned at mid-level scaffolding	✗	✓	✗
Performers at street level in front of open front-on wagon, and one listener at street level	✗	✓	✗

Table 12.1 (continued)

Settings	The Resurrection	Pentecost	The Assumption of the Virgin
Performers at street level in front of open front-on wagon, with audiences both standing and seated, but listeners positioned at mid-level scaffolding	✗	✓	✗
Performers on closed side-on wagon (Heaven), and one listener at street level	✗	✗	✓
Performers on closed front-on wagon (Heaven), and one listener at street level	✗	✗	✓
Performers on closed side-on wagon (Heaven), with audiences standing and seated, but listeners at the standing position	✗	✗	✓
Performers on closed front-on wagon (Heaven), with audiences standing and seated, but listeners positioned at top-level scaffolding	✗	✗	✓
Performers on closed side-on wagon (Heaven), with audiences standing and seated, but listeners positioned at mid-level scaffolding	✗	✗	✓

The next step was to source the audio samples to recreate the soundscape elements. With this aim in mind, the classification presented earlier in this chapter was followed, and it was decided that the sounds would capture the general street ambience, the sound of wagon wheels, animals, bells, weather conditions, and audiences. Sounds were either originally recorded or sourced from sound effects libraries.

Once the sonic aspects of the interactive experience had been decided on, work was conducted on producing vector graphic icons that would serve as visual representations of the different sounds. To help ensure the performance audio was at the center of the experience, the icons were arranged in the layout of a wheel (in reference to the wagon wheels), with the core performance audio placed at the center, and with the other sound elements encircling it.

Each element had two smaller accompanying icons that, when clicked, played either its respective soundscape audio (represented by a loudspeaker icon) or an associated oral history (speech bubble icon). The oral histories linked to each sound element had a thematic connection. For example, the weather icon was linked to oral histories that discussed the challenges of weather conditions in

York when performing the *York Mystery Plays* in modern times. Where more than one oral history recording was considered relevant and enriching to the user's experience, they were listed in a drop-down menu as "Oral His 1," "Oral Hist 2," etc. Small round icons labelled "Acoustics 1," "Acoustics 2," etc., were added around the performance audio icon, and so allowing the user to replace the dry performance audio with one of the auralisations.

Different soundscape sounds could be added, subtracted, and mixed together at the user's will. Clicking on the speech bubble of a soundscape element played an oral history file, but would pause all other active sounds. Alternatively, if one of the oral histories was active, playing a soundscape element would override the playback of the active oral history, pausing its audio. As a result of this logic, multiple sounds could be played together, but they would be paused when an oral history was activated. Conversely, only one oral history could be active at a time, and playing any other sound would override its playback.

Second Stage

Once the initial setup was finalized in terms of its components, interactivity, and initial layout, the research team started reconsidering the visual design. Although the initial stage had provided a simple design that was intuitive to use, its connection to medieval times was missing and would unlikely be grasped by someone not already familiar with the *York Mystery Plays*. A professional graphic designer, Wenqi Wan, was hired to rethink the visual design of the interface. It was at this stage that a greater connection to the world of gaming and simulation was integrated. Inspiration for the interface setup and visuals was drawn from Role-Playing Game (RPG) *The Elder Scrolls* and the strategy game *Age of Empires*.

Three avatars with medieval clothing were designed to represent each of the plays. The user had to click on a character to select a play and the selection activated a rosette-like background that further emphasized the medieval theme (see Figure 12.1). The chosen avatar would then present a speech bubble welcoming the user to the site and including a short explanation on the use of the interface. Moving forward, the instructions would then direct the user to the main part of the interface, which included the interactivity already described but with a different visual design (see Figure 12.2). The vector images were replaced by designs by Wenqi Wan, who incorporated stained glass window backgrounds to different icons, creating a strong visual connection to the medieval theme. As Reinhard discusses, visual imagery can be employed as "shorthand" for a historical period,

Figure 12.1: The Second Version of the interface presents each of the three plays with an avatar.

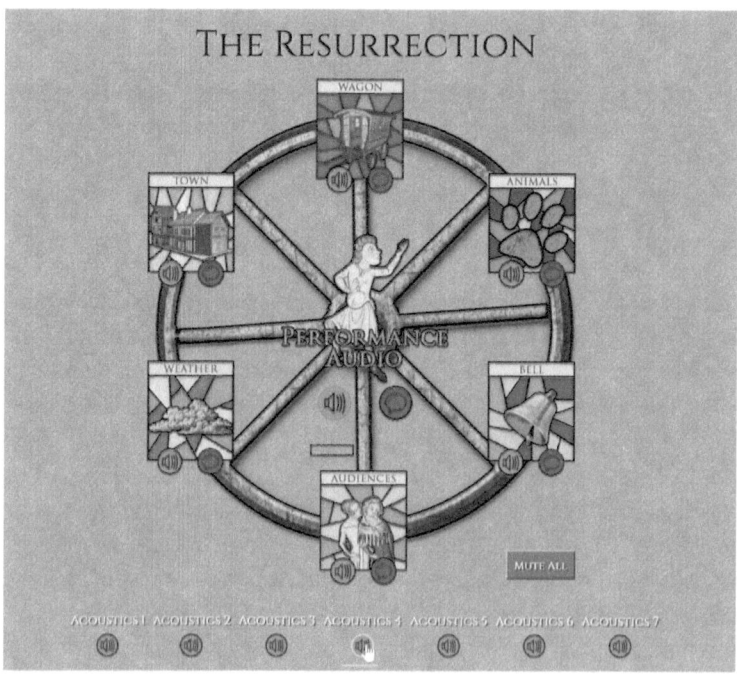

Figure 12.2: Updated visual design for the interface.

creating a connection without the need for textual explanation.[39] In this case, it was a connection that sought to draw the user into the interface. The buttons that generated the acoustical changes were moved to the bottom of the interface but still retained the generic labels of "Acoustics 1," "Acoustics 2," etc.

A menu could then be accessed to change plays and an *Aural Memories* tab provided access to additional oral histories that had not been mapped to the interface but were still considered of great value to the project. The aim was to produce an easy-to-use interface that did not require tutorials or lengthy introductions.

At this stage of the development, feedback was sought through a survey in order to determine what features were successful and what required further work. It is worth noting that the aim of the feedback was not to conduct a thorough qualitative or quantitative study, but to understand what had worked and what had not, so as to be able to progress with the design. The survey was completed by 31 participants. The features mentioned most favorably by survey participants included the ability to combine sounds together to shape their experiences, as well as listening to the oral history extracts, experimenting with different acoustical settings, and the overall freedom of choice.

When requesting feedback on what aspects needed improvement, the aspect most commented on was the lack of contextual information on the plays themselves and what was being heard. This meant some users were unsure as to the significance of the sounds and what was happening when they clicked on the different acoustic settings. Another aspect mentioned by survey participants was the need for additional instructions on how to use the interface, and that the lack of instructions had meant it was easy to miss out on certain parts of the experience.

When asked how engaging they found the RPG-like interface, results were mixed. Participants were given a 5-point Likert scale from 1 (Not engaging) to 5 (Very engaging), and, as can be seen in Table 12.2, the majority of participants scored it in a middle-point of the scale, demonstrating that work could be conducted to improve the engagement with the interface. Some contextualization for the responses on the interface was provided under a further comments section and these included not having noticed it, as well as feeling it was too old-fashioned and, as a result, not engaging. Further notes on the need for further contextualization of the sounds, as well as how the interface represented the outcomes of research, were also mentioned.

---

[39] Reinhard, *Archaeogaming*, 6 and 189.

Table 12.2: Likert-scale point percentages for the second stage of the interface.

Likert scale point	Percentage of survey participants
1 (Not engaging)	12.5%
2	15.63%
3	31.25%
4	21.88%
5 (Very engaging)	18.75%

Final Version

The final version sought to address the feedback received, in particular the lack of contextualizing information. The approach followed was to focus on the visual design further, as this was deemed key to providing the user with additional context: enabling them to grasp the aim of the project without having to read the website, specialist journal articles, or any substantive body of written text more generally. As Houghton warns, an over-reliance on textual explanations to provide information within historical digital games can end up obscuring the experience.[40] As a result, further work on the visual design was conducted alongside a focus on the journey the user takes through the interface.

A visual and interactive addition to aid contextualization was an icon on the main project website that linked directly to the interface, depicting a medieval town through timber-framed houses and the York Minster itself (see Figure 12.3). This first interactive element set the theme of the design and connected back to the project website, in which key background information could be accessed and appended to the more playful experience of building a soundscape.

On first entering the interface, the user is presented with an avatar next to a graphic representation of a page from an illuminated manuscript (see Figure 12.4), which states:

> Dear Friend, The Lord Mayor has issued the billets, we are bringing forth the wagons for the York Mystery Plays, will you join us in Stonegate?

---

[40] Houghton, "World, Structure and Play."

Figure 12.3: Image that introduces the interface to the project website visitor and acts as the gateway to the interactive experience.

Figure 12.4: An avatar next to a manuscript page introduces us to the context of the interface: a performance of the *York Mystery Plays* in Stonegate.

The phrasing used is based on the terminology present in manuscripts linked to the *York Mystery Plays*.[41] This addition was deemed crucial: placing the user of the interface in the context of the performances, while also introducing the location as Stonegate. A manicule at the bottom of the page, accompanied by the phrase "Take me there" (see Figure 12.4), allows the user to progress further.

The next step within the interface then shows a scroll-like version of the map of York (see Figure 12.5), indicating the position of the performance space in the intersection between Stonegate and Swinegate (now Little Stonegate). It is this particular area in Stonegate that the auralisations presented in the interface are based on, as the acoustic measurements and computer models were focused on that particular part of the street, whose selection was itself informed by historical documents.

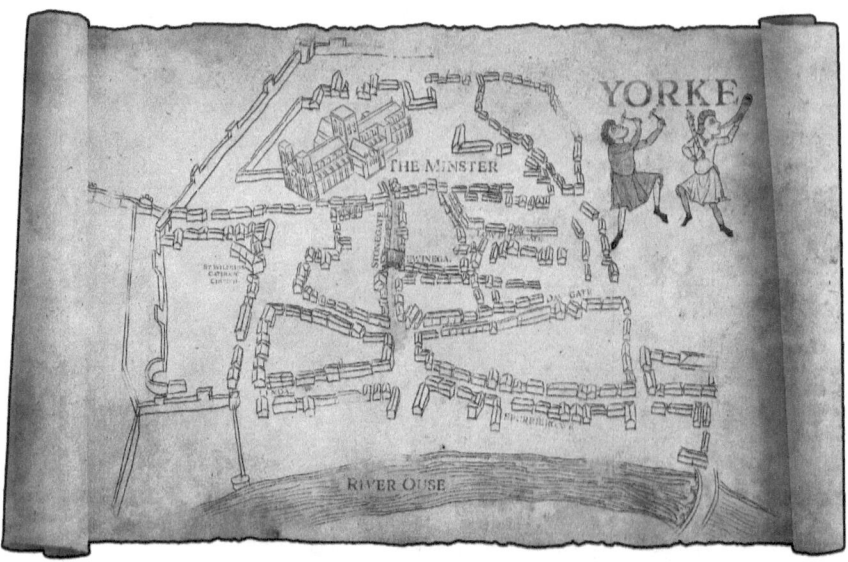

Figure 12.5: Map of York as a scroll and indicating the position of the wagon in the intersection between Stonegate and Swinegate.

Once the user clicks on the map, they are directed to a visual representation of the street space, featuring different choice of plays at the top, and the wagon wheel structure at the center (see Figure 12.6). The interface defaults automatically to the

---

41 A. Johnston and M. Rogerson, *REED*.

Figure 12.6: Final interface design for *The Soundscapes of the York Mystery Plays*.

play *The Resurrection* as, in terms of the chronological order of the full *York Mystery Plays* cycle, it is the first of the three plays.

A key addition was the replacement of a plain background with an image that would reflect the performance setting chosen by the user. A common background image was created that represented a generic medieval cobbled street with timber-framed structures to the sides—effectively, a stylized version of the computer model of Stonegate. Additions were made to the general representation depending on the acoustical setting selected, including: an added wagon structure, whose design and orientation matched the chosen user setting; varying positions for the performers (at street level, on top of the wagon, and at an upper "heaven" level of the wagon, to represent angelic singing, for example); and different audience positions—from simulations with only the performers and one listener (to eliminate the effect of audiences on the acoustics) to settings in which audiences were present both standing and on scaffolds, with an indication of the listener position simulated in each instance by highlighting listening audiences in red. These design changes were accompanied by a change from "Acoustics 1," "Acoustics 2" labels to short descriptions, such as "Street space" and "Side-on closed wagon," among others. The change in the background image as the user clicked on them would clarify the meaning of the setting and anchor the overall listening experience.

The visual changes sought to explore what Jenkins has referred to as Environmental Storytelling,[42] that is, how the elements in the design aid the narrative presented in a game. One could counter argue that there is no narrative in this interface but, as pointed out by Livingstone, Luchart, and Jeffrey,[43] we can consider the historical simulation, and its exploration, as a story being told. In this case, the graphic design style chosen, that of an illuminated manuscript, plus the aged map that says *Yorke*, and the background images, as well as the iconography of the wheel and the stained glass, all combine to tell the background story of the aural experiences of the *York Mystery Plays*. It is the piecing together of this information that aims to keep the user engaged through active interpretation.[44]

The only audio change made in this final stage was the re-recording of audience reactions, which were originally studio recordings, but were now replaced with binaural (in very simple terms, 3D audio over headphones) crowd recordings from an early modern drama outdoors performance. Finally, a playback bar was included for the performance audio, visualizing progress as well as enabling the user to navigate different sections of the file. Both these changes were a direct response to the survey feedback.

A "Help" button was added to the interface for those users requiring further explanations on its functionality, along with a note recommending the use of headphones. These changes were, again, in response to the survey feedback.

Upon the completion of the revised version, feedback was collected through a new anonymous survey, completed by 11 participants. When asked what they liked the most, once more participants commented on the ability to combine sounds and explore the different acoustical settings, as well as the excellent quality of the sound recordings, and its overall atmospheric potential. Interestingly, the number of positive comments on the interface increased, with praise being received for the visuals changing to match the audio being played, further contextualizing the hearing experience, alongside its graphical style and responsiveness.

Aspects noted as requiring further improvement included the addition of further context on the sounds being heard, as not all users were confident on the meaning of the acoustical settings, and their resulting effect on the performance

---

42 Henry Jenkins, "Game Design as Narrative Architecture," in *First Person: New Media as Story, Performance, Game*, ed. Noah Wardrip-Fruin and Pat Harrigan (Cambridge: MIT Press, 2004), 117–30.
43 Daniel Livingstone, Sandy Louchart, and Stuart Jeffrey, "Archaeological Storytelling in Games," *Proceedings of the 2016 Playing With History Workshop*, accessed April 6, 2021, http://www.digra.org/digital-library/publications/archaeological-storytelling-in-games/.
44 Harvey Smith and Matthias Worch, "What Happened Here? Environmental Storytelling," Paper presented at Game Developers Conference, March 11, 2010.

audio. Moreover, the interface design was noted as needing further work to increase general ease of use.

A Likert-scale rating for the interface was once more utilized, although this time the question was altered so it did not mention the RPG-style, so as to avoid confusing users that would not necessarily associate the work with RPG games. It can be noticed in Table 12.3 that higher ratings were given to the new interface.

Table 12.3: Likert-scale point percentages for the final stage of the interface.

Likert scale point	Percentage of survey participants
1 (Not engaging)	16.67%
2	8.33%
3	16.67%
4	41.67%
5 (Very engaging)	16.67%

When asked to compare the new version to the previous one, survey participants mentioned that they felt the contextualization of the performances through the visuals was an improvement and that it made the experience more engaging. There was also a mention that the route through the interface was also more satisfactory. However, there were also comments on the interface having become more cluttered and unfocused. There was an interesting suggestion on changing the interface to make it directly possible to activate sound sources through clicking on elements on the stage, and in the street space, which could help resolve the clutter of images on the screen.

Discussion, Conclusions, and Playing On

The reflection on the feedback provided by survey participants and the research team's analysis of the interface point towards the need to further contextualize the research the interactive experience is based on. Further contextualization would allow users to become more aware of the historical context of the performances, the relevance of the selected sounds, and the rationale behind the choices made.

Although the interface employs the notion of environmental storytelling to present the context, it still expects users to actively piece the information together. Feedback received suggests that the final design was successful, overall, in improving the contextualization of the sonic experiences, but this did not work for everyone, with some users still feeling confused and others left wanting to know more. The challenge faced is how to incorporate this information without over-cluttering the interface or relying on lengthy textual pieces. Some of the solutions explored in commercial games have included in-game encyclopaedias, as in *Age of Empires II: Definitive Edition*,[45] which includes a "History" tab under Settings, allowing the exploration of information under different heading categories, such as civilizations, historical periods, and military elements, alongside generic visual depictions. The information provided is not integral to the game, is not particularly easy to find, and provides no indication as to where the information is sourced from. Another game, *Crusader Kings II*,[46] questionably links its historical characters to relevant Wikipedia entries.

One interesting solution is provided by the much earlier *Cosmology of Kyoto*,[47] a combination of digital game and walking simulator, which features a *Reference* tab that is available throughout, and so accessing it can be considered as intrinsic to the experience. As the user progresses through the experience, the information available through the *Reference* tab changes as is appropriate to the context—ranging from the history of Kyoto itself to specific historical buildings and characters. Furthermore, it provides information linked to the historical period the game represents (tenth century), as well as present day information, and so directly linking past and present. *Cosmology of Kyoto* also allows for a reference-only optionality, in which there is no game experience and only the references are presented, which are organized in diverse ways: *Alphabetical, Thought and Religion, Politics and Economics, Lifestyle, Places and Buildings,* and *People and Literature*. A bibliography can also be accessed, and many entries are accompanied by historical images. Simulation and historical context are integrated smoothly throughout, and it is possible that a similar format might be suitable for further contextualizing experiences in other historically-themed simulations, regardless of whether their focus is on sound and acoustics.

In terms of the auditory experience, future work could be done to provide all audio assets in a binaural format, which may further immerse the listener in the experience. Moreover, although all performance elements (speech, music)

---

45 *Age of Empires II: Definitive Edition* (Xbox Game Studios, 2019).
46 *Crusader Kings II* (Paradox Interactive, 2012); Vinicius Marino Carvalho, "Videogames as Tools for Social Science History," *The Historian* 79, no. 4 (2017): 784–819.
47 *Cosmology of Kyoto* (Softedge, 1993).

were auralised to correspond to the source/listener combination being simulated, this was not the case for the soundscape elements, which were recorded outdoors directly but could not be matched to the acoustics being simulated. This was due to the difficulty in assigning a source position to such variable elements. However, further exploration of this possibility would help incorporate them more successfully to the auditory experience.

A further improvement to the interface could also be the incorporation of an option allowing the user to save and download their "mix" of sounds as an audio file for future use, a feature that is being explored by Dr Cobi van Tonder's project *Acoustic Atlas*, in which users can record their own voices combined with the acoustic characteristics of the sites included in the Atlas, before downloading the results.[48]

In addition to the improvements that can be made to the interactive interface, it is also worth exploring whether the concept can be expanded into a full game, in which players are assigned characters, have specific goals, and are rewarded for their achievements. Characters could be based on different generic medieval figures that might have attended the plays, from the wealthy attendee paying for a seat in the scaffolds to the casual passer-by, with each having a unique listening experience that can be explored. Additionally, the project could be expanded by incorporating the different performance sites of the *York Mystery Plays*, with the corresponding acoustical data. The transformation of the simulation into a game could open up the possibility of providing historical context through dialogue options between characters, as well as notices that could be read throughout the virtual environment.

The Soundscapes of the York Mystery Plays is the first web-based interface of its kind to present a playful means of engaging with acoustical heritage data. In the process, it articulates a critical view of the static, one-version approach towards acoustical heritage experiences that are commonly presented to general audiences, which fail to acknowledge the contradictions and unknowns inherent to the methods utilized. In response to this, the interface invites the user to choose one out of many possible pathways of experience, where what is chosen substantially affects the final outcome. By presenting multiple pathways it highlights that history is not reducible to a fixed narrative, and that our interpretation of the past presents multiple options. This invites the user to question their own notions of history, settling with the truth that we will never know for

---

[48] Cobi van Tonder, "Acoustic Atlas", accessed April 6, 2021, https://acousticatlas.de/; Cobi van Tonder and Mariana Lopez, "Acoustic Atlas – Auralisation in the Browser," 2021 Immersive and 3D Audio: from Architecture to Automotive (I3DA) (2021): 1–5, doi: 10.1109/I3DA48870.2021.9610909.

certain what the past sounded like. Finally, *The Soundscapes of the York Mystery Plays* also expands extant notions of what historical games and simulations can provide, moving away from a focus on visuals, political and economic simulations, to include aural experiences.

Although the present chapter has focused on a specific example, the techniques explored, and the lessons learnt, have a much wider relevance, for they invite researchers on acoustical heritage to consider alternative forms of presenting research outcomes and embracing interpretative transparency, while also inviting researchers in the field of historical games to widen their focus to embrace the importance of sonic histories research, both through the creation of new experiences and the exploration of already existing ones.

Funding: *The Soundscapes of the York Mystery Plays* project was possible thanks to funding by the British Academy (SG152109) and the Priming Funds initiative by University of York.

Bibliography

Álvarez-Morales, Lidia, Mariana Lopez, and Angel Álvarez-Corbacho. "The acoustic environment of York Minster's Chapter House." *Acoustics* 2, no. 1 (2020): 13–36.

Álvarez-Morales, Lidia, and Alvaro Cáceres Muñoz. *Cathedral's Treasures*. Accessed April 6, 2021. https://alvarocaceresmunoz.itch.io/cathedrals-treasures

Barron, M., and A. Marshall. "Spatial impression due to Early Lateral Reflections in Concert Halls: the derivation of a physical measure." *Journal of Sound and Vibration* 77, no. 2 (1981): 211–32.

Beadle, Richard, and Pamela King. *York Mystery Plays: a selection in modern spelling*. Oxford: Oxford University Press, 1995.

Bennett, Tony. *The Birth of the Museum: History, Theory, Politics*. London: Routledge, 1995.

Beranek, Leo. *Music, Acoustics and Architecture*. New York and London: John Wiley & Sons. Inc, 1962.

Beranek, Leo. *Concert and Opera Halls: how they sound*. New York: Acoustical Society of America, 1996.

Blasting, R. "The pageant wagon as iconic site in the York Cycle." *Early Theatre* 3, no. 1 (2000): 127–36.

Bogost, Ian. *Persuasive Games: The Expressive Power of Videogames*. London: MIT Press, 2007.

Carvalho, Vinicius Marino. "Videogames as Tools for Social Science History." *The Historian* 79, no. 4 (2017): 784–819.

Classen, Constance. "Foundations for an Anthropology of the Senses." *International Social Science Journal* 49 (1997): 401–12.

Crouch, David. "Paying to see the play: the stationholders on the route of The York Corpus Christi Play in the fifteenth century." *Medieval English Theatre* 13 (1991): 64–111.

Davidson, Clifford. *Corpus Christi Play at York: a context for religious drama*. New York: AMS Press, 2013.

"Defonic." Accessed April 6, 2021. http://defonic.com.

Denard, H. *The London Charter: for the computer-based visualisation of cultural heritage*. King's College London, 2009.

Elliott, Andrew B. R., and Matthew Wilhelm Kapell, eds. *Playing with the Past: digital games and the simulation of history*. London: Bloomsbury, 2013.

Elliott, Andrew B. R., and Matthew Kapel. "Introduction: To Build a Past that Will "Stand the Test of Time": Discovering Historical Facts, Assembling Historical Narratives." In *Playing with the Past: digital games and the simulation of history*, edited by Andrew B. R. Elliott and Matthew Wilhelm Kapell, 1–30. London: Bloomsbury, 2013.

Giles, Kate, Anthony Masinton, and Geoff Arnott. "Visualising The Guild Chapel, Stratford-upon-Avon: digital models as research tools in buildings archaeology." *Internet Archaeology* 32 (2012). Accessed April 6, 2021. https://doi.org/10.11141/ia.32.1.

Hamilakis, Yannis. *Archaeology and the Senses: Human Experience, Memory, and Affect*. New York: Cambridge University Press, 2013.

Holdenried, Joshua, and Nicolas Trépanier. "Dominance and the Aztec Empire: representations in *Age of Empires II* and *Medieval II: Total War*." In *Playing with the Past: digital games and the simulation of history*, edited by Andrew B. R Elliott and Matthew Wilhelm Kapell, 107–20. London: Bloomsbury, 2013.

Holter, Erika, Susanne Muth, and Sebastian Schwesinger. "Sounding out public space in Late Republican Rome." In *Sound and the ancient senses*, edited by Shane Butler and Sarah Nooter, 44–60. Oxon: Routledge, 2019.

Houghton, Robert. "World, Structure and Play: A Framework for Games as Historical Research Outputs, Tools, and Processes." *Práticas da História* 7 (2018): 11–43.

ISO 3382–1. Acoustics—Measurement of Room Acoustic Parameters. Part 1: Performance Rooms. Geneva: International Organization for Standardization, 2009.

Jenkins, Henry. "Game Design as Narrative Architecture." In *First Person: New Media as Story, Performance, Game*, edited by Noah Wardrip-Fruin and Pat Harrigan, 117–30. Cambridge: MIT Press, 2004.

Johnston, Alexandra, and Margaret Dorrell. "The Doomsday pageant of the York mercers, 1433." *Leeds Studies in English*, New Series V (1971): 11–35.

Johnston, Alexandra and Margaret Dorrell. "The York mercers and their pageant of Doomsday, 1433–1526." *Leeds Studies in English*, New Series VI (1973): 10–35.

Johnston, Alexandra, and Margaret Rogerson eds. *Records of Early English Drama: York* (REED). Toronto: University of Toronto Press, 1979.

Karabiber, Z. "A New Approach to an ancient subject: CAHRISMA project." Paper presented at the Seventh International Congress on Sound and Vibration, August 1, 2000.

King, Pamela. "Seeing and hearing: looking and listening." *Early Theatre* 3, no. 1 (2000): 155–66.

King, Pamela. "Poetics and beyond: noisy bodies and aural variations in medieval English outdoor performance." Paper presented at the 14th Triennial Colloquium of the Société Internationale pur l'etude du Théâtre Médiéval, Poznań, July 25, 2013.

Lefebvre, Henri. *The Production of Space*. Translated by Donald Nicholson-Smith. Oxford: Blackwell Publishing, 1974.

Livingstone, Daniel, Sandy Louchart, and Stuart Jeffrey. "Archaeological Storytelling in Games." *Proceedings of the 2016 Playing With History Workshop*. Accessed April 6, 2021. http://www.digra.org/digital-library/publications/archaeological-storytelling-in-games/

Lopez, Mariana. "An acoustical approach to the study of the wagons of the York Mystery Plays: structure and orientation." *Early Theatre* 18, no. 2 (2015): 11–36.

Lopez, Mariana. "Objective evaluation of a simulation of the acoustics of a medieval urban space used for dramatic performances." *Applied Acoustics* 88 (2015): 38–43.

Lopez, Mariana. "Using multiple computer models to study the acoustics of a sixteenth-century performance space." *Applied Acoustics* 94 (2015): 14–19.

Lopez, Mariana. "The York Mystery Plays: Exploring Sound and Hearing in Medieval Vernacular Drama." In *Sensory Perception in the Medieval West*, edited by Simon Thomson and Michael Bintley, 53–73. Turnhout: Brepols, 2016.

Lopez, Mariana. "Giving History a Voice." In *The Cambridge Companion to Music in Digital Culture*, edited by Nicholas Cook, Monique Ingalls and David Trippett, 147–49. Cambridge: Cambridge University Press, 2019.

Lopez, Mariana. "Heritage Soundscapes: contexts and ethics of curatorial expression." In *The St. Thomas Way and the Medieval March of Wales: Exploring place, heritage, pilgrimage*, edited by Catherine A. M. Clarke, 103–20. Leeds: Arc Humanities Press, 2020.

Lopez, Mariana, Marques Hardin, and Wenqi Wan. *The Soundscapes of the York Mystery Plays*. Accessed April 6, 2021. http://soundscapesyorkmysteryplays.com/interface/.

Lopez, Mariana, Sandra Pauletto, and Gavin Kearney. "The application of impulse response measurement techniques to the study of the acoustics of Stonegate, a performance space used in medieval English drama." *Acta Acustica united with Acustica* 99, no. 1 (2013): 98–108.

McCall, Jeremiah. *Gaming the Past: Using video games to teach secondary school history*. Oxon: Routledge, 2011.

McKinnell, J. "The medieval pageant wagons at York: their orientation and height." *Early Theatre* 3, no. 1 (2000): 79–104.

Meredith, Peter. "Development of the York Mercers' Pageant Waggon." *Medieval English Theatre* 1 (1979): 5–18.

Meredith, Peter. "The fifteenth century audience of the York Corpus Christi Play: Records and Speculation." In *'Divers toyes mengled': Essays on Medieval and Renaissance Culture in Honour of Andre Lascombes*, edited by M. Bitot, R. Mullini, and P Happé, 101–11 Tours: Université François Rabelais, 1996.

Miller, P., and J. Richards. "The good, the bad, and the downright misleading: archaeological adoption of computer visualization." In *Proceedings of the 22nd CAA Conference*, edited by J. Huggest and N. Ryan, 19–22. Oxford: ArchaeoPress, 1995.

Nielsen, Martin Lisa, Jens Holger Rindel, Anders Christian Gade, and Claus Lynge Christensen. "Acoustical computer simulations of the ancient Roman theatres." *Proceedings of the ERATO Project Symposium*, 20–36 (2006).

Nelson, Alan. "Easter week pageants in Valladolid and Medina del Campo." *Medieval English Theatre* 1 (1979): 62–70.

Okano, T., L. Beranek, and T. Hidaka. "Relations among interaural cross-correlation coefficient ($IACC_E$), lateral fraction (LF_E), and apparent source width (ASW) in concert halls." *Journal of the Acoustical Society of America* 104, no. 1 (1998): 119–31.

O'Neill, Brendan, and Aidan O'Sullivan. "Experimental archaeology and re-experiencing the senses of the medieval world." In *Routledge Handbook of Sensory Archaeology*, edited by Robin Skeates and Jo Day, 451–466. Oxon: Routledge, 2020.

Rastall, Richard. *Six Songs from the York Mystery Plays 'The Assumption of the Virgin.'* Devon: Antico Edition, 1984.

Rastall, Richard. "Heaven: The Musical Repertory." In *The Iconography of Heaven*, edited by Clifford Davidson, 162–96. Kalamazoo: Medieval Institute Publications, 1994.

Rastall, Richard. *The Heaven Singing: Music in Early English Religious Drama I*. Cambridge: D.S. Brewer, 1996.

Rastall, Richard. *Minstrels Playing: Music in Early English Religious Drama II*. Cambridge: D.S. Brewer, 2001.

Reinhard, Andrew. *Archaeogaming: An introduction to archaeology in and of video games*. New York: Berghahn Books, 2018.

Rindel, Jens Holger, and Martin Lisa Nielsen. "The ERATO Project and its contribution to our understanding of the acoustics of ancient Greek and Roman theatres." *Proceedings of the ERATO Project Symposium* (2006):1–10.

Rogerson, Margaret. "Raging in the streets of medieval York." *Early Theatre* 3, no. 1 (2000): 105–25.

Salen, Katie, and Eric Zimmerman. *Rules of Play: Game Design Fundamentals*. Cambridge: Massachusetts, MIT Press, 2003.

Shankland, R. S. "Acoustics of Greek theatres." *Physics Today* 26 (1973): 30–35.

Smith, Harvey, and Matthias Worch. "What Happened Here? Environmental Storytelling." Paper presented at Game Developers Conference, March 11, 2010.

Smith, Mark. *Sensory History*. Oxford: Bloomsbury, 2007.

Soulodre, G., and J. Bradley. "Subjective evaluation of new room acoustic measurements." *Journal of Acoustical Society of America* 98 (1995): 294–301.

Twycross, Meg. "The Flemish *Ommegang* and its pageant cars." *Medieval English Theatre* 2 (1980): 15–41.

van Tonder, Cobi. "Acoustic Atlas". Accessed April 6, 2021. https://acousticatlas.de/.

van Tonder, Cobi, and Mariana Lopez. "Acoustic Atlas – Auralisation in the Browser." *2021 Immersive and 3D Audio: from Architecture to Automotive* (I3DA) (2021): 1–5.

Vorländer, Michael. "Computer simulations in room acoustics: Concepts and uncertainties." *Journal of Acoustical Society of America* 133 (2013): 1203–13.

Walsh, M. "High places and travelling scenes: some observations on the staging of the York Cycle." *Early Theatre* 3, no. 1 (2000): 137–54.

Yuksel, Z., C. Binan, and R. Unver. "A research project in the intersection of architectural conservation and virtual reality: CAHRISMA." *Nineteenth International Symposium CIPA* (2003)

Ludography

Age of Empires. Ensemble Studios, 1997.
Age of Empires II: Definitive Edition. Xbox Game Studios, 2019.
Cosmology of Kyoto. Softedge, 1993.
Crusader Kings II. Paradox Interactive, 2012.
The Elder Scrolls. Bethesda Game Studios, 2014.

Robert Houghton
13 Beyond Education and Impact: Games as Research Tools and Outputs

Abstract: The potential of games as learning and teaching tools is increasingly difficult to deny. However, the possibility of using games as tools for scholarly historical research and communication is much less widely accepted. This chapter notes this discrepancy and highlights three emergent approaches towards the use of games in academic study through the use of a "Gamic Mode" of history, the creation and modification of games as simulacra to explore historical arguments, and the possibilities presented by roleplay as a means to engage with history and historiography. The similarities between the educational and scholarly potential of these games is emphasized throughout the chapter and it is ultimately argued that the varied approaches highlighted here represent the emergence and consolidation of a new historical method.

Introduction

The chapters of this volume have highlighted the vast and varied potential of games as learning and teaching tools. The impact of games within and outside an educational setting has been re-emphasized. The potency of carefully deployed commercial games has been highlighted as a tool for the consideration of modern perceptions of the Middle Ages, as an exploratory roleplaying environment, and as an alternative perspective on political and economic systems. The value of custom built games as introductory tools to a new period, theme or region, or as a way to explore deeper historical systems and arguments, has been demonstrated. The power of student led game design and modification has been highlighted as an alternative means of exploring and expressing analysis and debate. The applicability of these approaches within the heritage sector has also been underlined. These pieces contribute to a considerable and growing body of scholarship around the use of history games for teaching.

But the use, creation, and modification of games within the field of history can be taken further. The possibilities around the use of history games as research outputs and tools have been debated for some time and a growing number of scholars have considered theoretical and practical methods to utilize games in this manner. These approaches have often been met with skepticism: the use of games as historical research tools is rarely considered,[1] largely because of the common perception of games as a medium unsuited for scholarly history.[2] However, there is a growing recognition of the capacity of games to present serious history and to perform a useful function within the academy – albeit one very distinct from that of traditional research outputs and methods.[3] Indeed, games have been used for similar purposes within fields closely associated with history – most notably within Archaeology and Anthropology.[4]

The tentative acceptance of games as research tools rests in part on their growing use in these adjacent fields, but also in large part on their increasingly recognized value within educational methods.[5] The demonstrable capacity of games as teaching tools at undergraduate or even postgraduate levels of study highlights the capacity of these games as valuable approaches to complex historical and historiographical issues. The detailed worlds and mechanics presented

---

1 Annette Vowinckel, "Past Futures: From Re-Enactment to the Simulation of History in Computer Games," *Historical Social Research / Historische Sozialforschung* 34, no. 2 (2009): 322; Dawn Spring, "Gaming History: Computer and Video Games as Historical Scholarship," *Rethinking History* 19, no. 2 (2015): 209, https://doi.org/10.1080/13642529.2014.973714; Robert Houghton, "World, Structure and Play: A Framework for Games as Historical Research Outputs, Tools, and Processes," *Práticas Da História* 7 (2018): 12–13.
2 Vinicius Marino Carvalho, "Videogames as Tools for Social Science History," *Historian* 79, no. 4 (2017): 795–96, https://doi.org/10.1111/hisn.12674; Houghton, "World, Structure and Play," 14.
3 Jeremy Antley, "Going Beyond the Textual in History," *Journal of Digital Humanities* 1, no. 2 (2012), http://journalofdigitalhumanities.org/1-2/going-beyond-the-textual-in-history-by-jeremy-antley/; Carvalho, "Videogames as Tools," 818–19; Houghton, "World, Structure and Play," 35–41.
4 Shawn Graham, "TravellerSim: Growing Settlement Structures and Territories with Agent-Based Modeling," 2006, https://doi.org/10.17613/m6g29k; Gabriel Wurzer, ed., *Agent-Based Modeling and Simulation in Archaeology*, Advances in Geographic Information Science (Cham: Springer, 2015); Wendy H. Cegielski and J. Daniel Rogers, "Rethinking the Role of Agent-Based Modeling in Archaeology," *Journal of Anthropological Archaeology* 41 (March 2016): 283–98, https://doi.org/10.1016/j.jaa.2016.01.009; Shawn Graham, "Agent Based Models, Archaeogaming, and the Useful Deaths of Digital Romans," in *The Interactive Past: Archaeology, Heritage & Video Games*, ed. Angenitus Arie Andries Mol et al. (Leiden: Sidestone Press, 2017), 123–31.
5 Juan Francisco Jiménez Hiriart, "How to Be a 'Good' Anglo-Saxon: Designing and Using Historical Video Games in Primary Schools," in *Communicating the Past in the Digital Age: Proceedings of the International Conference on Digital Methods in Teaching and Learning in Archaeology (12th-13th October 2018)*, ed. Sebastian Hageneuer (Ubiquity Press, 2020), 149–50, https://doi.org/10.5334/bch; Robert Houghton, "Scholarly History through Digital Games: Pedagogical Practice as Research Method," in *Return to the Interactive Past: The Interplay of Video Games and Histories*, ed. Csilla E. Ariese-Vandemeulebroucke et al. (Sidestone Press, 2021), 137–55.

within some modern games can approach or exceed that of even the largest historical research projects. There is little reason in principle why suitably informed and critical consideration and development of historical games should not form a valid scholarly approach.

This chapter addresses the embryonic historiographical development of these approaches to research through games and connects them to the methods represented throughout the chapters of this volume. To this end, I will briefly define and outline the three most prominent emergent approaches to historical research through games – which may be termed "Gamic," "Simulacrum," and "Roleplaying" – and consider the ways in which the games and methods discussed throughout the course of this volume may be applied to create scholarly research games within each of these schools.

The "Gamic" Mode

The "Gamic" approach emerged as a reaction to the growing body of scholarship around the use of games in the history classroom and the accompanying discussion of their capability to represent history in a serious if not scholarly manner. In particular, this school of thought criticizes the ability of commercial games – and academic games which followed the same design principles – to conduct scholarly history. This reaction ran alongside the growth of digital modelling systems within the neighboring discipline of Archaeology, and seems to have been driven at least in part by a concern that this drive to simulation would infiltrate the field of history and challenge the authority of its traditional means of enquiry.[6] Proponents of this Gamic system echo the concerns raised by Galloway and de Groot that games can only represent a single, reductive, and unquestionable view of historical cause and effect and are therefore ill-equipped to explore and evaluate the complicated nuance of historical argument.[7] They deride the relevance of the counterfactual history which commercial games allow their players to create.[8] As such, while this school recognizes a potential for games

---

[6] Carvalho, "Videogames as Tools," 795–96.
[7] Alexander R. Galloway, *Gaming: Essays on Algorithmic Culture*, Electronic Mediations 18 (Minneapolis: University of Minnesota Press, 2006), 104; Jerome De Groot, *Consuming History: Historians and Heritage in Contemporary Popular Culture*, Second edition (London; New York: Routledge, Taylor & Francis Group, 2016), 7–8.
[8] Jerremie Clyde, Howard Hopkins, and Glenn Wilkinson, "Beyond the 'Historical' Simulation: Using Theories of History to Inform Scholarly Game Design," *Loading . . . The Journal of*

to conduct scholarly history, it maintains that such history cannot be conducted through the design approach of commercial companies.

The main proponents of the Gamic school – Clyde, Hopkins, and Wilkinson – defined a "gamic mode of history" as "the construction of scholarly historical arguments as scholarly games."[9] In doing so, they echo Kee's earlier design of a theoretical game where players would create historical arguments on the basis of the selection and interpretation of sources presented in the game.[10] They see this Gamic mode as distinct from the representation of history within typical digital games: in the Gamic mode the game is a historical argument, while Clyde et al. perceive historical digital games as attempts to reconstruct or simulate the past.[11] As such they reject the scholarly value of games like *Medal of Honour* which engage with history through unsubstantiated references to data and a focus on storytelling and world building over explanation of events.[12] They likewise reject simulation games such as *Civilization* which present models of history and allow players to alter past events as, by their reckoning, this is of no scholarly value.[13] Their hypothesized Gamic mode "communicates historical truths and simulate an argument rather than the past": games in this format are designed to represent the construction of arguments from accepted data points.[14]

This Gamic mode of history is presented as distinct from the traditional "textual mode" present within scholarly monographs and other written outputs,[15] but nevertheless openly and deliberately shares a number of qualities with these more traditional approaches. It emphasizes the importance of a constructed narrative within the Gamic mode to closely match the narrative structure of research within the textual mode.[16] Just as is the case with history in the textual mode, their Gamic history must be rooted in the primary sources and secondary literature, although digital elements like links to sources or the in-game presentation of documents may be introduced to facilitate and augment

---

the Canadian Game Studies Association 6, no. 9 (2012): 11, http://journals.sfu.ca/loading/index.php/loading/article/viewArticle/105.
9 Clyde, Hopkins, and Wilkinson, 3.
10 Kevin Kee, "Computerized History Games: Narrative Options," *Simulation & Gaming* 42, no. 4 (August 2011): 435–36, https://doi.org/10.1177/1046878108325441.
11 Clyde, Hopkins, and Wilkinson, "Beyond the 'Historical' Simulation," 6.
12 Clyde, Hopkins, and Wilkinson, 9–10.
13 Clyde, Hopkins, and Wilkinson, 10–11.
14 Clyde, Hopkins, and Wilkinson, 12.
15 Clyde, Hopkins, and Wilkinson, 3.
16 Clyde, Hopkins, and Wilkinson, 8.

this referencing.[17] Essentially, games produced through the Gamic approach reject many aspects of commercial games and instead emphasize their similarities to traditional scholarly outputs to justify their academic authority.

The Gamic school has influenced several areas of historical game theory. Perhaps most notably, Chapman's realist-conceptual descriptive scale for historical games rests in part on the approach to historical games outlined by this school.[18] Its ideas around the presentation of historiography rather than history through games have been considered in the construction of teaching games[19] and the broader theory of scholarly game creation.[20] Its ideas are of huge importance to understanding some of the ways in which games may communicate history and informs historical game design and study.

However, the practical application of the Gamic approach has been limited. Clyde, Hopkins, and Wilkinson produced *Shadows of Utopia: Exploring the Thinking of Robert Owen* – a digital game which provides an abstract exploration of Owen's historical theory designed for scholarly exploration and discussion.[21] Clyde and Wilkinson also created the tabletop *The History Game* which makes use of an abstract system of mechanics to represent and communicate the methodological construction of historical arguments.[22] More recently – and perhaps more visibly – Martínez constructed a digital game titled *Time Historians* which provides a more tangible setting of Ancient Egypt and tasks the players with gathering historical information; selecting, ignoring, and interpreting different data points, and collaboratively constructing historical arguments through game play.[23] Beyond these examples though, there has been limited impact of this influential theory in practice. Indeed, of the approaches discussed within this volume only Horswell's use of *Assassin's Creed* as an exploration of the construction of history can be particularly associated with the Gamic approach.

---

17 Clyde, Hopkins, and Wilkinson, 13.
18 Adam Chapman, *Digital Games as History: How Videogames Represent the Past and Offer Access to Historical Practice*, Routledge Advances in Game Studies 7 (New York, NY: Routledge, Taylor & Francis Group, 2016), 60–61.
19 Charalambos Poullis et al., "Evaluation of 'The Seafarers': A Serious Game on Seaborne Trade in the Mediterranean Sea during the Classical Period," *Digital Applications in Archaeology and Cultural Heritage* 12 (2019): 2, https://doi.org/10.1016/j.daach.2019.e00090.
20 Spring, "Gaming History," 208–10.
21 Clyde, Hopkins, and Wilkinson, "Beyond the 'Historical' Simulation," 11–13.
22 Jerremie Clyde and Glenn R. Wilkinson, "More Than a Game . . . Teaching in the Gamic Mode: Disciplinary Knowledge, Digital Literacy, and Collaboration," *The History Teacher* 46, no. 1 (2012): 45–66.
23 Manuel Alejandro Cruz Martínez, "The Potential of Video Games for Exploring Deconstructionist History" (PhD, University of Sussex, 2019).

There are several contributing reasons for this limited uptake. Gamic history focuses on the construction of arguments rather than the arguments themselves. This is a vitally important element of historical study, but one which is usually reduced to an auxiliary capacity even within traditional textual mode outputs: historiography is key to scholarly history, but the history itself almost always takes center stage. The fundamental distinction from commercial historical games which the Gamic approach demands is also an issue here. The method mandates unusual and abstract mechanics and storytelling along relatively narrow and rigid lines which limits the breadth of its applicability and perhaps makes the method less accessible to both historians and designers. Further, by tying history in games so closely to traditional academic outputs and methods, the proponents of Gamic history remove much of what makes games unique and innovative. The games produced through this method allow the exploration and development of a particular tool of historical analysis, but maintain the core elements of traditional textual history. They create games which can act as excellent teaching aids or as intriguing variants of traditional approaches, but ultimately (and actively) refrain from expanding a historical approach in a substantially new direction. The Gamic approach is informative and incredibly useful in certain circumstances, but this utility has remained rather narrow in practice.

The "Simulacrum" Approach

Although the roots of the "Simulacrum" school predate Clyde's work,[24] its dominant thinking crystallized in response to the Gamic mode,[25] and was designed to address many of the same core issues: to demonstrate the utility of historical games as scholarly outputs and tools; and to address the limitations of a simulation model of history. However, while the Gamic school calls for a new type of game, the Simulacrum school emphasizes the capacity of existing formats of historical digital games to serve as valid scholarly outputs simply through a more learned and academically rigorous approach to their construction, play and modification, and emphasizes the value of digital games as a unique medium of communication and analysis. As such, proponents of this system tend

---

24 Vowinckel, "Past Futures."
25 Antley, "Going Beyond the Textual"; Jeremiah McCall, "Navigating the Problem Space: The Medium of Simulation Games in the Teaching of History," *History Teacher* 1 (2012): 9–28; Carvalho, "Videogames as Tools"; Houghton, "World, Structure and Play."

to argue that attempts to create games which perform the same function to traditional historical outputs and which employ fundamentally the same methods substantially undermines the utility of the medium.[26]

In contrast with the Gamic mode, this approach embraces the potential utility of games' audio-visual environments as representations of material and physical culture and of geography, arguing that these elements of games may perform the functions of images, maps, and charts in innovative ways.[27] Within the Simulacrum approach, the veracity of these details is not an absolute concern: the point is to create an image which is informed by historical research and analysis, and which provides an environment which communicates this theory.[28] As a corollary of this, Staley has underlined the potential of games as alternatives to literary history in a more abstract manner – through the use of audio-visual storytelling techniques he has suggested that games may present a coherent account of historical events and analysis.[29]

More significantly, this approach accepts the value of game mechanics as systems-based explanations of history as opposed to the narrative form prescribed by the Gamic school.[30] Rather than viewing games as attempts to reconstruct historical events and systems, this school of thought sees games as theoretical models,[31] and argues that their mechanics should be seen as presentations of historical

---

[26] Houghton, "World, Structure and Play," 15–16.
[27] Spring, "Gaming History," 212; Houghton, "World, Structure and Play," 21–25.
[28] Blair Apgar, "Visiting the Unvisitable: Using Architectural Models in Video Games to Enhance Sense-Oriented Learning," in *The Middle Ages in Modern Games 2 (25 May – 28 May 2021): Twitter Conference Proceedings*, ed. Robert Houghton (Winchester: The Public Medievalist / University of Winchester, 2021); Andy Ashton, "The Medieval Influence: *Foundation* (Game)," in *The Middle Ages in Modern Games 2 (25 May – 28 May 2021): Twitter Conference Proceedings*, ed. Robert Houghton (Winchester: The Public Medievalist / University of Winchester, 2021); Tea de Rougemont, "Medieval Letterings – Gameplay, Argumentum and Conservation," in *The Middle Ages in Modern Games 2 (25 May – 28 May 2021): Twitter Conference Proceedings*, ed. Robert Houghton (Winchester: The Public Medievalist / University of Winchester, 2021).
[29] David J. Staley, *Computers, Visualization, and History: How New Technology Will Transform Our Understanding of the Past*, Second Edition, History, the Humanities, and the New Technology (Armonk, New York: M.E. Sharpe, 2014).
[30] McCall, "Navigating the Problem Space"; Antley, "Going Beyond the Textual"; Carvalho, "Videogames as Tools," 806–7; Houghton, "World, Structure and Play," 25–27.
[31] Douglas N. Dow, "Historical Veneers: Anachronism, Simulation, and Art History in Assassin's Creed II," in *Playing with the Past: Digital Games and the Simulation of History*, ed. Matthew Kapell and Andrew B. R. Elliott (New York: Bloomsbury Academic, 2013), 218–19; Andrew B. R. Elliott, "Simulations and Simulacra: History in Video Games," *Práticas Da História* 5 (2017): 29–31.

arguments rather than absolute claims to authoritative historical accuracy.[32] As Elliott has it, a historical game is not so much a simulation but "a simulacrum, a model which reflects modern ideas about the past even if those are not technically faithful to the historical facts."[33] Coltrain and Ramsay have repeated these ideas almost verbatim and suggested that they may be applied to the study of the humanities more generally.[34] Ultimately then, this approach constructs game rules and mechanics on the basis of historical arguments and maintains that the outputs may be valid scholarly materials on the basis of appropriate research,[35] referencing of primary and secondary sources,[36] and clarity of presentation of arguments and data.[37] As Wainwright and Ortega have demonstrated within the classroom,[38] critical play of historical games may be used to explore and question the arguments on which their mechanics are based, representing a fundamentally different communication and reception of these arguments, but one which may nonetheless be academically rigorous through the application of the appropriate skillset and historical and ludic literacies.[39]

By extension, the modification of the mechanics of historical games would therefore represent the construction of counter-arguments to those posed by the original game and could hence form a new medium for the conduct of historical debate.[40] This approach has been used pedagogically by Kee and Graham who rightly emphasize the educational potential for students to create their own historical arguments based on the modification of existing game mechanics.[41] The

---

32 Adam Chapman, "Privileging Form Over Content: Analysing Historical Videogames," *Journal of Digital Humanities* 1, no. 2 (2012): 42; McCall, "Navigating the Problem Space," 18; Chapman, *Digital Games as History*, 75; Carvalho, "Videogames as Tools," 812–13.
33 Elliott, "Simulations and Simulacra," 31.
34 James Coltrain and Stephen Ramsay, "Can Video Games Be Humanities Scholarship?," in *Debates in the Digital Humanities 2019*, ed. Matthew K. Gold and Lauren F. Klein (Minneapolis: University of Minnesota Press, 2019), 36–45, https://doi.org/10.5749/j.ctvg251hk.
35 Houghton, "World, Structure and Play," 26–27.
36 Carvalho, "Videogames as Tools," 811.
37 Antley, "Going Beyond the Textual."
38 A. Martin Wainwright, "Teaching Historical Theory through Video Games," *The History Teacher* 47, no. 4 (2014): 579–612; Stephen Ortega, "Representing the Past: Video Games Challenge to the Historical Narrative," *Syllabus* 4, no. 1 (2015): 1–13.
39 Houghton, "World, Structure and Play," 27–29.
40 Jakub Majewski, "The Potential for Modding Communities in Cultural Heritage," in *The Interactive Past: Archaeology, Heritage & Video Games*, ed. Angenitus Arie Andries Mol et al. (Leiden: Sidestone Press, 2017), 185–205; Houghton, "World, Structure and Play," 27–30.
41 Kevin Kee and Shawn Graham, "Teaching History in an Age of Pervasive Computing: The Case for Games in the High School and Undergraduate Classroom," in *Pastplay: Teaching and Learning History with Technology*, ed. Kevin Kee (University of Michigan Press, 2014), 270–91,

method could readily be adapted to an academic research environment and resolves a key issue around scholarly games: it enables the game to represent more than one perspective.[42]

A number of games have been developed using the theory and methods described within the Simulacrum school. Carvalho has led the construction of *The Triumphs of Turlough* which considers the political and military dynamics of medieval Ireland through mechanics based on his historical research and deployed through his theoretical work on scholarly games, making use of complexity theory to provide a less anthropocentric approach to history.[43] My game, *The Investiture Contest* – described in chapter ten – considers socio-political influence in northern Italy in the late eleventh century and serves as a forum for debate of the period and historical structures through its facilitation of user-modification, and was developed as both a teaching and a research tool.[44] Hepburn and Armstrong are currently developing the game *Strange Sickness* as a tool to communicate their research within public and academic circles.[45] Migliazzo, Morley, and Celico are constructing a range of games based on their individual research as practical demonstrations of their "Custom Design" approach to research games which has players explore and test the arguments set out through the mechanics of a game through play.[46] These games have acknowledged limitations, but demonstrate

---

https://doi.org/10.2307/j.ctv65swr0.17; Shawn Graham, "Rolling Your Own: On Modding Commercial Games for Educational Goals," in *Pastplay: Teaching and Learning History with Technology*, ed. Kevin Kee (University of Michigan Press, 2014), 214–27, https://doi.org/10.2307/j.ctv65swr0.

42 Houghton, "Scholarly History through Digital Games."

43 Carvalho, "Videogames as Tools"; Vinicius Marino Carvalho, "'The Triumphs of Turlough': A Scholarly Videogame about Medieval Ireland," in *The Middle Ages in Modern Games (30 June – 3 July 2020): Twitter Conference Proceedings*, ed. Robert Houghton (Winchester: The Public Medievalist / University of Winchester, 2020), 17–18, https://issuu.com/theuniversityof winchester/docs/final_mamg20_threads; Vinicius Marino Carvalho, "Analysing and Developing Videogames for Experimental History: Kingdom Simulators and the Historians," in *The Middle Ages in Modern Games 2 (25 May – 28 May 2021): Twitter Conference Proceedings*, ed. Robert Houghton (Winchester: The Public Medievalist / University of Winchester, 2021).

44 Robert Houghton, "'Losing Is Fun': Asymmetric Rules and Play for Teaching and Research," in *The Middle Ages in Modern Games (30 June – 3 July 2020): Twitter Conference Proceedings*, ed. Robert Houghton (Winchester: The Public Medievalist / University of Winchester, 2020), 19, https://issuu.com/theuniversityofwinchester/docs/final_mamg20_threads.

45 William Hepburn and Jackson Armstrong, "*Strange Sickness*: Running a Crowdfunding Campaign for a Historical Research-Based Game," in *The Middle Ages in Modern Games 2 (25 May – 28 May 2021): Twitter Conference Proceedings*, ed. Robert Houghton (Winchester: The Public Medievalist / University of Winchester, 2021).

46 Francesco Migliazzo, Jacob Morley, and Giuseppe Celico, "Presenting Your Research Through Games," in *The Middle Ages in Modern Games II (25 May – 28 May 2021): Twitter*

the substantial potential of this medium to act as historical research tools in a variety of manners distinct from traditional approaches.

Many of the teaching approaches discussed within this volume can readily be adapted for historical research purposes. *Akritas* as described by Stamou, Sotiropoulou, Mylonas, and Voutos represents the construction of historical arguments through game story and mechanics at a more basic but fundamentally similar manner to Carvalho's approach. The modding approach advocated by Champion, Nurmikko-Fuller, and Grant within *Skyrim* has demonstrable utility within the classroom but could be readily adapted to present academic research around culture, architecture, and landscape. Klaasen's in class development of *Virtus* and *Distaff* presents a method of the collaborative construction of arguments and debate through game design which may be granted greater authority through broader and deeper exploitation of primary sources and engagement with historiographical traditions. The soundscapes constructed within the *York Mystery Plays* by Lopez, Hardin, and Wan have undeniable educational and outreach impact, but these representations of acoustic transmission have practical applications within architectural, cultural, and religious historical study.

Variations of the Simulacrum approach have come to dominate thinking around scholarly history through games in recent years. The methods it describes are more practical and accessible than those of the Gamic school and have the potential to discuss historical themes and issues rather than simply the methods by which history is constructed. Perhaps most tellingly, Clyde and Wilkinson have diluted their Gamic approach, moving away from their earlier declaration that commercial games have no value for historical study to instead echo the Simulacrum school's vision of user modification of games as a means of historical analysis and debate.[47] Gamic history is still important and influential, but its applicability is much narrower and more limited than that of the Simulacrum school.

Conference Proceedings, ed. Robert Houghton (Winchester: The Public Medievalist / University of Winchester, 2021).

47 Jerremie Clyde and Glenn R. Wilkinson, "Rhetorical Replay and the Challenge of Gamic History: Silencing the Siren Song of Digital Simulation," in *Emerging Technologies in Virtual Learning Environments*, ed. Kim Becnel, Advances in Educational Technologies and Instructional (AETID) Book Series (Hershey PA: IGI Global, 2019), 180–82.

Roleplaying History

The use of Roleplaying for historical research is truly embryonic. While both the Gamic and Simulacrum schools have somewhat established processes and publications spanning around a decade, the "Roleplaying" school has only emerged in the last few years. This school has some notable similarities with the Simulacrum school, most fundamentally in that it accepts games as a new and viable means to explore history on their own terms. Indeed there is substantial overlap between the two and it remains to be seen if the Roleplaying school should be considered as distinct from the Simulacrum school or as an interesting offshoot.

In any event, the Roleplaying school is distinct for the approach through which it engages with history: while the Simulacrum school focuses on the creation and modification of the audio-visual and mechanical components of games as the means by which history is communicated, the Roleplaying school looks instead to the potential of games to allow their players to experience the character of the figures they represent and hence to understand their motivations and actions and the broader world in which they lived.

Roleplay within historical games is a rather understudied area. It does not fit within many of the frameworks constructed for the categorization and analysis of this media. Chapman's dichotomy between audio-visual realist simulations and mechanical conceptual simulations is perhaps the most influential framework for the discussion of historical games and its utility is impossible to deny, but the model nevertheless largely ignores the place of roleplay within these games.[48] Chapman, and his many followers, place roleplaying games squarely in the centre of this scale – neither quite realist nor conceptual – but do not typically discuss their unique qualities which games with roleplaying elements provide to their discussion of history. Nolden has highlighted this peculiarity and notes that roleplay and multiplayer elements may allow players to engage with history in new ways which go beyond Chapman's model.[49] It should be noted that Chapman has always emphasized that his model was not

---

48 Chapman, *Digital Games as History*, 59–89.
49 Nico Nolden, "Social Practices of History in Digital Possibility Spaces: Historicity, Mediality, Performativity, Authenticity," in *History in Games: Contingencies of an Authentic Past*, ed. Martin Lorber and Felix Zimmermann, Studies of Digital Media Culture 12 (Bielefeld: Transcript-Verl, 2020), 85–88; Nico Nolden, *Geschichte Und Erinnerung in Computerspielen: Erinnerungskulturelle Wissenssysteme* (De Gruyter Oldenbourg, 2020), https://doi.org/10.1515/9783110586053.

intended to be prescriptive,[50] but its application has often ignored this important nuance.

The omission of roleplay from Chapman's model is particularly significant as the potential of roleplay in history teaching has long been posited and various methods have been deployed in classrooms globally for several decades.[51] A key recent development within this pedagogical field has been the creation and expansion of the *Reacting to the Past* series of games which have gained particular traction within several universities in the USA.[52] A number of studies have demonstrated that games which permit and encourage roleplay may have a particularly prominent impact on their players' understanding of the past both within[53] and outside the classroom,[54] and so the genre is certainly worthy of further investigation.

The educational value of roleplay at tertiary level implies a potential for the approach as a scholarly historical research tool and a handful of adaptions and developments of this roleplay have emerged within medieval scholarly circles in recent years. Hayes, Cromwell, Dar, Ochała, and Scheerlinck have made use of a customized *Dungeons and Dragons* campaign to explore a collaboratively constructed vision of the early medieval Middle East as a means to highlight potential

---

[50] Chapman, *Digital Games as History*, 60–61.

[51] Sharon M. Fennessey, *History in the Spotlight: Creative Drama and Theatre Practices for the Social Studies Classroom / Sharon M. Fennessey* (Portsmouth, NH: Heinemann, 2000); Kathryn N. McDaniel, "Four Elements of Successful Historical Role-Playing in the Classroom," *The History Teacher* 33, no. 3 (May 2000): 357, https://doi.org/10.2307/495033.

[52] Thomas C. Buchanan and Edward Palmer, "Role Immersion in a History Course: Online versus Face-to-Face in Reacting to the Past," *Computers & Education* 108 (May 2017): 85–95, https://doi.org/10.1016/j.compedu.2016.12.008; Kathryn E. Joyce, Andy Lamey, and Noel Martin, "Teaching Philosophy through a Role-Immersion Game: Reacting to the Past," *Teaching Philosophy* 41, no. 2 (2018): 175–98, https://doi.org/10.5840/teachphil201851487.

[53] R. G. McLaughlan and D. Kirkpatrick, "Online Roleplay: Design for Active Learning," *European Journal of Engineering Education* 29, no. 4 (December 2004): 477–90, https://doi.org/10.1080/03043790410001716293; Robert McLaughlan and Denise Kirkpatrick, "Peer Learning Using Computer Supported Roleplay Simulations," in *Peer Learning in Higher Education: Learning from and with Each Other*, ed. David Boud, Ruth Cohen, and Jane Sampson (Hoboken: Taylor and Francis, 2014), 141–55, http://public.eblib.com/choice/publicfullrecord.aspx?p=1683620.

[54] Robert Houghton, "Where Did You Learn That? The Self-Perceived Educational Impact of Historical Computer Games on Undergraduates," *Gamevironments* 5 (2016): 27–28; Eve Stirling and Jamie Wood, "'Actual History Doesn't Take Place': Digital Gaming, Accuracy and Authenticity," *Game Studies* 21, no. 1 (May 2021), http://gamestudies.org/2101/articles/stirling_wood; Robert Houghton, "History Games for Boys? Gender, Genre and the Self-Perceived Impact of Historical Games on Undergraduate Historians," *Gamevironments* 14 (2021): 1–49, https://doi.org/10.26092/ELIB/918.

research questions.⁵⁵ Migliazzo, Morley, and Celico take an alternative approach with their "Road to Success" system whereby they encourage the use of roleplay as a means to communicate and text historical analysis, taking a game built around Migliazo's research into the interactions of the Italian city states as their core example.⁵⁶ This process shares core similarities with the Simulacrum methods described above, but differs fundamentally in its emphasis on players adopting the character of their role to explore historical environments rather than relying on the mechanics of the game to define arguments and analysis.

Several of the pedagogical approaches described throughout this volume may inform the development of scholarly games with a focus on roleplay. The use of *Skyrim* by DeVine and *Crusader Kings* by Kuran, Tozoglu, and Tavernari place a considerable emphasis on the adoption of historical character roles by students – an exploratory method which may be profitably transferred to academic study in a similar manner to the methods deployed by Hayes. Gottlieb and Clyde through their *Lost and Found* games, and Konshuh and Klaasen through their *Renaissance Marriage* game, take an approach which places somewhat more emphasis on game mechanics but nevertheless incorporates roleplay as a key element: an approach with similarities to the Road to Success model described by Migliazzo, Morley, and Celico which may provide an alternative and more flexible means to articulate and debate historical theories.

These roleplaying approaches to historical research and analysis are very much in the embryonic and formative stages of development. They typically overlap with the approaches described within the Simulacrum school, but they nevertheless represent an important new and underutilized subfield with substantial potential as implied by the growing use of roleplay within tertiary history education. The arguments they produce through play may be more abstract than those created through the Simulacrum approach, but this approach is more immediately flexible and does not rely on the construction of detailed and coherent rules.

Conclusion

There are, therefore, numerous and varied means by which games may be profitably employed for historical research – moving well beyond acting as simulations of the past. The Gamic approach may be used to explore the construction

---

55 Jennifer Cromwell et al., "'Dice on the Nile': Roleplaying History" (Manchester: Manchester Game Studies Network, 2021).
56 Migliazzo, Morley, and Celico, "Presenting Your Research Through Games."

and deconstruction of historical arguments in an abstract but nevertheless learned manner which closely approaches the communication methods of traditional written accounts. The Simulacrum school promotes the consideration of historical sites, events, and analysis through game world, mechanics, play, and modification in a more concrete manner through an emphasis on the unique properties of games to create a new approach to the communication of history distinct from that of monographs or scholarly articles. The emphasis on roleplay by a growing number of scholars highlights a new and distinct approach which encourages a more free-form interaction with scholarly history with less emphasis on rules and more concern for player interaction and interpretation.

These approaches almost invariably share core characteristics with teaching methods currently in use at a number of universities and other higher education institutions. This is not coincidental: the pedagogical possibilities presented by games frequently translate or transpose to methods applicable to scholarly research just as traditional methods of teaching research, analysis, and argument mirror academic approaches. If we accept games as viable teaching tools at graduate and postgraduate level, then we must at least consider their potential as tools for the communication and development of historical research. The difference between an educational and scholarly game is very similar to the distinction between a dissertation and a scholarly article. There may be distinctions in precise method, depth, and authority, but the form remains fundamentally analogous. As such, the educational methods deployed using history games – including those addressed within this volume – may easily form the basis for scholarly approaches.

It should be underlined that the divisions outlined within this chapter are by no means definitive, inflexible, or static. The categorization of these approaches into "schools" is in some ways premature given their emergent nature and, as is the case with Chapman's model,[57] this framework should be seen as descriptive and porous rather than prescriptive and absolute. There are overlaps in approach between each of these schools – most notably an emphasis on scholarly rigour in the collection of data and clear representation of arguments – and it is inevitable that some methods will straddle two or more of these groups or sit beyond the framework entirely. The development of the Simulacrum school was influenced by the emergence of the Gamic approach – even if this influence frequently manifested as a drive to justify the uniqueness of games as historical tools or to defend the scholarly validity of games in their own right. Leading figures within the Gamic school have in turn been influenced by the approaches of Simulacrum scholars, most notably in the recognition of game modification as a means of

---

57 Chapman, *Digital Games as History*, 60–61.

historical debate. Meanwhile, Roleplay has arisen as a method which mirrors or echoes many of the processes proposed within the Simulacrum approach. As illustrated above, the thinking within and around these schools is fluid and has changed substantially even over the past decade.

Nevertheless, it is important to emphasize that certain divergent trends and clusters of approaches are emerging even within this very young field. These carry advantages and disadvantages and, just as is the case within the classroom, are each better suited for particular scholarly research and approaches. As the fields around historical education and research through games grow and evolve, it becomes increasingly necessary to engage with the approaches of previous teachers and scholars, and we have reached the point where the categorization of these approaches is necessary even as any categorization must reduce nuance.

Ultimately, just as games present valuable and wide-ranging opportunities for pedagogical development, they highlight a new avenue for the communication, interrogation, and iteration of historical research. Just as ludic teaching methods stand apart from traditional educational approaches, the use of games for research is significantly different from typical means of historical scholarship. But just as these teaching approaches are still valid pedagogical tools when deployed through a sufficiently critical approach, games may act as effective and authoritative research tools when constructed and played with an appropriate degree of historical and ludic literacy. This requires a change in attitudes towards the legitimacy of games as representations of the past and discussions of history and the cultivation of a skill set somewhat distinct from regular historical expertise. Nevertheless, the growing use and success of games within the history classroom demonstrates a softening of these attitudes and highlights the accessibility of requisite game design and criticism abilities. The emergence of numerous scholarly historical games demonstrates a growing interest in these approaches and suggests a shift from theory to practice. These approaches are embryonic and prototypical, and their impact on general historical approaches should not be overstated: as Carvalho has highlighted, games will not revolutionise history.[58] But these shifts still represent important expansions of the tools available for the exploration of history. The development of games for teaching, engagement, and research are closely entwined and we should expect the expansion and diversification of each of these areas over the next decade.

---

58 Carvalho, "Videogames as Tools," 818.

Bibliography

Antley, Jeremy. "Going Beyond the Textual in History." *Journal of Digital Humanities* 1, no. 2 (2012). http://journalofdigitalhumanities.org/1-2/going-beyond-the-textual-in-history-by-jeremy-antley/.

Apgar, Blair. "Visiting the Unvisitable: Using Architectural Models in Video Games to Enhance Sense-Oriented Learning." In *The Middle Ages in Modern Games 2 (25 May – 28 May 2021): Twitter Conference Proceedings*, edited by Robert Houghton. Winchester: The Public Medievalist / University of Winchester, 2021.

Ashton, Andy. "The Medieval Influence: *Foundation* (Game)." In *The Middle Ages in Modern Games 2 (25 May – 28 May 2021): Twitter Conference Proceedings*, edited by Robert Houghton. Winchester: The Public Medievalist / University of Winchester, 2021.

Buchanan, Thomas C., and Edward Palmer. "Role Immersion in a History Course: Online versus Face-to-Face in Reacting to the Past." *Computers & Education* 108 (May 2017): 85–95. https://doi.org/10.1016/j.compedu.2016.12.008.

Carvalho, Vinicius Marino. "Analysing and Developing Videogames for Experimental History: Kingdom Simulators and the Historians." In *The Middle Ages in Modern Games 2 (25 May – 28 May 2021): Twitter Conference Proceedings*, edited by Robert Houghton. Winchester: The Public Medievalist / University of Winchester, 2021.

Carvalho, Vinicius Marino. "'The Triumphs of Turlough': A Scholarly Videogame about Medieval Ireland." In *The Middle Ages in Modern Games (30 June – 3 July 2020): Twitter Conference Proceedings*, edited by Robert Houghton, 17–18. Winchester: The Public Medievalist / University of Winchester, 2020. https://issuu.com/theuniversityofwinchester/docs/final_mamg20_threads.

Carvalho, Vinicius Marino. "Videogames as Tools for Social Science History." *Historian* 79, no. 4 (2017): 794–819. https://doi.org/10.1111/hisn.12674.

Cegielski, Wendy H., and J. Daniel Rogers. "Rethinking the Role of Agent-Based Modeling in Archaeology." *Journal of Anthropological Archaeology* 41 (March 2016): 283–98. https://doi.org/10.1016/j.jaa.2016.01.009.

Chapman, Adam. *Digital Games as History: How Videogames Represent the Past and Offer Access to Historical Practice*. Routledge Advances in Game Studies 7. New York, NY: Routledge, Taylor & Francis Group, 2016.

Chapman, Adam. "Privileging Form Over Content: Analysing Historical Videogames." *Journal of Digital Humanities* 1, no. 2 (2012): 42–46.

Clyde, Jerremie, Howard Hopkins, and Glenn Wilkinson. "Beyond the 'Historical' Simulation: Using Theories of History to Inform Scholarly Game Design." *Loading . . . The Journal of the Canadian Game Studies Association* 6, no. 9 (2012). http://journals.sfu.ca/loading/index.php/loading/article/viewArticle/105.

Clyde, Jerremie, and Glenn R. Wilkinson. "More Than a Game . . . Teaching in the Gamic Mode: Disciplinary Knowledge, Digital Literacy, and Collaboration." *The History Teacher* 46, no. 1 (2012): 45–66.

Clyde, Jerremie, and Glenn R. Wilkinson. "Rhetorical Replay and the Challenge of Gamic History: Silencing the Siren Song of Digital Simulation." In *Emerging Technologies in Virtual Learning Environments*, edited by Kim Becnel, 170–86. Advances in Educational Technologies and Instructional (AETID) Book Series. Hershey PA: IGI Global, 2019.

Coltrain, James, and Stephen Ramsay. "Can Video Games Be Humanities Scholarship?" In *Debates in the Digital Humanities 2019*, edited by Matthew K. Gold and Lauren F. Klein, 36–45. Minneapolis: University of Minnesota Press, 2019. https://doi.org/10.5749/j.ctvg251hk.

Cromwell, Jennifer, Alon Dar, Edmund Hayes, Grzegorz Ochała, and Eline Scheerlinck. "'Dice on the Nile': Roleplaying History." Manchester, 2021.

De Groot, Jerome. *Consuming History: Historians and Heritage in Contemporary Popular Culture*. Second edition. London; New York: Routledge, Taylor & Francis Group, 2016.

Dow, Douglas N. "Historical Veneers: Anachronism, Simulation, and Art History in Assassin's Creed II." In *Playing with the Past: Digital Games and the Simulation of History*, edited by Matthew Kapell and Andrew B. R. Elliott. New York: Bloomsbury Academic, 2013.

Elliott, Andrew B. R. "Simulations and Simulacra: History in Video Games." *Práticas Da História* 5 (2017): 11–41.

Fennessey, Sharon M. *History in the Spotlight: Creative Drama and Theatre Practices for the Social Studies Classroom / Sharon M. Fennessey*. Portsmouth, NH: Heinemann, 2000.

Galloway, Alexander R. *Gaming: Essays on Algorithmic Culture*. Electronic Mediations 18. Minneapolis: University of Minnesota Press, 2006.

Graham, Shawn. "Agent Based Models, Archaeogaming, and the Useful Deaths of Digital Romans." In *The Interactive Past: Archaeology, Heritage & Video Games*, edited by Angenitus Arie Andries Mol, Csilla E. Ariese-Vandemeulebroucke, Krijn H. J. Boom, and Aris Politopoulos, 123–31. Leiden: Sidestone Press, 2017.

Graham, Shawn. "Rolling Your Own: On Modding Commercial Games for Educational Goals." In *Pastplay: Teaching and Learning History with Technology*, edited by Kevin Kee, 214–27. University of Michigan Press, 2014. https://doi.org/10.2307/j.ctv65swr0.

Graham, Shawn. "TravellerSim: Growing Settlement Structures and Territories with Agent-Based Modeling," 2006. https://doi.org/10.17613/m6g29k.

Hepburn, William, and Jackson Armstrong. "*Strange Sickness*: Running a Crowdfunding Campaign for a Historical Research-Based Game." In *The Middle Ages in Modern Games 2 (25 May – 28 May 2021): Twitter Conference Proceedings*, edited by Robert Houghton. Winchester: The Public Medievalist / University of Winchester, 2021.

Hiriart, Juan Francisco Jiménez. "How to Be a 'Good' Anglo-Saxon: Designing and Using Historical Video Games in Primary Schools." In *Communicating the Past in the Digital Age: Proceedings of the International Conference on Digital Methods in Teaching and Learning in Archaeology (12th-13th October 2018)*, edited by Sebastian Hageneuer, 141–51. Ubiquity Press, 2020. https://doi.org/10.5334/bch.

Houghton, Robert. "History Games for Boys? Gender, Genre and the Self-Perceived Impact of Historical Games on Undergraduate Historians." *Gamevironments* 14 (2021): 1–49. https://doi.org/10.26092/ELIB/918.

Houghton, Robert. "'Losing Is Fun': Asymmetric Rules and Play for Teaching and Research." In *The Middle Ages in Modern Games (30 June – 3 July 2020): Twitter Conference Proceedings*, edited by Robert Houghton. Winchester: The Public Medievalist / University of Winchester, 2020. https://issuu.com/theuniversityofwinchester/docs/final_mamg20_threads.

Houghton, Robert. "Scholarly History through Digital Games: Pedagogical Practice as Research Method." In *Return to the Interactive Past: The Interplay of Video Games and Histories*, edited by Csilla E. Ariese-Vandemeulebroucke, Krijn H. J. Boom, Angenitus Arie Andries Mol, and Aris Politopoulos, 137–55. Sidestone Press, 2021.

Houghton, Robert. "Where Did You Learn That? The Self-Perceived Educational Impact of Historical Computer Games on Undergraduates." *Gamevironments* 5 (2016): 8–45.

Houghton, Robert. "World, Structure and Play: A Framework for Games as Historical Research Outputs, Tools, and Processes." *Práticas Da História* 7 (2018): 11–43.

Joyce, Kathryn E., Andy Lamey, and Noel Martin. "Teaching Philosophy through a Role-Immersion Game: Reacting to the Past." *Teaching Philosophy* 41, no. 2 (2018): 175–98. https://doi.org/10.5840/teachphil201851487.

Kee, Kevin. "Computerized History Games: Narrative Options." *Simulation & Gaming* 42, no. 4 (August 2011): 423–40. https://doi.org/10.1177/1046878108325441.

Kee, Kevin, and Shawn Graham. "Teaching History in an Age of Pervasive Computing: The Case for Games in the High School and Undergraduate Classroom." In *Pastplay: Teaching and Learning History with Technology*, edited by Kevin Kee, 270–91. University of Michigan Press, 2014. https://doi.org/10.2307/j.ctv65swr0.17.

Majewski, Jakub. "The Potential for Modding Communities in Cultural Heritage." In *The Interactive Past: Archaeology, Heritage & Video Games*, edited by Angenitus Arie Andries Mol, Csilla E. Ariese-Vandemeulebroucke, Krijn H. J. Boom, and Aris Politopoulos, 185–205. Leiden: Sidestone Press, 2017.

Martínez, Manuel Alejandro Cruz. "The Potential of Video Games for Exploring Deconstructionist History." PhD, University of Sussex, 2019.

McCall, Jeremiah. "Navigating the Problem Space: The Medium of Simulation Games in the Teaching of History." *History Teacher* 1 (2012): 9–28.

McDaniel, Kathryn N. "Four Elements of Successful Historical Role-Playing in the Classroom." *The History Teacher* 33, no. 3 (May 2000): 357. https://doi.org/10.2307/495033.

McLaughlan, R. G., and D. Kirkpatrick. "Online Roleplay: Design for Active Learning." *European Journal of Engineering Education* 29, no. 4 (December 2004): 477–90. https://doi.org/10.1080/03043790410001716293.

McLaughlan, Robert, and Denise Kirkpatrick. "Peer Learning Using Computer Supported Roleplay Simulations." In *Peer Learning in Higher Education: Learning from and with Each Other.*, edited by David Boud, Ruth Cohen, and Jane Sampson, 141–55. Hoboken: Taylor and Francis, 2014. http://public.eblib.com/choice/publicfullrecord.aspx?p=1683620.

Migliazzo, Francesco, Jacob Morley, and Giuseppe Celico. "Presenting Your Research Through Games." In *The Middle Ages in Modern Games II (25 May – 28 May 2021): Twitter Conference Proceedings*, edited by Robert Houghton. Winchester: The Public Medievalist / University of Winchester, 2021.

Nolden, Nico. *Geschichte Und Erinnerung in Computerspielen: Erinnerungskulturelle Wissenssysteme*. De Gruyter Oldenbourg, 2020. https://doi.org/10.1515/9783110586053.

Nolden, Nico. "Social Practices of History in Digital Possibility Spaces: Historicity, Mediality, Performativity, Authenticity." In *History in Games: Contingencies of an Authentic Past*, edited by Martin Lorber and Felix Zimmermann, 73–89. Studies of Digital Media Culture 12. Bielefeld: Transcript-Verl, 2020.

Ortega, Stephen. "Representing the Past: Video Games Challenge to the Historical Narrative." *Syllabus* 4, no. 1 (2015): 1–13.

Poullis, Charalambos, Marta Kersten-Oertel, J. Praveen Benjamin, Oliver Philbin-Briscoe, Bart Simon, Dimitra Perissiou, Stella Demesticha, et al. "Evaluation of 'The Seafarers': A Serious Game on Seaborne Trade in the Mediterranean Sea during the Classical Period."

Digital Applications in Archaeology and Cultural Heritage 12 (March 2019): e00090. https://doi.org/10.1016/j.daach.2019.e00090.

Rougemont, Tea de. "Medieval Letterings – Gameplay, Argumentum and Conservation." In *The Middle Ages in Modern Games 2 (25 May – 28 May 2021): Twitter Conference Proceedings*, edited by Robert Houghton. Winchester: The Public Medievalist / University of Winchester, 2021.

Spring, Dawn. "Gaming History: Computer and Video Games as Historical Scholarship." *Rethinking History* 19, no. 2 (2015): 207–21. https://doi.org/10.1080/13642529.2014.973714.

Staley, David J. *Computers, Visualization, and History: How New Technology Will Transform Our Understanding of the Past*. Second Edition. History, the Humanities, and the New Technology. Armonk, New York: M.E. Sharpe, 2014.

Stirling, Eve, and Jamie Wood. "'Actual History Doesn't Take Place': Digital Gaming, Accuracy and Authenticity." *Game Studies* 21, no. 1 (May 2021). http://gamestudies.org/2101/articles/stirling_wood.

Vowinckel, Annette. "Past Futures: From Re-Enactment to the Simulation of History in Computer Games." *Historical Social Research / Historische Sozialforschung* 34, no. 2 (128) (2009): 322–32.

Wainwright, A. Martin. "Teaching Historical Theory through Video Games." *The History Teacher* 47, no. 4 (2014): 579–612.

Wurzer, Gabriel, ed. *Agent-Based Modeling and Simulation in Archaeology*. Advances in Geographic Information Science. Cham: Springer, 2015.

List of Contributors

Erik Champion is an Enterprise Fellow at the University of South Australia. He is also an Honorary Professor at the Australian National University; an Honorary Research Fellow at the University of Western Australia; and Emeritus Professor at Curtin University. At Curtin he was UNESCO Chair of Cultural Heritage and Visualisation. He predominantly researches in the area of digital heritage, and serious games. Relevant books he has written include *Rethinking Virtual Places*; *Critical Gaming: Interactive History and Virtual Heritage*; and *Playing with the Past*. He has edited the books: *Virtual Heritage: A Guide*; *The Phenomenology of Real and Virtual Places*; and *Game Mods: Design, Theory and Criticism*; and co-edited *Cultural Heritage Infrastructures in Digital Humanities*.

Shawn Clybor is a curriculum designer and educational consultant with expertise in Eastern European history, social studies education, and game-based learning. Dr. Clybor began his career as an assistant professor before transitioning to the world of New York independent schools, where he spent ten years innovating approaches to history education and media literacy. He has published various articles and book chapters on game-based curriculum design and the cultural history of Czechoslovakia. He has also worked as a game designer at Charles Games in Prague, where he helped develop two award-winning serious games about the Second World War.

David DeVine is a member of the Adjunct Faculty in the Department of Composition and Literacy Studies at Austin Community College District, in Austin, TX, USA. His research interests are at the intersections between games, gaming pedagogies, and rhetorical practice. He is both an avid gamer and passionate teacher and looks to marry games to pedagogy wherever possible.

Owen Gottlieb is Associate Professor of Interactive Games and Media at the Rochester Institute of Technology. He is the Founder and Director of the Interaction, Media, and Learning Lab (IMLearning) rit.edu/learnlab. Gottlieb specializes in researching and designing interactive media experiences for learning, the application of interactive media for healing and wellness, interactive narrative, and the history of instructional design. His and his teams' internationally award winning learning games have been featured at the Smithsonian American Art Museum, Indiecade, Games for Change, Now Play This: London, International Meaningful Play, and numerous other venues. His most recent research project is in the history of late Cold War broadcast instructional design and includes recent presentations at SCMS and FSAC/ACÉC.

Katrina Grant is a senior lecturer in Digital Humanities at the Australian National University, with a specialisation in Art History. She has a special interest in the Digital Art History and the application of visualisation and mapping technologies to art history research, as well as the use of digital technologies in the galleries and museums sector for outreach and engagement. She is an expert on the representation of landscape in early modern Italy and the visual cultures performance and spectacle. Her recent book 'Landscape and the Arts in Early Modern Italy: Theatre, Gardens and Visual Culture' is published by Amsterdam University Press.

Marques Hardin is a creative technologist and researcher based in Cambridge, UK. He investigates ways in which immersive and interactive mediums can support knowledge exchange and promote social impact.

Mike Horswell completed his PhD in 2017 at Royal Holloway, University of London, and his book – *The Rise and Fall of British Crusader Medievalism*, c. *1825–1945* – was published by Routledge in 2018. A founding editor of the *Engaging the Crusades* series he is also the author of several articles and book chapters his work includes studies of crusading in the *Encyclopaedia Britannica* and Wikipedia, the 1999 Reconciliation Walk, and crusading imagery in digital games; he has forthcoming work considering reception studies, teaching medievalism, historiography and crusader statues. He has taught at Royal Holloway, King's College London, the University of Oxford and the University of Bayreuth and is a Fellow of the Royal Historical Society.

Robert Houghton is a senior lecturer in medieval history at the University of Winchester, with research foci around Italian socio-political networks and engagement with the Middle Ages through modern games. He has recently edited several volumes including *Playing the Crusades*, *The Middle Ages in Modern Culture* (with Karl Alvestad), *Conflict and Violence in Medieval Italy: 568–1154* (with Christopher Heath), and *Playing the Middle Ages: Pitfalls and Potential in Modern Games*. Robert is the Senior Games Editor at *The Public Medievalist*, leads the organisation of the *Middle Ages in Modern Games* annual Twitter conference and associated events and publications, and has consulted on a range of games including *Crusader Kings II* and *Rulers of the Sea*. His current work addresses the representation of the Middle Ages within computer games.

Frank Klaassen is a Professor of History at the University of Saskatchewan. His recent books include *Making Magic in Elizabethan England, The Magic of Rogues: Necromancers and Authority in Early Tudor England,* and *Everyday Magicians: Legal Records and Magic Manuscripts from Tudor England* (Penn State University Press). He was awarded the CARA (Medieval Academy) Award for Excellence in Teaching in part for his work with games in teaching.

Courtnay Konshuh is assistant professor in the history department at the University of Calgary. She works on history-writing and identity in the Anglo-Saxon world. Recent publications look at the compilation of the Anglo-Saxon Chronicles. Their article, "Constructing Early Anglo-Saxon Identity in the Anglo-Saxon Chronicles," was recently published in *The Land of the English Kin: Studies in Wessex and Anglo-Saxon England in Honour of Barbara Yorke*.

Mariana López is a Senior Lecturer in Sound Production and Post Production at University of York, where she's been working since 2016. Mariana's work focuses on two main fields: the study of historical soundscapes and acoustics; and the use of sound design to create accessible experiences for visually impaired film and television audiences. She is currently writing a book on acoustical heritage and soundscapes to be published by Routledge.

Phivos Mylonas is currently a tenured Full Professor by the Department of Informatics of the Ionian University, Greece and collaborates as a Senior Researcher with the Intelligent

Systems, Content and Interaction Laboratory, School of Electrical and Computer Engineering, Department of Computer Science of the National Technical University of Athens, Greece. His research interests include content-based information retrieval, visual context representation and analysis, knowledge-assisted multimedia analysis, issues related to multimedia personalization, user adaptation, user modeling and profiling. He has published very broadly and is a member of the Technical Chamber of Greece, the Hellenic Association of Mechanical & Electrical Engineers and a member of W3C.

Terhi Nurmikko-Fuller is a Senior Lecturer in Digital Humanities at the Australian National University, and a Research Fellow (2019–2022) at the Graduate School of Library and Information Sciences at the University of Illinois Urbana-Champaign. She was recently awarded the Gale Scholar Asia Pacific, Digital Humanities Oxford Fellowship 2022–23 at the Bodleian Libraries at the University of Oxford. Her research focuses on interdisciplinary experimentation into ways digital technologies can support and diversify research in the Humanities, Arts, and Social Sciences, and in relation to cultural heritage. Her new book "Linked Data for Digital Humanities" (Routledge) is coming out in 2022. When not researching, Terhi can be found running trails or playing video games.

Anna Sotiropoulou has worked as a high-school professor of informatics for 12 years and she is currently working as Laboratory Teaching Staff in the Department of Informatics, Ionian University. Her research interests include digital humanities, medieval history (focusing on Muslim Iberia), database applications for archaeology.

Klio Stamou is preparing her Doctoral Thesis at the Department of History, Ionian University, in the field of learning environments with the application of the theory and methods of collaborative learning. Her professional and research interests focus on the elaboration of linguistic features of modern speech, the repositories of digital objects and their representation, the design and development of educational activities, scenarios and serious games, the semantic analysis of textual contents and participation in related scientific and technical activities.

Eve Stirling is a Principal lecturer and design researcher at Sheffield Hallam University Art and Design department. Her research uses practice based and visual research methods to explore the everyday (often digital) lives of participants. Current research focuses on design fiction and the sustainable and inclusive use of secondary data exploring pathways to zero.

Mehmet Şükrü Kuran is currently working in Airties Wireless Networks, Research department as a Staff Research Engineer. His research interests are wireless networks, WiFi technologies, quality of service in computer networks, game studies, and usage of computer games in higher education. His recent publications include "Multimedia Traffic Classification with Mixture of Markov Components – Elsevier Ad Hoc Networks", A Survey on Modulation Techniques in Molecular Communication via Diffusion – IEEE Surveys and Tutorials", and "Journey of Next Generation Boardgames and Eurogames in Turkey, Chapter in Game Studies from Turkey and in Turkey – Nobel Publishing.

Ahmet Erdem Tozoğlu has been working in Abdullah Gul University Faculty of Architecture since 2014. He was in the University of Chicago as a visiting researcher with the financial support of TUBITAK international post-doctoral research scholarship to conduct his research project in 2018–19 academic year. His research interests include architecture and urbanism, Ottoman Society, Culture, and Architecture, Art and Architecture of Muslim Societies, Medieval History, Architectural Historiography. He is the author of many national and international articles, book chapters and conference papers, and participating research projects.

Yorghos Voutos is a PhD candidate at the Department of Informatics of the Ionian University in the field of Geospatial Semantics. He has many years of professional experience in research projects in the field of environmental, cultural and educational studies. His research work has been published and presented through papers (collective and individual) in reputable international and Greek scientific journals and conferences. He has many years of involvement with civil society in voluntary activities and active participation in NGOs in the fields of culture and environment. In addition, he has experience in alternative tourism and in his recreational time he is involved in outdoor activities.

Wenqi Wan is an art director and a concept artist, who has contributed to more than 20 feature films with 12 years industry experience. After receiving the Postproduction in Visual Effects Master's degree from University of York, Wenqi Wan started his film career at ViridianFX. He has designed concept art for sci-fi and fantasy films such as Deus (Stone 2022) and Dark Encounter (Strathie 2019). He is also the visual designer for some visual experimental features, such as Macbeth (Monkman 2018).

Jamie Wood is Professor of History and Education at the University of Lincoln (UK), where he has taught since 2013. He has published extensively on the historical writings of Isidore of Seville, bishops in Visigothic Hispania, and education in late antiquity. His current project explores political, economic, and religious connections between the Iberian Peninsula and the Byzantine world in the fifth and sixth centuries. Jamie has also led several digital education projects at Lincoln and beyond, including recent work on students' online reading practices.

Index

Accuracy *see Authenticity*
Acoustic Atlas 273
Action, action-adventure 29, 50, 95
Africa 78, 92, 96
Age of Empires series 7, 115, 257, 263, 272
Agency 12, 32–36, 39, 138, 219, 231, 238, 242–243
Akritas 113–228, 288
Americas 92, 229
Ancestry *see Heritage*
Anno series 95
Anthropology 132, 280
Apples to Apples 169
Arabia, Arabic 57, 114, 126, 179 *see also* Middle East
Archaeology 2, 9, 177, 255–256, 280–281
Architecture 17, 30, 60, 113, 175, 177–178, 182–188, 192, 288
Asia 33, 96, 100, 126
Assassin's Creed series 7, 10, 17, 29, 47–67, 76 fn 29, 77, 95, 147, 184, 196–197, 283
Attentat 1942 134–135
Austria *see Holy Roman Empire*
Authenticity 1, 30, 32–35, 39, 47–49, 58–60, 64, 89–93, 95, 103, 119, 147, 161, 167, 175, 177, 184, 237, 243, 286

Battle *see Warfare*
Bavaria 207, 211, 221, 224 *see also* Germany
Byzantium, Byzantine 17, 113–129, 185, 187, 213, 216

Call of Duty series 7
Cards Against Humanity 7
Castille *see Iberia*
Cathedral's Treasures 256
Christianity, Christians 50–54, 56, 90–92, 96, 103–104, 125–126, 134, 178, 180–181, 249–277 *see also Religion*
– Catholicism 90–91, 96, 98–100, 102–104, 159–160, 205–207
– Protestantism 93, 207

City-building games 95
Civilization series 8–9, 11, 13, 78 fn 29, 88–89, 91–92, 115, 203, 282
Clash Royale 115
Class (social) 9, 18, 95, 240, 242
Classical period 69–76, 83
Collaboration, collaborative gaming 34–35, 115, 121–122, 131–151, 209, 282, 288, 290 *see also Teamwork*
Colonialism, colonization 4, 14, 39 77, 80, 90, 92–93
Competition 12, 14, 34, 84, 131–132, 134, 144, 149–150, 155–156, 162, 176, 212, 236
Cooperation *see Collaboration*
Cosmology of Kyoto 272
Crazy Taxi 5
Crusader Kings series 17, 87–109, 272, 291
Crusades 17, 31, 47–67, 88, 99, 191 fn 50, 191 fn 151, 191 fn 52, 230
Czechia 134

Denmark 179
Deus Ex 55
Diplomacy 122, 124–125
Distaff 229, 231, 235, 239–241, 243–244, 288
Dragon Age 55, 77
Dungeons & Dragons 77–78, 135, 145, 290

Early modern period 89–93, 107, 270
ECO 84
Economics, economy 8, 87–88, 90, 95–97, 97 fn 14, 106, 108, 114, 119–120, 147–148, 151, 156, 204, 220, 238, 257, 272, 274, 279
Egypt 10, 50, 193, 193 fn 63, 195 fig. 9.3, 283
– Cairo (Fustat) 17, 131, 134, 136, 142, 146, 148
Emotion 122, 137–139, 147, 166, 215
Empathy 69–86, 119, 135–139, 149–151, 177
Empire 14, 33, 69, 78, 90, 92, 93, 113, 123–128, 179, 185, 206, 213 *see also Nation*

Engagement (of player / student) 5, 34, 37, 40, 57, 70, 72–75, 75 fn 25, 77, 79, 81, 85, 98, 116–117, 120–123, 131, 135, 139, 142, 147–149, 151, 155–158, 161–163, 165–166, 168–170, 175–176, 178–179, 182–183, 185, 196–197, 202–203, 205, 207–209, 213–215, 217–219, 232–234, 239–240, 242–243, 251, 255–256, 265–266, 270–271, 273, 282, 288–289, 293
England 50, 54, 181, 186, 191 fn 50, 242, 259
Escapism 29, 77, 136, 155
Ethnicity *see Race*
Eurocentrism 14, 107
Europa Universalis series 8, 89–90, 107
Excommunication 98–99, 103

Fallout 9
Fantasy 15, 39, 69–72, 76–80, 83–84, 94, 175–176, 179 fn 12, 182, 185–187, 189, 191, 197
Feudalism 90–92, 96–102, 104–105, 194
Fidelity 32, 120, 147–148
France 50, 54, 179, 186, 191 fn 50, 221, 223,
– Brittany 179
– Paris 50

Game mechanics 5, 7–11, 14, 16, 18, 36, 60, 77–78, 81–82, 89–108, 118, 141, 143, 145, 147–150, 157, 162, 165–166, 168–169, 175, 201–205, 207–210, 212–213, 217–220, 229, 231–234, 236–244, 257, 280, 283–288, 291–292
Gee, James Paul 70, 72–73, 75–76, 139
Gender 14, 18, 79, 103, 126–127, 156, 159–160, 169–170, 177–179, 177 fn 10, 205, 229, 231, 233–234, 238, 240, 242
– Male 14, 72, 99, 124, 126–127, 177–179, 177 fn 10, 181, 231, 233–236, 242
– Female 73, 103, 114, 124, 127, 159, 177, 177 fn 10, 179, 231, 234–238, 242–243
Geography 73, 103, 114, 124, 127, 159, 177, 177 fn 10, 179, 231, 234–238, 242–243
Germany 207, 211, 221, 223–224 *see also Bavaria*
Greece 50, 73, 113–114, 125, 127–128, 259

Hearts of Iron IV 89, 99
Heritage 18, 33, 47, 49, 54, 78, 81, 98, 118, 125, 146, 179, 192–193, 197, 224, 249–252, 255–260, 273–274, 279
Historiography 18, 33, 47, 49, 54, 78, 81, 98, 118, 125, 146, 179, 192–193, 197, 224, 249–252, 255–260, 273–274, 279
Holy Roman Empire 50, 90, 93
Houghton, Robert 1–26, 48–49, 95 fn 13, 105, 201–227, 258, 266, 279–297

Iberia 90–92
Immersion 18, 33, 47, 49, 54, 78, 81, 98, 118, 125, 146, 179, 192–193, 197, 224, 249–252, 255–260, 273–274, 279
Imperator Rome 93
India 96, 100, 104
Indigenous peoples 178, 229
Industrial age 89, 177, 181, 189
Ireland 91, 287
Islam, Muslims 18, 33, 47, 49, 54, 78, 81, 98, 118, 125, 146, 179, 192–193, 197, 224, 249–252, 255–260, 273–274, 279, *see also Religion*
Italy 18, 33, 47, 49, 54, 78, 81, 98, 118, 125, 146, 179, 192–193, 197, 224, 249–252, 255–260, 273–274, 279
– Canossa 206–207, 211, 213–214, 218, 221–24
– Florence 30, 162, 224
– Milan 30, 211, 214, 221, 223–24
– Ravenna 30, 211, 214, 221, 223–24
– Rome 7, 30, 35, 71, 74, 114, 126, 177, 179, 185, 192, 207, 211, 223–224, 259–60
– Venice 185, 213, 216

Japan 88
Judaism, Jews 104, 131, 134, 136, 139–144, 147, 149, 151 *see also Religion*

Kingdom Come: Deliverance 93, 95
Kingdom of Heaven 52–53, 57, 60
Knights *see Military*

Landscape *see Geography*
Latin 73, 179–181

Law, legal matters 69, 74, 83, 97–99, 102, 131, 134–136, 140–141, 143–144, 146–147, 149–150, 159, 162, 168, 179
Lost & Found 17, 131–154, 291

Maps 7, 30, 60, 96, 100, 106, 209, 211–212, 216, 268, 270, 285
Magic: The Gathering 135
Medal of Honour 282
Media literacy 70, 132, 148, 150–151, 286, 293
Mediterranean 50, 139–140, 179
Middle East 48, 50, 96, 290
Military 17, 34, 50–51, 53, 58, 61 fig. 3.1, 64, 73, 80, 88, 95–97, 113, 120, 124–127, 176, 179, 186, 191, 191 fn 50, 229, 272, 287
Minecraft 84, 197
Mods, modding 10–11, 16–18, 30, 34, 100, 175–199, 175 fn 3, 187, 189–194, 193 fn 60, 193 fn 64, 195 fig. 9.3, 196 fig. 9.4, 197, 201–220, 232–233, 279, 284, 286–289, 292
Mongolia 56, 100
Morality 14, 138, 164, 192, 192 fn 59
Morocco 90 92
Multiplayer 72, 84, 212, 289
Museums 16, 113, 125, 131, 177, 185–186, 190, 197, 233–234, 238–239, 238 fn 7, 245, 251
Myths, mythology 34, 53–57, 81, 94, 105, 143, 178, 182–183, 194, 229, 235

Narrative 14, 33, 36, 40, 51, 59, 78, 117–120, 126–127, 131, 134, 148, 151, 156, 175–178, 181, 191–193, 205, 209, 216, 254, 260, 270, 273, 282, 285
Nation 15, 32–33, 38, 87–89, 92, 96, 106–107, 118, 179 *see also Empire*
Nationalism 9, 78, 80, 183
Near East *see Middle East*
Normans 38, 213
Norse, Nordic 96, 99, 104, 178, 182–184, 186
Norway 179, 184–185

Ottoman Empire 90, 93, 179

Papacy, popes, antipopes 8–9, 15, 32, 64, 69, 87–88, 91, 95–97, 97 fn 14, 99–100, 103–106, 119–120, 160, 182, 207, 210, 212, 215, 223, 257, 272, 274, 279, 287
Patrician 8
Period (historical), periodization 3, 6–7, 10–11, 13, 15, 18, 37, 87, 89–91, 93, 94–95, 106, 113, 123, 125, 128, 131, 136, 141, 144, 149–150, 160, 180, 182–185, 189, 203, 205, 207, 210, 212, 215, 220, 232, 240, 243, 253, 263, 272, 279, 287, *see also Classical period, Early modern period, Industrial age, Renaissance period*
Persia 56, 93
Playing History 2: Slave Trade 5
Pokémon Go! 176
Politics 8–9, 15, 32, 64, 69, 87–88, 91, 95–97, 97 fn 14, 99–100, 103–106, 119–120, 160, 182, 207, 210, 212, 215, 223, 257, 272, 274, 279, 287
Portugal *see Iberia*

Race 18, 71, 77–81, 83, 126, 177 fn 10, 178–180, 182–183, 194
Racism 14, 71, 77–79, 229
Reacting to the Past series 290
Religion 14, 51–53, 90–93, 96, 98–99, 103–106, 103 fn 16, 108, 124, 131, 134–135, 140–141, 146, 180–181, 193, 252, 272, 288 *see also Christianity, Islam, Judaism, Papacy*
Renaissance period 31, 50, 76, 155–171
Rhetoric 17, 57, 69–86, 143, 215, 258
Roleplay, roleplaying games (RPGs) 9, 11–12, 18, 29–30, 33, 57, 76 fn 29, 95, 139, 143, 151, 159–161, 163–165, 177, 192–194, 211, 213–215, 217, 219–220, 257, 263, 265, 271, 279, 281, 289–293
Russia 114

Saami 178
Saladin 50, 52–53
Scandinavia 178–179, 184, 186, 191 fn 50
Shadows of Utopia: Exploring the Thinking of Robert Owen 283

Simulation 18, 33, 35, 38, 95–96, 115–116, 142–145, 150, 155–171, 157 fn 5, 168, 175–176, 180, 193–194, 210, 217, 219, 229–230, 249, 251–252, 257–258, 263, 272, 284, 286, 289
Single-player 30, 34, 84, 95, 176
Skyrim 17, 69–86, 175–199, 175 fn 1, 288, 291 *see also* The Elder Scrolls
Snake Oil 169
Solitaire 176
Soldiers *see* Military
Sound 18, 32, 126–127, 178, 249–277, 288
Strange Sickness 287
Strategy (games) 10, 29–30, 38–39, 87–90, 95–96, 98, 100, 106–108, 131, 134, 139, 144, 161, 176, 214, 216, 240, 251, 257, 263
Svoboda 1945: Liberation 134
Sweden 179

Teamwork, teams 30, 34–35, 58, 121–122, 131, 134, 158, 163–165, 168, 176, 197, 211, 214–215, 221–224
Technology 8, 14, 84, 87–88, 93, 96, 106, 108, 113–115, 163, 182, 197, 259
Tecumseh Lies Here 10
Templars 49–55, 57, 59, 61 fig. 3.1
Tetris 5
The Elder Scrolls 84, 180, 257, 263 *see also* Skyrim
The Guild series 95
The History Game 10, 283

The Investiture Contest 18, 201–227, 287
The Renaissance Marriage Game 17, 155–171, 291
The Triumphs of Turlough 287
The York Mystery Plays 18, 249–277, 288
Time Historians 10, 283
Tolkien, J.R.R. 69, 76–77, 94, 230
Tomb Raider 70, 78
Total War 7–8, 89, 93, 96
Trade 90, 96, 106, 179–180, 191, 194
Tropes (historical, fantastical) 3, 6, 12–14, 16, 53, 56, 71, 76–77, 95, 176–178, 189, 192
Twine 11

United States 50, 139, 141 *see also* Americas

Victoria II 93
Vikings 50, 95, 178–179, 183, 185–186
Violence 13–14, 51–53, 78–80, 83–84, 156, 160–162, 191, 197, 205 *see also* Warfare
Virtus 229, 231 fn 5, 233, 235, 239–240, 243–245, 288

Warfare 8, 32, 50–53, 58, 61 fig. 3.1, 73, 79–82, 88, 97–99, 114, 119–120, 125–128, 177, 214, 220 *see also* Violence
World of Warcraft 72–73, 84

www.ingramcontent.com/pod-product-compliance
Lightning Source LLC
Chambersburg PA
CBHW020221170426
43201CB00007B/281